Reflective Teaching in the
Primary School

Reflective Teaching in the Primary School

A Handbook for the Classroom

Third edition

Andrew Pollard

CASSELL

Cassell

Wellington House
125 Strand
London WC2R 0BB

370 Lexington Avenue
New York
NY10017 - 6550

First published 1997

Reprinted 1997, 1998

British Library Cataloguing-in Publication Data

A catalogue record for this book is available from the British Library.

ISBN   0–304–338699(hb)
       0–304–70011 (pb)

Typeset by Pantek Arts, Maidstone, Kent.
Printed and bound in Great Britain by Redwood Books, Trowbridge, Wiltshire

CONTENTS

PREFACE

This third edition of *Reflective Teaching in the Primary School* has been thoroughly revised to accommodate the enormous changes which have occurred in education during the mid-1990s.

There are three particularly important substantive elements of this revision. First, there has been a complete update concerning curriculum and assessment following the 1995/96 implementation of the Dearing Review of the National Curriculum and assessment procedures. Second, the issues associated with the new models of school inspection have been addressed, particularly with reference to the OFSTED model used in England. Third, a new chapter has been provided focusing on social differentiation and 'equal opportunities' – issues which have an enduring effect on the experiences of many teachers and pupils.

Additionally, the whole text and each section of Further Readings has been updated to highlight the latest and most helpful writing and research on educational issues. Readers will also notice the redesign of the book which makes it even easier to use.

A final important feature of the third edition is the way in which it is now supported by a reader. *Readings for Reflective Teaching in the Primary School* (which I will refer to in this text as '*Readings*') provides direct access to many of the materials recommended in this text. Indeed, with over 130 readings combining influential publications and the very latest research, it is a unique resource. It has been designed as a precise complement to this book, and specific cross-referencing opportunities are indicated by an icon in the margin and the number of the reading, in bold, in the text.

The book is intended to provide flexible and comprehensive support for school-based and school-focused teacher education, in a form which is suitable for a wide range of circumstances. Suggested *Practical Activities* and annotated *Notes for Further Reading* are designed to provide support for self-directed or group study with or without the support of tutors or teacher mentors. It is hoped that the framework and its contents will provide continuous resources for teachers, students and tutors at all stages of professional development.

However, the book is meant to be used selectively, depending on judgements of what is needed. Put another way, it should be possible to differentiate among and within the activities and resources which the book offers and to use them, appropriately and specifically, to support the professional development of oneself and others.

The book, together with the companion *Readings*, should thus be an excellent resource for students, teachers, mentors and tutors and can be used in almost any form of professional development activity.

My thanks to those who have offered comments, criticisms and suggestions regarding previous editions. These are extremely helpful and readers of this new edition are invited to continue to maintain the feedback loop so that the book can be effectively developed in the future.

Andrew Pollard
University of Bristol
February 1996

ACKNOWLEDGEMENTS

Working on the third edition of this book at a time of educational change has been a challenging experience. However, it has been informed by the work of a great many people from schools, local education authorities, colleges and universities both within the UK and elsewhere. The commitment, knowledge, insights and skills which educationalists collectively offer constitute a resource of very high quality, which the book tries to represent. It follows that the biggest acknowledgement should be to all those people who have done such a magnificent job in recent years in developing and supporting a thinking and reflective teaching profession in difficult circumstances.

This new edition has been produced at great speed and without the involvement this time of my co-author in the first edition, Sarah Tann. I would like to acknowledge with gratitude Sarah's contribution to that first book. The change of authorship in this, third, edition recognizes how our work has now moved in different directions.

I would particularly like to thank Sarah Butler for her commitment in producing the manuscript, of the present book, so efficiently. I am very grateful, too, to the Cassell team, particularly Naomi Roth, Charlotte Ridings and Huw Neill, who have worked very hard to develop the book and its linkage with the *Readings*. Thanks too to Gill Riordan for her excellent work on the index.

Finally, I would like to thank the following authors and publishers for permission to reproduce previously published materials:

Avon Education Authority for Figure 8.1.

Robin J. Alexander for Table 7.1, from *Primary Teaching* (1984). London: Holt, Rinehart & Winston.

Barry Fraser and Darrell Fisher for the short form of 'My Class Inventory', from their *Assessment of Classroom Psychological Environment: Workshop Manual* (1984). Bentley: Western Australian Institute of Technology.

Croom Helm Ltd and Patrick Easen for material from his *Making School-Centred INSET Work* (1985). London: Croom Helm.

Inner London Education Authority, for the 'Me at School' form designed by members of the Junior School Project team based at the Research and Statistics Branch.

Curriculum Council for Wales for Figure 7.3, from *The Whole Curriculum 5–16 in Wales* (1991).

Neville Bennett and Elizabeth Dunne for Figure 11.1, from *Managing Classroom Groups* (1992). London: Simon & Schuster.

Longman Group UK Ltd for Figure 11.2, from S. Alladina and V. Edwards (eds) *Multilingualism in the British Isles* (1991).

Paula Johnson and Scholastic Publications Ltd for drawings from 'Assessing the Links', *Junior Education*, October 1992.

John Davies and the University of the West of England for material from a School Development Programme on *Equal Opportunites* by Jo Elliot, Ian Menter, Terry Mortimore, Elizabeth Newman, Andrew Pollard, Pat Triggs, Lizzie White and Bev Woodroffe (1991), RCPE, Bristol Polytechnic.

Jenny Wills for material in Practical Activity 15.3.

INTRODUCTION

The main aim of this book is to support student teachers, school mentors and teachers who wish to reflect upon teaching in a systematic fashion. It is hoped that processes of enquiry, reflection and sharing could help to account for achievements, to analyse anxieties and to identify areas for future professional development.

The book is designed as a handbook which can be easily dipped into and from which ideas can be taken and developed. Selected issues, particular procedures and related *Practical Activities* are set out so that analysis and practical suggestions are readily accessible. Each chapter also contains a section of *Notes for Further Reading*. This is an annotated list of particular books which are recommended to readers to extend study of certain issues and procedures. These suggestions are supported by the companion book, *Readings for Reflective Teaching in the Primary School*, which provides easy access to extracts from over 130 key educational sources. Direct cross-referencing is indicated by the icon of an open book, as in this margin.

However, this book is intended to be more than a practical guide to the self-evaluation of classroom practice and the work of students, mentors and teachers. The analysis and activities have been set within a theoretical framework which attempts to link classroom practice and educational theory with current educational, political and social debates. Thus, this book offers a broad context – the context of the 'extended professional' – within which to reflect upon teaching.

When Sarah Tann and I began writing the first edition of this book in the mid-1980s, we fully recognized that all forms of action inevitably involve people in making judgements based on values and commitments – and this is certainly true for teachers. We therefore wanted to produce a framework which recognized the necessity of professional judgements by individual teachers and yet was also informed by a set of value-commitments that would command widespread support in moral and ethical terms.

We considered many of the documents which have flowed from government agencies in recent years, reflecting wide-ranging concerns about the quality of educational provision. However, at a more fundamental level, we felt a particular need to emphasize the links between education, human rights and democracy. In this respect one can learn a great deal from looking at the Universal Declaration on Human Rights and the European Convention on Human Rights, which were both developed in the post-war years. More recently, there has been a specific educational Recommendation from the Council of Europe's Committee of Ministers, entitled *Teaching and Learning about Human Rights in School* (Council of Europe, 1985), to which Great Britain is a signatory. It is worth citing some parts of this document here.

There are two statements on the curriculum:

> The understanding and experience of human rights is an important element of the preparation of all young people for life in a democratic and pluralistic society. It is a part of social and political education, and it involves intercultural and international understanding. (1.1)

> Concepts associated with human rights can, and should, be acquired from an early stage. For example, the non-violent resolution of conflict and respect for other people can already be experienced within the life of a pre-school or primary class. (1.2)

In terms of both knowledge to be acquired and the climate within schools in which such work should take place, it is stated:

> The study of human rights in schools should lead to an understanding of, and sympathy for the concepts of justice, equality, freedom, peace, dignity, rights and democracy. Such understanding should be both cognitive and based on experience and feelings. Schools should thus provide opportunities for pupils to experience affective involvement in human rights and to express their feelings through drama, art, music, creative writing and audio-visual media. (3.3)
>
> Democracy is best learned in a democratic setting where participation is encouraged, where views can be expressed openly and discussed, where there is freedom of expression for pupils and teachers, and where there is fairness and justice. An appropriate climate is, therefore, an essential complement to effective learning about human rights. (4.1)

For teacher education, the task is also spelt out clearly:

> The initial training of teachers should prepare them for their future contribution to teaching about human rights in their schools. For example, future teachers should:
> (i)   be encouraged to take an interest in national and world affairs:
> (ii) be taught to identify and combat all forms of discrimination in schools and society and be encouraged to confront and overcome their own prejudices. (5.1)

These are challenging ideas, but ones which have to be faced if we are to provide the best possible quality of education for all the children in our society. The work of a professional educator thus involves a heavy degree of social responsibility. I hope that this book will help its readers to reflect on these concerns, as well as to improve their 'practice' more generally.

This book has three parts. Part 1 is entitled 'Becoming a Reflective Teacher'. It offers a theoretical rationale for the approach (Chapter 1) and provides an analysis of the relationship between individuals, education and society (Chapter 2). It concludes with a review and examination of ways of investigating classrooms (Chapter 3).

Part 2, 'Being a Reflective Teacher', represents the classroom-focused, practical core of the book. Each chapter is devoted to a particular aspect of the teaching–learning process. Each has the same structure: a significant issue is discussed, practical activities for classroom investigation are presented, follow-up points are suggested and guidance for further reading is given.

The issues selected in Part 2 are ones which are basic to classroom life – examining ourselves, our values, aims and commitments (Chapter 4); classroom relationships (Chapter 5); considering how children learn (Chapter 6); reviewing National Curriculum structures (Chapter 7): school and classroom planning of what to teach (Chapter 8); organizing a classroom (Chapter 9); classroom management (Chapter 10); communication skills (Chapter 11); assessment (Chapter 12); social consequences and provision of equal opportunities (Chapter 13).

Part 3 looks 'Beyond Classroom Reflection' to consider reflective teaching and innovation in schools as a whole (Chapter 14). In this part, the place and responsibilities of reflective primary school teachers in society (Chapter 15) are also reconsidered.

PART 1

BECOMING A REFLECTIVE TEACHER

CHAPTER 1

Reflective teaching and competence

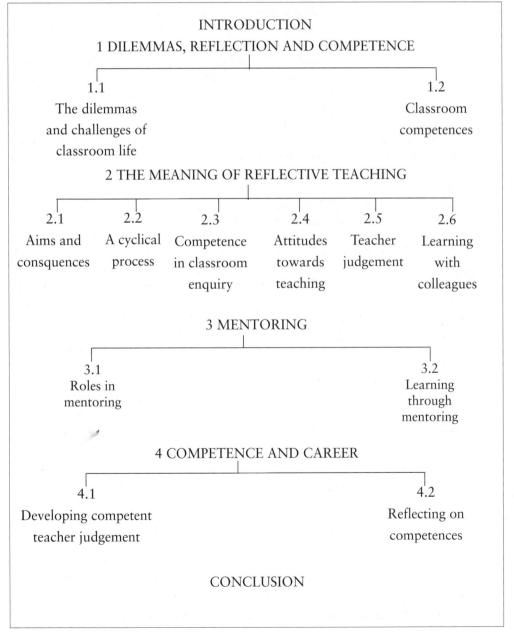

INTRODUCTION

1 DILEMMAS, REFLECTION AND COMPETENCE

1.1
The dilemmas
and challenges of
classroom life

1.2
Classroom
competences

2 THE MEANING OF REFLECTIVE TEACHING

2.1
Aims and
consquences

2.2
A cyclical
process

2.3
Competence
in classroom
enquiry

2.4
Attitudes
towards
teaching

2.5
Teacher
judgement

2.6
Learning
with
colleagues

3 MENTORING

3.1
Roles in
mentoring

3.2
Learning
through
mentoring

4 COMPETENCE AND CAREER

4.1
Developing competent
teacher judgement

4.2
Reflecting on
competences

CONCLUSION

INTRODUCTION

This book is based on the belief that teaching is a complex and highly skilled activity which, above all, requires classroom teachers to exercise judgement in deciding how to act. Reflective teaching is seen as a process through which the capacity to make such professional judgements can be developed and maintained.

The book also relates directly to the practical 'competences' which are increasingly required of teachers and which, in many respects, represent a constructive clarification of the particular skills, knowledge and understandings of the profession. However, when discussing competence, there is a tendency to concentrate on practical and technical matters with little reference to values, aims and consequences. Such consequences could be of a personal nature, for example, the effects of a classroom teachers's practice on a child's self-image. They could be of an academic nature, for example, concerning a child's intellectual achievement, or they could be of a social nature, for example, relating to the cumulative effects of school experience on a child's life chances.

The view taken in this book is that teaching concerns values, aims, attitudes and consequences as well as skills, knowledge and competence. Indeed, I shall argue that there is a constructive relationship between the *state* of classroom competence and the *processes* of reflection through which competence is developed and maintained.

This proposition simplifies a number of issues, but it remains at the core of the approach which has been taken in this book. We see successive levels of competence in teaching: those which student teachers may attain at the beginning, middle and end of their courses; those of the new teacher after his or her induction to full-time school life; and those of the experienced, expert teacher. Given the nature of teaching, professional development and learning should never stop. Indeed, the process of reflection feeds a constructive spiral of professional development and competence. This should both be personally fulfilling for teachers, but also lead to a steady increase in the quality of the education which is offered to children. This argument is represented diagrammatically in Figure 1.1.

This chapter has three main parts. The first introduces some of the dilemmas which teachers face and some of the issues surrounding competences. In the second part, six key characteristics of reflective teaching are identified and discussed. The final part focuses on developing successive levels of competence throughout a teaching career and also looks at some criticisms of competency approaches.

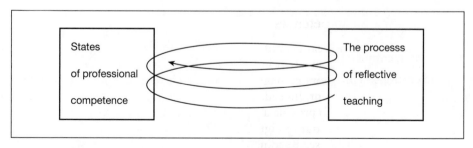

Figure 1.1 *The spiral of professional development and competence*

1 DILEMMAS, REFLECTION AND COMPETENCE

1.1 The dilemmas and challenges of classroom life

The complicated nature of educational issues and the practical demands of class-room teaching ensure that a teacher's work is never finished. When practicalities, teaching competence, personal ideals and wider educational concerns are considered together, the job of rising to the challenges and reconciling the numerous requirements and possible conflicts often seems to be overwhelming. As an infant teacher explained:

> I love my work but it's a constant struggle to keep it all going. If I focus on one thing I have to neglect another. For instance, if I talk to a group or to a particular child then I have to keep an eye on what the others are doing; if I hear someone read then I can't help with maths problems or be in a position to extend other children's language when opportunities arise; if I put out clay then I haven't got room for painting; if I get a lot of creative writing going then I can't also concentrate on maths; if I go to evening courses then I can't prepare as well for the next day; if I spend time with my family then I worry about my class but if I rush around collecting materials or something then I feel guilty for neglecting the family. It's not easy... but I wouldn't do anything else.

Such dilemmas are frequently expressed – not only by experienced teachers, but even more by student teachers.

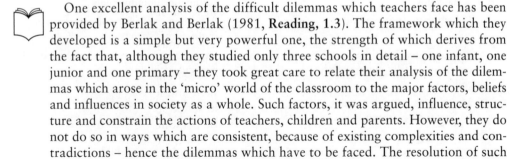

One excellent analysis of the difficult dilemmas which teachers face has been provided by Berlak and Berlak (1981, **Reading, 1.3**). The framework which they developed is a simple but very powerful one, the strength of which derives from the fact that, although they studied only three schools in detail – one infant, one junior and one primary – they took great care to relate their analysis of the dilemmas which arose in the 'micro' world of the classroom to the major factors, beliefs and influences in society as a whole. Such factors, it was argued, influence, structure and constrain the actions of teachers, children and parents. However, they do not do so in ways which are consistent, because of existing complexities and contradictions – hence the dilemmas which have to be faced. The resolution of such dilemmas calls for teachers to use professional judgement to assess the most appropriate course of action in any particular situation.

But what are the major dilemmas which have to be faced? Table 1.1, presents a version of some of them. This book is intended to provide a practical guide to ways of reflecting on such issues and it offers strategies and advice for developing the necessary classroom competences to resolve them.

1.2 Classroom competences

There has been a great deal of discussion in recent years about the need to ensure that teachers are competent in the skills, knowledge and understanding required for effective classroom management, pupil assessment, subject teaching and professional development. Indeed, competency criteria have been set by governments in many countries to provide a framework for teacher training. For instance, those for Scotland are set out in Figure 1.2 (for the comparable list of competences for England and Wales, see **Reading, 1.8**).

Table 1.1 *Common dilemmas faced by teachers*

Treating each child as a 'whole person'	Treating each child primarily as a 'pupil'
Organizing the children on an individual basis	Organizing the children as a class
Giving children a degree of control over their use of time, their activities and their work standards	Tightening control over children's use of time, their activities and their work standards
Seeking to motivate the children through intrinsic involvement and enjoyment of activities	Offering reasons and rewards so that children are extrinsically motivated to tackle tasks
Developing and negotiating the curriculum from an appeciation of children's interests	Providing a subject curriculum which children are deemed to need and which 'society' expects them to receive
Attempting to integrate various subjects of the curriculum	Dealing systematically with each discrete subject of the curriculum
Aiming for quality in schoolwork	Aiming for quantity in schoolwork
Focusing on basic skills or on cognitive development	Focusing on expressive or creative areas of the curriculum
Trying to build up co-operative and social skills	Developing self-reliance and self-confidence in individuals
Inducting the children into a common culture	Affirming the variety of cultures in a multi-ethnic society
Allocating teacher time, attention and resources equally among all the children	Paying attention to the special needs of particular children
Maintaining consistent rules and understandings about behaviour and schoolwork	Being flexible and responsive to particular situations
Presenting oneself formally to the children	Relaxing with the children
Working with 'professional' application and care for the children	Working with consideration of one's personal needs

Such competency criteria are very helpful in defining goals for students, tutors and teachers who are engaged in initial teacher education and, of course, others could be developed for the initial period of induction into full-time work or for in-service stages of professional development.

However, we need to be clear about the status of such competency criteria. The example following describes the skills, knowledge and understanding which have been deemed to be appropriate for teachers in the particular context of Scotland in the 1990s. Those required where a national curriculum and legally defined assessment procedures exist may well differ from those which are called for where such structures do not exist; those called for where class sizes are very high (as in

Core Professional Competences:
from the Initial Teacher Training Guidelines for Teacher Training Courses,
Scottish Office, 1992

2.1   *Competences relating to Subject and Content of Teaching*

The new teacher should be able to:

–   demonstrate a knowledge of the subject or subjects forming the
         content of his or her teaching which goes beyond the immediate
         demands of the school curriculum;
–   plan: for example to prepare coherent teaching programmes which
         ensure continuity and progression, taking into account national,
         regional and school curriculum policies and plan lessons within these
         teaching programmes;
–   present the content of what is taught in an appropriate fashion to
         pupils;
–   justify what is taught from knowledge and understanding of curricu-
         lum issues and of child development.

2.2   *Competences relating to the Classroom*

         2.2.1 *Communication*

The new teacher should be able to:

–   present what he or she is teaching in clear language and a stimulat-
         ing manner;
–   question pupils effectively, respond and support discussion.

         2.2.2 *Methodology*

The new teacher should be able to:

–   employ a range of teaching strategies appropriate to the subject or
         topic and the pupils in his or her classes;
–   identify suitable occasions for teaching the class as a whole, in
         groups, in pairs or as individuals;
–   have expectations which make demands appropriate to pupils being
         taught;
–   have an awareness of the learning difficulties or the special educa-
         tional needs of some pupils;
–   to take into account cultural differences among pupils;
–   encourage pupils to take initiatives in and become responsible for,
         their own learning;
–   select and use in a considered way a wide variety of resources,
         including information technology;

- evaluate his or her practice;
- justify the methodology being used.

2.2.3 *Class Management*

The new teacher should have a knowledge of the principles which lie behind the keeping of good discipline and should be able to:

- deploy a range of approaches to create and maintain a purposeful, orderly and safe environment for learning;
- manage pupil behaviour by the use of appropriate rewards and sanctions and be aware when it is necessary to seek advice;
- maintain the interest and motivation of the pupils for whom he or she has responsibility;
- evaluate his or her own actions in managing pupils.

2.2.4 *Assessment*

The new teacher should:

- have an understanding of the principles of assessment and the different kinds of assessment which may be used;
- be able to judge how pupils perform against standards defined for the particular group of pupils;
- be able to assess and record systematically the progress of individual pupils;
- be able to provide regular feedback to pupils on their progress;
- be able to use assessment to evaluate and improve teaching.

2.3   *Competences relating to the School*

The new teacher should:

- have a knowledge of the system in which he or she is working and in particular of the organization and management systems of schools, or school policies and development plans and where they impinge on his or her teaching;
- be able to discuss with parents the progress of their children;
- be able to communicate with members of other professions concerned with the welfare of pupils and with members of the community served by the school, as well as with colleagues within the school and its associated schools;
- be aware of sources of help and expertise within the school and how they can be used;
- be aware of cross-curricular aspects of school work and able to make an input into these;
- have interests and skills which can contribute to activities with pupils outside the formal curriculum.

2.4   *Competences related to Professionalism*

The new teacher should:

–   have a working knowledge of his or her pastoral, contractual, legal
         and administrative responsibilities;
–   be able to make a preliminary evaluation of his or her own profes-
         sional progress.

However, professionalism implies more than a mere series of competences. It
also implies a set of attitudes which have particular power in that they are
communicated to those being taught:

–   a commitment to the job and to those affected by the job;
–   a commitment to self-monitoring and continuing professional devel-
         opment;
–   a commitment to collaborate with others to promote pupil achieve-
         ment;
–   a commitment to promoting the moral and spiritual well-being of
         pupils;
–   a commitment to the community within and beyond the school;
–   a commitment to views of fairness as expressed in multi-cultural and
         other non-discriminatory policies.

Figure 1.2 *Core professional competences (from the* Initial Teacher Training
Guidelines for Teacher Training Courses, *Scottish Office, 1992)*

many parts of the world) may vary from those needed when much smaller classes
or groups are taught; those required in the early 1990s are unlikely to remain constant into the next century. To illustrate this point, it is interesting to consider the
requirements made of apprenticed 'pupil teachers' in England about one hundred
and fifty years ago (Figure 1.3).

I want to argue, then, that officially endorsed competency criteria are context
specific. They reflect the cultures, values and the priorities of decision-makers. In
the case of teacher education, they describe a particular repertoire of skills,
knowledge and understanding which has been deemed appropriate for the particular time and circumstances in which a new generation of teachers are to be trained.
This specificity brings both benefits and difficulties, and these are represented in
Figure 1.4 (see p.11), as elaborated from work by Whitty and Willmott (1991).

There has been considerable concern in some quarters about the use of
competences in teacher education, and there have been some unfortunate and
unsuccessful experiences in the United States. Nevertheless, the advantages of
having a clear specification of goals for teacher education are very significant.
They could provide a framework both for greater partnership between schools
and higher education training institutions and for rational, career-long staff
development.

> *Regulations respecting the education of pupil teachers.*
> *Minutes of the Committee of Council on Education, 1846.*
>
> *Qualifications of candidates:*
>
> To be at least 13 years of age.
>
> To not be subject to any bodily infirmity likely to impair their usefulness.
>
> To have a certificate of moral character.
>
> To read with fluency, ease and expression.
>
> To write in a neat hand with correct spelling and punctuation, a simple prose narrative read to them.
>
> To write from dictation sums in the first four rules of arithmetic, simple and compound: to work them correctly, and to know the table of weights and measures.
>
> To point out the parts of speech in a simple sentence.
>
> To have an elementary knowledge of geography.
>
> To repeat the Catechism and to show that they understand its meaning and are acquainted with the outline of Scripture history. (Where working in schools connected with the Church of England only.)
>
> To teach a junior class to the satisfaction of the Inspector.
>
> Girls should also be able to sew neatly and to knit.

Figure 1.3 *Regulations respecting the education of pupil teachers, 1846*

However, we can reassert our point that they represent states of teaching capacity to be attained. They do not define or prescribe the process by which these states of competence are to be developed. For the latter, the process of 'reflective teaching' is essential.

2 | THE MEANING OF REFLECTIVE TEACHING

The notion of reflective teaching, around which this book is based, stems from Dewey (1933, **Reading, 1.1**) who contrasted 'routine action' with 'reflective action'. According to Dewey routine action is guided by factors such as tradition, habit and authority and by institutional definitions and expectations. By implication it is relatively static and is thus unresponsive to changing priorities and circumstances. Reflective action, on the other hand, involves a willingness to engage in constant self-appraisal and development. Among other things, it implies flexibility, rigorous analysis and social awareness.

Benefits of competency approaches	Difficulties of competency approaches
May provide clear goals for students	May be hard to agree definitions of competence
May clarify the roles of schools and of colleges in the training process	May lead to a fragmented reductionism of the holistic capacity to teach
May give employers greater confidence in what beginning teachers can do	May be difficult to agree valid and reliable criteria for assessment
May give beginning teachers more confidence in themselves	May emphasize outcomes rather than learning processes in training

Figure 1.4 *Benefits and disadvantages of competency approaches*

Dewey's notion of reflective action, when developed and applied to teaching, is very challenging. In this section, we review its implications by identifying and discussing what has been identified as six key characteristics. These are:

1. Reflective teaching implies an active concern with aims and consequences, as well as means and technical efficiency.

2. Reflective teaching is applied in a cyclical or spiralling process, in which teachers monitor, evaluate and revise their own practice continuously.

3. Reflective teaching requires competence in methods of classroom enquiry, to support the development of teaching competence.

4. Reflective teaching requires attitudes of open-mindedness, responsibility and wholeheartedness.

5. Reflective teaching is based on teacher judgement, which is informed partly by self-reflection and partly by insights from educational disciplines.

6. Reflective teaching, professional learning and personal fulfilment are enhanced through collaboration and dialogue with colleagues.

Each of these six characteristics will now be considered more fully.

2.1 Aims and consequences

Reflective teaching implies an active concern with aims and consequences as well as means and technical efficiency.

This issue relates first to the immediate aims and consequences of classroom practice for these are any teacher's prime responsibility. However, classroom work cannot be isolated from the influence of the wider society and a reflective teacher must therefore consider both spheres. Two examples from the United Kingdom will illustrate the way in which changes outside schools influence actions within them.

During the 1960s and the early 1970s the education provided in many primary schools was guided by a particular philosophy of 'child-centredness'. This philosophy has a long history, but in the post-war years it drew particular support from the work of child psychologists, such as Piaget (Piaget, 1926, 1950, **Reading, 6.3**), and received official legitimation in the Plowden Report (CACE, 1967, **Reading, 7.6**). At the time, there appeared to be a broad consensus about the nature of 'good practice' in primary schools. However, child-centredness was the subject of much criticism in later years. For instance, it was accused of preventing rigorous thinking about the curriculum and of providing a relatively closed system of professional beliefs – an 'ideology'.

Whatever view is taken on this issue, the fact remains that the broad consensus on the characteristics of 'good practice', which appeared to exist briefly, was shattered during the 1970s. There were cases where schools lost the confidence of parents (e.g. William Tyndale) and research projects which produced controversy about teaching methods (Bennett, 1976). Where there once seemed to be 'answers', there were 'issues to debate' and many competing opinions, aims and values.

The second example of the breakdown of consensus follows from the first, for in the midst of such debates and challenges, successive Conservative governments from 1979 introduced far-reaching and cumulative changes in all spheres of education. Many of these reforms were opposed, at each stage, by professional organizations (e.g., Haviland, 1988; Arnot and Barton, 1992) but with no noticeable effect on political decision-making. For instance, in the summer of 1992, three professionals who had been highly influential in the early development of the educational reforms, the former Chief Inspector of Schools, the architect of the assessment arrangements and the former director of the National Curriculum Council for England, made public statements regarding their concern about the extent of political influence. Indeed, the allegation was again made that educational policy was being influenced by a closed system of beliefs – an 'ideology' – but this time under the control of a small number of right-wing politicians.

Meanwhile, teachers and pupils in schools and classrooms worked to implement the new forms of curriculum, assessment, accountability, management and control which had been introduced – despite the fact that, in many respects, they were opposed to the principles on which the reforms were based.

Such real and stark examples of the contestation of aims and values in education raise questions concerning the relationship between professionals, parents and policy-makers. It is possible to start from the seemingly uncontroversial argument that, in a democratic society, decisions about the aims of education should be 'democratically' determined. It has been suggested (White, 1978) that teachers should accept a role as active 'interpreters' of political policy. That most teachers accept this argument is shown by the way in which they implemented legislation even when they did not support it – though in the late 1980s an unusual number of teachers did leave the profession.

However, such a stance is very different from the idea of the autonomous professional with which many teachers have traditionally identified. Yet it can be argued that the existence of unconstrained autonomy is only reasonable and practical if ends, aims and values are shared in some sort of social consensus. Obviously, in such circumstances, judgements about the technical effectiveness of various types of teaching would best be derived from the educator on the spot.

However, as soon as questions about educational aims and social values are seriously raised then the position changes. In a democratic society, the debate appropriately extends to the political domain and this, of course, is what has happened recently.

This does not mean, though, that teachers, even as interpreters of policy, should simply 'stand by' in the procedure. Indeed, there are two important roles which they can play. In the case of the first, an appropriate metaphor for the teacher's role is, as White suggested, that of 'activist'. This recognizes that primary school teachers are individual members of society who, within normal political processes, have rights to pursue their values and beliefs as guided by their own individual moral and ethical concerns. They should thus be active in contributing to the formation of public policy. Second, whilst accepting a responsibility for translating politically determined aims into practice, teachers should speak out, as they have done, if they view particular aims and policies as being professionally impracticable, educationally unsound or morally questionable. In such circumstances the professional experience, knowledge and judgements of teachers should be brought to bear on policy-makers directly – whether or not the policy-makers wish for or act on the advice which is offered. Indeed, it is not unreasonable to suggest that, within a modern democratic society, teachers should be entitled to not only a hearing, but also some influence, on educational policy.

The reflective teacher should thus acknowledge the political process and be willing to contribute to it both as a citizen and as a professional.

2.2   A cyclical process

Reflective teaching is applied in a cyclical or spiralling process, in which teachers monitor, evaluate and revise their own practice continuously.

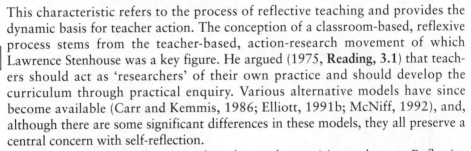

This characteristic refers to the process of reflective teaching and provides the dynamic basis for teacher action. The conception of a classroom-based, reflexive process stems from the teacher-based, action-research movement of which Lawrence Stenhouse was a key figure. He argued (1975, **Reading, 3.1**) that teachers should act as 'researchers' of their own practice and should develop the curriculum through practical enquiry. Various alternative models have since become available (Carr and Kemmis, 1986; Elliott, 1991b; McNiff, 1992), and, although there are some significant differences in these models, they all preserve a central concern with self-reflection.

Teachers are principally expected to plan, make provision and to act. Reflective teachers also need to monitor, observe and collect data on their own and the children's intentions, actions and feelings. This evidence then needs to be critically analysed and evaluated so that it can be shared, judgements made and decisions taken. Finally, this may lead the teacher to revise his or her classroom policies, plans and provision before beginning the process again. It is a dynamic process which is intended to lead through successive cycles, or through a spiralling process, towards higher quality teaching. This model is simple, comprehensive and certainly could be an extremely powerful influence on practice. It is consistent with the notion of reflective teaching, as described by Dewey, and provides an essential clarification of the procedures for reflective teaching.

Figure 1.5 represents the key stages of the reflective process.

2.3 Competence in classroom enquiry

Reflective teaching requires competence in methods of classroom enquiry, to support the development of teaching competence.

I will identify three types of competence – gathering information, analysis and evaluation – each of which contributes to the cyclical process of reflection (see section 2.2). I focus on these because they provide the foundation for strategic thinking and planning for future provision. In the cyclical process, this is followed by action and by further evaluation and reflection, before the whole cycle begins again – spiralling towards higher quality teaching.

Empirical competence. This relates to the essential issue of knowing what is going on in a classroom or school. It is concerned with collecting data, describing situations, processes, causes and effects with care and accuracy. Two sorts of data are particularly relevant. Objective data, such as descriptions of what people actually do, are important, but so too are subjective data which describe how people feel and think – their perceptions. The collection of both types of data calls for considerable skill on the part of any classroom investigator, particularly when they may be enquiring into their own practice.

Analytical competence. This form of competence is needed to address the issue of how to interpret descriptive data. Such 'facts' are not meaningful until they are

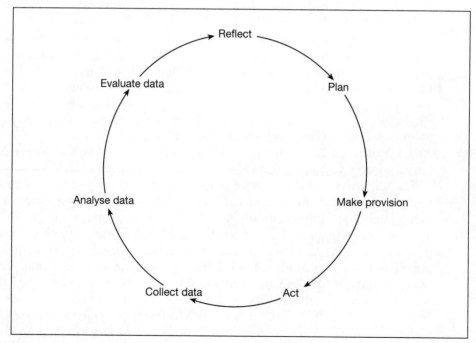

Figure 1.5 *The process of reflective teaching*

placed in a framework which enables a reflective teacher to relate them one with the other and to begin to theorize about them.

Evaluative competence. Evaluative competences are involved in making judgements about the educational consequences of the results of the practical enquiry. Evaluation, in the light of aims, values and the experience of others, enables the results of an enquiry to be applied to future policy and practice.

Further practical discussion on competence in classroom enquiry is offered in Chapter 3 of this book and in *Readings*. However, such competence is not sufficient in itself for a teacher who wishes to engage in reflective teaching. Certain attitudes are also necessary and need to be integrated and applied with enquiry skills.

2.4 Attitudes towards teaching

Reflective teaching requires attitudes of open-mindedness, responsibility and wholeheartedness.

Open-mindedness
As Dewey put it, open-mindedness is an

> active desire to listen to more sides than one, to give heed to facts from whatever source they come, to give full attention to alternative possibilities, to recognize the possibility of error even in the beliefs which are dearest to us.
>
> (Dewey, 1933, p. 29)

Open-mindedness is an essential attribute for rigorous reflection because any sort of enquiry which is consciously based on partial evidence only weakens itself. We thus use it in the sense of being willing to reflect upon ourselves and to challenge our assumptions, prejudices and ideologies as well as those of others. However, to be open-minded regarding evidence and its interpretation is not the same thing as declining to take up a value-position on important social and educational issues. This point brings us to the second attribute which Dewey saw as a prerequisite to reflective action – 'responsibility'.

Responsibility
Intellectual responsibility, according to Dewey, means,

> to consider the consequences of a projected step; it means to be willing to adopt these consequences when they follow reasonably .... Intellectual responsibility secures integrity.
>
> (Dewey, 1933, p. 30)

The position which is implied here is clearly related to the issue of aims which were discussed above. However, in Dewey's writing the issue is relatively clearly bounded and he seems to be referring to classroom teaching and to school practices only. Zeichner has taken this considerably further when, in considering teacher education, he points out that

> Because of the intimate relationships between the school and the social, political and economic contexts in which it exists, any consideration of the consequences to which classroom action leads must inevitably take one beyond the boundaries of the classroom and even of the school itself and beyond the consideration of educational

> principles alone. ... An exclusive focus on the level of the classroom and on educa-
> tional principles alone does not enable the student teacher to contemplate the kinds
> of basic structural changes that may be necessary for his or her responsibility to be
> fully exercised. The attention of student teachers remains focused on the amelioration
> of surface symptoms in individuals and not on an analysis of the social conditions
> that stand behind, and at least partially explain, the existence of those symptoms.
>
> (Zeichner, 1981/82, pp. 6–7)

Here, Zeichner is asserting the inevitable consequence of relating means and ends
in education with systematic open-mindedness. Moral, ethical and political issues
will be raised and must, he argues, be considered so that professional and personal
judgements can be made about what is worthwhile. It clearly follows that a simple
instrumental approach to teaching is not consistent with reflectiveness (see also
Reading, 3.2).

Wholeheartedness

'Wholeheartedness', the third of Dewey's necessary attitudes, refers essentially to
the way in which such consideration takes place. Dewey's suggestion was that
reflective teachers should be dedicated, single-minded, energetic and enthusiastic.
As he put it,

> There is no greater enemy of effective thinking than divided interest .... A genuine
> enthusiasm is an attitude that operates as an intellectual force. When a person is
> absorbed, the subject carries him on.
>
> (Dewey, 1933, p. 30)

Together, these three attitudes are vital ingredients of the 'professional' commitment
which needs to be demonstrated by all those who aim to be reflective teachers.

2.5 Teacher judgement

*Reflective teaching is based on teacher judgement, which is informed partly
by self-reflection and partly by insights from educational disciplines.*

Teacher knowledge has often been criticized. For instance, Bolster (1983) carried
out an analysis of teachers as classroom decision-makers and concluded that
teacher knowledge commonly has certain negative characteristics. In particular, he
suggested that, since teacher knowledge is specific and pragmatic, it is resistant to
change. Bolster argued that teacher knowledge is based on individual experiences
and is believed to be of value if it 'works' in practical situations. However, since it
'works', there is little incentive to change, even in the light of evidence supporting
alternative ideas or practices. On this analysis there is little need for teacher judgement, since teachers will stick to routinized practices.

However, Bolster's position does not seem to recognize adequately the very real
strengths of the knowledge which teachers can develop. For an alternative view it
is possible to draw on Donald Schön's work (1983, **Reading, 1.2**) on the characteristics of 'reflective practitioners'. Schön contrasted 'scientific' professional work
such as laboratory research, with 'caring' professional work such as education. He
called the former 'high hard ground' and saw it as supported by quantitative and
'objective' evidence. On the other hand, the 'swampy lowlands' of the caring professions involve more interpersonal areas and qualitative issues. These complex

'lowlands', according to Schön, tend to become 'confusing messes' of intuitive action. He thus suggested that, although such 'messes' tend to be highly relevant in practical terms, they are not easily amenable to rigorous analysis because they draw on a type of knowledge-in-action – knowledge that is inherent in professional action. It is spontaneous, intuitive, tacit and intangible but, it 'works' in practice.

Schön also argued that it is possible to recognize 'reflection-in-action', in which adjustments to action are made through direct experience. As he put it:

> When someone reflects-in-action, he [*sic*] becomes a researcher in the practice context. He is not dependent on the categories of established theory and technique, but constructs a new theory of the unique case. His enquiry is not limited to a deliberation about means which depends on a prior agreement about ends. He does not keep means and ends separate, but defines them interactively as he frames a problematic situation. He does not separate thinking from action.... His experimenting is a kind of action, implementation is built into his enquiry.
>
> (Schön, 1983, p. 68)

Such ideas have received powerful empirical support in recent years, with the sophistication of teachers' classroom thinking and 'craft knowledge' being increasingly recognized and understood by researchers (e.g., Elbaz, 1983; Calderhead, 1987, 1988, **Reading, 1.8**; Cortazzi, 1990, **Reading, 4.2**; Olson, 1991; Brown and McIntyre, 1992). It is clear that effective teachers make use of judgements all the time, as they adapt their teaching to the ever changing learning challenges which their circumstances and pupils present to them.

However, there is a danger too in this affirmation of the sophistication of much teacher thinking, for a justifiable emphasis on the value and merits of teacher-generated classroom knowledge could devalue the enriching strengths of other forms of educational insight. Many of these derive from research or analysis undertaken by people outside classrooms. They may be based on comparative, historical or philosophical research, on empirical study with large samples of classrooms, teachers, pupils or schools, on innovative methodologies or on developing theoretical analyses. Whatever its character, such educational research has the potential to complement, contextualize and enhance the detailed and practical understandings of teachers.

It is thus clearly worthwhile to maximize the potential for *collaboration* between teachers and researchers in relevant disciplines. For such collaboration to be successful it must be based on a frank appreciation of each other's strengths and weaknesses. While recognizing the danger of unjustified generalization, these strengths and weaknesses are identified below (see Figure 1.6).

We arrive, then, at a position which calls for attempts to draw on the strengths of teachers and researchers and, by doing so, overcome the weaknesses which exist in both positions. This is what we mean by the statement of the fifth characteristic of reflective teaching, that it should be based on 'informed teacher judgement'. The collaborative endeavour which is implied here underpins this whole book.

2.6 Learning with colleagues

Reflective teaching, professional learning and personal fulfilment are enhanced through collaboration and dialogue with colleagues.

The value of engaging in reflective activity is almost always enhanced if it can be carried out in association with other colleagues, be they students, teachers or tutors. The circumstances in primary schools, with the isolation of classes and very high proportions of contact-time with children, have constrained a great deal of such educational discussion in the past – though this is gradually changing as whole-school professional development assumes a greater priority. On teacher education courses, reflection together in seminars, tutor-groups and workshops, at college or in school, should bring valuable opportunities to share and compare, support and advise in reciprocal ways.

 Collaborative work capitalizes on the social nature of learning (Vygotsky, 1978, **Reading, 6.4**). This is as significant for adults as it is for children (see Chapter 6) and it works through many of the same basic processes.

Collaboration produces discussion and action together. Aims are thus clarified, experiences are shared, language and concepts for analysing practice are refined, the personal insecurities of innovation are reduced, evaluation becomes reciprocal and commitments are affirmed. Moreover, openness, activity and discussion grad-

	Strengths	Weaknesses
Researchers' knowledge	Often based on careful research with large samples and reliable methods	Often uses jargon unnecessarily and communicates poorly
	Often provides a clear and incisive analysis when studied	Often seems obscure and difficult to relate to practical issues
	Often offers novel ways of looking at situations and issues	Often fragments educational processes and experiences
	Often practically relevant and directly useful	Often impressionistic
Teachers' knowledge	Often communicated effectively to practitioners	Often relies too much on situations which might be unique
	Often concerned with the wholeness of class-room processes and experiences	When analysing, is sometimes unduly influenced by existing assumptions

Figure 1.6 *Comparison of researchers' and teachers' knowledge*

ually weave the values and self of individuals into the culture and mission of the school or course. This can be both personally fulfilling and educationally effective (Nias, 1989a, **Reading, 4.1**).

In the 1990s, when the development of coherence and progression in school policies and practice have become of enormous importance, collaborative work is also a necessity. At one level, it is officially endorsed by the requirement to produce 'school development plans', a process which has been seen as 'empowering' (Hargreaves and Hopkins, 1991, **Reading, 14.3**). More detailed work on the nature of primary school cultures, whilst affirming the enormous value of whole-school staff-teams working and learning together, have also shown the complexity and fragility of the process (Nias *et al.*, 1992, **Reading, 14.2**).

Whatever their circumstances, however, reflective teachers are likely to benefit from working, experimenting, talking and reflecting with others. Apart from the benefits for learning and professional development, it is usually both more interesting and more fun!

3 | MENTORING

Mentoring is the provision of support for the learning of one person through the guidance of another person who is more skilled, knowledgeable and experienced, particularly in relation to the context in which the learning is taking place.

The importance of mentoring in modern initial teacher education reflects two trends. First, there is the growing professional recognition and understanding of the complexity of teachers' capabilities and of the need to study, practice and develop these within real school contexts. Second, governments have required an increasing proportion of time on initial training courses to be spent in practical work in schools.

Mentoring, and being guided by a mentor, provides excellent opportunities for the development of both practical skills and reflective understanding. After all, that is the essential rationale for what is normally an officially designated relationship between a student teacher and an experienced teacher, underpinned by a 'partnership' arrangement between a school and the higher education institution which validates a student's course.

3.1 Roles in mentoring

Agreement about roles and relationships within such arrangements is obviously crucial if their benefits are to be maximized, and this is true for teacher mentors, student teachers and higher education tutors. If the roles are clear, then the learning potential of such situations are very considerable indeed.

The role of the mentor has been usefully analysed by Yeomans and Sampson (1994, **Reading, 1.5**). They suggest that it has three dimensions:

Structural: working across the school as planner, organizer, negotiator, inductor for the student placement;

Supportive: working with the student as host, friend and counsellor;

Professional: working with the student as trainer, educator and assessor.

The role of the tutor from the higher education institute can also be seen in terms of these three dimensions. Structurally, tutors must negotiate and facilitate the placement with the student, school and mentor. They must then support the relationship between the student and mentor as it develops, so that the potential benefits of that learning relationship are forthcoming. Professionally, they must contribute to the educational process with their comparative experience and knowledge from reading and research. In the assessment phase they must draw on their comparative judgement.

The role of the student is perhaps the most important. After all, mentoring, tutoring and school experience is directed to support student learning, and the student's approach to the new challenges he or she will meet is of enormous significance. Again, we can identify three dimensions of the role. Structurally, students need to present themselves and organize their activities so that they become accepted within the school. In terms of support, it is helpful if students are receptive to the efforts which the mentor and tutor make and are willing to develop a constructive relationship with them. Professionally, it is vital that the student adopts an active approach to the development of skills and understanding, that the learning value is extracted from classroom experiences and that advice is received openly. A student can also contribute a great deal to any necessary assessment phase, through the quality of his or her self-evaluation activities.

3.2 Learning through mentoring

If roles, relationships and channels for communication are established and open, then the potential for constructive professional learning is considerable. Focusing specifically on this, Peter Tomlinson (1995) has provided a very useful summary of four major forms of student learning activity and mentoring assistance, and these are set out in Figure 1.7.

This is an exciting agenda in which the mentor provides support at each stage of the teaching cycle (see Figure 1.5). Indeed, in many ways the mentor–student relationship is very close to that which is discussed in relation to social constructivist models of learning (see Chapter 6, section 1.3). Thus the mentor 'assists the performance' and 'scaffolds the understanding' of the student learner, as he or she constructs his or her own skills and understanding in the classroom context. Initially, the student will need direct support by explanation, modelling and guidance with the analysis of issues and with evaluation. Gradually, however, he or she will become sufficiently confident to teach more independently. Greater challenges will be faced (larger groups, longer teaching sessions, more complex teaching aims) and the student will begin to monitor his or her performance more independently. Collaborative teaching will reinforce these emergent skills and understandings as the student experiences the response of the mentor within specific teaching situations.

The mentor is thus uniquely placed to support the student in Tomlinson's first three ways (learning from others, learning from their own teaching, collaborating with others). Tutors from higher education institutions are likely to be able to make a particular contribution to the fourth element of exploring key concepts and broader issues.

1. Assisting students to learn from other people teaching by:

   - explaining the planning
   - guiding observation of the action
   - modelling and prompting monitoring
   - modelling and prompting reflection

2. Assisting students to learn through their own teaching activities by:

   - assisting their planning
   - supporting their teaching activity
   - assisting monitoring and feedback
   - assisting analysis and reflection

3. Progressively collaborative teaching involving:

   - progressive joint planning
   - teaching as a learning team
   - mutual monitoring
   - joint analysis and reflection

4. Exploring central ideas and broader issues through:

   - direct research on pupil, colleague, school and system contexts
   - reading and other inputs on teaching and background issues
   - organized discussion and tutorial work on these topics

Figure 1.7 *Major forms of student learning activity and mentoring assistance* (Tomlinson 1995)

4   COMPETENCE AND CAREER

4.1   Developing competent teacher judgement

In this section we look at career development and competence. This is important, if only because much present provision in this area is so haphazard. However, as Alexander *et al.*, (1992) argued so clearly, the future of primary education is partially dependent on improving the quality and targeting of support for teacher development in initial, induction and in-service stages of careers. To explore some of these issues, I have simplified some work by Elliott (1991a), who drew on Dreyfus (1981).

Dreyfus suggested that understanding and judgement in complex interpersonal situations is based on four basic capacities:

1. Recognizing issues;
2. Discerning which issues are important;
3. Understanding the situation as a whole;
4. Making decisions.

Dreyfus and Elliott mapped five stages in the development of these capacities for situational understanding and judgement. I have simplified these to just three, those of the 'novice', the 'competent' and the 'expert'. These three stages can then be related to the four capacities for situational understanding and decision-making (Table 1.2). The value of the model is that it highlights key factors in the *development* of competence. This can be applied to teaching.

Table 1.2 *Stages in the development of competence*

	Recognizing the issues	Discerning important issues	Understanding the whole situation	Making a decision
Novice	Out of context	No	Analytically	Rationally
Competent	In context	Yes	Analytically	Rationally
Expert	In context	Yes	Holistically	Intuitively

Novice teachers tend to need to proceed carefully, having only a limited understanding of the issues with which they are about to engage, and having to think hard about both the various features of their classroom situation and how best to act in it. Sometimes there is also a tendency for such teachers to seek security by conforming to the norms and culture of the school (Menter, 1989).

Competent teachers have had more experience and know classroom situations better. They can thus interpret and respond to events with more confidence, even though they still have to work at their decision-making.

Expert teachers work at a higher level of competence, understanding the various dimensions of school and classroom contexts so well that many of their decisions become almost intuitive. Where appropriate, they are also able to face the dilemmas of teaching with more self-confidence, to experiment with, and analyse, their own practice.

Of course, as with many developmental models, this model simplifies great complexity. For instance, for any one teacher it is very likely that levels of competence and self-confidence regarding different aspects of the teaching role will vary. More specific needs for professional development will need to be identified and met – a role which is increasingly being met by collegiate systems of appraisal (Bollington *et al.*, 1990, **Reading, 3.6**).

As I argued in the introduction to this chapter, reflective teaching is important as the process through which ascending levels of competence, in whatever sphere, can be developed. At a novice stage, reflection on one's practice can be unsettling and perhaps even painful at times. On the other hand it is part of the learning process and can also be affirming. At more competent stages there is a considerable danger that people may level out their aspirations for professional competence, and decide to coast along in routinized ways. Reflective practice will help to develop beyond this. As expert stages are reached, reflective teaching is likely to be an accepted part of the repertoire of teachers who are constantly asking questions of themselves and seeking to increase the quality of their provision.

Reflective teaching thus provides a means of constantly evaluating, developing and refining competences. It provides an essential underpinning for professional judgement, development and the provision of high quality education.

4.2 Reflecting on competences

Having suggested the value of defining competences and the role of reflective processes in developing them, it is appropriate to consider some avenues of critique. Several are suggested by the 'difficulties' identified in Figure 1.4. However, we can also approach this using a comparative strategy and by thinking about generic competences drawn from the world of industry.

A great deal of work on competences has been carried out in businesses, particularly with regard to productivity and management. Among the early influential studies are those of McBer and Company in the 1970s, summarized in a book *Three Factors of Success in the World of Work* by Klemp (1977). Klemp's key suggestion is that it is possible to distinguish three basic generic types of competence which are needed in acting appropriately in complex situations involving problem-solving and decisons. These should thus apply to many types of occupation – including teaching. Klemp suggests that there are:

- *Cognitive abilities* – for instance, understanding, analysing and communicating information, reflecting on experience
- *Interpersonal abilities* – for instance, empathizing with, relating to and supporting others
- *Motivational abilities* – for instance, personal goal setting, risk-taking and commitment to achieve; networking, goal-sharing and teamwork

The Practical Activity 1.1 applies these three categories to structure a critique of competences for teacher education.

The development and maintenance of appropriate types of cognitive, interpersonal and motivational competence is obviously necessary for high quality teaching – but, as we have seen, teachers crucially need the professional judgement to select from their repertoire of teaching competences, as appropriate, to meet the needs of the children whom they teach.

Practical activity 1.1

Aim: To consider how Klemp's three generic types of competence relate to the competences required of teachers or student teachers in your country or your course.

Method: Consider each of the competences listed in the official teacher education documentation of your country, or of your course. Classify them in terms of Klemp's cognitive, interpersonal and motivational abilities.

Follow-up: How appropriate, for teacher professionals, is the emphasis which you have found? Do you recognize these holistic qualities in teaching? Are they recognized by those who support your professional development?

Perhaps the major fear of those who oppose the use of competency statements in teacher education is that it will lead to itemization and fragmentation of what, when it is working well, is the holistic art of teaching. Teaching is only partly amenable to rational analysis, and, particularly in work with young children, the intangible contribution of rapport, intuition and imagination will often defy detailed analysis. This should not be seen as a weakness. Indeed, it is a necessary aspect of human interaction and part of what makes teaching fulfilling.

CONCLUSION

We have considered ways in which *states* of classroom competence can be defined and the benefits of doing so. We have also discussed the way in which reflective teaching provides a *process* through which successive levels of competence can be developed and maintained. We have outlined six characteristics of reflective teaching.

Some readers may well be wondering if this isn't all just a bit much to ask. How is the time to be found? Isn't it all 'common sense' anyway? I would respond in two ways. First, it must be accepted that engaging constantly in reflective activities of the sort described in this book would be impossible. The point however, is to use them, as appropriate, as *learning experiences*. Such experiences should lead to conclusions which can be applied in new and more routine circumstances. Second, there is certainly what some may see as a good deal of 'common sense' in the logic of the process of reflective teaching, but this resonance should be seen as a strength. When reflective teaching is used as a means of professional development it is extended far beyond this underpinning. The whole activity is much more rigorous – carefully gathered evidence replaces subjective impressions, open-mindedness replaces prior expectations, insights from reading or constructive and structured critique from colleagues challenge what might previously have been taken for granted. 'Common sense' may well endorse the value of the basic, reflective idea but, ironically, one outcome of reflection is often to produce critique and movement beyond the limitations of common-sense thinking. That, in a sense, is the whole point, the reason why it is a necessary part of professional activity. The aim of reflective practice is thus to support a shift from routine actions rooted in common-sense thinking to reflective action stemming from professional thinking.

Teachers can confidently expect to achieve an appropriate state of professional competence through adopting processes of reflective teaching – and the remainder of this book is designed to provide support in precisely that process.

Notes for further reading

The dilemmas in educational decision-making, which suggest that reflection is a continually necessary element of teaching, are analysed in:

Berlak, H. and Berlak, A. (1981)
Dilemmas of Schooling,
London: Methuen.

📖 Reading, 1.3

Two works by Dewey which have influenced our thinking are:

Dewey, J. (1916)
Democracy and Education,
New York: Free Press. Reading, 1.1

Dewey, J. (1933)
How We Think: A Restatement of the Relation of Reflective Thinking to the Educative Process,
Chicago: Henry Regnery. Reading, 1.1

The work of Zeichner on reflective teaching is also very stimulating. See, in particular:

Zeichner, K. (1981–2) Reflective teaching and field-based experience in pre-service teacher education, *Interchange*, **12**, 1–22.

Tabachnich, R. and Zeichner, K. (eds) (1991)
Issues and Practices in Inquiry-Oriented Teacher Education,
London: Falmer. Reading, 3.7

On the potential gains, embracing both practical competence and social emancipation, which are claimed to derive from self-evaluation and classroom enquiry see:

Stenhouse, L. (1983)
Authority, Education and Emancipation,
London: Heinemann. Reading, 3.1

Carr, W. and Kemmis, S. (1986)
Becoming Critical,
London: Falmer Press. Reading, 3.2

Elliott, J. (1991b)
Action Research for Educational Change,
Buckingham: Open University Press. Reading, 1.7

Smyth, J. (1991)
Teachers as Collaborative Learners,
Buckingham: Open University Press.

For a range of views on the nature of professional knowledge and its relationship to more theoretical analyses see:

McNamara, D. and Desforges, C. (1978) The social sciences, teacher education and the objectification of craft knowledge, *British Journal of Teacher Education,*
4 (1), 17–36.

Schön, D. (1983)
The Reflective Practitioner: How Professionals Think in Action,
London: Temple Smith. Reading, 1.2

Van Manen, M. (1990)
The Tact of Teaching: The Meaning of Pedagogical Thoughtfulness,
London, Ontario: Althouse Press.

Calderhead, J. (1988)
Teachers' Professional Learning,
London: Falmer. also Reading, 1.8

Brown, S. and McIntyre, D. (1992)
Making Sense of Teaching,
Buckingham: Open University Press.

For case-studies of teachers' practical reasoning see:

Elbaz, F. (1983)
Teacher Thinking: A Study of Practical Knowledge,
London: Croom Helm.

Clandinin, D. J. (1986)
Classroom Practice: Teacher Images In Action,
London: Falmer Press.

Cortazzi, M. (1990)
Primary Teaching How It Is: A Narrative Account,
London: David Fulton.
📖 Reading, 4.2

Cooper, P. and McIntyre, D. (1996)
Effective Teaching and Learning: Teachers' and Students' Perspectives,
Buckingham: Open University Press.

On the collaborative learning in primary schools see:

Nias, J., Southworth, G. and Campbell, P. (1992)
Whole-School Curriculum Development in the Primary School,
London: Falmer.
📖 Reading, 14.2

Biott, C. and Nias, J. (1992)
Working and Learning Together for Change,
Buckingham: Open University Press.

The field of competences in teacher education is a rapidly developing one. For very useful reviews of the issues, see:

Whitty, G. and Willmott, E. (1991)
Competence-based teacher education: approaches and issues,
Cambridge Journal of Education,
21 (3), 309–18.

Hustler, D. and McIntyre, D. (1996)
Developing Competent Teachers: Approaches to Professional Competence in Teacher Education,
London: David Fulton.

The most developed investigation of teaching competences for primary education is that of the Leverhulme Primary Project at the University of Exeter. See:

Bennett, S. N. and Carré, C. (eds) (1993)
Learning to Teach,
London: Routledge.
📖 Reading, 1.4

For an analytical view of the relationship of competency and professionalism, see Chapter 8 of:

Elliott, J. (1991b)
Action Research for Educational Change,
Buckingham: Open University Press.
📖 Reading, 1.7

The holistic, intuitive and contextualized competence, which Elliott characterizes 'expert', is also often described as reflecting the 'art' of teaching. For an influential perspective on this, including the concept of 'connoisseurship', see:

Eisner, E. W. (1979)
The Educational Imagination,
New York: Macmillan.

The key documents for Scotland, England and Wales which specify competences for initial teacher education are:

Scottish Office Education Department (1992)
Revised Guidelines for Teacher Training Courses,
Scottish Office Education Department: Edinburgh.

Department for Education/Welsh Office (1992)
Initial Teacher Training (Secondary Phase),
DFE Circular 9/92, WO Circular 35/92,
London: DFE.

Department for Education (1993)
The Initial Training of Primary School Teachers: New Criteria for Course Approval,
London: DFE.   📖 **Reading, 1.6**

For a sustained attempt to identify competences of reflective teaching, see:

Hextall, I., Lawn, M., Menter, I., Sidgwick, S. and Walker, S. (1991)
Imaginative projects: arguments for a new teacher education,
Evaluation and Research in Education,
5 (1) and (2), 79–95.

Recent approaches to teacher education and training are premised on large proportions of school-based initial teacher education and on close partnership between higher education institutions and schools. For a collection of papers which reviews the issues involved in such partnership, see:

Booth, M., Furlong, J. and Wilkin, M. (1990)
Partnership in Initial Teacher Training,
London: Cassell.

The government agency which is responsible for teacher training is the Teacher Training Agency. See:

Teacher Training Agency (1995)
Corporate Plan, 1995,
London: TTA.

The role of experienced teachers in mentoring students in school is of enormous importance in modern teacher education programmes. For useful books on this, see:

Yeomans, R. and Sampson, J. (eds) (1994)
Mentorship in the Primary School,
London, Falmer Press.   📖 **Reading, 1.5**

McIntyre, D. and Hagger, H. (1996)
Mentors in Schools: Developing the Profession of Teaching,
London: David Fulton.

Tomlinson, P. (1995)
Understanding Mentoring: Reflective Strategies for School-Based Teacher Preparation,
Buckingham: Open University Press.

Furlong, J. and Maynard, T. (1995)
Mentoring Student Teachers: The Growth of Professional Knowledge,
London: Routledge.

For international comparisons of changes in teacher education which track a tightening of state control in many countries, see:

Popkewitz, T. (ed.) (1993)
Changing Patterns of Power: Social Regulation and Teacher Education Reform in Eight Countries,
New York: State University of New York Press.

Given the influence of Dewey on reflection in professional life, and the intellectual openness advocated by him, we should be prepared to engage with those who espouse very different views. For a direct attack on Dewey and on educationalists, see:

O'Hear, A. (1991)
Education and Democracy: Against the Educational Establishment,
London: Claridge.

CHAPTER 2

Social contexts, teachers and children

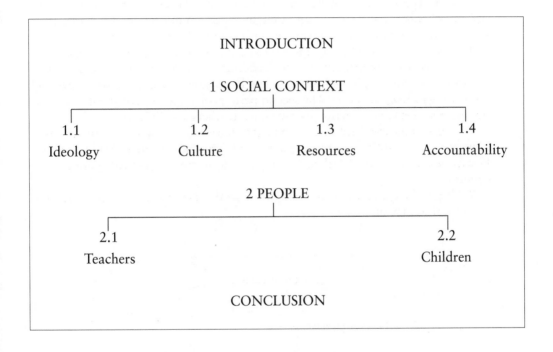

INTRODUCTION

This chapter is intended as an introduction and as a brief review of a wide-ranging set of issues which are important for teachers in primary schools. It provides a context for the much more specific factors regarding teaching and learning which will be considered in the various chapters of Part 2. Figure 2.1 represents the way in which the relationships between these factors have been conceptualized in this book.

I will argue that the influence of social context pervades everything that happens in schools and classrooms and that, as suggested in Chapter 1, awareness of such issues is an important contributing element of reflective teaching.

The second purpose of the chapter is to establish a theoretical model concerning the relationships of individuals and society. Indeed, the chapter is very deliberately in two parts. The first, 'social context', emphasizes the ideas, social structures and resources which *affect* action. The second part, 'people', is concerned with the various factors which *enable* action by individual teachers and children.

Of course, this argument can be applied to the education system of any country. However, for illustrative purposes, this chapter focuses on the United Kingdom. Please see the Notes for Further Reading for suggested sources concerning other countries.

We begin the chapter by discussing the social context and by introducing the theoretical framework.

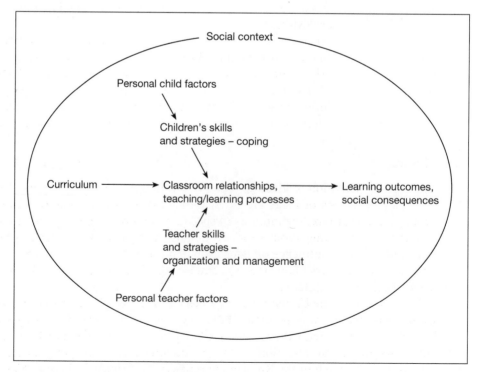

Figure 2.1 *Factors in classroom teaching and learning*

1 SOCIAL CONTEXT

A particular theoretical position underpins this chapter and, indeed, the book as a whole. At the core of this position is the concept of a dialectical relationship between society and individuals. This suggests the existence of a constant interplay of social forces and individual actions. On the one hand, the decisions and actions which people make and take in their lives are constrained by social structures and by the historical processes which brought about such structures. On the other hand, each individual has a unique sense of self, derived from his or her personal history or biography. Individuals have a degree of free will in acting and in developing understandings with others. Sets of these understandings, which endure over time, form the basis of cultures. Such understandings can also lead to challenges to established social structures and thus to future changes.

For example, there are differences between various social groups in terms of power, wealth, status and opportunities (Halsey, 1986; Goldthorpe, 1987; Reid, 1989; Government Statistical Service, 1991). However, individuals, each with their own background and sense of self, will react to such factors in a variety of ways. Some in powerful positions might wish to close ranks and defend themselves by suggesting that their position is inherited by right or earned by merit. Some among those who are less fortunate may accept the social order or even aspire to success in its terms. Others may try to contest it for, of course, to be able to question existing social arrangements is a fundamental right in our democratic societies.

 There is, thus, an ebb and flow in social change, a process of tension and struggle. At opposite poles are action and constraint, voluntarism and determinism, biography and history (Mills, 1959, **Reading, 2.1**).

A reflective teacher has responsibilities within this process which should not be avoided. With this in mind, we will now discuss four aspects of the social context which are particularly significant for practice in primary schools: ideology, culture, resources and accountability. The influence of each can be traced at national, regional, local and school levels so that, although such issues sometimes seem distant, they affect children and teachers in classrooms in very real ways.

1.1 Ideology

A dictionary definition of ideology states that it means a 'way of thinking'. However, particular sets of ideas are often used, consciously or unconsciously, to promote and legitimize the interests of specific groups of people. Indeed, if a particular way of thinking about society is dominant at any point in time it is likely to be an important influence on education and on teachers' actions. It may produce a particular curriculum emphasis and even begin to frame the ways in which teachers relate with children.

For instance, in the United States of America of the 1950s, the Cold War, anti-Communist feeling was so great that it not only led to the now discredited inquisitions of the McCarthy Committee but also to a range of nationalistic practices in schools, reinterpretations of history and pressures to compete, particularly after the 1957 launch of the Russian Sputnik satellite. Similarly, in the USSR and

Eastern-bloc countries, before the revolutionary changes which swept Eastern Europe in 1989, pupils were taught highly selective views of history, of the values and achievements of their societies. They too were encouraged to compete, particularly to sustain exceptional international achievements in areas such as science and sport. In both cases, despite widely differing circumstances, it can be seen that the ideologies of key political elites interacted with the 'common-sense thinking' of the wider population to create particular ideological climates (see the work of Gramsci, 1978, for an analysis of such hegemonic phenomena). Although the influence of these ideological periods was enormous, they passed.

The ideologies which more specifically influence primary education also come and go. As we saw in Chapter 1, the 1960s' and 1970s' professional ideology of child-centredness (Alexander, 1984) has gradually been supplanted. However, many commentators have suggested that the educational policies of successive Conservative governments since 1979 were based on the influence of 'New Right' ideologies and pressure groups (e.g. Gamble, 1986; Whitty, 1989; Quicke, 1988). The most influential of these pressure groups, often with interlocking memberships, were the Hillgate Group (e.g. 1987), the Adam Smith Institute (1984), the No Turning Back Group of MPs (1986), the Centre for Policy Studies (e.g. Cox and Marks, 1982; Lawlor, 1988), the National Council for Educational Standards (e.g. Marks and Pomian-Srzednicki, 1985) and the Campaign for Real Education (e.g. Yeo, 1992; Marks, 1992).

One important belief of the members of these groups is that educational standards need to be raised and that the best way to do this is to provide more parental choice and school accountability, so that educational provision is subject to market forces. Another belief is that basic skills of literacy should be prioritized and taught traditionally and that key elements of British history and culture should be emphasized.

In the 1980s and early 1990s such ideas were taken up by many in the media and there were repeated 'moral panics' (Cohen, 1972) in which public concern was orchestrated, for instance, over issues such as reading, spelling, 'failing schools', Shakespeare and teaching methods.

Civil servants and educationalists had, in the post-war years, tended to moderate such political activity, when it relatively infrequently occurred. This in itself was a reflection of the influence of policy-making professionals' own ideologies and 'assumptive world' (McPherson and Raab, 1988). However, they were unable to assert such influence in the late 1980s, and there was a considerable struggle for control between politicians, civil servants and professionals over education policy (Ball, 1990). By the early 1990s it was absolutely clear that the politicians had won, with reorganizations at the Department of Education, an apparent reduction in the scale and independence of Her Majesty's Inspectors, reorganizing of the national bodies for curriculum and assessment and dismissal of the protests of teachers' professional associations.

In terms of examining the intended effects and likely consequences of recent changes, some historians have argued (for example, Simon, 1985, 1992) that, by such means, attempts are made to make the education system more effective as a means of 'social control'. In other words, existing social and class structures are to be accepted and reproduced. Indeed, authors such as Althusser (1971) have seen education systems within capitalist societies as 'ideological state apparatuses' which are designed for precisely this purpose (see also **Reading, 13.1**). On the other hand, sociologists such as Collins (1977), Kogan (1978) and Archer (1979, **Reading, 15.1**) have argued that educational policies and provision are the product of competing interest groups and that control and power is more diffuse.

In any event, the recent legislation from central government has radically challenged what previously had been, in effect, a very decentralized system, so that the priorities, structures, centres of control and accountability have all been restructured. Teachers are now regularly required to respond to the direction of central government as new priorities supplant old ones.

The dominant patterns of thinking about primary school practice have thus changed considerably in recent years. However, awareness of the concept of ideology makes it more likely that the values or interests that may lie behind another round of proposals, for instance from 'New Labour', will be considered by reflective teachers. It is also worth remembering that societies and dominant ideologies are never static. At some point in time, critique and experience lead to re-evaluation, counter-proposals, development and change (see Bowe and Ball with Gold, 1992, **Reading, 2.4**). There will be no end to this story.

Nor should we forget that no one, including ourselves, is immune to the influences of ideologies. For instance, professional ideologies are likely to always remain strong among teachers – they represent commitments, ideals *and* interests. Reflective teachers should be open-minded enough to critique constructively their own beliefs, as well as those of others.

1.2 Culture

Cultures can be seen as sets of shared perspectives and as the products of people acting together. Cultures can develop from collective activity and from the creative responses of groups to situations. Furthermore, it must also be recognized that cultures endure over time and can thus represent sets of ideas, perspectives, values and practices into which individuals are likely to be socialized. The playground cultures of children provide an example here. In one sense, children in friendship groups develop unique and particular ways of perceiving school life. Indeed, they use these as a means of understanding school and coping with it (Davies, 1982, **Reading, 4.6**; Pollard, 1987b; Clarricoates, 1987). Yet, at the same time, continuities in children's culture, from generation to generation, seem to provide a context which young children absorb (Opie and Opie, 1959; Slukin, 1981).

Several other kinds of culture are likely to affect teachers. For instance, the community which the school serves provide another cultural context. This is bound to influence and be influenced by the perspectives of parents, children and teachers. Few communities, however, can be characterized as single, united entities. Among the many divisions which may exist are those relating to race, language, religion, social class, sexuality and to political or personal values. The existence of such cultural diversity is particularly important in many inner-city schools and reflective teachers are likely to explore the relationship between cultures in the home and in the school very carefully indeed. A great deal of research has shown problems arising when working-class cultures are regarded as being deficient by those in schools (for example, King, 1978; Sharp and Green, 1975) and institutionalized forms of racism are likely to result if teachers fail to take appropriate account of

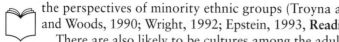

the perspectives of minority ethnic groups (Troyna and Hatcher, 1992; Grugeon and Woods, 1990; Wright, 1992; Epstein, 1993, **Reading, 13.5**).

There are also likely to be cultures among the adults within each school. Those which are particularly important for teachers are the professional ones which develop out of the staff-room – that backstage area where tensions are released, feelings are shared and understandings about school life are developed. This is the territory of the classroom teacher, and the resulting teacher cultures usually provide a source of solidarity and sympathy when facing the daily pressures of classrooms (Nias *et al.*, 1989, **Reading, 4.1**). While colleagues may be stimulating and supportive of experimentation, they can also become protective of existing practices and inhibit innovation. Furthermore, there is sometimes a tendency for staff-room talk to avoid important educational issues which might be contentious and might thus begin to break down the sense of solidarity which teacher cultures are, in a sense, collaboratively created to provide (Sedgwick, 1988; Pollard, 1987a).

Despite this element of constraint and limitation in some aspects of teacher cultures, it should be remembered that they develop in response to particular conditions and work experiences in a school. One crucial factor here is the availability and nature of resources, and it is to this issue that we now turn.

1.3 Resources

Adequate resources are essential in education and we will distinguish four types here: people, buildings, equipment and materials. In both quality and quantity, these resources have an impact on what it is possible to do in schools and classrooms (House of Commons, 1986; Stewart, 1986). A very consistent feeling from teachers is that class size is a major factor in determining educational practice and there is much research which supports this proposition (e.g. Glass *et al.*, 1979, see also **Reading, 9.1**).

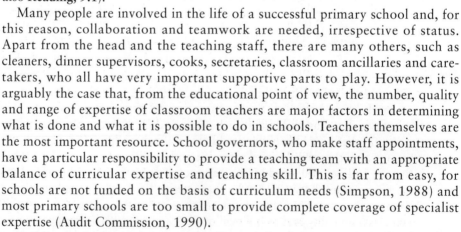

Many people are involved in the life of a successful primary school and, for this reason, collaboration and teamwork are needed, irrespective of status. Apart from the head and the teaching staff, there are many others, such as cleaners, dinner supervisors, cooks, secretaries, classroom ancillaries and caretakers, who all have very important supportive parts to play. However, it is arguably the case that, from the educational point of view, the number, quality and range of expertise of classroom teachers are major factors in determining what is done and what it is possible to do in schools. Teachers themselves are the most important resource. School governors, who make staff appointments, have a particular responsibility to provide a teaching team with an appropriate balance of curricular expertise and teaching skill. This is far from easy, for schools are not funded on the basis of curriculum needs (Simpson, 1988) and most primary schools are too small to provide complete coverage of specialist expertise (Audit Commission, 1990).

Buildings are also an important influence on what goes on in schools. At its most obvious, buildings constrain decisions about numbers and types of classes because of the number and nature of the classrooms which are available. This often affects class sizes and forms of curriculum and teaching organization. The quality of the school environment will also be influenced by aesthetic considerations, and schools vary considerably in terms of the degree of consideration which is given to this issue. Many schools still date from the last century, particularly in rural and inner-city areas. These are often built on a 'central' model, with classes leading from a large hall, or on a 'linear' model, with classes ranged along a corridor. Buildings from the early 1970s are particularly notable for 'open-plan' designs. Adequate maintenance of school buildings is recognized as being important but appropriate budget allocations are not always possible. Reflective teachers are likely to be concerned about the quality of the learning environment within their school and will aim to maximize the learning potential of the buildings and space which they have available. In one sense, buildings have an obvious fixed quality and are a source of constraint; on the other hand, it is surprising what uses and activities creative imaginations can produce.

Equipment is very significant in primary education because it is often through the use of equipment that young children are able to get appropriate learning experiences in school. This ranges from hall and playground requirements to the instruments for music-making, the artefacts for historical work and the wide-ranging resource needs of the modern science, maths and English curricula.

Materials such as paper, pencils, creative and artistic materials, are the bread-and-butter consumables of a school. The quality of learning experiences will be directly affected by such provision. However, budgeting for them is often not easy.

Since the 1988 Education Reform Act, all schools have 'locally managed' budgets. Income is distributed annually from each LEA or direct from central government, on the basis of a formula. This formula allocates a certain amount for each pupil on roll, plus certain other amounts in respect of social disadvantage, special educational needs or school size. Expenditure is the responsibility of the headteacher and governors. However, school managers often have relatively small sums to spend at their discretion, once fixed costs are taken out of the overall budget (see Audit Commission, 1991). For instance, in primary schools the salaries of teachers and other staff often amount to around 80 per cent of the budget, and costs of building maintenance and school running costs may come to another 10 per cent. Thus in 1995/6, a medium-sized primary school in Bristol, with 145 children on roll and a total budget of £226,100, could only preserve £13,000, 6 per cent of its budget, to spend directly on educational equipment, books and materials (see Chapter 14, section 1).

All resources have to be paid for and, on a national basis, education is a significant expense. For instance, the total cost of education in 1991/2 was £29 billion, or 14 per cent of all government spending. Primary education in England and Wales alone costs almost £5 billion. At the local level education is by far the largest item in council budgets: about 70 per cent in some cases, of which the most significant item is teachers' salaries.

Resourcing levels vary somewhat between local education authorities, for the levels of government support, the degree of priority given to education and the exact form of the funding formula differs from one LEA to another. Further resource differences emerge due to the fact that a considerable contribution to total school incomes can be made by parental fund-raising. For instance, HMI (DES, 1985b) reported a variation for single schools between £70 and £9,000 per annum and the Audit Commission (1991) reported schools receiving between £1 and £96 extra per pupil per year. It seems likely that social divisiveness will be increased by such parental funding because of the wide differences in the distribution of parental wealth and incomes in different local areas and regions of the country.

Thus, the level of resourcing in particular classrooms is dependent on a combination of school-based decisions, numbers of pupils on roll and the priority given to education by national and local governments. A good deal of political, as well as professional, judgement is involved at all points (Hewton, 1986; Kingdom, 1991; Byrne, 1992; see also Dale, 1996, **Reading, 15.6**).

While resources structure the material conditions in which teachers work, the actions which they might take are also likely to be influenced by the degree of autonomy which they feel they have. For this reason, we now focus on the issue of accountability.

1.4 Accountability

Teachers in the public education system are paid, through national and local taxation systems, to provide a professional service. However, the degree of accountability and external control to which they have been subject has varied historically and has been subject to considerable change in recent years.

In the first part of this century, the payment-by-results system of the late 1800s, although superseded, still left a legacy in the form of imposed performance requirements in reading, writing and arithmetic (see also **Reading, 7.4**). Handbooks of suggestions for good practice were published regularly, as guidelines, but were not enforceable. However, from the 1920s teachers began to develop greater professional autonomy and in this they benefited from the acquiescence of successive governments (Lawn and Ozga, 1981). In particular, the independence of headteachers within their schools, and of class teachers within their classrooms, emerged to become established principles. After the Second World War, as professional confidence grew, this independence extended into the curriculum: so much so that, in 1960, it was described by Lord Eccles, Minister for Education, as a 'secret garden' into which central government was not expected to intrude. Such confidence was probably at a high point in the early 1970s.

Since then, the changing ideological, economic and political climate has resulted in teachers coming under increasing pressure: first to increase their 'accountability'; and second, to demonstrate their competence. These developments were presented as a necessary reduction in the influence of the 'producers' (seen as teacher unions, administrators and theorists) and as enabling educational provision to be shaped by the 'consumers' (seen as parents and industry, though with little direct reference to children themselves). In England, following the Education Reform Act of 1988, the government set up two organizations to implement this transformation – the National Curriculum Council (NCC) and the School Examination and Assessment Council (SEAC). They were replaced in 1993, by a single body – the School Curriculum and Assessment Authority (SCAA).

Some of the products of these trends can now, in the late 1990s, be seen. For instance, regarding accountability, both the rights and the numbers of governors drawn from parents, industry and the community have been increased, governors must present an annual report to parents and parents have their 'rights' enshrined by the government in a 'Parents' Charter' (DES, 1992a). Information from both standardized and teacher assessment of pupils must now be published to parents, together with written, annual reports. These results, and school attendance figures, can, it is claimed, be used to judge the effectiveness of schools (see Chapter 12, section 2.6). In 1992 Her Majesty's Inspectorate, a widely respected and independent body which had advised on both particular schools and the system for over one hundred and fifty years, was scaled down and reorganized within the Office for Standards in Education (OFSTED), which contracts teams of inspectors (including non-educationalists) with the aim of making a public report on every individual school in a four-yearly cycle (see Chapter 14, section 2).

On the issue of teacher appraisal, despite constructive negotiations within the profession (National Steering Group, 1989) and a significant increase in both LEA appraisal schemes and methods of school-based, self-evaluation, a national appraisal was imposed in England and Wales. Pressure for linkage of appraisal to salary levels remains strong.

In an historical review of such developments, Grace has suggested:

> We are now in a period where the social and political context of state-provided schooling in Britain is reminiscent in a number of ways of the climate of reaction in the 1860s. There is a growing emphasis upon tighter accountability; a required core curriculum and a concentration upon basics. The role and strength of the inspectorate is being reappraised and changes can be expected in the ideology and practice of inspection at all levels. Both teacher training and the work of teachers in schools are to be subject to more surveillance and to the application of more specific criteria for the assessment and evaluation of competence.
>
> (Grace, 1985, p. 13)

Accountability is thus an important aspect of social context because it highlights both legal requirements and areas of independent and consultative decision-making. Nor should we forget that, underlying all the specific measures which we have reviewed, is the conception of market competition 'forcing up standards'. Thus the greatest influence on accountability is supposedly the 'market'. Whether market strategies achieve their intended results or not, there is no doubt that accountability measures have enormous implications for each teacher's work experience (see Menter *et al.*, 1996, **Reading, 14.5**). This is likely to remain an area of much flux and considerable contest, particularly between the government and teacher unions.

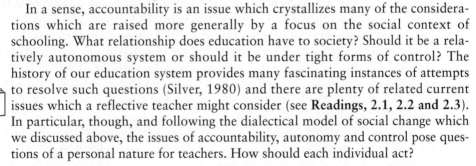

In a sense, accountability is an issue which crystallizes many of the considerations which are raised more generally by a focus on the social context of schooling. What relationship does education have to society? Should it be a relatively autonomous system or should it be under tight forms of control? The history of our education system provides many fascinating instances of attempts to resolve such questions (Silver, 1980) and there are plenty of related current issues which a reflective teacher might consider (see **Readings, 2.1, 2.2 and 2.3**). In particular, though, and following the dialectical model of social change which we discussed above, the issues of accountability, autonomy and control pose questions of a personal nature for teachers. How should each individual act?

2 | PEOPLE

Within the dialectical model, which conceptualizes the constant interaction of social structures and individuals, personal factors are the counterpart of social context. For instance, classroom life can be seen as being created by teachers and children as they respond to the situations in which they find themselves. Thus, as well as understanding something of the factors affecting the social context of schooling, we also need to consider how teachers and children respond. We begin by focusing on teachers.

2.1 Teachers

Teachers are people who happen to hold a particular position in schools. I make no apologies for wishing to begin by asserting this simple fact, for it has enormous implications. Each person is unique, with particular cultural and material experiences making up his or her 'biography' (Sikes *et al.*, 1985). This provides the seed-bed for their sense of 'self' and influences their personality and perspectives (Mead, 1934). The development of each person continues throughout life, but early formative experiences remain important. Indeed, because personal qualities, such as having the capacity to empathize and having the confidence to project and assert oneself, are so important in teaching, much of what particular teachers will be able to achieve in their classrooms will be influenced by them. Of even greater importance is the capacity to know oneself. We all have strengths and weaknesses and most teachers would agree that classroom life tends to reveal these fairly quickly (Nias, 1989a, **Reading, 4.1**). Reflective teaching is, therefore, a great deal to do with facing such features of ourselves in a constructive and objective manner and in a way which incorporates a continuous capacity to change and develop.

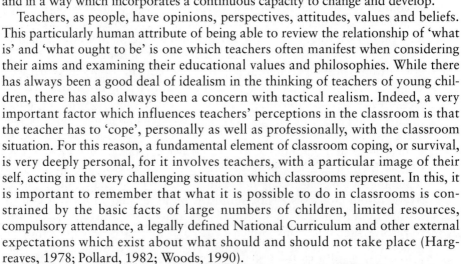

Teachers, as people, have opinions, perspectives, attitudes, values and beliefs. This particularly human attribute of being able to review the relationship of 'what is' and 'what ought to be' is one which teachers often manifest when considering their aims and examining their educational values and philosophies. While there has always been a good deal of idealism in the thinking of teachers of young children, there has also always been a concern with tactical realism. Indeed, a very important factor which influences teachers' perceptions in the classroom is that the teacher has to 'cope', personally as well as professionally, with the classroom situation. For this reason, a fundamental element of classroom coping, or survival, is very deeply personal, for it involves teachers, with a particular image of their self, acting in the very challenging situation which classrooms represent. In this, it is important to remember that what it is possible to do in classrooms is constrained by the basic facts of large numbers of children, limited resources, compulsory attendance, a legally defined National Curriculum and other external expectations which exist about what should and should not take place (Hargreaves, 1978; Pollard, 1982; Woods, 1990).

In such circumstances, teachers face acute dilemmas between their personal and professional concerns and the practical possibilities (Berlak and Berlak, 1981, **Reading, 1.3**). They are forced to juggle with their priorities as they manage the stress which is often involved (Dunham, 1992; Cole and Walker, 1989) and as they come to terms with the classroom situation.

The final set of personal factors about teachers to which attention will be drawn relates to their position as employees. The first aspect of this is that teachers are workers and have legitimate legal, contractual and economic interests to maintain, protect and develop (Lawn and Ozga, 1981; Lawn and Grace, 1987). Some balance has to be struck between educational expectations and what it is reasonable to ask of people who happen to earn their living from teaching. It should never be forgotten that teachers also have their own personal lives outside the classroom. Both male and female teachers have family responsibilities, as well as other interests which may be important to their own personal development. In a very real sense then, teachers, especially the females who make up the vast majority of primary teachers, experience the pressure of having two 'jobs' (Evetts, 1990; Acker, 1989).

2.2 Children

As with the personal factors associated with teachers, the most important point to make about children is that they are thinking, rational individuals (James and Prout, 1990). Each one, of the almost five million primary school pupils in the UK, has a unique 'biography'. The way in which they feel about themselves, and present themselves in school, will be influenced by their understandings of previous cultural, social and material experience (Richards and Light, 1986; Bruner, 1986). Their sense of 'self' and their emerging personality will be at relatively early stages of their development – a fact which may well leave each child rather vulnerable when confronted with the challenges of school life (Barrett, 1989; Cleave and Brown, 1992).

Perhaps the most important fact for teachers to consider is the huge range of attributes and experiences which children may bring to school. Factors, such as sex, social class, race, language development, learning styles, health and types of parental support, are so numerous and so complex in their effects that, although broad but important generalizations about patterns of advantage and disadvantage can be made (Rutter and Madge, 1976; Osborn *et al.*, 1984), it is foolish to generalize in specific terms about their ultimate consequences. This caution is made even more necessary if it is acknowledged that factors in children's backgrounds can influence, but not determine, consequences. Nevertheless, children are faced by many challenges in the modern world. For instance, the Institute for Fiscal Studies (1995) reported that 3.7 million children in the UK were growing up in families living on, or below, the poverty line (being dependent on Income Support benefits or with a household income below this level). A report by the Joseph Rowntree Foundation (1995) showed that income inequality widened rapidly from 1977 to 1990, with the lowest paid being worse off in both absolute and relative terms. The family circumstances in which children develop are becoming increasingly diverse, with UK marriages at their lowest number since the 1920s (Central Statistical Office, 1995). Other factors also have important impacts, such as the growing diversity of cultures and social groups in our societies; the multiple influences of new forms of mass media.

However, coming between children's backgrounds, biographies and experiences and their educational development is the whole issue of how children actually respond to their circumstances and, indeed, of how teachers provide for them. Like teachers, children have to learn to cope and survive in classroom situations in which they may well feel insecure. We would argue that children's culture and the support of a peer group are considerable resources in this. However, such cultural responses by children can also pose dilemmas in class when children try to satisfy personal interests by attempting to please both their peers and their teacher. Creative strategies are called for and these may cover a range from conformity through negotiation to rejection. Once again then, we should highlight the importance of the subjectivity of the perspectives which teachers and children develop as they interact. Such perspectives are likely to be a great influence on the motivation which children feel and on the ways in which learning is approached (Pollard with Filer, 1996).

Above all, though, we must never forget that children are placed in the role of 'pupils' for only part of each day (Calvert, 1975). It is no wonder that families and peer groups are important to them. A reflective teacher, therefore, must aim to work with parents and with an understanding of child culture.

CONCLUSION

The intention in this chapter has been to discuss the relationship between society as a whole and the people who are centrally involved in primary education. This is because school practices and classroom actions are influenced by the social circumstances within which they occur. I have also argued that individuals can have effects on future social changes, though the degree of influence ebbs and flows at different phases of history.

A theoretical framework of this sort is important for reflective teachers. The provision of high-quality education is enhanced when social awareness is developed and when individual responsibilities for professional actions are taken seriously.

This fundamental belief in the commitment, quality and role of teachers underpins the book. At a time when central control over education has been tightened and when teacher morale is sometimes low, the analysis is, essentially, optimistic. High-quality education is not possible without the commited professionalism of teachers and, at some point, the extent of unilateral government interventions will recede, to be replaced, we must hope, by greater recognition of professional expertise and by a new partnership.

Notes for further reading

These suggestions concentrate on the theoretical framework which has been introduced, rather than on the topics through which it has been illustrated. The latter are all covered in more detail elsewhere in the book, and can be accessed via the index. (See also the parallel chapter in *Readings*.)

On the theoretical framework which has been introduced, with its juxtaposition of social context and individuals, two classic books may be helpful. Chapter 1 of Mills and Chapters 4 and 5 of Berger are particularly relevant.

Berger, P. L. (1963)
Invitation to Sociology: A Humanistic Perspective,
New York: Doubleday.

Mills, C. W. (1959)
The Sociological Imagination,
Oxford: Oxford University Press.

Reading, 2.1

For more recent, but equally stimulating, texts, try:

Giddens, A. (1989)
Sociology,
Cambridge: Polity Press.

☐ Reading, 2.3

Bauman, Z. (1990)
Thinking Sociologically,
Oxford: Blackwell.

For a readable analysis of modern British society, which illustrates aspects of this framework, see:

Halsey, A. H. (1986)
Change in British Society,
Oxford: Oxford University Press.

For a more international challenge, try:

Miliband, R. (1991)
Divided Societies,
Oxford: Oxford University Press.

Three very different illustrations of the uses of the basic framework are provided by:

Connell, R. W., Ashden, D. J., Kessler, S. and Dowsett, G. W. (1982)
Making the Difference: Schools, Families and Social Divisions,
Sidney: Allen & Unwin.

Humphries, S. (1982)
Hooligans or Rebels?,
Oxford: Blackwell.

Grace, G. (1978)
Teachers, Ideology and Control,
London: Routledge & Kegan Paul.

Humphries is based on oral histories and analyses the education of working-class children. Connell *et al.* is an analysis of school processes and Australian society.

Two case-studies of primary schools which specifically attempt to trace links between individual actions and the wider social context are:

Pollard, A. (1985)
The Social World of the Primary School,
London: Cassell.

☐ Reading, 4.7

Sharp, R. and Green, A. (1975)
Education and Social Control,
London: Routledge & Kegan Paul.

General reviews which locate education and primary school practices within a social and historical context are:

Pollard, A. (1996)
An Introduction to Primary Education,
London: Cassell.

Clarkson, M. (1988)
Emerging Issues in Primary Education,
London: Falmer.

Cunningham, P. (1988)
*Curriculum Change in the Primary School since 1945:
Dissemination of the Progressive Ideal,*
London: Falmer.

and for Europe as a whole:

Husen, T., Tuijnman, A. and Halls, W. (eds) (1992)
Schooling in Modern European Society,
Oxford: Pergamon.

Galton, M. and Blyth, A. (1989)
Handbook of Primary Education in Europe,
London: David Fulton.

For Australia:

Henry, M., Taylor, S., Knight, J. and Lingard, R. (1990)
Understanding Schooling,
London: Routledge.

For the USA:

Spring, J. (1991)
American Education: An Introduction to Social and Political Aspects,
New York: Longman.

Keeping abreast of new developments and policies is a considerable challenge. However, there are a number of useful newspapers and magazines for the UK:

Times Educational Supplement (weekly).
Education (weekly).
Child Education (monthly).
Junior Education (monthly).
Primary Life (termly).

Legal requirements have also been changing rapidly and access to reliable, accurate and regularly updated sources of information can be invaluable. The National Association for Headteachers and the National Union of Teachers supply such services for their members in the form of ring binders of information. An independent resource for all teachers, with a quarterly update routine and dealing with all legislation, management, staffing, special educational needs and day to day issues which occur in schools, is:

The Head's Legal Guide,
London: Croner Publications.

How should teachers act? An accessible Canadian book which urges teachers to have faith in themselves, collaborate and act in the face of centralized control is:

Fullan, M. and Hargreaves, A. (1992)
What's Worth Fighting for in Your School?,
Buckingham: Open University Press.

CHAPTER 3

Investigating classrooms

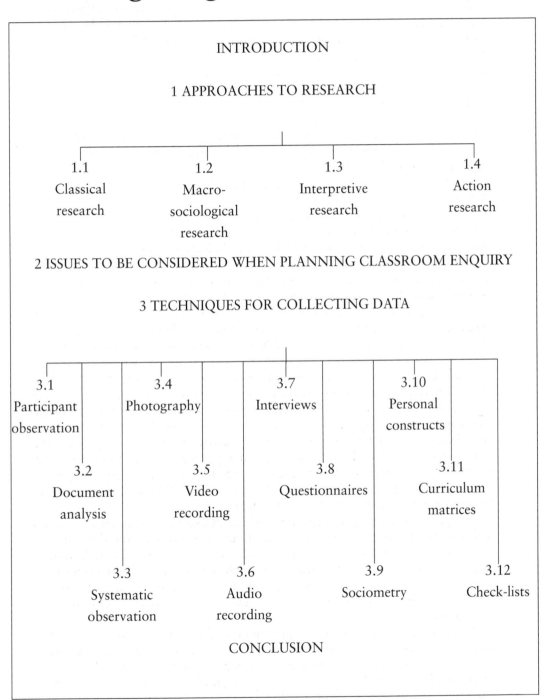

INTRODUCTION

1 APPROACHES TO RESEARCH

1.1	1.2	1.3	1.4
Classical research	Macro-sociological research	Interpretive research	Action research

2 ISSUES TO BE CONSIDERED WHEN PLANNING CLASSROOM ENQUIRY

3 TECHNIQUES FOR COLLECTING DATA

3.1 Participant observation

3.2 Document analysis

3.3 Systematic observation

3.4 Photography

3.5 Video recording

3.6 Audio recording

3.7 Interviews

3.8 Questionnaires

3.9 Sociometry

3.10 Personal constructs

3.11 Curriculum matrices

3.12 Check-lists

CONCLUSION

INTRODUCTION

The relationship between 'researchers' and teachers has often been an uneasy one. Teachers have identified a number of reasons for this state of affairs. First, teachers claim that researchers do not seem to focus on the kinds of concerns which teachers actually have. Second, researchers appear to be rather distant: they come to do research about teachers and their classrooms, but without clearly explaining the purpose or the methods. Third, the results are often presented through complicated statistical procedures or are embedded in technical language. Unfortunately, many teachers have disclaimed such research as 'less than useful' (Cane and Schroeder, 1970; Freeman, 1986), and the Teacher Training Agency (TTA) seem to be rather ambivalent about existing work and wish to prioritize research which is of more *direct* relevance to 'effective classroom and training practice' (TTA, 1995).

Constructive alternatives to this situation include researchers working alongside teachers in more collaborative ways, or teachers becoming their own researchers into classroom practice. In the latter case, this means that teachers need to develop the necessary techniques to enquire into their own classrooms and have to be able to interpret and evaluate their findings appropriately.

Such developments raise important issues, the first of which relates to the nature of research itself. Research is traditionally characterized as being 'objective' – reliable, valid, generalizable and credible (Shipman, 1981). If research were done by involved insiders, such as teachers in their own classrooms, would such enquiries still be able to meet these criteria? If not, would this matter? In particular, could such research, which would be likely to be small-scale, provide a basis for theoretical explanations and generalizations? Again, if not, would it matter?

Such questions and doubts have been raised for many years about the feasibility of teachers becoming 'teachers-as-researchers'. However, more and more teachers have begun to gather evidence of their classroom practices routinely. Indeed, teachers are frequently aware of the discrepancies between their 'espoused theory' and their actual practice, and between their own descriptions of the practice and the descriptions made by others of the same practice (Elbaz, 1983; Cortazzi, 1990). Most of us realize how difficult it can be to 'see' what we are doing while we are in the middle of doing it. However, because it is difficult, it does not mean that it is not possible or that it is not worthwhile to try!

The model of a reflective teacher, as outlined in Chapter 1, suggests that critical reflection and systematic investigation of our own practice should become an integral part of our daily classroom lives. Such self-examination should lead to an improvement in our teaching judgements and help us to have a more professional control over our own development and that of others. Self-appraisal and professional awareness should provide the basis for a professional autonomy and educational quality.

If this is to happen, then an appreciation of the major issues involved in research and some knowledge of the main enquiry techniques available are essential. This chapter has been written as an introduction to such matters. Readers are strongly advised to follow up issues and techniques in which they may be particularly interested via the Notes for Further Reading and Chapter 3 of *Readings*.

The chapter begins by examining two issues: the nature of traditional forms of research and the status of the main alternative forms. There is then a section on what are essentially 'research design' issues for classroom enquiry. Finally the chapter reviews a range of possible research techniques which teachers could use in their own classrooms.

1   APPROACHES TO RESEARCH

 Four main research approaches to education can be identified (see also **Reading, 3.5**). The first is the 'classical' scientific model which has traditionally laid great emphasis on quantitative data – for instance, by classifying and measuring behaviour. This approach is sometimes called 'positivistic'. A second approach is offered by some sociologists and focuses on structural features of society – for example, social inequalities, which are frequently measured and quantified. Such features are also examined in relationship to their historical, economic, cultural and political contexts. This may be referred to as a 'macro-sociological' approach. Forms of comparative education could be associated with this. The third approach is 'interpretive' research, which emphasizes the qualitative aspects of each situation being researched – for instance, by analysing people's perceptions. It is sometimes referred to as being 'phenomenological'. The final approach is one which has been developed in recent years by curriculum specialists working alongside teachers. This 'action research' is concerned with self-evaluation and the direct improvement of classroom practice.

1.1   Classical research

The classical model is based on the research style which has served the physical sciences for many years. Its characteristic stages are:

- to recognize and define a problem
- to develop a hypothesis
- to design a controlled research procedure to test the hypothesis
- to accumulate observations
- to analyse the data
- to interpret the data and form generalizable explanations

The hallmarks of this classical model are, therefore, that the investigation has a hypothesis, which is testable and replicable, which provides an explanation and is generalizable. When such research is referred to as 'scientific', it is usually to highlight two features which are believed by some to be crucial: that it is 'systematic' in the way the research is carried out and that it is 'objective' in the interpretation of the data collected and in the conclusions drawn. How far such research is 'scientific' in practice and whether this is still a suitable model for some areas of the physical sciences (for example, astrophysics or microbiology) is in dispute in the scientific community itself (Capra, 1982).

When this model is transferred to the social sciences, certain inadequacies are evident. For instance, it is very much more difficult to test a hypothesis in a classroom situation with the same rigour as one might expect in a laboratory experiment. It is more difficult because we cannot isolate the variables being examined and we cannot control all the myriad factors which might influence the test. In addition, we are dealing with human beings for whom we must have proper ethical concern about the way in which they, as with all living things, are treated. Further, because of the complexity of the classroom and because of the ethics of any such research, any 'experiment' can never be replicated exactly. Researchers have had to rely on sophisticated statistical methods to try to measure the impact of variables. Notwithstanding this, the difficulties weaken the claim that such research can provide generalizable explanations. For all these reasons, the argument runs, such study cannot properly be called scientific research.

Nevertheless, there has been a long tradition in education research of following the classical model as exactly as is humanly possible. For example, much of the laboratory-based psychological testing and measurement research has been of this nature (for example, Cattell and Kline, 1977). Similarly, the extensive work on teacher effectiveness in classrooms in the USA during the 1960s and 1970s (for example, Flanders, 1970) used systematic observation techniques. These are still positively regarded for some purposes (for example, Galton *et al.*, 1980; Pollard *et al.*, 1994).

1.2 Macro-sociological research

The second, 'macro-sociological', approach has many features which distinguish it from the 'classical' model. In the first place, it is far more wide-ranging, for it is based on the assumption that specific situations, practices and perspectives can only be understood in relationship to their historical, economic, cultural and political contexts. Comparative and historical studies provide one form of this (e.g. Altbach and Kelly, 1986; Green, 1990). In its sociological form it rejects narrow forms of positivistic empiricism which tend to prevent such wide-ranging factors being considered, and uses various forms of theorizing to try to make sense of social structures, their processes and development. Among a number of forms of theorizing, the most important influences on educational analysis have been structural functionalism (for example, Parsons, 1951, 1959), structural Marxism (for example, Bowles and Gintis, 1976, **Reading, 13.1**), Weberianism (for example Collins, 1977; Archer, 1979, **Reading, 15.1**) and cultural Marxism (for example, Apple, 1982). The latter offers ways of examining the tensions and dialectical forces of change or development within education and society. In recent years variants of such forms of analysis have been powerfully applied to educational policy-making (for example see Whitty, 1985; Ball, 1990; Dale, 1989; see **Readings, 2.4, 2.5, 15.5** and **15.6**).

One major criticism that has often been made of both classical scientific and macro-sociological styles of research is that they fail to address the subjective perceptions of the people who are the subjects of study. This concern has led to the development of an alternative 'interpretive' form of sociological research.

1.3   Interpretive research

The origins of this 'interpretive' approach can be traced to anthropology and the concern to understand, describe and analyses the cultures of particular societies and groups. Among the ethnographic methods which were developed are participant observation and interviewing. These techniques (which we will discuss in more detail later) are explicitly 'qualitative', rather than 'quantitative', and are concerned with opinions and perceptions rather than only observable facts or behaviour. Interpretive researchers tend to aim, in the first place, simply to describe the perspectives, actions and relationships of the people whom they are studying. Typically, they study a limited number of cases in depth and try to achieve a view of the whole situation in a way which is seen to be valid by the participants. This process often requires the personal involvement of the researcher and is rarely a neat, linear progression of research stages. The approach is pragmatic and flexible, as the researcher seeks data and understanding (Burgess, 1984; Hammersley and Atkinson, 1983; Woods, 1986). The outcome of such research is usually a detailed case-study within which concepts, relationships and issues are identified and analysed. Glaser and Strauss (1967) provided the classic statement of the challenge of such work when they argued that interpretive sociologists should start from the grounded base of people's perspectives and, through the simultaneous collection, classification and analysis of data, should develop systematic and theoretically refined perspectives of the social institutions and relationships which they study. Some examples of such work are available concerning primary education (King, 1978; Pollard, 1985, **Readings, 4.7 and 5.3**; Hartley, 1985, 1992; Grugeon and Woods, 1990; Troyna and Hatcher, 1992, **Reading, 13.6**; Nias *et al.*, 1989, **Reading, 14.2**, 1992; Pollard with Filer, 1996).

Interpretive research has strengths and weaknesses, as with the classical model. Indeed, in many respects, they can be seen as complementary. For instance, a phenomenological researcher's 'generation' of theory may be balanced by a positivistic researcher's 'testing' of theory; qualitative data on perspectives may be balanced by quantitative data on behaviour; and a focus on detailed whole cases may be balanced by generalization from sampling across cases.

Whatever their differences and the degree of their complementarity, these alternative approaches to social science each share one important feature: they have all tended to distance themselves from actual practice. It is only recently that a direct concern with practical action has emerged (Finch, 1986; Shipman, 1985; Woods and Pollard, 1988). It has been argued that to understand thoroughly is a pre-condition of acting effectively, and there is clearly some merit in this point. However, a quite different approach has also been developed, which seeks to improve and understand practice through the direct action and involvement of practitioners.

1.4   Action research

'Action research' was origniated by Lewin (1946). His model for change was based on action *and* research. It involved researchers, with teachers or other practitioners, in a cyclical process of planning, action, observation and reflection before beginning the whole process all over again.

Further development of this model was instigated by Stenhouse (1975, **Reading, 3.1**) and elaborated by Elliott and Adelman (1973) in their work with the Ford Teaching Project, based at the Centre for Applied Research in Education at the University of East Anglia. It was this generation of researchers who coined the term 'teacher-as-researcher' to refer to the participants in the movement they helped to create. This encouraged teachers to assume the role of researcher in their own classrooms as part of their professional, reflective stance.

The approach is sometimes criticized for encouraging a focus on practical classroom ideas while wider, structural factors are accepted as unproblematic (e.g. Barton and Lawn, 1980/81; Whitty, 1985). However, Carr and Kemmis (1986, **Reading, 3.2**) argue that such work provides a means of 'becoming critical'. They suggest that action-research involves

- the improvement of practice
- the improvement of the understanding of the practice by the practitioners
- the improvement of the situation in which practice takes place (p. 165)

Overall, they, like Stenhouse (1982), see the potential of action research as being 'emancipatory': releasing practitioners from 'the often unseen constraints of assumptions, habits, precedents, coercion and ideology' (Carr and Kemmis, 1986, p. 192). There are now some excellent published examples of teachers' action

research (Nixon, 1981; Hustler *et al.*, 1986; Webb, 1991) (see also **Readings, 3.3** and **3.4**).

In this section we have identified four major forms of research: the classical or positivistic, the macro-sociological, the interpretive or qualitative and, lastly, action research. The position which has been adopted in this book borrows a great deal from action research in terms of the processes of enquiry which has been suggested. In addition, its sense of purpose draws on macro-sociological awareness. With regard to specific substantive topics, the findings and methods of both positivistic and interpretive approaches to research are used as well. However, regardless of whichever approaches to research or enquiry are adopted, there are certain basic questions which have to be addressed and these form the subject of the next section.

2 · ISSUES TO BE CONSIDERED WHEN PLANNING CLASSROOM ENQUIRY

Before any research can begin there are general decisions to be taken concerning the overall design of the study. The most significant of these design issues will be discussed below.

1. *Which facet of classroom life should be investigated and why?* Identifying the issue for investigation is sometimes a problem in itself. We do not always have a particular topic in mind, but merely want to explore first and see what emerges. Dillon (1983) offered a threefold categorization of the kinds of prob-

lems that might be explored: existing problems which we can already recognize; emergent problems which we discover in our initial investigations; and potential problems which we anticipate might develop if we took a particular course of action. The issue chosen for investigation may emerge from any of these three types of problem.

2. *What data to collect and how?* This decision is very important, for it must be remembered that no data can ever wholly represent the events or phenomena which are studied. Therefore, data should be selected which are valid indicators of what it is we want to study. Judgements about which data to collect are thus crucial, so that we do not distort the 'picture'. It is important to remember that what we choose to collect and how we will collect it affect what we find and, therefore, our understanding of the situation. Thus, however objectively we try to collect data, the choice of methods inevitably results in some distortion. One way of limiting this problem is to use several methods so that data on a single issue are collected in several ways. This is known as 'methodological triangulation'. However, our choice must, to a certain extent, be determined by what is feasible, given the time we can set aside to collect data and the time we can spend analysing it.

3. *How can we analyse, interpret and apply the findings?* The basic strategy is to look for patterns, for places where regularities and irregularities occur. In order to do this, the data have to be sorted using various sets of criteria. All patterns of frequencies, sequences and distributions of activity are likely to be of interest. In addition, it is also important to look for spaces and omissions – where something does not occur which might have been expected. Where examples of co-occurrence exist, they can be misinterpreted as implying a cause – effect relationship. Such judgements should be viewed with caution until further data reinforce the pattern.

The important question of interpreting findings leads us into the issue of the relationships between research and the theoretical explanations to which it can lead. I would argue that theorizing is an important and integral part of reflective teaching. This is because it represents an attempt to make sense of data and experience. It is also an opportunity to develop creative insights and an occasion to consider any discrepancies between 'what is' and 'what ought to be'. In a sense, we are all theorists in our everyday lives in the ways in which we develop hunches and use our intuition. This might be a starting-point, but, as reflective teachers, we would need to go further. In particular, we would want to generate theory relatively systematically and consciously. One way of doing this is to engage in a continuous process of data collection, classification and analysis of our own practice. The 'theory' which emerges is likely to be professionally relevant and may also offer insights with regard to other cases. This kind of theory resembles what Glaser and Strauss (1967) refer to as 'grounded' in that it is developed from and grounded in our own experiences.

Such theorizing is particularly important for conceptualizing teaching and learning processes and for developing a language with which they can be discussed and refined. Indeed it has been argued that the lack of such an appropriate conceptual vocabulary is a serious constraint on professional development (Hargreaves, 1978).

Grounded theory, developed from the study of individual cases, is valuable. However, such particular 'micro' studies can only offer a partial analysis of social and educational structures, processes and practices. This is where macro-sociological models can help by offering explanations which may challenge 'common-sense' assumptions and place particular events in a wider context (for example, Apple, 1982; Archer, 1979; Bourdieu and Passeron, 1977; Carnoy and Levin, 1985; Halsey, 1986; Whitty, 1985; Simon, 1985, 1992; see *Readings*, Chapters 2 and 15). Such studies may well raise more issues than they resolve, but they are likely to make an important contribution to the sense of commitment and social responsibility which we have identified as being characteristic of reflective teaching. A particularly useful insight from Mills (1959, **Reading, 2.1**) is his observation of the way in which people often worry about 'private troubles' without seeing how they manifest 'public issues'. There is nothing then to prevent reflective teachers from developing their own theories and conceptualizations of the relationships between education, the individual and society.

For the most part though, reflective teachers are likely to be concerned more directly with specific aspects of their practice. This calls for the use of a range of techniques for gathering data, which we will now review.

3 TECHNIQUES FOR COLLECTING DATA

For many teachers, busy teaching, it is difficult to collect the information we need to make the necessary day-to-day decisions and judgements, much less the information needed for anything more systematic and research-like. Our usual impressionistic data are collected sporadically and are often incomplete. They are selective and are probably based on what we have found in the past to be useful (one of the reasons it is so difficult to break out of old habits). They also tend to be subjective, because we have so few chances of discussion to help us to see things from any other viewpoints. If we could manage it, the most helpful forms of data might be:

- descriptive (rather than judgemental)
- dispassionate (not based on supposition or prejudice)
- discerning (so that they are forward-looking)
- diagnostic (so that they lead us into better action)

That data should be as valid and reliable as we can make it must be accepted, but technicalities should not blind us to some relatively simple underlying processes in research. Essentially, these boil down to *looking, listening and asking*, though, of course, with an unusual degree of care in selection and use.

In Figure 3.1 a simple distinction is used between 'looking, listening and asking' to produce an overview and typology of the data-gathering techniques which are introduced at various places in the book. We may also distinguish between those which occur routinely in classroom life and those which must be undertaken specially. Whilst, for the most part, the former are more convenient to use, the latter often produce more structured data which may be easier to analyse.

	LOOKING	LISTENING	ASKING
ROUTINELY OCCURRING	Participant observation (C3, 3.1) Document analysis (C3, 3.2) *Marking pupils' work* (C12, 3.1) *Analysis of pupil diaries or logs* (C12, 3.2)	***Active listening*** (C11, 2.4)	***Questioning*** (C11, 2.2) *Setting tasks* (C12, 3.5) *Testing* (C12, 3.6)
		Discussing (C11, 2.3) *Conferencing* (C12, 3.3)	
SPECIALLY UNDERTAKEN	Systematic observation (C3, 3.3) Photography (C3, 3.4)	Audio recording (C3, 3.6)	Interviewing (C3, 3.7) *Concept mapping* (C12, 3.4) Questionnaires (C3, 3.8) Sociometry (C3, 3.9) Personal constructs (C3, 3.10) Curriculum matrices (C3, 3.11) Checklists (C3, 3.12)
	Video recording (C3, 3.5)		

Figure 3.1 *A typology of data-gathering methods and their location in this book*

There are many uses for such techniques and they can be applied to the issues considered in all the chapters of this book. However, there are methods which are particularly appropriate for gathering evidence for the assessment of children's learning. Such methods are *italicized* in Figure 3.1. Where **bold italic** is used, the methods are discussed in the communication chapter, Chapter 11. Where *plain italic* is used, the methods are discussed in the assessment chapter, Chapter 12. The other, more generally applicable forms of data gathering, are introduced below.

References for further consideration of data-gathering issues are provided in the Notes for Further Reading section at the end of this chapter.

3.1 Participant observation

Participant observation refers to a way of actively, carefully and self-consciously describing and recording what people do whilst one is, oneself, part of the action. Personal involvement is not necessarily seen as a weakness if the benefits of direct experience are complemented by care in avoiding judgements. The emphasis, in the first place, should be on description. Recording is usually done in the form of field notes which contain detailed descriptions of events, incidents or issues. Such field notes may record individual or group activity. They may record conversations together with features of the situations in which conversations or events took place. The participant observer will also often try to discuss the situation observed to elicit the participants' interpretations of events. Thus the observer's, teacher's and the children's views will be sought, and a process of triangulation may be employed.

Although this may be a time-consuming procedure, such records can contain a wealth of information and can be applied very flexibly. Over a period of recording, it is normally possible to discern recurring themes which may lead to a greater understanding of the complex whole of a classroom environment. This technique, because it is relatively open-ended, can be particularly comprehensive and responsive to the unique features of the situation.

However, field notes can generate an enormous quantity of wide-ranging data from which it may be difficult to draw conclusions. On studying such notes, the teacher may identify specific insights which it might prove fruitful to follow up in greater detail. The follow-up could then be in terms of a further set of more *focused observations* designed to test out an emerging idea. Alternatively, the teacher may decide to use another technique to provide a further source of insights.

3.2   Document analysis

It can be revealing to examine official documents. For instance, this is a very important aspect of policy analysis and of historical and comparative work. In such approaches, official documents will be 'interrogated' with questions to generate an analysis. Do there appear to be any hidden aims, as well as those which are explicit? What are the underlying assumptions which are embedded in the document? Which groups are likely to gain from the document? Which groups are likely to lose? Does the document reflect the influence of any particular interest group, or a combination of concerns? How has it been created? Who was consulted? Who was not? How is this reflected in its final form?

During the recent period of Conservative governments of the United Kingdom there has been a steady flow of education documents on which this form of analysis can be used (e.g. DES, 1987, 1992c; DFE, 1992; OFSTED, 1995). Those associated with other political parties may be just as interesting. For instance, compare the tone of successive Labour Party statements (1994, **Reading, 7.11**, 1995). Glossy designer production features, should, of course, be questioned in the same way as the content.

At a school level, examination of documents might include the brochure for parents containing introductory information. Similarly, curriculum policy documents (for example, maths, English or science policies) should provide some insights to collective staff thinking – their aims, values, commitment. The contents of such documents are likely to indicate the assumptions held by their author(s) about how children learn, what they should learn, why, and how it should be taught. Similarly useful and indicative documents are annual school development plans.

Working papers, which might have been produced for staff meetings, may also throw light on the issues discussed during the formation of school policies and development plans. Similarly, minutes of governors' and parents' meetings, documents from community organizations, communications from the school to the community (for example, notice-boards/letters/bulletins) can also be of value to the reflective teacher.

However, it is worth remembering that even school documents tend to be relatively 'official' products and may thus gloss over internal debates which took place in the process of their creation. It is important, therefore, to read 'between the lines' and to be aware of what is not considered as well as the issues that are included. For instance, written planning devices, such as school policy documents, attempt to describe what is expected in terms of the intended curriculum. They do not, of course, reflect what is actually conveyed through the 'hidden' curriculum. Distinguishing between these two aspects is a very important task for a reflective teacher (see Chapters 5, 7 and 13).

3.3 Systematic observation

This is a way of observing behaviour in classrooms by using a schedule, or list of categories, of probable behaviour. The categories are chosen by the observer or reflective teacher who has decided which ones are important to the issue in hand. Each category is then 'checked off' as the behaviour is observed. The technique assumes that the teacher has already carried out sufficient preliminary, exploratory investigations to be able to decide which behaviours are relevant. Nevertheless, having devised the schedule, it can be a very quick and easy-to-administer technique for collecting information.

There are two main differences in the use of such schedules. First, there are those which are 'checked off' each time there is any sign of the listed behaviours. This is called a 'sign' system. The other type of schedule is 'checked off' at prede-termined time intervals and can be referred to as a 'timed' system.

Information collected in this way can easily be quantified, and the frequencies and distribution patterns of the listed behaviours can be calculated. It might be useful, for example, in finding out how much use is made of the book corner and who seems to use it most. It can be used to find out how individual children, per-haps with special educational needs, seem to spend their day. It could be used to note how teachers distribute their time among different children; which children seek attention; which ones avoid it; or which ones 'get forgotten'. Another common use is to measure the possible differences in the ways teachers interact with boys and with girls.

To reduce the possibility of misrepresenting the behaviour which is seen, it is often considered advisable to use categories which can be clearly identified and involve little interpretation by the teacher (that is, low-inference categories rather than those which involve high levels of inference). An example of a low-inference category would be 'child talks to neighbour' rather than 'child helps neighbour'. Further, to make it easier to code quickly in a busy classroom situation, it is advis-able to use categories which do not overlap – exclusive rather than inclusive categories. Exclusive categories would be 'teacher asks open question', 'teacher expands child's response', rather than 'teacher discusses'.

Such information can indicate frequencies and patterns in what happens but it cannot explain why. The technique is designed to be selective, but might distort the pic-ture. It relies on the appropriateness of the predetermined categories on the schedule.

3.4 Photography

Recording what happens inside a classroom, by any of the next three techniques, provides a very valuable source of information, for they 'fix' events which are so fleeting. This is particularly valuable because no one can have ears and eyes everywhere and even the most alert of teachers misses a great deal of what goes on.

Photography is a relatively unobtrusive form of visual recording, especially if fast film (with a high ASA/ISO rating) is used so that flash is not needed. Photography, of course, only captures frames of action rather than the sequence of action itself, though stop-frame techniques can overcome this to some extent (Adelman and Walker, 1975). A particular advantage is the ease of use of photographs once they are developed. They can provide an excellent basis for discussion with others.

3.5   Video recording

Video recording is particularly helpful in providing contextual information in classrooms and in capturing non-verbal behaviour as well as some speech. Sampling selections must be made, and, before filming, it is important to think through exactly what is required. The presence of cameras is likely to affect some children and may distort the normality of the classroom, but, if done periodically, the novelty usually soon wears off. Modern video cameras, with automatic focusing and low-light adjustment facilities make videoing a relatively easy task.

This is a convenient and very powerful form of data. The quality of the soundtrack is usually the weakest point.

3.6   Audio recording

Audio recording of a class discussion is a common and simple procedure. However, tape recorders often only pick up a few of the children, or perhaps only the teacher's voice. Nevertheless, the procedure can provide excellent information about the amount, type and distribution of teacher talk – a very worthwhile, though often salutary experience.

Recording small groups or pairs of children is technically easier if background noise can be controlled and can similarly provide valuable insights into the language strategies used and into social dynamics. Children usually forget about the recorder, though its presence may affect some – either to put on a performance or to clam up. Time could be allowed for familiarization.

A radio-microphone or portable recorder could also be worn by an individual child for a period of time. The main advantage of this is that the quality of the recording is frequently excellent.

It must be remembered that it takes time to play back tapes: at least three times the length of the recording is often needed to study effectively and to distinguish who said what. Still more time will be needed for transcription.

Photography, video and audio recording capture and record what is said or done. They can, therefore, be used to produce high quality descriptive data, leaving us to analyse and infer our own explanations. We could also discuss them with the participants and thus gain insights into their interpretations of the same events or we could discuss them with other colleagues. Each of these uses is likely to make a powerful contribution to reflection.

3.7 Interviews

Interviews are structured or semi-structured discussions which can be used to find out what people think or do, and why. The interviewer can explore and negotiate understandings because of the possibility of immediate feedback and follow-up. However, because of the person-to-person situation, some people may feel threatened – by the interviewer or, if it is a group interview, by other participants. The success of this technique of data collection rests heavily on the relationship established and on the way in which the event is conducted. Interviews can be used with varying degrees of formality and structure. The term 'interview' is usually reserved for the more formal, more structured one-to-one situations. As the event becomes more informal and less structured, it may be more appropriately seen in terms of a 'conference' or discussion.

3.8 Questionnaires

This form of data collection uses questions and statements to stimulate responses to set items. Questionnaires are usually given to the respondents to fill in (which, therefore, demands a certain level of writing skill). The technique can be used for collecting factual information as well as opinions. Hence, it may provide data about what people do or think, and also why.

The format of a questionnaire can be closed (e.g. asking for specific data or yes/no responses) or open (e.g. asking for general and discursive responses). Open forms of response encourage relatively free answers which has the advantage of enabling the respondents to express their thoughts and priorities in their own way. However, it also makes greater demands on the respondents' writing abilities and poses the problem of how to categorize a wide range of replies which such an item may well evoke.

The wording and design of questionnaires is important, so that the respondents do not misunderstand, or are led to respond in any particular way. For example, some words are emotive and can exaggerate responses. Sometimes people react differently to a positive statement compared to a negative statement. Questionnaires can be filled in independently of the teacher and thus not interrupt the flow of teaching time. On the other hand, they could be completed through discussion with individual children.

Questionnaires can be useful in a variety of ways, such as to provide information to include on school records. They can be used to try to discover how respondents feel about aspects of classroom life: for example, for feedback on a particular lesson or topic of work. Questionnaires can also be used for evaluative purposes at the end of a unit of work. They encourage children to reflect on their recent learning experiences and to comment on them by answering specific questions to focus their response. The answers may be required as written sentences, by ticking boxes, or by ringing a word/number on a rating scale (e.g. hard/quite hard/just right/easy, or, from 'exciting' 5–4–3–2–1 'boring'). For younger children, scales have been devised which require the child to colour the face which shows how they feel – in response to a statement which is read out by the teacher: the faces range from happy to neutral, bored, worried or angry.

3.9 Sociometry

Sociometric techniques have been developed to help children and teachers gain insights into friendship patterns (Evans, 1962). The basic procedure is to ask children, in confidence, to name three children from their class with whom they would like to work or play. This can also, with care, be extended to ask children to identify anyone with whom they would not like to work or play. The friendship groupings which emerge from an analysis of these choices as a whole can then be represented in diagrammatic form, known as a sociogram (see Practical Activity 4.15). Such representations provide a visual display of social relationships: mutual pairs and groups (where choices are reciprocated); clusters of friends (though not all with reciprocated choices); isolates and even rejectees.

However, this technique does not tell the whole story. In particular, it provides a static picture of friendships, and given the dynamic nature of the social relationships of some children, this needs to be borne in mind. Nevertheless, the data are structured and descriptive and can provide a starting point for analysing further aspects of relationships between children.

3.10 Personal constructs

This is a structured method of indirectly finding out about the way people think and feel about each other. Personal constructs are evident in our thinking when, for example, we appraise or comment on children. They can be identified by asking teachers to comment about children in their class.

The usual procedure is to produce small name cards for each child in the class, successively to draw three names and to ask the teacher first to identify which two are most alike, and then to explain why. In this way it is possible to elicit relatively instinctive reactions and the actual 'constructs', or criteria, which are used by the teacher. Such a procedure is usually more effective than asking teachers to consider, in abstract, what constructs they think they might use to distinguish children. Having obtained such a list, it is then possible to classify the constructs – for example, those which are academic, physical or social.

The patterns which may emerge could indicate underlying assumptions that the teacher has about what school is for and how he or she perceives children. However, construct elicitation only provides information which the respondents choose to give. It may provide information about what respondents say they feel, but in itself is unlikely to indicate why they feel it or to describe what they actually do.

3.11 Curriculum matrices

Different forms of matrix can be used for both planning and review purposes. Given the complexity of modern curriculum planning, the two-dimensional character of matrices gives them enormous utility, particularly where coherence, progression and interrelation of provision is necessary.

For instance, a matrix could be used be used for school and classroom planning purposes, for locating units for study and organizing resources. Matrices could also be used to review balance, breadth, coherence and progression amongst the components of the curriculum – for example, in terms of concepts, knowledge, skills and attitudes. For examples of matrices used in these ways, see Chapter 8.

Matrices are often enormously useful to represent relationships and to aid planning and review. However, it is vital that the two axes are appropriately conceptualized. Additionally, one must always bear in mind that educational provision cannot often, in reality, be reduced simply to two dimensions.

3.12 Check-lists

Check-lists provide a simple and practical form of record which has been tried and tested by generations of teachers (Clift *et al.*, 1981). Indeed, check-lists have been developed in sophisticated ways to support a variety of teaching concerns: early learning skills (Ainscow and Tweddle, 1984); curriculum planning (Johnson *et al.*, 1992); assessment (Merttens and Vass, 1990). Targets, competencies or other attainments can be clearly listed and ticks, crosses or other symbol systems can be used to record children's achievements against these criteria. However, judgements should be checked with evidence before a check-list is completed. Sometimes check-lists are completed relatively impressionistically, which may not always be accurate.

The process of devising a check-list can also be helpful in clarifying aims, so that they can be itemized and shared with others.

CONCLUSION

This chapter has provided a brief introduction to some of the theoretical issues and practical techniques of undertaking classroom research as reflective teachers. We would advise readers to follow up other more detailed references, such as those given below. However, 'doing research' is not just about collecting data. The next stage is to be able to interpret the data and to design further investigations to refine our understandings. We need to be able to relate our findings to those of others and to consider our results in the context of the current debates about educational issues. Finally, as reflective teachers and collaborating professionals, we need to be able to turn our data into action and articulate what we are doing and why to others.

Part 2 of this book is designed to help to put this reflection into practice.

Notes for further reading

These notes are more extensive than those provided for some other chapters. It is important that suggestions on methodology are followed up to provide detailed information on techniques prior to their use. See also Chapter 3 of *Readings*.

Gathering information about the existing state of knowledge on educational issues is obviously important. Databases, abstracts, journals and research indices are available in good libraries. See, for instance:

National Foundation for Educational Research
Register of Educational Research in the United Kingdom,
London: Routledge.

Educational Resources Information Center (ERIC)
United States Department of Education.

British Education Index,
Leeds: Leeds University Press.

For statistical data on education in the UK see the latest edition of the sources below. The first is exceptionally well presented and comprehensive for all counties in the UK.

Steedman, J. and MacKinnon, D. (1991)
The Education Factfile,
London: Hodder and Stoughton.

Government Statistical Service
Statistical Bulletin, (published monthly);
Education Statistics for the United Kingdom (published annually),
London: DFE.

For general overviews and discussion of the most common research methods used in the study of education, see:

Cohen, L. and Manion, L. (1994)
Research Methods in Education (4th edn),
London: Croom Helm.

📖 Reading, 3.5

Wragg, E. C. (1993)
An Introduction to Classroom Observation,
London: Routledge.

Open University (1992)
Principles of Social and Educational Research,
Course DEH313. Milton Keynes: Open University.

To focus thinking on important research issues see:

Hammersley, M. (1986)
Controversies in Classroom Research,
Milton Keynes: Open University Press.

Shipman, M. (1981)
The Limitations of Social Research,
London: Longman.

Shipman, M. (ed.) (1985)
Educational Research: Principles, Policies and Practice,
London: Falmer Press.

Walford, G. (1991)
Doing Educational Research,
London: Routledge.

The classical 'scientific' research tradition is discussed in:

Popper, K. R. (1968)
The Logic of Scientific Discovery,
London: Hutchinson.

For useful guides to the application of this approach in education see:

Borg, W. R. (1981)
Applying Educational Research: A Practical Guide for Teachers,
New York: Longman.

Cohen, L. (1976)
Educational Research in Classrooms and Schools:
A Manual of Materials and Methods,
London: Harper & Row.

An excellent and extensive series of pamphlets on particular methods is provided by:

Rediguides,
Nottingham University School of Education.

Systematic observation is particularly well covered by:

Croll, P. (1986)
Systematic Classroom Observation,
London: Falmer.

Statistical analysis would be helped by books such as:

Cohen, L. and Holliday, M. (1979)
Statistics for Education,
London: Harper & Row.

Anderson, A. J. B. (1989)
A First Course in Statistics,
London: Routledge.

For a quite different critical perspective see:

Radical Statistics Education Group (1982)
Reading Between the Numbers:
A Critical Guide to Educational Research,
London: BSSRS publications.

The methods which are appropriate to macro-sociological approaches are, in one way, properly seen as being those involved in conceptualizing the links between individuals, classroom practices and wider social structures. The classic book is:

Mills, C. W. (1959)
The Sociological Imagination,
New York: Oxford University Press.   📖 **Reading, 2.1**

For examples of sociological, historical and comparative work respectively, see:

Whitty, G. (1985)
Sociology and School Knowledge,
London: Methuen.

Green, A. (1990)
Education and State Formation,
London: Macmillan.

Combs, P. H. (1985)
The World Crisis in Education:
The View from the Eighties,
Oxford: Oxford University Press.

A rather different approach to macro-sociology issues is through the collection of survey data. A book for guidance in this method is:

Fink, A. and Kosecoff, J. (1986)
How to Conduct Surveys:
A Step by Step Guide,
London: Sage.

Excellent examples of work using a survey approach are:

Halsey, A. H., Heath, A. F. and Ridge, J. M. (1980)
Origins and Destinations,
Oxford: Oxford University Press.

Osborn, A. H., Butler, N. R. and Morris, A. C. (1984)
The Social Life of Britain's Five-Year-Olds,
London: Routledge & Kegan Paul.

Interpretive research has a long history. A general collection of papers, in which the major methodological issues are discussed, is:

Burgess, R. G. (ed.) (1982)
Field Research: A Sourcebook and Field Manual,
London: Allen & Unwin.

Further discussions of these issues can be found in:

Burgess, R. G. (1984)
In the Field: An Introduction to Field Research,
London: Allen & Unwin.

Hammersley, M. and Atkinson, P. (1983)
Ethnography: Principles in Practice,
London: Tavistock.

For a feminst approach to ethnography, see:

Ely, M. (1990)
Doing Qualitative Research: Circles within Circles,
London: Falmer.

Analysis can be a particular problem, but see the first few chapters of:

Strauss, A. and Corbin, J. (1990)
Basics of Qualitative Research,
New York: Sage.

There are two books on qualitative methods which have been specially written for teachers who want to engage in their own studies:

Woods, P. (1986)
Inside Schools,
London: Routledge & Kegan Paul.

Hitchcock, G. and Hughes, D. (1995)
*Research and the Teacher: A Qualitative
Introduction to School-Based Research* (2nd edn),
London: Routledge.

On the question of obtaining high quality data from children, see:

Fine, G. A. and Sandstrom, K. L. (1988)
Knowing Children: Participant Observations with Minors,
New York: Sage.

Pollard, A. (1987c)
Studying children's perspectives: a collaborative approach.
In G. Walford, *Doing Sociology of Education,*
London: Falmer.

For the study of language, see:

Edwards, A. D. and Westgate, D. P. G. (1987)
Investigating Classroom Talk,
London: Falmer.

The action research approach is introduced in **Readings, 3.1, 3.2, 3.3** and **3.4**. There are also many good books, each of which provides advice on the use of a variety of methods:

Hopkins, D. (1986)
A Teacher's Guide to Classroom Research,
Milton Keynes: Open University Press.

Walker, R. (1986)
Doing Research: A Handbook for Teachers,
London: Routledge.

Altrichter, H., Posch, P. and Somekh, B. (1993)
*Teachers Investigate Their Work: An Introduction
to the Methods of Action Research*,
London: Routledge.

Open University (1980)
Curriculum in Action: Practical Classroom Evaluation,
Milton Keynes: Open University Press.

For guidance on the principles and design of an action research study for classroom or school use:

Elliott, J. (1991b)
Action Research for Educational Change,
Buckingham: Open University Press.

McNiff, J. (1988)
Action Research: Principles and Practice,
London: Routledge.

Winter, R. (1989)
*Learning From Experience: Principles and
Practice in Action-Research*,
London: Falmer.

Illustrations of action research studies are becoming more easily available. See for instance:

Barr, M., D'Arcy, P. and Healy, M. K. (eds) (1982)
*What's Going On? Language/Learning Episodes
in British and American Classrooms, Grades 4–13*,
Montclair: Boynton/Cook.

Dadds, M. (1995)
*Passionate Enquiry and School Development:
A Story about Teacher Action Research*,
London: Falmer.

Hustler, D., Cassidy, T. and Cuff, T. (eds) (1986)
Action Research in Schools and Classrooms,
London: Allen & Unwin.

Nixon, J. (ed.) (1981)
A Teachers' Guide to Action Research,
London: Grant McIntyre.

Webb, R. (ed.) (1991)
Practitioner Research in the Primary School,
London: Falmer.

Vulliamy, G. and Webb. R. (1992)
Teacher Research and Special Educational Needs,
London: David Fulton.

BEING A REFLECTIVE TEACHER

CHAPTER 4

Who are we, as teachers and pupils?

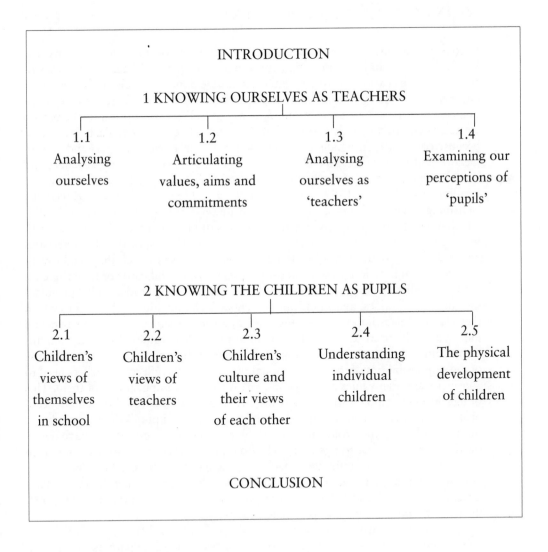

INTRODUCTION

1 KNOWING OURSELVES AS TEACHERS

1.1	1.2	1.3	1.4
Analysing ourselves	Articulating values, aims and commitments	Analysing ourselves as 'teachers'	Examining our perceptions of 'pupils'

2 KNOWING THE CHILDREN AS PUPILS

2.1	2.2	2.3	2.4	2.5
Children's views of themselves in school	Children's views of teachers	Children's culture and their views of each other	Understanding individual children	The physical development of children

CONCLUSION

INTRODUCTION

In the first section of this chapter we focus on ourselves as teachers and pay particular attention to three central issues: the qualities of ourselves as unique individuals; our strengths and weaknesses in taking on the role of teacher; and the values and commitments which we hold. The second section focuses on understanding children as pupils.

1 KNOWING OURSELVES AS TEACHERS

In considering ourselves as teachers, the first step is to consider the person we are. We could do this in terms of social, cultural and educational background, experience and qualifications, position, interests and personality. Such factors make up our 'personal biography' and together they can be seen as contributing to the development, within each of us, of a unique sense of 'self': a conception of the person we are. Social psychologists argue that this sense of self is particularly important because of the way in which it influences our perspectives, strategies and actions (Secord and Backman, 1964; Rosenberg, 1989). This is as true for teachers and children in classrooms as it is for anyone else (Hargreaves, 1972; Nias, 1989a, **Reading, 4.1**; Claxton, 1989; Kohl, 1986) . Each individual is thus seen as having a 'self-image' which is based on a personal understanding of the characteristics which he or she possesses and on an awareness of how others see his or her 'self'. Individuals may also have a sense of an 'ideal self', that is, of the characteristics which they may wish to develop and of the type of person which they might want to become. An individual's self-esteem is, essentially, an indicator of the difference between their self-image and their ideal self. The concept of ideal self introduces the question of values, aims and commitments which individuals hold and to which they aspire. This is important because individuals in society, including teachers and pupils, actively interpret their situation in terms of their values, aims and commitments. Furthermore, teachers' values have considerable social significance because of the responsibilities of their professional position. Thus reflective teachers need to consider their own values carefully and be aware of the implications of them. This brings us to a second set of factors which are to do with the 'roles' which are occupied by a teacher – or by a pupil too. Whilst teachers and pupils do not simply act out particular ascribed roles, it is certainly the case that expectations have developed about the sort of things that each should do. These expectations come from many sources: for example, headteachers, parents, governors, school inspectors, government and the media. Unfortunately expectations are frequently inconsistent. Thus teachers and pupils have to interpret these pressures and make their own judgements about the most appropriate actions.

Few teachers, however committed, can hope to fulfil all their aims if the context in which they work is not supportive. For instance, some parents may have a different set of educational priorities from our own; staff may take up another value-position; the established practices of the school may not support the particular styles of teaching which we would wish to adopt; we may disagree with some aspects of government policy or the resources which we need may not be available. For reasons such as these, teachers must continually adapt: they must both know themselves and the situations in which they work, and they must be able to make astute strategic judgements as they seek to achieve personal and professional fulfilment and to resolve the dilemmas posed by idealism and pragmatism.

Such reflection is a personal process and is very effective when undertaken with a self-aware integrity. However, such professional self-development is now complemented, as a national requirement for England and Wales, by teacher appraisal systems in each Local Education Authority. 'Appraisal' is a formal procedure through which reflection on personal goals and teaching roles is managed by LEAs and headteachers. In England and Wales, following extensive discussion across the teaching profession (ACAS, 1986), appraisal was deliberately not linked to pay so that there was no hindrance to openness. Such procedures are professionally constructive and often require teachers to identify goals on which they may be appraised and to review their personal development and professional capacities in terms of their job descriptions (see **Reading, 3.6**). Such job descriptions will, of course, fit within the framework of the school's overall structure and development plans (see Chapter 14).

Appraisal procedures thus provide a more formal contribution towards the process of knowing oneself as a person, establishing a clear set of values, aims and commitments, and understanding the context in which we work. These are three essential elements in any reflective consideration of teaching and they are examined in more detail below. Because they are three absolutely fundamental issues, we discuss them outside the context of appraisal schemes with which they may, or may not, be associated.

1.1 Analysing ourselves

A recent study of primary school teachers by Nias (1989a, **Reading, 4.1**) has shown that most people enter the profession with a strong sense of personal identity and of personal values. Nias reported that this sense of self was so strong that many teachers saw themselves as 'persons-in-teaching' rather than as 'teachers' as such. Clearly, if this is so, then the openness and willingness to change and develop, which is implied by the notion of reflective teaching, is dependent on the qualities and degree of confidence of each teacher's sense of self and the relationship of 'self' to 'role'. One issue of particular interest is the argument which Nias makes about achieving personal fulfilment from teaching. She suggests that this is most likely when there is a congruence between each teacher's personal sense of self and the ways in which they are expected to present their self in school – their public display.

This raises a number of important points, particularly the need to develop self-knowledge. Easen (1985) has provided a useful framework for developing such understanding. He suggests that we can distinguish between a set of characteristics which we see as being part of ourselves (as representing our self-image) in contrast to a set of attributes which other people attribute to us on the basis of observation and interaction with us. There is also an unknown area of potential for self-development.

Using a model of this sort one can distinguish between the following:

- our public display: aspects of ourselves which we recognize and others also see
- our blind spots: aspects of ourselves which others see but we do not recognize

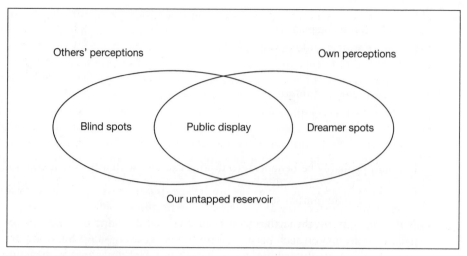

Figure 4.1 *Diagram to show seen and unseen aspects of 'self'*

● our dreamer spots: aspects of ourselves which we know are there, or would like to be there, but of which others are unaware

● our untapped reservoir: our unknown potential, of which we are also unaware

These aspects are indicated in Figure 4.1.

Understanding oneself is not something which one can simply 'do' and complete in a single activity. It is something which develops over time. In Practical Activity 4.1 our main purpose is simply to draw attention to the centrality of such self-awareness for the reflective teacher.

Practical activity 4.1

Aim: To analyse dimensions of our 'selves'.

Method: Think of specific and memorable incidents in which you were centrally involved. Try to identify the most prominent characteristics of yourself which they reveal.

Try to identify:

1.	Dreamer spots...	1.
	(parts you would like to develop)	2.
		3.
2.	Blind spots...	1.
	(parts you do not often face up to)	2.
		3.

3.	Public display...	1.	
	(how you try to present yourself)	2.	
		3.	
4.	Untapped reservoir...	1.	
	(parts you think might be there)	2.	
		3.	

It would probably be beneficial to do this exercise with a friend. It could help you to deepen your understandings, share and explain your perceptions, whilst providing mutual support.

Follow-up: Clearly, the challenge of being a reflective teacher is intimately bound up with reflection on such personal issues. It is about replacing blind spots with insights, about developing dreams and ideals into realities, about tapping potential and facilitating learning.

However, it is necessary to consider the fact that developing such self-awareness can involve a process of self-discovery which may, at times, be threatening and painful. The work of Carl Rogers (1961, 1969, 1980) is useful here. Rogers writes as a psychotherapist who has developed what he calls a 'person-centred' approach to his work. His central argument is

> that individuals have within themselves vast resources for self-understanding and for altering their self-concepts, basic attitudes and self-directed behaviour. (1980, p. 115)

In addition to the focus on inner self-development, Rogers also suggests that personal development is facilitated by the genuine acceptance by others. This has great relevance for professional and personal development in teaching. In particular, it points to the importance of working collaboratively with colleagues and developing open, trusting relationships. Such relationships should not only provide an alternative source of insights into our own practice but should also provide the support to face and deal with whatever issues may be raised.

1.2 Articulating values, aims and commitments

In beginning to consider personal values, it is important to establish a basic point: that our perspectives and viewpoints influence what we do both inside and outside the classroom. The values we hold are frequently evident in our behaviour, and thus, in our teaching.

Identifying values and aims is difficult, and so, too, is trying to identify what to look for in the classroom that would tell us whether we were putting our aims into practice. Reflective teachers need both to identify values, aims and commitments and to consider indicators of their actual implementation. Only then will they be able to judge whether what they do really matches what they say they believe.

Many attempts have been made to group such beliefs and to link them to educational ideologies (see Chapter 2, section 1.1). These value-positions and ideological perspectives can be labelled in many different ways – itself a challenging activity for a reflective teacher. The six positions identified below are, or have been, particularly important.

Social democracy. This is characterized by an egalitarian value-position and a focus on the potential of education as an instrument of gradual social change. This was a prevalent ideology in the post-war years and, for a period, seemed to have a degree of all-party support in the UK.

Liberal romanticism. An example of this is the highly individualistic, 'child-centred' view of education, focusing on the unique development of each child, a view which values diversity and individual difference. This is the ideology which was endorsed by the Plowden Report (CACE, 1967, **Reading, 7.6**).

Traditional educational conservatism. A perspective that emphasizes the transmission of established social values, knowledge and culture through a subject-orientated approach and which also has a particular emphasis on upholding 'standards'. This was the explicit ideology of the Black Papers (e.g. Cox and Dyson, 1969) and was an important element of the thinking of the

1970s and 1980s (Boyson, 1975; Hillgate Group, 1987; Scruton, 1986; Lawlor, 1988, **Reading, 7.9**) which influenced the Education Reform Act (1988).

Economic pragmatism. An instrumental approach focusing on the individual's acquisition of useful skills. The term 'vocationalism' is sometimes used where the emphasis shifts, perhaps at times of high unemployment, to directing individuals to acquire skills economically useful to society. In England and Wales this approach is evident in much provision for post-16 education and in the vocational training sponsored by industry through local Training Enterprise Councils.

Social reconstructionism. An approach which is based on a commitment to develop education as a means of combating inequalities in society. Proponents support positive action regarding such issues as sexism, racism, homophobia, social class, disability, rights and the distribution of power and wealth. Some 1980s policies of the Inner London Education Authority reflected this approach before it was disbanded, and the commitments, if not the actions, are reflected in UK laws (e.g. Race Relations Act 1976, Sex Discrimination Act 1975) and international conventions (e.g. European Convention on Human Rights, United Nations Convention on the Rights of the Child, see **Reading, 15.4**).

Neo-liberal conservatism. A set of beliefs, going back to Adam Smith, about the efficiency of free market forces in allocating resources and raising standards in the provision of goods and services (No Turning Back Group of MPs, 1986; Sexton, 1987, 1988; Chubb and Moe, 1990). As O'Keeffe (1988) put it:

If you do not like the groceries at one supermarket, try another. The system which has utterly out performed all others in history in the production of a wide range of goods and services needs trying out in education too.

In the 1980s, this ideology was applied in education in combination with that of traditional educational conservatism, to produce a radical set of 'New Right' ideas which see educational provision as a market and parents as consumers. Among the many implications of this conception are the reduction of the importance of local educational planning (e.g. through LEAs in the UK) and increasing the importance of information for consumers on pupil and school performance (see Dale, 1996, **Reading, 15.5**). These ideas have been very influential in the 1990s restructuring of education in countries such as New Zealand, Australia and the United States of America, as well as in the UK.

New Labourism. An attempt, initiated by Tony Blair in the mid 1990s, to set a new social democratic agenda for the Labour Party, and aimed to distance new policies both from previous Labour Party commitments and from the neo-liberal conservatism of John Major's government. Characterized by 'toughness' regarding the quality of public services (Labour Party, 1995), but also by a strong commitment to inclusivity through the concept of the 'stakeholder society' (Hutton, 1995).

Such value-positions deserve serious consideration and, where any set of beliefs is dominant, it can rarely be ignored. However, reflective teachers should aim to develop their own clearly defined personal perspective as a guide to everyday action and practical policies. The lack of explicitly conceived values and aims often results in an inconsistent commitment to implement any relevant policy.

Approaching this in another way, Eisner and Vallance (1974) distinguish three main dimensions upon which varied value-positions are held. They suggest these are best represented as continua:

individual ←→ society

(i.e. whether education should be geared to meet individuals' needs and demands, or whether educational provision should be planned to meet the needs of society)

values ←→ skills

(i.e. whether education should focus on developing children's sense of values in a moral and ethical context, or on developing their skills and competencies)

adaptive ←→ reconstructive

(i.e. whether education should prepare individuals to fit into the present society, or should equip them to change and develop it)

By identifying these three dimensions, it may be possible to clarify where each of us stands regarding our value-positions. For example, a student teacher might place herself at the 'individual' extreme of the first dimension, tend towards the 'skills' extreme of the second dimension and feel most comfortable with the 'adaptive' extreme of the third dimension. Such a person would, therefore, be committed to an educational system which aimed at developing individuals with the skills and competencies to fit into the given present society. She would feel less ethical concern for the needs of society as a whole or desire to consider the possibilities and processes of change.

The importance of identifying our value-positions is threefold. First, it can help us to assess whether we are consistent, both in what we, as individuals, believe and in reconciling differences which may exist in a school between colleagues working together. Second, it can help us in evaluating and responding to external pressures and changes to our work as teachers. Third, it can help us to assess whether what we believe is consistent with how we actually behave: that is, whether our 'philosophy', or value-system, is compatible with our actual classroom practice. For instance, although official and professional support was given to child-centred teaching methods throughout most of the 1970s, there is considerable evidence that, in practice, they were not nearly so widespread as was once thought. Both HMI (DES, 1978a) and the ORACLE survey (Galton *et al.*, 1980, **Reading, 9.2**) found only limited evidence for 'progressive practices'. Such gaps between aspirations and actual achievements are very common in all walks of life, but for a reflective teacher it is particularly important to examine them. One useful way of monitoring such issues in ourselves is to identify and focus on key indicators of our value-positions which we would expect to be reflected in our school and classroom practices.

In a sense, the whole of this book is dedicated to helping us to identify additional indices, such as those listed in Table 4.1, whereby we can analyse more precisely our own behaviour and its consequences in the light of our own beliefs.

It is also important to feel able to interrogate the texts and actions of others and to identify their value-positions. Practical Activity 4.2 provides a sample text for this exercise. (See also Practical Activities 4.3 and 4.4)

Table 4.1 *Characteristics of pedagogy*

Progressive	Traditional
1. Teacher as guide to educational experiences (e.g. pupils participate in curriculum planning)	1. Teacher as distributor of knowledge (e.g. pupils have no say in curriculum planning)
2. Active pupil role (e.g. learning predominantly by discovery techniques)	2. Passive pupil role (e.g. accent on memory and practice and rote)
3. Intrinsic motivation (e.g. enjoyment and fulfilment emphasized, interests followed)	3. Extrinsic motivation (e.g. rewards and punishments used: points and penalties)
4. Integrated subject matter and flexible timetable	4. Separate subject matter and rigid timetable
5. Concerned with personal/social/ academic potential: accent on co-operative group work, and creative expression	5. Concerned with academic standards: accent on competition and correct expression
6. Continuous informal forms of monitoring	6. Periodic formal testing and assessments
7. Teaching not confined to classroom base	7. Teaching confined to classroom base

Practical activity 4.2

Aim: To identify value commitments and ideologies through consideration of educational policy statements.

Method: We suggest that a variety of policy statements are discussed with colleagues with a view to identifying both underlying value positions and practical implications. We provide an example from parts of a pamphlet by the Hillgate Group (1987), entitled '*The Reform of British Education*'.

The Goal

Radical policies ... can be successfully implemented only if they are motivated by a clear and defensible goal.

The aim, we believe, is to offer an independent education to all, by granting to all parents the power, at present enjoyed only by the wealthy, to choose the best available education for their children. This aim can be accomplished only by offering schools the opportunity to liberate themselves from Local Authority control.

Conclusion

An autonomous educational system ... will prepare pupils for genuine and nationally approved examinations. We see this as the best way to perpetuate knowledge, to preserve our heritage, to improve standards, and – last but not least – to move forward into the new areas of competence that are expected of children in our time, and without which our country must fall behind its competitors. Parents, we believe, will gradually become aware of the advantages of a devolved system of education, and will eventually welcome it. But what about teachers? We believe that the situation of teachers will inevitably improve, as schools begin to control their own budgets, and salaries become flexible. Genuine competition will of course be painful at first, for those whose incompetence will be revealed by it. But good teachers will soon be sensible of the rewards, and in time their pay and conditions will be transformed so as to enable them to enjoy once again that professional and social status which is theirs by right, but which – thanks largely to the labyrinthine educational bureaucracies and the resulting sustained militant action – has been gradually eroded. As the bureaucracies dwindle, so will the money available to spend in schools increase. And as school expenditure increases, so will teachers begin to enjoy their new-found responsibilities.

Follow-up: Discussion of such documents should bring questions about educational aims and commitments into the open, and thus expose them to debate (see also **Reading, 14.6**).

Practical activity 4.3

Aim: To identify individual value-positions.

Method: Try to place yourself along each of the three continua discussed above and clarify where your 'position' is.

Follow-up: Having tried to do this, you may find other dimensions need to be added as well – or taken away. This exercise can be extended so that a whole group could identify its 'positions'. Then it is possible to clarify areas of conflict and reassess policy issues in the light of such discussions. Consider the implications each 'position' may have for teaching styles. A reflective teacher will also need to consider to what extent classroom behaviour is consistent with expressed beliefs.

Practical activity 4.4

Aim: To identify general aims which you hold for the children's learning.

Method: List your 'top ten' aims, and number them in order of importance.

Follow-up: How do your aims relate to your 'value-position'? How do your aims compare with your colleagues'? What are the implications of any similarity or difference?

1.3 Analysing ourselves as 'teachers'

Any set of aims makes certain demands of a teacher. In this section, we will consider the personal demands of the relationships between a teacher and the other adults with whom they work. This theme will be further developed in Part 3 of this book. Relationships between teachers and children will also be discussed briefly here, but are the main focus of Chapter 5.

I suggested earlier, following Nias (1989a, **Reading, 4.1**), that being a teacher involves accepting particular responsibilities and establishing particular kinds of relationships with the people with whom we work. These have to be achieved within the context of other people's expectations of a 'teacher'.

The first set of relationships with other adults to be considered here are those with parents. Educationalists have argued that the learning experiences which are provided by parents and teachers should not be separated by conventional, but artificial, boundaries of 'home' and 'school' (Cullingford, 1985; Grant, 1989; Stacey, 1991; Pollard with Filer, 1996). Parents should thus participate more fully in their children's education than in the past and teachers should regard parents as 'partners' in the educational process. Some teachers see such moves as a threat and as having de-professionalizing implications. For others they are seen as a welcome and positive change where home and school work together for the greater benefit of each child.

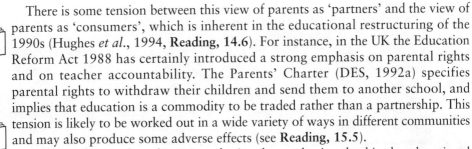

There is some tension between this view of parents as 'partners' and the view of parents as 'consumers', which is inherent in the educational restructuring of the 1990s (Hughes *et al.*, 1994, **Reading, 14.6**). For instance, in the UK the Education Reform Act 1988 has certainly introduced a strong emphasis on parental rights and on teacher accountability. The Parents' Charter (DES, 1992a) specifies parental rights to withdraw their children and send them to another school, and implies that education is a commodity to be traded rather than a partnership. This tension is likely to be worked out in a wide variety of ways in different communities and may also produce some adverse effects (see **Reading, 15.5**).

Other professionals and quasi-professionals are also involved in the educational process. For instance, with further moves towards the integration of pupils with special educational needs – resulting initially in the UK from the Warnock Report (DES, 1978b), the 1981 Education Act and latterly continuing reductions in the level of local education authority funding for centrally provided services – we can expect other specialist staff to be working in the classroom, and liaison with social services and health professionals to grow in significance. Similarly, the high cost of teachers and tight school budgets are leading to rising class sizes and may produce increases in the numbers of relatively cheap, non-teaching ancillary staff who are employed in classrooms. Hence, teachers increasingly have to be able to manage not only themselves and their children, but also a team of other adults as well. 'Room management' studies (e.g. Thomas, 1992; **Reading, 9.7**) suggest that adults work most effectively in classrooms when their roles are distinct, complementary and clear – both to themselves and the pupils.

A final set of relationships that we have to be able to develop is with other teaching colleagues on the school staff. The introduction of National Curriculum in the UK and of procedures for whole-school planning (see Chapter 14) have been a tremendous spur in this direction in the 1990s. The need for curriculum progression and continuity has produced increased professional trust and co-operation among school staffs (Pollard *et al.*, 1994). Most schools have identified staff who act as curriculum co-ordinators and leaders so that a source of particular expertise is available within the school. As the subject knowledge demands of the National Curriculum become recognized, it is also likely that staff co-operation will develop further, to support more teaching of particular subjects by specialist staff (Alexander *et al.*, 1992; Practical Activity 4.5).

Practical activity 4.5

Aim: To consider the advantages and disadvantages of other adults working in the classroom.

Method:
1. List the different adults who might work in a primary classroom, their status (e.g. parent, ancillary, etc.).
2. List the qualities that you would look for in the different adults whom you would like to take up particular roles in your classroom.
3. List the possible kinds of tasks they might do. Try to identify advantages/ disadvantages, possibilities/limitations of their involvement.

This may best be done if you have had experience of these kinds of situations, or with colleagues who can perhaps share their experiences with you. Are the suggested roles likely to be distinct, complementary and clear – both to adults and the pupils?

Follow-up: From such an exercise, it may be possible to draw up proposals for maximizing the potential of such classroom support and for minimizing possible problems.

Changes in the professional role of teachers may make considerable demands on our personal and social attributes, as well as on our pedagogic skills and competencies. They also make demands on our willingness and capacity for change. We need, therefore, to consider our aims in the light of the many demands which are made upon us (Practical Activity 4.6).

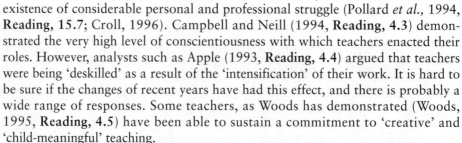

Practical activity 4.6

Aim: To identify the demands that teaching makes of us as individuals.

Method: Divide the page into two vertical columns. In the left-hand column, make a list of the aims you have for yourself as a teacher, as you did in Practical Activity 4.4. In the right-hand column, make a list of the personal qualities, skills, knowledge or competences which are needed to implement each aim. Perhaps reference back to the discussion of competences in Chapter 1 would be helpful.

Follow-up: Review the qualities, skills, knowledge and competences which are required. Consider which ones would be easy for you and which ones might be more difficult. Try to identify steps that could be taken to help to meet your particular challenges.

Studies of primary school teachers at work in the early 1990s demonstrated the existence of considerable personal and professional struggle (Pollard *et al.,* 1994, **Reading, 15.7**; Croll, 1996). Campbell and Neill (1994, **Reading, 4.3**) demonstrated the very high level of conscientiousness with which teachers enacted their roles. However, analysts such as Apple (1993, **Reading, 4.4**) argued that teachers were being 'deskilled' as a result of the 'intensification' of their work. It is hard to be sure if the changes of recent years have had this effect, and there is probably a

wide range of responses. Some teachers, as Woods has demonstrated (Woods, 1995, **Reading, 4.5**) have been able to sustain a commitment to 'creative' and 'child-meaningful' teaching.

Of course, meeting the challenges of teaching is not a once-and-for-all process and professional development should continue throughout a teaching career. This is likely to have three main phases – initial training, induction in the very early years of teaching and a long phase of sustained and continuous development programmes, as appropriate, thereafter. Whilst the initial phase will be structured by a partnership between a teacher education institution and schools, the induction phase is likely to be more exclusively school-based. The third, continuous phase may well be linked to processes of appraisal and to the gradual evolution of a career, perhaps, for some, complemented by the experience of a break from school teaching to bring up a family.

Whatever the actual career pattern, the process of professional development should be broadly similar – that of the continuous identification, development and refinement of skills, knowledge and competences (Calderhead, 1988, **Reading, 1.8**). Reflective teachers should aim to develop a coherent and progressive professional development programme which meets both their short-term needs and their career aspirations.

Perhaps the most important aspect of analysing self involves considering whether what it is 'to be a teacher' is compatible with how we see ourselves 'as a person'. For some, there may be a conflict between these two images, particularly for student teachers who may be more used to thinking of themselves as 'learners'. For example, certain aspects of 'being a teacher' have been described as being willing to take a leadership role, to be 'in authority'. This may result in a conflict between personal values and aims and other people's expectations of a teacher's role.

A final aspect, which at many different times in our teaching lives we need to consider, is the question of what part 'being a teacher' is going to play in our lives. We have to decide how we are going to balance the demands of the job with our own personal needs, with regard for example, to our own family, social life and interests (Evetts, 1990). As we have seen, recent years have been times of great stress for teachers (Dunham, 1992; Cole and Walker, 1989) and it is doubtful if such an imbalance in personal/professional matters can be sustained in the long term.

1.4 Examining our perceptions of 'pupils'

Just as it was important to understand what we expect of ourselves as 'teachers', so, too, it is important to understand what we expect of 'pupils'.

All of us are likely to have preconceptions and prejudices about what children should be like as pupils. For instance, it has been found that teachers are affected by the sex, race or social class of the children and even by their names (Meighan, 1981). If, as teachers, we hold such preconceptions, it can result in treating children in different ways, according to these preconceptions. Children then tend to respond differently, which reinforces our original preconceptions. Such labelling, or stereotyping, can lead to a phenomenon known as a 'self-fulfilling' prophecy and could result in considerable social injustices (Brophy and Good, 1974; Nash, 1976; Sharp and Green, 1975), particularly if they emerge in official assessment (Filer, 1993). The reflective teacher, therefore, needs to question the bases for any differential treatment of the children in the class. This means examining the evidence upon which we base our conceptions of individual children. We need to try and ensure that opinions are based on impartial assessment and on systematic and careful observation and discussions, rather than on prejudiced or haphazard impressions (see also Chapter 13 and **Readings, 5.7** and **13.8**).

Teachers do, of course, have to develop ways of understanding, organizing and grouping children in order to respond effectively to their educational needs. Within the classroom, however, this should be done with regard for the purposes of each particular situation or learning activity. An inflexible form of classroom organization is almost bound to disadvantage some children unnecessarily (Practical Activities 4.7 and 4.8).

Practical activity 4.7

Aim: To find out our response to members of our class.

Method: Write down the names of the children in your class (without refer-ring to the register or any lists). Note which order you have listed them in and which names you found hard to remember.

Follow-up: What does the order tell you about which children are more mem-orable than others, and for what reasons? How does this reflect those you get on best with, those with problems, those who present you with problems, children who are withdrawn, those you would like to forget...? Are there any differences between those of different sex, race, ability or social class?

Practical activity 4.8

Aim: To understand our perceptions of 'pupils'.

Method: Use the list from Practical Activity 4.7 of the children in your class-room to generate the 'personal constructs' which you employ. To do this, look at each adjacent pair of names and write down the word that shows how those two pupils are most alike. Then write down another word which shows how they are most different.

Follow-up: When you have done this with each pair, review the characteristics that you have identified.

1. What does this suggest to you about the characteristics by which you dis-tinguish children? What additional qualities do the children have which these constructs do not seem to reflect and which perhaps you do not use?

2. Consider the constructs and note any patterns which might exist: for exam-ple whether some constructs are used more with boys than girls, with children from different class/race/religious backgrounds. There may also be a variety of constructs which relate to such things as academic ability, physical attributes or behaviour towards teachers or other children.

2 KNOWING THE CHILDREN AS PUPILS

Developing an understanding of the children as pupils requires that a reflective teacher should empathize with what it is like to be a 'pupil' at school as well as develop personal knowledge of and rapport with individual children.

2.1 Children's views of themselves in school

However, what children think of themselves is also important and will influence their approach to learning. Some may be highly anxious and continually undervalue themselves. Others may seem overconfident. Some may be very well aware of their own strengths and weaknesses whilst others may seem to have relatively naive views of themselves. Children may be gregarious, or loners, or they may be lonely. For instance Pollard with Filer (1996) traced the home, playground and classroom experiences of a small group of children through their primary school careers. They argued that such experiences contribute to a sense of identity and thence to confidence and achievement in learning. Table 4.2 (see pp. 81–2) provides a summary for one of the children in their study for a three-year period from the ages of 5 to 7 (see also Practical Activity 4.9).

Practical activity 4.9

Aim: To consider the influence of relationships in home, playground and classroom on the sense of identity and learning of a child.

Method: Select a child on whom to focus. Draw up a matrix, similar to that used by Pollard with Filer (1996), but for an appropriate period. Use records, observation and discussion to complete gradually each cell of the matrix. This may take some time and enquiry to do appropriately.

Follow-up: Consider your matrix as a whole. How is the child's view of his/her self influenced by others? Hos does his/her view of self influence the approach taken to learning? Are there any specific implications for providing for this child or overall conclusions for understanding children more generally?

Practical Activity 4.10 suggests a quick way of gathering evidence about the feelings of a whole class.

Practical activity 4.10

Aim: To identify how children feel about themselves in a school context.

Method: Children can be asked to complete 'Me at School' sheets (Mortimore *et al.*, 1986). They should be completed by each child individually and can be administered to a whole class simultaneously. Each item can be read by the teacher in turn. Children should put a cross in the box which is 'most true for me'.

The children's responses will give an indication of their overall feelings about themselves at school and the items can be scored and aggregated. Scoring is from one to five for items 1, 3, 5, 6, 7 and 9. It is from five to one for items 2, 4, 8, 10 and 11. If an item is missed, code 0. If a more specific analysis is required then the following groups of items can be identified.

- 3, 7 and 10 relate to relationships with other children
- 1, 2 and 8 relate to anxiety
- 4, 5 and 9 relate to learning
- 6 and 11 relate to behaviour

ME AT SCHOOL

MY NAME _____

TODAY'S DATE _____

	Always	Usually	Sometimes	Usually	Always	
1. I am happy and contented	☐	☐	☐	☐	☐	I am unhappy nervous or worried
2. I find it difficult when I am put in new situations or meet new people	☐	☐	☐	☐	☐	I find it easy when I am put in new situations or meet new people
3. I am easygoing and it takes a lot to make me lose my temper	☐	☐	☐	☐	☐	I am irritable and quarrelsome
4. I find it hard to concentrate on work and I am easily distracted	☐	☐	☐	☐	☐	I can concentrate on my work and I am not easily distracted
5. I am keen to learn and I am interested in finding out about things	☐	☐	☐	☐	☐	I am not very interested in learning or finding out about things
6. I am well behaved and I do what my teacher tells me to do	☐	☐	☐	☐	☐	I am naughty and I don't do what my teacher tells me to do
7. I am helpful and kind to other children	☐	☐	☐	☐	☐	I bully or am spiteful towards other children
8. I'd rather be on my own than be with other children	☐	☐	☐	☐	☐	I'd rather be with other children than be on my own
9. I keep going if work is hard and I like to try and find the answer to difficult problems	☐	☐	☐	☐	☐	I give up easily if work is hard and I don't like trying to find the answer to difficult problems
10. Other children think I am unkind and spiteful	☐	☐	☐	☐	☐	Other children think I am kind and helpful
11. My teacher thinks I am naughty and don't do as I'm told	☐	☐	☐	☐	☐	My teacher thinks I am well behaved and I do as I am told

Table 4.2 *Factors and processes in a boy's approach to learning from 5 to 7 years old*

	Home relationships	Peer group relationships	Teacher relationships	Identity	Learning
Reception class	One younger sister. Both 'strong characters' – sparks. Confidence unpredictable; can back off or respond with frustration to Neil's pace. Parents resist putting on pressure.	Jointly most popular child in class. A close but volatile relationship with Richard. Neil's group of friends acknowledge friendship with girls in interview.	One of the oldest in class but achieving well below chronological age. 'Total confidence'. Likes to 'play' not 'work'. Able but minimalist approach to academic tasks. 'Strong-willed'. 'Doesn't like being told what to do.'	Very popular, confident, strong-willed. Difficult to discipline/ volatile relationships at school	Minimalist approach to school. Tendency to angry frustration sometimes at home. Withdraws from some challenges.
Year 1 class	Shows increase in determination/ persistence. Home writing for own needs contrasts with school writing. Mother pleased with school. Changeable relationships with sister. Volatile. Some jealousy? Mother explains, discusses moods of children.	Peer group not as astute as Neil so cannot extricate self from trouble. Neil and his group very scathing and dismissive of girls.	Average age for the class but working at or above this level. 'Boisterous', 'a leader', 'assured', 'noisy', 'a bit devious', 'potentially a deviant', 'works slowly as a tactic'.	Moderately popular. A leader. Assured. A bit devious. Socially astute.	Motivated by extrinsic rewards at school – stages, product, parental approval. Engages in learning selectively at school. Likes the 'fun' and stages of maths and reading. Hates 'boring' writing. Becoming product-orientated. Support from parents as appreciative audience sought.

Table 4.2 *Factors and processes in a boy's approach to learning from 5 to 7 years old*

	Home relationships	Peer group relationships	Teacher relationships	Identity	Learning
Year 2 class	Still changeable relationship with sister – supportive/ belittling, mostly good. Very creative at home now. Mother teaches Neil at home – supportive of school methods. Neil difficult to discipline, sometimes verbally aggressive with mother.	Male-orientated in street play. Suffers divided loyalties between two best friends who don't get on well. Richard leaves. Friendship with Stephen wanes. Starts playing with Daniel and says Daniel will be 'my best friend next year'.	Relatively young in class but achievement level much higher. Good rapport with teacher. Knows and relates to other teachers in school.	Sees himself as 'clever' and as a producer of a lot of work. Observant, perceptive, a mimic. Confident relationships with teachers. Difficult to discipline/ volatile relationships at home.	Individual forays into new learning at home. Rapid development of writing in all respects. Avoids artistic/ practical activities in favour of filling books.

A central strategy in the development of positive self-concepts among the children in school lies in encouraging individuals to identify qualities within themselves which they can value (**Readings, 5.6** and **4.8**). It is important to provide opportunities where a wide range of qualities can be appreciated. In classrooms where competitive achievement is greatly emphasized, some children may quickly come to regard themselves unfavourably, or else learn to resent and oppose the values and the teacher. It is, however, possible to create a climate where many different qualities are valued and where children are encouraged to challenge themselves to improve their own individual performance. In this way the dignity of the individual child can be protected and individual effort and engagement rewarded. (These ideas are extended in Chapter 5, section 3 and Chapter 10, section 3.)

One of the ways of establishing such a climate is to encourage children to evaluate their own work and to set their own personal goals (see Practical Activity 4.11).

2.2 Children's views of teachers

If we are trying to negotiate a positive working relationship with children, it is important to know how each of the individuals involved in the relationship view one another. It is, therefore, important to know how children perceive their teachers.

Practical activity 4.11

Aim: To encourage children to evaluate themselves and to review their work.

Method: This can be done informally. For example, when a story is brought for marking the child can be asked for his or her opinion on it. More formally, perhaps at the completion of a project, children could fill in a comment form to indicate what they had liked best/least about it, what they had found easy/difficult about it, what they had learnt from it (content and skills), what they think they need to practise more or try harder at, etc. Another excellent strategy, if the children can write freely, is to ask them to keep a journal in which they can review their achievements on a regular basis.

Follow-up: Such procedures will reveal specific difficulties which children experience and help the teacher to match future tasks appropriately. However, it is necessary to consider what difficulties some children might experience. How could the teacher help them to articulate their own needs?

A considerable amount of evidence has been collected in this area (Blishen, (1969); Makins, (1969); Meighan, (1978); Pollard, (1993). Much of the evidence suggests that children like teachers who 'make them learn'. They expect teachers to teach, by which they seem to mean to take initiatives, to be in control and to provide interesting activities. On the other hand, they also like teachers who are prepared to be flexible, to respond to the different interests of the individuals in the class and to provide some scope for pupil choice. Children dislike teachers who have favourites or who are unpredictable in their moods. Most children like a teacher who can sometimes 'have a laugh'. Overall, it seems that children like teachers who are firm, flexible, fair and fun (see Practical Activities 4.12, 4.13, 4.14).

2.3 Children's culture and their views of each other

So far the focus has been on the teacher, the child and their mutual perceptions. However, it is most important to remember that, although the teacher is a central figure, classrooms are a meeting place for many children – indeed, Jackson (1968, **Reading, 5.5**) referred to 'the crowd' as being a salient feature of classroom life. How children learn to cope with being one of a crowd and how they relate to each other is of consequence. This can affect how well the children settle in the class socially, and, in turn, may affect their learning. There is, thus, a social dimension to classroom life.

Children's culture has been described by Davies (1982, p. 33) as the result of children 'constructing their own reality with each other' and 'making sense of and developing strategies to cope with the adult world' (**Reading, 4.6**). It thus reflects the children's collective perspectives and actions, many of which can be interpreted as defensive responses to children's relative dependence on adults.

Practical activity 4.12

Aim: To find out children's criteria for a 'good teacher'.

Method: Hold a discussion (with the whole class, or in small groups which can then report back to the whole class) on what makes a 'good teacher'. Perhaps the discussion could be couched in terms of suggestions for a student on how to become a good teacher. Discussions with children on such a topic must obviously be handled very carefully and only with the agreement of any teachers who are involved.

Follow-up: Such information can be interesting in two ways:

1. It reveals something of the children's expectations of what it is to be a good 'teacher'.
2. It can contribute to reflection on our own effectiveness as teachers and in implementing our values, aims and commitments. It could also lead to a reconsideration of those values, aims and commitments.

Practical activity 4.13

Aim: To provide an opportunity for children to analyse the teaching they experience.

Method: At the end of each year, when children often receive reports from teachers, it would also be possible for the children to write evaluative reports on their teacher, or on the work they have done that term. They could comment on what they have enjoyed and why, and what they have not enjoyed and why.

Follow-up: Of course this activity could be carried out much more frequently. Pupil evaluations could be of particular interest to student teachers at the end of their period of teaching in school.

Practical activity 4.14

Aim: To find out children's views on school.

Method: Children could be asked to write a story about their ideal school, or about what they would do if they were the headteacher of their school.

Follow-up: Consider the pattern of ideas which emerges. Is there any consensus? What practical suggestions emerge? What implications do the children's views have for us? How should we respond?

Children's play is, therefore, an important means by which they can identify with each other, establish themselves as members of a group, try out different roles and begin to develop independence and responsibility. Young children often make friends with those who are immediately accessible and with whom they share common experiences (Rubin, 1980). Typically, their friends are children who live close by, who are in their class or who are the children of their parents' friends. When peer groups begin to form, each individual is likely to have to establish their membership of the group in a number of ways. Each member may be expected to contribute and conform to the norms which are shared by the group: for example, liking similar games, toys and TV programmes; supporting the same football team or pop group; liking the same fashions. Group members will also be expected to be loyal to each other, 'stand up for their mates', play together and share things.

A further feature of children's culture is status. As children try to establish their individual identities among their peers each will be valued in particular ways. Sometimes this value will be based on prowess in the playground: for example in skipping, football, fighting. In addition, the identity which children develop through their schoolwork and their relationships with parents, siblings and teachers may influence the way children are perceived by their peers. Where this is the case, there are clear implications for us as teachers. This process of differentiation of children, in terms of their status with both teachers and with other children, affects their own self-image. The process starts during the early years at school and has been found to increase during children's school lives (Breakwell, 1986; Pollard with Filer, 1996). It may lead to a polarization of pro-school and anti-school cultures (Lacey, 1970). Hence, the status and self-image of the children have significant consequences for the children's development during their school years – and these can last into their adult lives (**Reading, 13.8**).

Teachers may wish to know something of the patterns of children's friendships in order to use this information to sustain a positive learning atmosphere and so that friendships can be considered when deciding on grouping arrangements in classrooms (**Readings, 4.7, 9.3 and 9.4**). For reasons of this sort, trying to establish the friendship patterns within the classroom may be of particular interest. Many teachers feel that they 'know' their class well and several friendship groupings may be clearly identifiable. Nevertheless, friendship is very complex, and with younger children may be highly fluid. Constructing a sociogram as suggested in Practical Activity 4.15 can capture some of this complexity.

Friendships can be a source of much pain and distress. It is also easy to fail to notice things, such as that an outgoing child may actually lack a particular friend of his or her own. Sociometric analysis can help in developing this sort of awareness and sensitivity but there are other ways. For instance, Slukin (1981) spent many hours watching children in their playgrounds. He observed their 'playground code' which encompassed things such as ways of behaving, establishing status and resolving disputes. Playground observation, in a consciously focused way, could be valuable in understanding such issues (see also Blatchford, 1989).

One particularly issue which could be watched for is that of bullying (Elliott, 1992; Tattum and Lane, 1989). This is an unacceptable aspect of child culture and often reflects both its tendency to emphasize conformity and its concern with status, as well as, frequently, the relative insecurity of the perpetrators. Thus children who are different in some way – new to school, overweight or possibly have an unusual accent or simply a different culture – are picked on physically and verbally and are excluded by other children as their unacceptability for cultural membership is asserted or as a pecking order is maintained. In one of its worst forms this can degenerate into overt racism.

Adult intervention must be firm but sensitive to the realities of the social situation. All children need to have friends, to play with and feel accepted by others. The teacher's task is therefore to stop the bullying whilst facilitating the entry of the 'victim' into an appropriate niche within the child culture.

2.4 Understanding individual children

Just as we looked at personal and personality factors in the teacher, so a similar kind of 'biographical' knowledge about each child is valuable in understanding children as individual people and as learners. There are two unique longitudinal studies of children's learning and careers through primary school (Pollard with

Practical activity 4.15

Aim: To try to identify the class friendship patterns.

Method: It is possible to construct a sociogram to indicate friendships.

1. Each child can be asked, confidentially, to write down the names of the three people in his or her class with whom he or she would most like to play, or, with whom he or she would most like to do a particular classroom activity.

2. If desired, each child could also be asked for the names of those with whom he or she would least like to play or work.

3. Having collected the data, friendship groupings can then be picked out and plotted. It is often easier to start with the reciprocal choices, where these are also positive (i.e. two or more children name each other as children with whom they would like to play, or work).

4. Where the choices are positively reciprocated, write down the names, linked with a double-headed arrow (i.e. ←→).

5. Where the choice is not reciprocated link the names with a single-headed arrow (i.e. →).

6. Where a negative choice is reciprocated, i.e. there is mutual dislike, link the names with a dotted, double-headed arrow (←·····→).

7. Where a negative choice is one-way link the names with a dotted, single-headed arrow (·····→).

From the diagram thus created (which will probably take more than one attempt) it should now be possible to isolate various features, such as:

- Clusters (ie three or more pupils who show mutual, positive relationships – a clique).

- Pairs (i.e. two pupils who show mutual choices).

- Isolates (i.e. those whom no one positively chooses but towards whom no one displays negative feelings).

- Rejectees (i.e. those who are negatively identified and actively disliked).

Follow-up: A number of questions need to be considered:

1. Are there any isolates or rejectees? If this results in any negative behaviour on the part of any children, what can a teacher do to help all the children in their social development, so that they learn to handle differences in positive ways and try to find ways by which they can accept each other? At the same time, it is important to remember that some children may choose to be outsiders for a time: they may be very cautious in establishing relationships and may, at first, prefer to be loners.

2. Have groups emerged which are based on race, social class, ability or sex? To what extent are these a reflection of criteria used in the school?

3. Have the friendship patterns discovered got any implications for classroom management policies (e.g. seating and collaborative group work activities)? Is understanding a particular individual, or group, enhanced by greater knowledge of their place in the children's social structure?

Filer, 1996; Pollard and Filer, forthcoming). These books provide very detailed case-studies of individual pupils as they develop through their primary school, and document the ways in which family, friends and relationships with successive teachers influence learning progress and the emergent identity of each child (see Table 4.2 and also **Reading, 4.8**).

Many schools collect basic information about each child's medical history and educational progress, but such records, although sometimes helpful, rarely convey an impression of the 'whole child'. As a move in this direction, profiles, portfolios or 'records of achievement' may be kept in some schools. These forms of record tend to focus on each child's progress, together with examples of the work at different ages. However, they are often enhanced by information about hobbies and interests, abilities and tastes, and materials which reflect each child's social attitudes, behaviour, out-of-school achievements and family context. Perhaps each child also helps in decisions about what to include.

Such records may provide an excellent starting-point for understanding each child, in terms of his or her material, social and cultural circumstances as well as his or her development in school. They thus provide a context for understanding children. However, such records cannot replace the awareness which will come from personal contacts with children and their parents (Practical Activity 4.16).

It is often argued that the 'needs' of the learner should be seen as the starting-point for teaching and learning policies. However, the notion of appropriate needs is a very problematic one, since it begs questions about prior aims, and judgements about what is worthwhile (Dearden, 1968; Barrow, 1984; see also **Reading, 13.7**). Nevertheless, it may be valuable for us as reflective teachers to articulate what we see as the basic 'needs' of every child which we commit ourselves to trying to meet. Maslow (1954) identified three classes of needs:

Practical activity 4.16

Aim: To construct a biographical perspective of a child.

Method:

1. Present open-ended opportunities where a child can write, draw, talk or otherwise communicate about herself or himself. Discussions about friends, experiences, family or about favourite books or TV characters can be revealing. Make notes.

2. Observe and take notes on the child's general behaviour in the playground and in the classroom. Consider how the child interacts with other children and how he or she tackles learning tasks.

3. If possible, discuss the child with parents and other teachers. Make notes.

4. Summarize your key understandings and your areas of uncertainty. Consider the child's strengths and areas of need.

Follow-up: Accumulating such information can take time and will only develop gradually. Nevertheless, it could provide a valuable profile of the specific and unique characteristics of an individual. Then it is necessary to consider what implications it has for shaping the educational provision that is appropriate for the child.

- primary needs...for food, sleep and shelter
- emotional needs...for love and security
- social needs...for acceptance by peers

This is not dissimilar from those suggested by Kellmer-Pringle (1974), who identified four basic types of needs for young children:

- the need for love and security
- the need for new experiences
- the need for praise and recognition
- the need for responsibility

Within each of these general areas, it would be possible to identify many further needs. This could be attempted in the specific context of one's class, though one would have to be careful to guard against adversely labelling the children in the process (Practical Activity 4.17).

2.5 The physical development of children

The issue of the physical development of children has been relatively neglected by educationalists in recent years. At one time it was a central issue in teacher education courses, with the pioneering work of Tanner at the London Institute for Child Health (see Tanner, 1978) being highly influential. It was on the basis of such work that mass screening procedures were introduced into the United Kingdom. These are carried out in schools by visiting medical staff using measures such as height and weight as indicators of child health.

Practical activity 4.17

Aim: To identify some needs of a selected number of children in one's class and to establish an order of priority.

Method: List the children's names and beside each name record your judgement of that child's key needs.

Follow-up:

1. Consider which criteria you used in deciding 'key' needs. Was your choice based on the fact that you value certain needs more than others and believe them to be of greater importance in themselves?

2. Examine the needs that you have listed and see if any pattern exists across the class which could form a common basis for planning activities.

3. Identify needs which are specific to individual children and consider how you could make provision for them.

Health has always been strongly associated with social conditions (Rutter and Madge, 1976) and perhaps it has been the general rise in average standards of living since the 1970s which has reduced the prominence of the issue. However, in Britain in the 1980s and 1990s, poverty levels for those out of work have steadily worsened and the health of children in poor families is being affected (DHSS, 1989; National Children's Homes, 1991).

Children develop physically at very different rates, particularly at puberty, and such differences can affect both children's capacity for new learning and their self-confidence. Differential rates of development should, therefore, be carefully considered by teachers, particularly when a national curriculum and assessment procedures make no explicit allowance for such variations.

There are also concerns about the diet and lack of physical exercise of many children (see Practical Activity 4.18). In general, children consume far too much fat and sugar and the exercise which they get is not sustained or sufficient to ensure healthy development of muscles and heart. Environmental issues, such as lead poisoning in cities and the thinning of the ozone layer, are obviously additional concerns.

What, too, do children think of their own health and health care at home and school? Mayall (1995) researched this question in London schools and found that children were aware of many important health issues and were capable of taking more responsibility than they were normally offered by adults (**Reading, 4.9**).

A further set of issues in understanding children draw on psychology, for studies of the development of children's thinking have had an enormous impact on teaching in schools. This work is considered in Chapter 6.

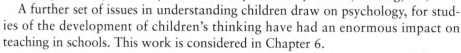

Practical activity 4.18

Aim: To evaluate the exercise taken by children in your class.

Method: We suggest that a simple daily record sheet is developed such as the one below.

The task for the children could be:

If you had any exercise at these times, please write in what you did.

After getting up...

Getting to school...

First lesson...

Playtime...

Second lesson...

Dinner-time...

Third lesson...

Story-time...

Getting home...

At home before supper...

At home after supper...

This could be completed retrospectively by each child for one week, perhaps at the start of each day regarding the day before.

Follow-up: Analyse your results. You should be able to see patterns in the type, amount and timing of activities. Perhaps there will be differences between boys and girls, or between children with gardens at home and those without. Do you judge that the amount of exercise is sufficient for healthy physical growth at the age of your children?

CONCLUSION

The process of engaging in activities such as those suggested in this chapter should help us as teachers to place our aims in a realistic personal perspective. If the many unconscious influences on our teaching can be made explicit, it is easier to identify where we are being most successful and where perhaps our aims and our practice do not match as well as they might. It is also possible, by trying to make the implicit explicit, to be more aware of how we get to know children and of the evidence upon which we base our understanding. Furthermore, by becoming more aware of the children's perceptions of us as teachers, of their culture and of their perspectives on themselves and each other, we are more likely to be able to take account of their needs when planning and making provision for classroom activities.

Notes for further reading

Two accessible and insightful introductions to the importance of considering the 'self' of teachers and children are:

Hargreaves, D. H. (1972)
Interpersonal Relationships and Education,
London: Routledge & Kegan Paul.

Lawrence, D. (1987)
Enhancing Self-Esteem in the Classroom,
London: Paul Chapman.   Reading, 5.6

A stimulating sociological analysis of these matters is:

Goffman, E. (1959)
The Presentation of Self in Everyday Life,
Garden City: Doubleday.

In the book below, Easen provides many suggestions for coming to understand our 'selves' more clearly:

Easen, P. (1985)
Making School-Centred INSET Work,
London: Croom Helm.

The following book is a particularly sensitive account of the challenges which are posed for primary school teachers:

Nias, J. (1989a)
Primary Teachers Talking,
London: Routledge.   📖 **Reading, 4.1**

A considerable amount of work on teacher biography has been conducted in recent years. This illustrates links between the personal and professional spheres of activity and demonstrates effects on careers. Among the best are:

Ball, S. J. and Goodson, I. F. (1985)
Teachers' Lives and Careers,
London: Falmer.

Connell, R. W. (1985)
Teachers' Work,
London: Allen & Unwin.

Sikes, P. J., Measor, L. and Woods, P. (1985)
Teachers' Careers,
London: Falmer.

For fascinating data on the social background of primary school student teachers, see:

EATE (1991)
Student Primary Teachers: Their Economic and Industrial Background, Understanding and Attitudes,
EATE Dissemination Study No 2,
Bath: EATE, University of Bath.

On questions of aims, values and commitments, there are a number of distinctive philosophical analyses. Contrast for example:

Peters, R. S. (1966)
Ethics and Education,
London: Allen & Unwin.

Bantock, G. H. (1980)
Dilemmas of the Curriculum,
Oxford: Martin & Robinson.

O'Hear, A. (1981)
An Introduction to the Philosophy of Education,
London: Routledge.

Barrow, R. and Woods, R. (1988)
An Introduction to Philosophy of Education,
London: Routledge.

Bottery, M. (1990)
The Morality of the School,
London: Cassell.

The most recent research on primary teachers' aims is reported in:

Pollard, A., Broadfoot, P., Croll, P., Osborn, M. and Abbott, D. (1994)
Changing English Primary Schools?
London: Cassell.

Campell, J. and Neill, S. R. St J. (1994)
Primary Teachers at Work,
London: Routledge.

Croll, P. (ed.) (1996)
Teachers, Pupils and Primary Schooling: Papers from the PACE Project,
London: Cassell.

For an excellent historical analysis which demonstrates the importance of considering aims and value positions within their social context, see:

Grace, G. (1978)
Teachers, Ideology and Control,
London: Routledge & Kegan Paul.

Two books which will provide an interesting comparative perspective on teachers and teaching are:

Neave, G. (1992)
The Teaching Nation: Prospects for
Teachers in the European Community,
Oxford: Pergamon.

Newman, J. W. (1990)
America's Teachers,
New York: Longman.

Teaching is, of course, work and teachers are employees with both contractual duties and rights which need to be protected. For an historically informed analysis of the ways in which teachers organize collectively to protect their interests and influence policy in the UK, see:

Barber, M. (1991)
Education and the Teacher Unions,
London: Cassell.

Many people feel that teacher associations in the UK would be greatly strengthened if they could form a General Teaching Council. For an elaboration of this aspiration, see:

Sayer, J. (1992)
The Future Governance of Education,
London: Cassell.

On teacher appraisal see:

ACAS (1986)
Report of the Appraisal/Training Working Group,
London: ACAS.

Hopkins, D. and Bollington, R. (1989)
Teacher appraisal for professional development,
Cambridge Journal of Education,
19(2), 163–82.   ◌ Reading, 3.6

Teacher stress and 'burn-out' are increasingly common. For supportive books on this, see:

Dunham, J. (1992)
Stress in Teaching,
London: Routledge.

Claxton, G. (1989)
Being a Teacher: A Positive Approach to Change and Stress,
Milton Keynes: Open University Press.

Cockburn, A. (1996)
Teaching Under Pressure: Looking at Primary Teachers' Stress,
London: Falmer Press.

The majority of primary school teachers are women, and research suggests that their work experience is neither easy nor equitable. See:

Evetts, J. (1990)
Women in Primary Teaching: Career, Contexts and Strategy,
London: Routledge.

De Lyon, H. and Migniuolo, F. (1989)
Women Teachers: Issues and Experiences,
Milton Keynes: Open University Press.

Accounts of research on effects of teachers' expectations on pupils are provided in:

Tizard, B., Blatchford, P., Burke, J., Farquhar, C. and Plewis, I. (1988)
Young Children at School in the Inner City,
Hove: Lawrence Erlbaum Associates
Reading, 13.2

Mortimore, P., Sammons, P., Stoll, L., Lewis, D. and Ecob, R. (1988)
School Matters: The Junior Years,
Wells: Open Books.
Reading, 5.7

For reports of case-studies see:

Hartley, D. (1985)
Understanding the Primary School,
London: Croom Helm.

Pollard, A. (1985)
The Social World of the Primary School,
London: Cassell.
Reading, 4.7

Waterhouse, S. (1991)
First Episodes: Pupil Careers in the Early Years of School,
London: Falmer.

King, R. (1989)
The Best of Primary Education? A Sociological Study of Junior Middle Schools,
London: Falmer.

On children's 'needs' see:

Kellmer-Pringle, M. (1974)
The Needs of Children,
London: Hutchinson.

For philosophical discussions of the difficulties in identifying needs – in particular of the values which must be inherent in any such attempt – see:

Dearden, R. F. (1968)
The Philosophy of the Primary Education,
London: Routledge & Kegan Paul.

Barrow, R. (1984)
Giving Teaching Back to Teachers,
Brighton: Wheatsheaf.

There are a number of interesting books on children's culture, friendships and perspectives. Collections which illustrate such work are:

Pollard, A. (ed.) (1987b)
Children and their Primary Schools: A New Perspective,
London: Falmer.

James, A. and Prout, A. (eds) (1990)
Constructing and Reconstructing Childhood:
Contemporary Issues in the Sociological Study of Childhood,
London: Falmer.

Waksler, F. C. (ed.) (1991)
Studying the Social Worlds of Children: Sociological Readings,
London: Falmer.

Pollard, A., Thiessen, D. and Filer, A. (1997)
Children and the Curriculum: The Perspectives
of Primary and Elementary School Pupils,
London: Falmer.

Other useful books which focus on specific issues are:

Calvert, B. (1975)
The Role of the Pupil,
London: Routledge & Kegan Paul.

Rubin, Z. (1980)
Children's Friendships,
London: Fontana.

Slukin, A. (1981)
Growing Up in the Playground,
London: Routledge & Kegan Paul.

Blatchford, P. (1989)
Playtime in the Primary School: Problems and Improvements,
London: Routledge.

Davey, A. (1983)
Learning to be Prejudiced,
London: Edward Arnold

Willes, M. (1982)
Children into Pupils,
London: Routledge & Kegan Paul.

On the particular problem of bullying, see:

Olweus, D. (1989)
Aggression in the Schools,
New York: Wiley.

Tattum, D. P. and Lane, D. A. (1989)
Bullying in Schools,
Stoke on Trent: Trentham Books.

Elliott, M. (ed.) (1992)
Bullying: A Practical Guide to Coping for Schools,
London: Longman.

On racism in schools, see:

Commission for Racial Equality (1987)
Learning in Terror: A Survey of Racial Harassment in Schools,
London: CRE.

Wright, C. (1992)
Race Relations in the Primary School,
London: David Fulton.

Troyna, B. and Hatcher, R. (1992)
Racism in Children's Lives: A Study of Mainly White Primary Schools,
London: Routledge.   📖 Reading, 13.6

The books below are more wide-ranging in their coverage of pupil culture:

Davies, B. (1982)
Life in the Classroom and Playground,
London: Routledge & Kegan Paul.   📖 Reading, 4.6

Goodnow, J. and Burns, A. (1985)
Home and School: A Child's Eye View,
Sydney: Allen & Unwin.

Pollard. A. (1995)
The Social World of the Primary School,
London: Cassell.   📖 Reading, 4.7

Woods, P. (1990)
The Happiest Days? How Pupils Cope with School,
London: Falmer.

For unique longitudinal studies of social influences on pupil learning and careers at school, see:

Pollard, A. with Filer, A. (1996)
The Social World of Children's Learning,
London: Cassell.

Pollard, A. and Filer, A. (forthcoming)
The Social World of Pupil Careers,
London: Cassell.

On children and their physical development, see:

Tanner, J. M. (1978)
Education and Physical Growth,
London: University of London Press.

National Children's Homes (1991)
Poverty and Nutrition Survey,
London: National Children's Homes.

Brierley, J. (1992)
Growth in Children,
London: Cassell.

Mayall, B. (1995)
Negotiating Health: Children at Home and Primary School,
London: Cassell.   📖 Reading, 4.9

CHAPTER 5

How are we getting on together?

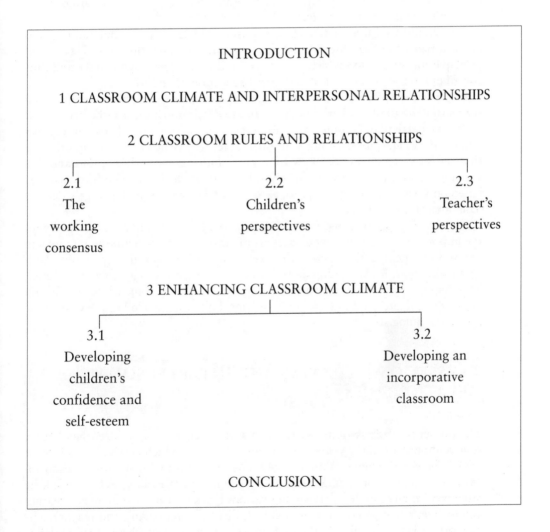

INTRODUCTION

1 CLASSROOM CLIMATE AND INTERPERSONAL RELATIONSHIPS

2 CLASSROOM RULES AND RELATIONSHIPS

2.1	2.2	2.3
The working consensus	Children's perspectives	Teacher's perspectives

3 ENHANCING CLASSROOM CLIMATE

3.1	3.2
Developing children's confidence and self-esteem	Developing an incorporative classroom

CONCLUSION

INTRODUCTION

The quality of classroom relationships is commonly regarded as being very important – for instance, see the Elton Report on discipline in schools (DES, 1989b, **Reading, 10.9**) – but it is also extremely intangible. As we suggested in Chapter 2, it has played a prominent part in the child-centred ideology which has influenced primary practice for many years. There are good reasons for this, for good classroom relationships are considered to be important in facilitating learning, in providing both teachers and children with a sense of self-fulfilment and, in addition, in underpinning the positive, purposefully disciplined working atmosphere which all teachers aim to create.

Nor should we forget that such relationships reflect certain values and help to define a type of moral order for the classroom. In so doing, they model codes and principles of interaction which have wider and longer-term significance and thus contribute to the social, ethical and moral education of children.

However, despite its importance, the issue of classroom relationships often seems to defy analysis. Perhaps this is because relationships are the product of such very particular, complex and subtle personal interactions between teachers and children. Despite such inherent difficulties, the issue is of such significance that reflective teachers are likely to have it almost constantly in mind and this chapter sets out a framework for consideration of the issue. The framework is based on various analytic models of classroom relationships and is largely derived from interpretive studies.

This chapter is structured in three main parts. It is particularly concerned with the importance of the mutual awareness of classroom rules, with the monitoring of children's perspectives and with developing positive and incorporative classroom strategies. It also addresses the issue of our own feelings towards children. The chapter begins, in a more general way, by considering some of the insights on classroom climates and interpersonal relationships which have been developed by social psychologists.

1 CLASSROOM CLIMATES AND INTERPERSONAL RELATIONSHIPS

The influence of classroom environments on teachers and children has been a research topic for many years. One obvious question which emerged was how to define the 'environment'. Withall (1949) answered this by highlighting the 'socio-emotional climate' as being particularly significant (**Reading, 5.1**). Indeed, he attempted to measure it by classifying various types of teacher statement – learner supportive, problem structuring, neutral, directive, reproving and teacher self-supportive. Understanding of the topic moved on when researchers began to define classroom environment in terms of the perception of teachers and children, rather than relying on outside observers (see Moos, 1979; Walberg, 1979). Further developments in this field have been comprehensively reviewed by Fraser (1986). He also provides a way for teachers to investigate the climate in their own classrooms, the 'My Classroom Inventory' (Fraser and Fisher, 1984). This can give direct and structured feedback on children's feelings about classroom life which could be obtained, for example, at the beginning and end of a school year (see Practical Activity 5.1).

Practical activity 5.1

Aim: To 'measure' overall classroom environment at a particular point of time.

Method: Each child will need a copy of the inventory below. As a class (or in a group) the children should be asked to circle the answer which 'best describes what their classroom is like'. The items could be read out in turn for children to give a simultaneous, but individual response. Scoring of answers can be done using the 'teacher's' column. 'Yes' scores 3 and 'No' scores 1 except where reversed scoring is indicated (R). Omitted or indecipherable answers are scored 2.

There are five scales, made up by adding various items, as follows:

Satisfaction (S)	Items 1, 6, 11, 16, 21
Friction (F)	Items 2, 7, 12, 17, 22
Competitiveness (CM)	Items 3, 8, 13, 18, 23
Difficulty (D)	Items 4, 9, 14, 19, 24
Cohesiveness (CH)	Items 5, 10, 15, 20, 25

Follow-up: Mean scores for each scale will provide some indication of the quality of the overall classroom climate and may raise issues for further consideration. (It should be noted that the inventory reproduced here is a short form of a longer inventory and is not a statistically reliable measure of the feelings of individuals.)

NAME _____

SCHOOL _____

CLASS _____

Remember you are describing your *actual* classroom	Circle your answer	For teacher's use
1. The pupils enjoy their school work in my class	Yes No	
2. Children are always fighting with each other	Yes No	
3. Children often race to see who can finish first	Yes No	
4. In our class the work is hard to do	Yes No	
5. In my class everybody is my friend	Yes No	

6. Some pupils are not happy in class	Yes No	R
7. Some of the children in our class are mean	Yes No	
8. Most children want their work to be better than their friend's work	Yes No	
9. Most children can do their schoolwork without help	Yes No	R
10. Some people in my class are not my friends	Yes No	R
11. Children seem to like the class	Yes No	
12. Many children in our class like to fight	Yes No	
13. Some pupils feel bad when they don't do as well as the others	Yes No	
14. Only the smart pupils can do their work	Yes No	
15. All pupils in my class are close friends	Yes No	
16. Some of the pupils don't like the class	Yes No	R
17. Certain pupils always want to have their own way	Yes No	
18. Some pupils always try to do their work better than the others	Yes No	
19. Schoolwork is hard to do	Yes No	
20. All of the pupils in my class like one another	Yes No	
21. The class is fun	Yes No	
22. Children in our class fight a lot	Yes No	
23. A few children in my class want to be first all of the time	Yes No	
24. Most of the pupils in my class know how to do their work	Yes No	R

The use of instruments such as the 'My Class Inventory' can provide a helpful description of children's collective feelings and thus go some way towards representing the classroom climate. However, such techniques arguably fail to grasp either the subtleties of the interpersonal relationships to which many primary school teachers aspire, or the dynamic complexity of teacher–pupil interaction.

One excellent source of insights on relationships is the work of Rogers (1961, 1969, 1980) on counselling. He suggests that three basic qualities are required if a warm, 'person-centred' relationship is to be established – acceptance, genuineness and empathy. If we apply this to teaching, it might suggest that acceptance involves acknowledging and receiving children 'as they are'; genuineness implies that such acceptance is real and heart-felt; whilst empathy suggests that a teacher is able to appreciate what classroom events feel like to children. Rogers introduced the challenging idea of providing 'unconditional positive regard' for his clients and perhaps this can also provide an ideal for what teachers should offer children. Good relationships are, according to Rogers, founded on understanding and on 'giving'.

Rogers's three qualities have much in common with the three key attitudes of the reflective teacher, discussed in Chapter 1. Being able to demonstrate acceptance and genuinely empathize requires 'open-mindedness' and a 'wholehearted' commitment to the children. It also necessitates 'responsibility' when considering the long-term consequences of our feelings and actions. However, this analysis is not really adequate as a guide to classroom relationships because additional factors are involved. For a number of reasons, the warmth and positive regard which teachers may wish to offer their class can rarely be 'unconditional'. In the first place, they are constrained by their responsibility for ensuring that the children learn adequately and appropriately. Second, the fact that they are likely to be responsible for relatively large numbers of children means that issues of class management and discipline must always condition their actions. Third, the fact that they, themselves will have feelings, concerns and interests in the classroom means that they, too, need to feel the benefit of a degree of acceptance, genuineness and empathy if they are to give of their best. Good relationships in classrooms must, then, be based on each teacher having established a framework for order and having earned the respect of the children (Woods, 1987, **Reading, 5.2**). Without this, a mutual positive regard between a teacher and his or her class of children is unlikely to be developed. Instead, the children are likely to regard the teacher as 'soft', 'weak' or as 'muddled'.

If, as reflective teachers, we are to take full account of the interpersonal climate in our classrooms, we need a form of analysis which goes beyond description and measurement. It needs to recognize both the speed at which things can happen in classrooms and the inevitable power relationships between teachers and children. One such form of analysis, we suggest, is offered by adopting an interpretive approach and, in particular, by using the concept of a 'working consensus'.

2   CLASSROOM RULES AND RELATIONSHIPS

Classroom order and discipline, as the Elton Report (DES, 1989b, **Reading, 10.9**) repeatedly emphasized, is most constructively based on good relationships and a sense of community. The concept of 'working consensus' (Hargreaves, 1972) helps us to identify the factors involved in the dynamic relationships between teacher and children.

2.1   The working consensus

A working consensus is based on a recognition of the legitimate interests of other people and on a mutual exchange of dignity between the teacher and the children in a class. Embedded in this is a tacit recognition of the coping needs of the other and a shared understanding that the 'self' of the other will not be unduly threatened in the classroom (Pollard, 1985, **Reading, 5.3**).

In a classroom, both teachers and children have the capacity to make life very difficult for each other and a pragmatic basis for negotiation thus exists. However, a positive relationship, or working consensus, will not just appear. To a very great extent, the development and nature of this relationship will depend on initiatives made by teachers, as they try to establish rules and understandings of the way they would like things to be in their classrooms. Children expect such initiatives from teachers and they are unlikely to challenge their teacher's authority to take them, so long as the teacher acts competently and in ways which children regard as 'fair'. However, it is also the case that, through negotiating the working consensus, the children recognize the greater power of the teacher. As they do so they also expect that the teacher's power will be partially circumscribed by the understandings which they jointly create within the classroom. Hopefully, these teacher initiatives will be based on appropriate principles and values.

Understandings and 'rules' develop in classrooms about a great many things. These might include, for example, rules about noise levels, standards of work, movement, interpersonal relationships. The first few weeks of contact with a class – the period of 'initial encounters' (Ball, 1981a) – is a particularly important opportunity during which a teacher can take initiatives and introduce routines and expectations (Hamilton, 1977). This is often a 'honeymoon period' when teachers attempt to establish their requirements and the children opt to play a waiting game. However, both the 'rules' and the teacher's capacity to enforce them are normally tested by the children before long, for children usually want to find out 'how far they can go' and 'what the teacher is like' when pressed.

As a working consensus is negotiated, both overt and tacit rules are produced. These are normally accepted by the majority of the class and become taken for granted.

Whilst some classroom rules are overt there are many more which are tacit. Awareness of this is very important for all teachers, but it is especially necessary for a student teacher, who is likely to be working with children who have already established a set of understandings with their normal class teacher. Two things have to be done: the first is to find out what the rules are; the second is to check that when attempting to enforce and act within them, student teachers are doing so in ways which will be regarded as 'fair'. This is essential if teachers are to establish the legitimacy of their actions in the eyes of the children. The concept of 'fairness' is vitally important in establishing a working consensus. Because of this, reflective teachers need to develop a variety of ways of monitoring children's perspectives and the criteria by which they make judgements about teachers. For this reason, a number of possible techniques are suggested in Practical Activity 5.2.

Practical activity 5.2

Aim: To identify the overt and tacit content of classroom rules.

Method: Asking the children is an obvious first step. With care, this can be done either in discussion or might be introduced as a written activity. Children usually enjoy such activities, but they will obviously tend to produce more information on the overt rules that on the tacit ones.

The best way to gather information on tacit rules is to study the patterns which exist in what people do. Observation, using a notebook to record such patterns, is one possibility. Another way is to record the events which lead to children being reminded of 'the way we do things here' or of being 'told off'. These could be noted during observation, or a video-cassette recording could be made of a session for later analysis.

Follow-up: Knowing the overt and tacit content of rules in a classroom makes it easier to evaluate social situations accurately, to act with the competence of a 'member' and to use such rules in achieving goals.

To be unaware of classroom rules and understandings is likely to produce a negative response from the children, because actions which they regard as incompetent or unfair will almost inevitably be made (Practical Activity 5.3).

In addition to the content and legitimacy of classroom rules, on which practical activities have been suggested, there are several other aspects of rules which can also be productively considered. In particular, the 'strength' and the 'consistency' of rules can be identified.

Practical activity 5.3

Aim: To check that we are acting in ways which are regarded as being 'fair'.

Method: Again, the only really valid source of information on this is the children. Whilst it is possible to discuss the issue openly with them, it is probably less contentious and as satisfactory to watch and note their responses to teacher actions. This should be a continuous process for teachers who are sensitive to the way their children feel about school, but it is worthwhile to focus on the issue from time to time. Both verbal and non-verbal behaviour could be noted and interpreted – the groans and the expressions of pleasure, the grimaces and the smiles. From such information, and from the awareness to be gained from such an activity, it should be possible to analyse classroom actions in terms of the classification which is discussed below.

One obvious but important point to note here is that not all the children will feel the same about teacher actions. This requires careful consideration (see Chapter 10, section 3).

Follow-up: The feedback which this activity should produce could contribute to the smooth running of the classroom and to the maintenance of the working consensus. If rules which were previously established are being broken by a new teacher, then the children are likely to become resentful. If classroom rules are not being maintained and enforced by the teacher, then the children may well consider the teacher to be 'soft' and may try to 'play him or her up' for a 'laugh' at their expense.

The strength of rules indicates the extent to which situations or events are 'framed' by expectations. This concept is referred to as 'rule-frame' (Pollard, 1980). It relates to the way in which action is constrained by understandings of appropriate behaviour which are developed for particular situations. For instance, one might compare the strong rule-frame which often exists in a hushed library, with the weak rule-frame which often exists in classrooms during wet dinner-breaks. For some purposes, such as a transition between phases of a session, one might want the rule-frame to be strong thus ensuring very tight control. On other occasions, such as during an indoor playtime, a weak rule-frame may be perfectly acceptable and may allow children considerable choice. Situations of difficulty often arise where a strong rule-frame is expected by a teacher but children act as if the rule-frame is weak. If this happens, a teacher has to act quickly to clarify and define the situation and to re-establish the rules in play.

Teachers can influence the degree of rule-frame by their actions, statements and movements. For example, an active, purposeful entry to a classroom is a clear signal that a teacher wants to get attention and one which will normally tighten the frame immediately. Conversely, acting rather casually, or withdrawing into conversation with a visiting adult, will usually cause the rule-frame to weaken and may result in children relaxing in their approach to activities.

The ability of a teacher to manage the strength of rule-frame has a great deal to do with classroom discipline. In particular, skillful management provides a means of pre-empting serious difficulties through giving clear expectations about acceptable behaviour. By its very nature, though, the development of such understandings cannot be rushed and frequently needs to be reviewed explicitly by teachers and children.

The degree of consistency with which rules are maintained provides an underlying structure for learning sessions. Conversely, teacher inconsistency tends to reduce the integrity of the working consensus and the sense of fairness on which it is based. This, in turn, can lead to a variety of subsequent control difficulties.

Relationships between teacher and children, which derive from a working consensus, have important implications for discipline and control. Figure 5.1 provides a simple model which may help us to reflect on the types of action which teachers and children may make in classrooms when a working consensus exists. The most important distinction is between actions which are bounded by the understandings of the working consensus and those which are not. Five basic 'types of action' can be identified.

Teacher acts				Child acts
Unilateral acts	Acts within the working consensus			Unilateral acts
Non-legitimate censure	Legitimate routine censure	Conformity	Legitimate routine deviance	Non-legitimate rule-framed disorder

Figure 5.1 *A classification of types of teacher and child classroom action*

Non-legitimate censure. This is the type of teacher action which children dislike and cannot understand. It often occurs when a teacher loses his or her temper or feels under great pressure. The effect of such actions is that the children feel attacked and unable to cope. They perceive teacher power being used without justification. Such actions lie outside the bounds of the working consensus and are likely to lead to a breakdown in relationships.

Routine censure. This is the typical teacher response to children's routine deviance – a mild reprimand. It will be regarded by the children as legitimate, in so far as such a reprimand will not threaten the dignity of a child nor be employed inappropriately. Censures of this type are within the bounds of the working consensus.

Conformity. These actions, by teachers or children, are 'as expected'. They are according to the tacit conventions and agreements of the working consensus.

Routine deviance. This is the type of mischief or petty misdemeanour which is accepted as being part of the normal behaviour of children. Talking too loudly, 'having a laugh' and working slowly are examples. Such activities are partly expected by teachers and are not normally intended by children as a threat. They are thus within the bounds of the working consensus.

Non-legitimate rule-framed disorder. This is a type of child action which teachers dislike and find hard to understand. It often occurs when a child or a group of children feels unable to cope with a classroom situation and thus seeks to disrupt it. Children are particularly prone to do this if they perceive themselves to have been treated 'unfairly' or feel that their dignity has been attacked. Action of this type usually reflects the cultural rules of peer groups and can be used to build up a type of 'solidarity' or an alternative source of positive self-esteem.

Many of the suggested activities below are designed to assist in the analysis of classroom relationships, using this basic classification. The central argument in what follows is that 'good relationships' are based on the existence of a negotiated sense of acceptability and fairness which teachers and children share. It is therefore important to begin with considering various ways of understanding children's perspectives.

2.2 Children's perspectives

Teaching can only be regarded as successful if the learners are learning. Generally speaking, for this to be achieved, the learners have to be motivated and achieve a sense of self-fulfilment through their classroom activities. They have to be involved in the process of learning and they have to appreciate that the effort which is required of them is worthwhile. It is thus very valuable to collect data from children on the subject of how they feel about the classroom activities in which they are required to engage. This information supplies a basic type of feedback on children's motivation and can be set alongside other diagnostic information about their learning achievements and difficulties – see Pollard *et al.*, 1994 for evidence of pupils' views of the National Curriculum in England and Jackson, (1968, **Reading, 5.5**) for insights into the challenges that they face in classrooms.

The method suggested in Practical Activity 5.4 involves direct comparison between classroom activities in different areas of the curriculum. Such comparisons are useful because they often highlight hidden issues.

Practical activity 5.4

Aim: To gather information on how children feel about curricular activities which they undertake in school.

Method: One method, suitable for children for whom writing is not difficult, is simply to ask them to write a comparison of two activities which you choose. It may be worth structuring this at the beginning by getting the children to make notes under headings such as the ones below:

	Good things	Bad things
Activity 1		
Activity 2		

An alternative method would be to carry out a similar exercise verbally. There is no reason why even very young children cannot participate in discussions about the activities which they like and dislike. Fairly open questions might be used such as, 'Can you tell me about the things that you like doing best at school?' and 'Can you tell me about the things which you don't like doing?' These, if followed up sensitively by further enquiries to obtain reasons (and the results recorded), should soon show up the children's criteria and patterns in their opinions about your provision. The recording is important, for when there is no record to analyse it is very easy to fail to appreciate fully the messages one may be being offered.

Follow-up: This activity should yield data of considerable importance for future planning and provision, and should be analysed to identify any patterns in the children's perspectives. If some children seem to be poorly motivated, to lack interest or to dispute the value of an activity, then the situation must be reconsidered and remedial measures taken.

Another important aspect of children's perspectives is their views on their own teacher – already introduced, in a general way, in Chapter 4. This is a fairly well-researched issue and enquiry into it can yield good summary data on the way children feel about the quality of relationships and education in their classroom. Obviously, for professional and ethical reasons, teachers should only collect such information in their own classroom, or with the permission of other people who may be concerned. Research has consistently shown that children like teachers who are kind, consistent, efficient at organizing and teaching, patient, fair and who have a sense of humour. They dislike teachers who are domineering, boring, unkind, unpredictable and unfair. Strict/soft are two common constructs which children use, with 'strict but fair' often being positively valued. 'Softness' is usually regarded as a sign of weakness.

Predictability is also usually important and children are often expert interpreters of the 'moods' of their teachers. Indeed, more generally, children's feedback to their teachers has been found to be both relatively accurate and reliable (see Practical Activity 5.5).

Practical activity 5.5

Aim: To gather feedback from children about how they feel about their teacher.

Method: A direct method may be best for this activity, but it should be timed carefully to come at the end of a session or series of activities – perhaps at half-term or at the end of a topic. The children are simply asked to rate their teacher on a scale such as the one below:

'Most of the time my teacher is...'

SOFT	1	2	3	4	5	STRICT
UNFAIR	1	2	3	4	5	FAIR
BORING	1	2	3	4	5	INTERESTING
SERIOUS	1	2	3	4	5	FUN
MOODY	1	2	3	4	5	NOT MOODY

Follow-up: The results of any activities designed to elicit children's points of view should provide considerable food for thought for a reflective teacher.

2.3   Teacher's perspectives

So far a number of suggestions have been made about how a teacher can take account of the perspectives, feelings and position of children. Now it is time to change the focus on to ourselves as teachers for, as was discussed in Chapter 4, the self-image of a teacher is just as important to maintain as the self-image of the child. Good teaching has never been easy, for to some extent it has always meant placing the learner's needs before the teacher's. However, classroom relationships are a very special and subtle phenomenon. On the one hand the nature of the working consensus is related to disciplinary issues and problems which are likely to confront the teacher. On the other hand, the quality of the relationships can, potentially, provide a continuous source of personal pleasure and self-fulfilment for a teacher.

If our own feelings as teachers are also an important factor in maintaining a positive working consensus, then ways of monitoring our feelings may be useful (Practical Activity 5.6).

Practical activity 5.6

Aim: To monitor and place in perspective our own feelings on classroom relationships.

Method: Probably the best way to do this is by keeping a diary. This does not have to be an elaborate, time-consuming one, but simply a personal statement of how things have gone and of how we felt.

The major focus of the diary in this case will obviously be on relationships. It is very common for such reflections to focus in more detail on particular disciplinary issues or on relationships with specific individuals.

Diary-keeping tends to heighten awareness and, at the same time, it supplies a document which can be of great value in reviewing events.

Follow up: Once a diary has been kept for a fortnight or so, some time should be set aside to read it carefully and to reflect upon it with a view to drawing reasonably balanced conclusions regarding ourselves and our planning of future policies in the classroom. It would be better still to discuss the issues which are raised with a colleague or friend.

3   ENHANCING CLASSROOM CLIMATE

So far in this chapter I have argued that the nature of classroom climates and the quality of interpersonal relationships are fundamental to establishing a positive learning environment. Having identified ways of improving our understanding of both teachers' and children's perspectives of these issues, it is now time to consider ways of enhancing other aspects of the learning environment.

3.1   Developing children's confidence and self-esteem

Children often feel vulnerable in classrooms, particularly because of their teacher's power to control and evaluate. This affects how children experience school and their openness to new learning. A considerable responsibility is thus placed on teachers to reflect on how they use their power and on how this use affects children.

There are two basic aspects of this. First there is the positive aspect of how teachers use their power constructively to encourage, to reinforce appropriate child actions and to enhance self-esteem (Lawrence, 1987, **Reading, 5.6**). Secondly, however, there is the potential for the destructive use of such power. The second issue thus concerns the manner in which teachers act when 'rules' are broken. This can be negative and damaging, but skillful and aware teachers will aim to make any necessary disciplinary points yet still preserve the dignity of each child. Activities are suggested below to monitor each of these aspects, starting with 'being positive'.

'Being positive' involves constant attempts to build on success. The point is to offer suitable challenges and then to make maximum use of the children's achievements to generate still more. This policy assumes that each child will have some successes. Sometimes a child's successes may be difficult to identify. Such difficulties often reveal more about the inability of an adult to understand and diagnose what a child is experiencing. As the psychologist Adler argued many years ago (Adler, 1927), irrespective of the baseline position, there is always an associated level of challenge – a target for learning achievement – which is appropriate and which can be the subject of genuine praise. It may range from producing a vivid story to correctly forming a letter of the alphabet, or from helping another child to sustaining a period of attention and concentration in story-time. The appropriateness of the achievement is a matter for a teacher to judge, but the aim should be to encourage all children to accept challenges and achieve successes (Merrett and Wheldall, 1990, **Reading, 5.8**; see Practical Activity 5.7).

Practical activity 5.7

Aim: To assess the degree and type of positive reinforcement given to children.

Method: There are many possibilities here.

1. Self-monitoring, that is trying to remain conscious of the need to praise efforts and achievements which children make. This involves actively looking for possibilities, but they must be genuine. The essence of this activity is expressed in the phrase 'Catch 'em being good'. Awareness is also likely to be heightened if the learning stages of each child and the tasks in which he or she is engaged are thoroughly appreciated and matched (see Chapter 8). With regard to our own tendencies to 'be positive' or otherwise, a diary-type record is well worth keeping for a period.

2. Observing by colleagues. A colleague who is able to sit in on a session to observe will be able to provide invaluable feedback. A suggested observational schedule is:

Child's initial action	Teacher's reinforcing action	Child's response

A discussion would be very helpful after the session particularly to identify any patterns in children's responses and to consider whether any other appropriate opportunities for reinforcement are being missed.

3. Analysis of displays of children's work. Questions which might be asked include: Are the genuine efforts of all children represented? Does the quality of the display indicate that the work is valued?

4. Analysis of written feedback to children. Children's workbooks provide a permanent record of teacher responses to their efforts. A tally of 'types of comment' is an easy exercise. Some headings might be:

	Child A	Child B	Child C	Child D
Encouragement given a phrase a sentence				
Diagnostic advice given				
Extension proposed				
No comment given				
Discouragement given				

Follow-up: There is a simple point to be made in considering attempts to be positive as a whole. If, as an outcome of this monitoring, it is found that some children do not receive adequate reinforcement, bearing in mind their apparent needs, then the teacher should both check that opportunities for praise are not missed and make provision so that genuine opportunities occur. These can then be monitored. This is another, motivational, aspect of the 'match' (see Chapter 8, section 3.3) which is very important for the personal development of any child.

This brings us to 'avoiding destructive action'. This is the second aspect of the teacher's use of power – the way in which control is used. On this issue, we want to focus on the dangers of 'flashpoints' in classrooms – situations in which teachers 'lose their head' and start to act unilaterally. All teachers would probably agree that a class of children has to be under control if purposeful and productive activities are to take place. However, a teacher's power can be exercised in many ways. In most situations teachers try to be calm, firm and fair – they act within the bounds of the working consensus and use various types of legitimate 'routine censure' to maintain discipline.

Unfortunately, there is a well-documented tendency for teachers to reprimand children over-personally when telling them off in the heat of the moment, rather than focusing positively on the activity in which they should have engaged. The effect of this can be that the children may feel attacked and humiliated so that, rather than conforming more, the children 'want to get back at' the teacher who has 'picked on' them 'unfairly'. Here, the problem is that the teacher's action is 'unilateral' and lies outside the understandings of the working consensus. The normally recommended way of enforcing authority whilst at the same time protecting the self-esteem of each child is to focus on the action of the children for condemnation rather than on the children themselves (Hargreaves *et al.*, 1975, **Reading, 10.7**). A reprimand can then be firmly given, but the self-image of each child is left relatively intact. Each child can then conform with dignity if he or she so wishes, and the incident is contained within the bounds of the working consensus. This will be discussed further in Chapter 10 where we focus on classroom management and on further aspects of discipline.

Thus, reflective teachers are likely to attempt to use their power positively and constructively, and they will be particularly aware of the potential damage to relationships which can be done by over-hasty reactions to some classroom crises.

A further type of reflection on relationships concerns the degree of involvement by children, which brings us to the notion of what may be called the 'incorporative classroom'.

3.2 Developing an incorporative classroom

An 'incorporative classroom' is one which is consciously designed to enable each child to act as a full participant in class activities and also to feel him or herself to be a valued member of the class. This is what most teachers would wish but there is plenty of evidence that, in the context of curriculum pressures, large class sizes and the requirements of many assessment procedures, it is difficult to achieve. One feature which often causes problems is that there are variations in both the quantity and quality of teacher attention which is given to different categories of children.

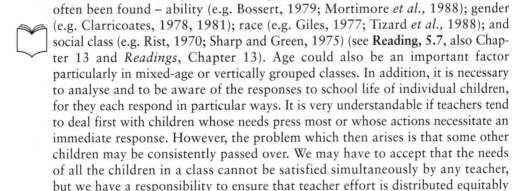

There are four fairly obvious categories around which such variations have often been found – ability (e.g. Bossert, 1979; Mortimore *et al.*, 1988); gender (e.g. Clarricoates, 1978, 1981); race (e.g. Giles, 1977; Tizard *et al.*, 1988); and social class (e.g. Rist, 1970; Sharp and Green, 1975) (see **Reading, 5.7**, also Chapter 13 and *Readings*, Chapter 13). Age could also be an important factor particularly in mixed-age or vertically grouped classes. In addition, it is necessary to analyse and to be aware of the responses to school life of individual children, for they each respond in particular ways. It is very understandable if teachers tend to deal first with children whose needs press most or whose actions necessitate an immediate response. However, the problem which then arises is that some other children may be consistently passed over. We may have to accept that the needs of all the children in a class cannot be satisfied simultaneously by any teacher, but we have a responsibility to ensure that teacher effort is distributed equitably (Practical Activity 5.8).

Practical activity 5.8

Aim: To identify if, when interacting with children, there are any patterns in the quantity, quality, or purpose of teacher–child contacts.

Method: To assess the *quantity of interaction*, it may be advisable to enlist the help of a colleague as an observer. Alternatively a video recording of a session could be made for later personal analysis. A simple schedule will be required on which to record contacts. This could distinguish between contacts with girls/boys, racial groups, attainment groups, etc., or even with particular individuals. It is then possible to make a tally of the different kinds of contacts. Decisions about whether to try to record all contacts or whether to adopt a time-sampling technique will have to be taken (see Chapter 3). If the latter is chosen, some practice is essential for the observer. It is also possible to focus on an individual child and to monitor the contacts with just that child.

To assess the *quality of contacts* requires a different approach. By quality we might have in mind, following Rogers (1980), the 'genuineness, acceptance and empathy' that is conveyed through the contact. Subjective interpretations are more likely to play a dominant part in this analysis, so it is probably helpful to use a video, or for an observer to make field notes concerning the nature of contacts made. Sharing perceptions with others afterwards is a valuable way of trying to interpret this aspect of the contacts.

Regarding the *purpose of contacts*, a schedule can be devised which lists different kinds of contact. This should be in terms of descriptive and visible actions (low inference), which do not overlap (exclusive categories): for example, 'instructional', 'managerial', 'social' and 'other' contacts. Data might then be collected by time-sampling or a tally. The results could then be analysed to try to identify any different patterns of contact between girls/boys, different races, attainments, abilities or personalities.

Follow-up: If patterns in teacher–child contact are identified, they need to be evaluated against the specific aims which we have for the class as a whole and for that particular child or children. By monitoring such patterns we become more aware of them and thus more able to change them if so desired.

Classes also vary in the degree to which differences between children and their abilities are valued. Such differences between people must inevitably exist, but a contrast can be drawn between classes in which the strengths and weaknesses of each child are recognized and in which the particular level of achievement of each child is accepted as a starting-point, and classes in which specific qualities or abilities are regarded as being of more value than others in absolute terms. In the case of the latter, the stress is often on achievements rather than on the effort which children may have made; the ethos is often competitive rather that co-operative; the success of some children is made possible only at the cost of the relative failure of others. The overall effect is to marginalize some children whilst the work of others is praised and regarded as setting a standard to which other children should aspire.

Quality of work and standards of achievement are crucially important considerations, but there are also many other factors to bear in mind. For instance, we would suggest that an incorporative classroom will produce better classroom relationships and more understanding and respect for others than one which emphasizes the particular success of a few. Such issues are particularly significant when specific assessment knowledge is gathered. In the United Kingdom the outcomes of both teacher assessment and of standardized assessment testing now produce relatively formalized 'results' and must be handled very carefully if they are not to threaten the self-esteem of lower-achieving children. Of course, children who are less academically successful may have considerable other strengths and achievements and these can be recognized, and celebrated, in 'pupil portfolios' or 'records of achievement'.

Thus, there are some central questions about how children are valued which should be answered by a reflective teacher. Among them are those which are suggested in Practical Activity 5.9. This time it takes the form of a check-list.

Overall then, teachers wishing to sustain an incorporative classroom will set out to provide opportunities for children to feel valued and to 'join in'. At the same time they will attempt to eliminate any routines or practices which would undercut such aims by accentuating the relative weaknesses of some children

Practical activity 5.9

Aim: To consider the degree to which the classroom is structured and run so that each of the children can fully identify with class activities.

Method: There are several indicators which might be considered:

1. Which is emphasized most: the absolute achievement of children or the efforts which are made?

2. How wide-ranging are the pupil achievements which are valued? Does every child experience at least some success?

3. In decisions about the curriculum, are the interests of each of the children recognized and given appropriate attention? Is the previous experience of the children drawn on as the planned National Curriculum is adapted to the needs of the class?

4. How is the work of the class represented – in classroom displays, in assemblies, in more public situations? Are there some children whose work features more often and others whose work is seen less often?

5. Are children helped to learn to respect each other?

6. Does any unnecessary and divisive competition take place?

7. Is assessment activity and its reporting handled sensitively?

Follow-up: Having completed your review, what can you do to increase the sense of inclusion for all pupils?

(Prutzman *et al.*, 1978; Putnam and Burke, 1992; see also Clegg and Billington, 1994, **Reading, 9.5**).

CONCLUSION

Apart from increasing the happiness and educational achievement of individual children, teachers who are attentive to the particular needs of individuals and develop good relationships with the class as a whole are likely to find that they encounter fewer disruptive incidents. Perhaps, too, an expectation of being caring towards each other may spread among the children and be of longer-term benefit for society more generally.

Finally, there are often some children with whom more specific efforts to develop good relationships may need to be made. Such cases might include particularly able children who may become bored; children who find school-work difficult and may become frustrated; children who have special educational needs; children who are new to the class or school; and children who have been upset by events in their lives over which they have little control, such as a bereavement, a breakup of their parents' marriage, parental unemployment or even sexual or physical abuse. Such children need very sensitive and empathic attention and they may need special help to express their feelings, to put them in perspective, to realize that their teacher and others care about them and to feel that they have tangible and appropriate targets to strive for in their lives. Such care may enable children to take control of their situation, with the support of their teacher, to the extent that this is possible. However, teachers should guard against being amateur therapists. Child psychologists and social workers are available and they should be invited to give advice if circumstances require their help.

Notes for further reading

For Withall's classic study on 'socio-emotional climate', see:

Withall, J. (1949)
The development of a technique for the measurement
of social-emotional climate in classrooms,
Journal of Experimental Education,
17, 347–61.   see also **Reading, 5.1**

One of a number of classic books by Carl Rogers on 'person-centred' theory is:

Rogers, C. (1969)
Freedom to Learn,
New York: Merrill.

More general overviews of research on classroom relationships are provided by:

Brophy, J. E. and Good, T. L. (1974)
Teacher–Student Relationships,
New York: Cassell.

Rogers, C. and Kutnick, P. (1990)
The Social Psychology of the Primary School,
London: Routledge.

For social–psychological detail on rules as guides to behaviour see:

Collett, P. (ed.) (1977)
Social Rules and Social Behaviour,
Oxford: Blackwell.

Harré, R. (1974) Rule as a scientific concept,
In T. Mischel, (ed.) *Understanding Other Persons*,
Oxford: Blackwell.

On rules in educational contexts see:

Hargreaves, D. H., Hestor, S. K. and Mellor, F. J. (1975)
Deviance in Classrooms,
London: Routledge & Kegan Paul.

The interpretive approach to classroom relationships which has informed much of this chapter, is discussed in detail in:

Pollard, A. (1985)
The Social World of the Primary School,
London: Cassell.   📖 Reading, 5.3

Other closely related accounts can be found in:

Delamont, S. (1990)
Interaction in the Classroom,
London: Routledge.

Woods, P. (1983)
Sociology and the School: An Interactionist Viewpoint,
London: Routledge & Kegan Paul.

The original use of the concept of working consensus is well worth following up. It can be found in:

Hargreaves, D. H. (1972)
Interpersonal Relationships and Education,
London: Routledge & Kegan Paul.

The 'art' of maintaining relationships while teaching is described by:

Woods, P. (1987)
Managing the primary school teacher's role,
In S. Delamont, (ed.) *The Primary School Teacher*,
London: Falmer.

Woods, P. and Jeffrey, B. (1996)
Teachable Moments: The Art of Teaching in Primary Schools,
Buckingham: Open University Press.

On children's confidence and self-esteem the books below provide a conceptual overview, a research review and practical ideas respectively:

Lawrence, D. (1987)
Enhancing Self-Esteem in the Classroom,
London: Paul Chapman.   📖 Reading, 5.6

Burns, R. B. (1982)
Self-Concept Development and Education,
London: Routledge & Kegan Paul.

Cranfield, J. and Wells, H. (1976)
100 Ways to Enhance Self-Concept in the Classroom,
Englewood Cliffs, NJ: Prentice-Hall.

For fascinating studies in which collaborative learning methods were developed so that relationships became 'the basis for learning', see:

Salmon, P. and Claire, H. (1984)
Classroom Collaboration,
London: Routledge & Kegan Paul.

Biott, C. and Easen, P. (1994)
Collaborative Learning in Staffrooms and Classrooms,
London: David Fulton.

Other constructive and stimulating books which will support the development of classroom relationships are:

Orlick, T. (1979)
Cooperative Sports and Games Book: Challenge without Competition,
London: Readers & Writers.

Humphreys, T. (1995)
A Different Kind of Teacher,
London: Cassell.

Prutzman, P., Burger, M. L., Bodenhamer, G. and Stern, L. (1978)
The Friendly Classroom for a Small Planet,
New Jersey: Avery Publishing.

Putnam, J. and Burke, J. B. (1992)
Organising and Managing Classroom Learning Communities,
New York: McGraw Hill.

Ingram, J. and Worrall, N. (1993)
Teacher-Child Partnership: The Negotiating Classroom,
London: David Fulton.

The growing literature on personal and social education is also relevant here. For an excellent introduction, see:

Pring, R. (1984)
Personal and Social Education in the Curriculum,
London: Hodder & Stoughton.

For a compendium of work on personal and social education in primary schools, see:

Lang, P. (ed.) (1988)
Thinking About Personal and Social Education in the Primary School,
Oxford: Blackwell.

For a view of how schools should support the context of the National Curriculum and OFSTED see:

Inman, S. and Buck, M. (1995)
Adding Value: Schools' Responsibility for Pupils' Personal Development,
Stoke: Trentham Books.

The importance of interpersonal relationships in classrooms and schools is repeatedly asserted in:

DES/WO (1989)
Discipline in Schools,
Report of the Committee of Enquiry chaired by Lord Elton,
London: HMSO.   ☐ **Reading, 10.9**

For suggestions of other books on classroom discipline, see the Notes for Further Reading of the chapter on classroom management – Chapter 10.

CHAPTER 6

How are we supporting children's learning?

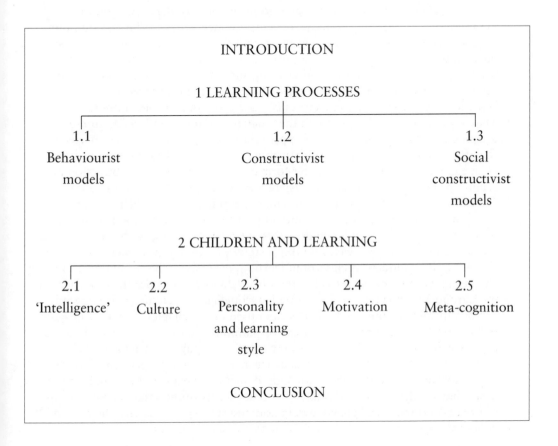

INTRODUCTION

1 LEARNING PROCESSES

1.1	1.2	1.3
Behaviourist models	Constructivist models	Social constructivist models

2 CHILDREN AND LEARNING

2.1	2.2	2.3	2.4	2.5
'Intelligence'	Culture	Personality and learning style	Motivation	Meta-cognition

CONCLUSION

INTRODUCTION

Learning can be considered as the process by which skills, attitudes, knowledge and concepts are acquired, understood, applied and extended. Children also learn about their feelings towards themselves, towards each other and towards learning itself. Learning is thus partly a cognitive process, and partly social and affective. Successful learning, may result in confidence, pleasure and in a sense of achievement. However, failure may result in low self-esteem, apathy, avoidance or aggression.

Of course, all teaching is about developing, deepening and extending pupil thinking. There must be both engagement with the child's understanding and support for its extension, hence the importance of diagnostic assessment and of the teacher's subject knowledge. Pupil learning should thus not be confused, as it so often is, with mere completion of tasks. Indeed, in the routinized work of many classrooms, children may complete a task 'correctly' but have learnt nothing new. They may also learn things which the teacher did not intend. Such unintended learning could be productive – an appropriate match to their current needs. On the other hand, they might also learn things which could cause them problems later, e.g. incorrect spellings or letter-formation skills, inefficient subtraction procedures or inaccurate information. There is no doubt, then, that effective learning is greatly enhanced by appropriate teaching. Learning cannot be left to chance.

In this chapter a framework is introduced for considering and investigating some of the ways in which learning occurs in primary schools. We begin by setting the scene in a practical way, by taking stock of existing practices using three simple analytic models of classroom learning processes. The second part of the chapter moves the focus on to children directly and we consider the influence on the learning of individuals of factors such as 'intelligence', culture, learning stance, personality and cognitive style. The issues raised in this chapter are taken up again in Chapter 8, in the practical context of planning a curriculum which matches cognitive and motivational aspects of school tasks to pupils' learning needs.

A specific word about the role of language in learning is appropriate here for there is probably no more significant factor. Indeed, that is the reason why a whole chapter of this book is devoted to it (Chapter 11). The issue permeates this chapter. The use of language within teaching and learning situations is thus a recurring theme. It will be seen to have a pivotal role in social constructivist approaches.

1   LEARNING PROCESSES

Learning is a highly complex aspect of human capacity and one which, even now, is not fully understood. Philosophers and psychologists have worked to analyse and research it for centuries and this will undoubtedly continue. The result is that there are many alternative theories which attempt to describe the learning process. Most rest on an element of valuable insight, but, it follows, each has both strengths and weaknesses. Over the years, many theories have influenced teaching methods and, having been tested by the realities of classroom practice, have left their mark as part of the pedagogic repertoire of teachers. As an influential report on primary school teaching methods argued, the key professional judgement concerns the 'fitness for purpose' of different methods (Alexander *et al.*, 1992).

We can simplify this complex field by identifying just three theories of learning which have been of particular influence on primary schools.

1.1 Behaviourist models

This theory suggests that living creatures, animal or human, learn by building up associations or 'bonds' between their experience, their thinking and their behaviour. Thus as long ago as 1911, Thorndike expressed both the 'law of effect':

> The greater the satisfaction or discomfort, the greater the strengthening or weakening of the bond.

and the 'law of exercise':

> The probability of a response occurring in a given situation increases with the number of times that response has occurred in that situation in the past.

Thorndike was confident and claimed that these 'laws' emerged clearly from 'every series of experiments on animal learning and in the entire history of the management of human affairs' (Thorndike, 1911, p. 244).

A variety of versions of behaviourism were developed and provided the dominant perspective on learning until the 1960s. Perhaps the most significant of these later psychologists was Skinner (e.g. 1968, **see Reading, 6.1**) who, through his work with animals, developed a sophisticated theory of the role in learning of stimulus, response and consequence.

The influence of behaviourist theory in education has been immense for, in the early part of the century, it provided the foundations of work on a 'science of teaching' based on whole-class, didactic approaches through which knowledge and skills were to be taught. The 'law of effect' was reflected in elaborate systems and rituals for the reward and punishment of pupil responses. The 'law of exercise' was reflected in an emphasis on practice and drill.

Behaviourist learning theory casts the learner in a relatively passive role, leaving the selection, pacing and evaluation of learning activity to the teacher. Subject expertise can thus be transmitted in a coherent, ordered and logical way, and control of the class tends to be tight – because, the children are often required to listen. There is a problem, however, in whether such teaching actually connects with the learner's existing understanding.

Teaching which has been influenced by behaviourism can been seen in all primary schools. The importance of reinforcing children's work and effort is well established and, of course, there is still much use made of negative sanctions – strategies which reflect the 'law of effect'. The use of practice tasks is also widespread (Bennett *et al.*, 1984, **Reading, 8.7**), particularly for teaching aspects of the core curriculum such as numerical computation, spelling and writing, and this type of work reflects the influence of the 'law of exercise'. The use of teacher-controlled explanation and of question and answer routines are important parts of any teacher's pedagogic repertoire. They will be found, for instance, in school assemblies, when new topics are being introduced and when taking stock of achievements. The idea of building progressive steps in learning (e.g. Gagné, 1965, **Reading, 6.2**) is, of course, directly reflected in the organization of the national curricula of the UK and other countries into 'levels'.

Figure 6.1, represents the roles of children and adult in behaviourist–influenced teaching and learning processes. Some particular points could be noted. First, there is a high degree of adult control in the process; deciding on the subject matter, providing instruction, pacing the lesson, correcting and assessing pupil responses. In principle, this makes it relatively easy for teacher expositions and explanations to be logical, coherent, linear and progressive as subject matter or skills are introduced to the pupils. This is likely to be of great benefit to those learners for whom such teaching is appropriate. Second, this approach lends itself to the teaching of large groups or whole classes, in which circumstances large numbers of children can benefit from teacher expertise.

However, there are also some difficulties in teaching in this way. The most important is the question of connecting with the existing understanding of children. In this respect, the strength of subject exposition can also be a weakness if a child does not recognize subject divisions as being relevant to daily experiences. Such a mismatch can reduce motivation and achievement as the child cannot use the knowledge which is offered to build a meaningful understanding. In such circumstances, learning tends to be superficial and fragmented. This problem may be made acute when large groups are taught because it is very hard for a teacher to 'pitch' the lesson appropriately for all learners. If this proves to be a problem, pupil motivation can be adversely affected.

The influence of behaviourism has been greatest on what are commonly termed 'traditional' teaching methods, and particularly those associated with whole-class, subject-based teaching. It is a relatively simple model and it is unfortunate that the value which it does have, when used appropriately, tends to be generalized by non-educationalists. Perhaps this is because of its association with tight discipline and strong subject teaching. However, as we have seen, these can also be weaknesses. The responsibility of teachers is to interact with children so that they actually learn, not simply to expose them to subject matter and drill.

Use of teaching methods based on behaviourism must, therefore, be fit for their purpose (Practical Activity 6.1).

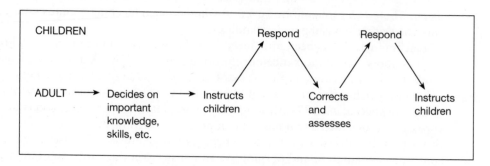

Figure 6.1 *A behaviourist model of roles in the teaching–learning process*

Practical activity 6.1

Aim: To consider the influence and strengths of behaviourist psychology when applied to children's learning and primary school practice.

Method: Review the learning situations and teaching methods, influenced by behaviourism, which your class has experienced during a school day.

Note each learning situation, each teaching method and then consider the reasons for its use.

Learning situation	Teaching methods used	Reason for choice of teaching methods

Follow up: Consider the influence, strengths and weaknesses of behaviourist learning theory on teaching and learning in your school. Are the teaching approaches used 'fit for their purpose'?

1.2 Constructivist models

This theory suggests that people learn through an interaction between thought and experience, and through the sequential development of more complex cognitive structures. The most influential constructivist theorist was Piaget (e.g. 1926, 1950, see **Reading, 6.3**), whose ultimate goal was to create a 'genetic epistemology' – an understanding of the origin of knowledge derived from research into the interaction between people and their environment.

In Piaget's account, when children encounter a new experience they both 'accommodate' their existing thinking to it and 'assimilate' aspects of the experience. In so doing they move beyond one state of mental 'equilibration' and restructure their thoughts to create another. Gradually, then, children come to construct more detailed, complex and accurate understandings of the phenomena they experience.

Piaget proposed that there are characteristic stages in the successive development of these mental structures, stages which are distinctive because of the type of cognitive 'operation' with which children process their experience. These stages are:

- the sensori-motor stage (approximately birth to 2 years)
- the pre-operational stage (approximately 2–7 years)
- the concrete operations stage (approximately 7–12 years)
- the formal operations stage (approximately 12 years onwards)

In each of the first three stages the role of the child's direct experience is deemed to be crucial. It is only in the formal operations stage that abstract thinking is believed possible. In the sensori-motor and pre-operational stages children are thought to be relatively individualistic and unable to work with others for long. Children are believed to behave rather like 'active scientists', enquiring, exploring and discovering as their curiosity and interests lead them to successive experiences. Play and practical experimentation has a crucial role in this process (Piaget, 1951).

The influence of constructivist theory in primary education was considerable following the report of the Plowden Committee (Central Advisory Council for Education, 1967, **Reading, 7.6**) in which it was suggested that:

> Piaget's explanation appears to fit the observed facts of children's learning more satisfactorily than any other. It is in accord with what is generally regarded as the most effective primary school practice, as it has been worked out empirically.

(CACE, 1967, para 522).

'Child-centred' teaching approaches, based on interpretations of Piaget's work, were adopted with enormous commitment by teachers in the late 1960s and 1970s. Great imagination and care was put into providing varied and stimulating classroom environments from which children could derive challenging experiences (e.g. Marsh, 1970). Sophisticated forms of classroom organization, such as the 'integrated day' (Walton, 1971; Brown and Precious, 1968, **Reading, 9.8**) were introduced and developed to manage the problem of providing individual children with appropriate direct learning experiences. Despite these efforts, empirical research showed that constructivist methods were not greatly reflected in the actual practice of teachers of older primary children, (Galton *et al.*, 1980, **Reading, 9.2**). Constructivism has always been more influential in work with younger pupils with whom the benefits of working from children's interests, from play and from practical experience are relatively clear-cut (Anning, 1991; Dowling, 1992; Moyles, 1994).

There have been a number of criticisms of Piaget's work, particularly because of the way in which seeing children's development in sequential structured stages can lead to underestimation of their capacities. Psychologists, such as Donaldson (1978) and Tizard and Hughes (1984), have demonstrated that children's intellectual abilities are far greater than those reported by Piaget. Such findings emerge when children are observed in situations which are meaningful to them. In such circumstances they have also shown considerably more social competence at young ages than Piaget's theory allows. From a different perspective, sociologists such as Walkerdine (1983, 1988) have argued that Piaget's stages became part of a child-centred ideology and a means through which teachers classify, compare and thus control children. Critics have also suggested that this form of constructivism overemphasizes the individual too much and ignores the social context in which learning takes place. In so doing, the potential of teachers, other adults and other children to support each child's learning is underestimated.

Constructivist learning theory, as adapted by educationalists, casts the learner in a very active and independent role, leaving much of the selection, pacing and evaluation of the activity to the child to negotiate. There is considerable emphasis on pupil interests and some compromise on the specifics of curriculum coverage. In its place, there tends to be more emphasis on learning concepts and skills through work on pupil-chosen topics.

Teaching which has been influenced by constructivism can be seen in all primary schools. It is reflected in the provision of a rich, varied and stimulating environment, in individualized work and creative arts, the use of practical apparatus, the role of play and imagination in media such as sand, water and clay, as well as in simulated play-contexts such as the 'home corner'. It may also be reflected in exercises and tests of 'readiness' for new stages of reading, or in direct Piagetian tests of young children for one-to-one correspondence and conservation of number. Above all, however, the influence of constructivism is reflected in the ways in which teachers relate with children. Perhaps this is an unintended legacy, but the nature of constructivism, with its close identification with the challenges which the learner faces, has influenced the quality of the affinity between primary school teachers and children.

Figure 6.2 represents the roles of child and adult in constructivist-influenced teaching and learning processes. Some particular points could be noted, in particular the negotiation of pupil activity and the emphasis placed on direct experience in learning. Together, these have the enormous strength, in principle, of creating high levels of pupil motivation and engagement. In the right circumstances, creativity and other forms of pupil achievement can reach exceptional levels of excellence. However, coverage of a particular curriculum is hard to monitor and the diversity of individual pupil interests tends to produce relatively complex forms of classroom organization as a range of activities is provided. Research shows that teachers then tend to be drawn into managing this complex environment rather than teaching.

The influence of constructivism has been greatest on what are commonly called 'progressive' teaching methods, and particularly those associated with play and with early-years education. It is a relatively difficult model for non-educationalists to interpret in practice, since the provision derived from it tends to be multifaceted with a great deal of varied child activity. It is thus vulnerable to caricature in the media, despite acceptance of the value of direct experience in learning. However,

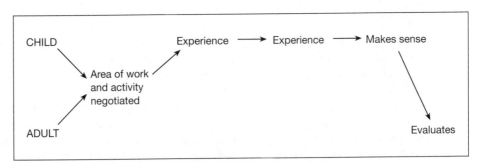

Figure 6.2 *A constructivist model of roles in the teaching–learning process*

the responsibility of teachers is to interact with children so that they actually learn, not simply to respond to ill-founded external misunderstandings.

Professional judgement is again required, for the use of teaching methods based on constructivism must be 'fit for their purpose' (Practical Activity 6.2).

Practical activity 6.2

Aim: To consider the influence and strengths of constructivist psychology when applied to children's learning and primary school practice.

Method: Review the learning situations and teaching methods, influenced by constructivism, which your class has experienced during a school day.

Note each learning situation, each teaching method and then consider the reasons for its choice.

Learning situation	Teaching methods used	Reason for choice of teaching methods

Follow-up: Consider the extent, strengths and weaknesses of the constructivist influence on teaching in your school. Are the teaching methods used 'fit for their purpose'?

1.3 Social constructivist models

This is another constructivist theory but, this time, one which strongly suggests the importance for learning of the social context and of interaction with others.

The most influential writer on this approach has been Vygotsky (1962, 1978, **Reading, 6.4**), whose publications in Russian actually date from the 1930s. The increasing availability of Vygotsky's work in English coincided with reappraisals of the strengths and weaknesses of Piagetian theory. Psychologists such as Bruner (1986), Wood (1988) and Wertsch (1985) have been able to demonstrate the considerable relevance of Vygotsky's work to modern education and this has coincided both with complementary empirical work by other child psychologists and with curriculum development initiatives by primary school teachers. Social constructivist theory is, it seems, beginning to provide a new model of effective practice.

We will focus on just two of the insights originating from Vygotsky. The first concerns what Vygotsky calls the 'zone of proximal development' (the ZPD) (1978, **Reading, 6.4**). This is:

> The distance between the actual developmental level (of the child) as determined through problem solving and the level of potential development as determined through problem solving under adult guidance or in collaboration with more capable peers.
>
> (Vygotsky, 1978, p. 86)

The ZPD concerns each child's potential to 'make sense'. Given a child's present state of understanding, what developments can occur if the child is given appropriate assistance by more capable others? If support is appropriate and meaningful, then, it is argued, the understanding of children can be extended far beyond that which they could reach alone.

Such assistance in learning can come in many ways. It may take the form of an explanation by or discussion with a knowledgeable teacher; it may reflect debate among a group of children as they strive to solve a problem or complete a task; it might come from discussion with a parent or from watching a particular television programme. In each case, the intervention functions to extend and to 'scaffold' the child's understanding across their ZPD for that particular issue. An appropriate analogy is that of building a house. Scaffolding is needed to support the process as the house is gradually constructed from its foundations – but when it has been assembled and all the parts have been secured the scaffolding can be removed. The building – the child's understanding – will stand independently.

The second key insight originating in Vygotsky's work concerns the role of the culture and the social context of the learner in influencing his or her understanding (Bruner, 1990, **Reading, 6.8**). This influence starts in informal ways from birth. Thus infants and young children interact with their parents and family and, through experiencing the language and forms of behaviour of their culture, also assimilate particular cognitive skills, strategies, knowledge and understanding (Richards and Light, 1986; Dunn, 1988). Cognition, language and forms of thought thus depend on the culture and social history of the learner as well as on any particular instruction which may be offered at any point in time. This influence of culture on learning continues throughout life (Rogoff and Lave, 1984); indeed, it is what makes learning meaningful. Ideas, language and concepts derived from interaction with others thus structure, challenge, enhance or constrain thinking. Whatever role they play, they cannot be excluded from our consideration. Thus, learning is social as well as individual. We therefore have to look at the context in which learning takes place in schools as well as at the nature of specific learning tasks.

The influence of social constructivist theory in education has been considerable since the early 1980s. Perhaps this is because the approach seems to recognize both the needs of learners to construct their own, meaningful understandings and the strength of teaching itself. Indeed, a key to the approach lies in specifying constructive relationships between these factors. As Tharp and Gallimore (1988, **Reading, 6.5**) put it, learning can be seen as 'assisted performance'.

Teaching which is influenced by social constructivism can be seen in many primary schools and is particularly associated with various processes of group work or review. Thus, for instance, investigational work in science, maths or technology often involves small groups of children in collaborative problem-solving. Sometimes discussion between the children augments their experience and they 'scaffold' each other's thinking; sometimes the thinking of the group is challenged by the intervention of the teacher. Processes of review can formalize this somewhat. Thus we have 'process writing', in which children develop their work through successive drafts, sharing them and eliciting comments from the teacher and other children at each stage, until they reach the point of 'publication'. The comments along the way provide a supportive challenge to the writer and scaffold his or her thinking so that the quality of the work is refined. A very similar process may occur in design work, where an initial sketch may be discussed, refined, developed to a prototype and refined again, before finally being completed. Again, the input of the teacher and others in supporting and extending thinking is crucial – the learner's performance is 'assisted'. They cross their ZPD.

Classrooms can be organized to build review processes into their routines. Thus, for example, schools influenced by a High/Scope approach (Hohmann *et al.*, 1979) maintain a regular cycle of planning, doing and reviewing to structure pupil thinking about classroom activities. More intuitive processes of review take place in most classrooms, often at the ends of sessions, to take stock, structure, affirm and draw together the threads of previous activities.

Figure 6.3 elaborated from Rowland (1987, **Reading, 6.11**), represents the roles of children and adult in social constructivist teaching and learning process. The figure shows some key social constructivist processes in classrooms analytically. Negotiation, focused perhaps on a National Curriculum topic, is followed by activity and discussion by children. However, the teacher then makes a constructive intervention – a role which Rowland named as that of the 'reflective agent'. This draws attention to the fact that any intervention must be appropriate. It must connect with the understandings and purposes of the learners so that their thinking is extended. If this is to happen, teachers need to draw on both their subject knowledge and their understanding of children. They must make an accurate, and reflective, judgement themselves about the most appropriate form of input and, in this, various techniques of formative assessment (see Chapter 12) are likely to be helpful. If such judgements are astute then the input could take the children's thinking forward, across the ZPD and beyond the level of understanding which they would have reached alone. Clearly

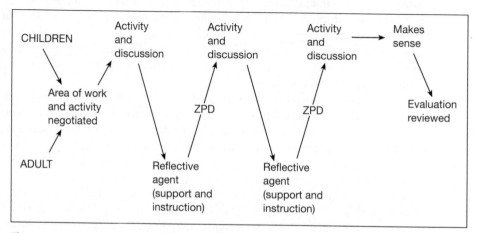

Figure 6.3 *A social constructivist model of roles in the teaching–learning process*

there could be successive cycles of this process (see **Reading, 6.10** for an example of a child constructing understanding with adult support).

The influence of social constructivist ideas are implicit in much of the documentation of the National Curriculum in the UK and for the last decade have progressively underpinned the work of curriculum associations and teacher-based curriculum innovation in all subjects. The role of language and of discussion is paramount in learning in each area. However, whilst social constructivism might, in a sense, seem to embody the most valuable educational implications of both behaviourism and constructivism, it provides little relief from the pressures of class size or from the wide range of curricular objectives to which primary school teachers are increasingly subject. These challenges remain. The result is that primary school teachers will continue to have to make judgements and compromises as they face the tension between how they may like to teach, and how they feel it is possible to teach in their particular circumstances. The practical implications of social constructivism are undoubtedly great, for it is an approach which will test the subject knowledge, judgement and organizational capacity of most teachers. Nevertheless, it is an approach with enormous strengths and should undoubtedly be in the repertoire of a reflective teacher.

Use of teaching methods based on social constructivism must, therefore, be fit for their purpose and circumstances (Practical Activity 6.3).

Practical activity 6.3

Aim: To consider the influence and strengths of social constructivist psychology when applied to children's learning and primary school practice.

Method: Review the learning situations and teaching methods, influenced by social constructivism, which your class has experienced during a school day.

Note each learning situation, each teaching method and then consider the reasons for its choice.

Learning situation	Teaching methods used	Reason for choice of teaching methods

Follow-up: Consider the extent, strengths and weaknesses of the social constructivist influence on teaching in your school. Are the teaching methods used 'fit for their purpose'?

Figure 6.4 provides a very simple summary of some of the key points in the previous discussions.

So far in this chapter we have considered three key theoretical influences on learning and teaching in primary schools. We now move on, in section 2, to consider some issues which are likely to produce differences between individual children as they approach learning in school.

2 CHILDREN AND LEARNING

2.1 'Intelligence'

Teachers meet the specific needs of children by knowing them well. It is thus right and proper that concepts to describe the attributes of pupils should exist. However, such concepts should be accurate, discriminating and capable of impartial application. Notions of 'intelligence' are common, but they can lead towards dangerous stereotyping and generalization.

The validity of the concept of intelligence has been in dispute among psychologists for many years. As one expert in the field recently commented:

> Intelligence provides a rich source of confusions, augmented by the fact that psychologists fail to agree about even the most basic issues, such as how the term should be defined and whether or not it can be regarded as providing an explanation as well as a description of human variability.

> (Howe, 1991)

When it comes to attempting to measure intelligence the field is even more difficult, which is perhaps not surprising since no one is precisely sure what it is!

However, the concept is very powerful since it has passed into our culture to denote a generalized form of ability. It is part of our language and it influences our ways of thinking about children. For instance, parents often talk about their children in terms of 'brightness' or 'cleverness', and teachers routinely describe children and classroom groupings in terms of 'ability'. The concept of intelligence is important, too, because it is often used in the rhetoric of politicians and the media when they communicate with the public. It is thus routinely assumed that there *is* both a generalized trait of intelligence and that it is possible to measure it objectively.

Of course, such beliefs underpinned the UK use in the 1950s and 1960s of intelligence tests, at 11+, to select children for secondary education. Belief in the context-free, objectivity of such testing was severely undercut by studies at the time, such as those by Simon (1953) and Squibb (1973). More recent research in areas where 11+ is still used, such as in Northern Ireland, continues to show the lack of objectivity of the measurement. For instance, Egan and Bunting (1991) recorded gains of 30 to 40+ points, out of a total possible 100 points, for a coached group of 11-year-olds compared with an uncoached group. The results showed clearly that children can be taught to do intelligence tests and that it is not possible to identify or measure some context-free generalized ability with any confidence. Such tests are therefore likely to disadvantage systematically those who receive less coaching or experience a less advantageous cultural background.

	Behaviourism in classrooms	Constructivism in classrooms	Social constructivism in classrooms
Image of learner	• Passive • Individual	• Active • Individual	• Active • Social
Images of teaching and learning	• Teacher transmits knowledge and skills	• Teacher gives child opportunity to construct knowledge and skills gradually through experience	• Knowledge and skills are constructed gradually through experience, interaction and adult support
	• Learning depends on teaching	• Learning can be independent of teaching	• Learning comes through the interdependence of teacher and children
Characteristic child activities	• Class listening to an adult	• Individuals making, experimenting, playing or otherwise doing something	• Discussing an issue with an adult or other child/ren
	• Class working on an exercise		• Problem-solving with a group
Some characteristics	• Draws directly on existing subject knowledge in a logical, linear manner	• Uses direct experience and allows children to explore in their own way at their own pace	• By structuring challenges can clarify thinking and produce meaningful understanding
	• When matched to existing understanding, can be a fast and effective way to learn	• Can build confidence and practical understanding which clarifies thinking and produces insight	• Encourages collaboration and language development
Some issues	• May not connect with existing understanding and may thus lead to superficiality	• Has major resource and organizational implications	• Has major resource and organizational implications
	• Difficult to motivate all children in class	• Management of classroom often dominates actual teaching	• Requires a very high level of adult judge-ment, knowledge and skill
	• Difficult to adapt structure of subject matter to varied pupil needs	• Assumes high level of motivation and autonomy from children	• Assumes high level of social and linguistic maturity from children

Figure 6.4 *Some features of behaviourist, constructivist and social constructivist models of learning applied to primary schools*

The debate about the nature and origins of intelligence also continues. Psychologists such as Kline (1991) argue, on the basis of complex statistical factor analysis, that general ability remains a valid concept to describe inherited attributes. Neurobiologists are also making very fundamental discoveries about factors which enhance or inhibit brain functioning. On the other hand, Howe (1990) used experimental and biographical evidence from different cultures to argue that there are many types of ability, and that generalized measures, such as IQ scores, are misleading. According to Howe, the origins of exceptional abilities lie in an interaction of intellectual, motivational and temperamental factors produced within a social and cultural context, and this may, itself, enhance or inhibit achievement. As Howe puts it:

> Faced with a new task, the chances of a person being successful depend on a myriad of contributing influences. These include the person's existing knowledge in relation to the particular task, existing cognitive skills, interest, motivation, attentiveness, self-confidence and sense of purpose, to mention only a few.

(Howe, 1990, p 221)

The idea that there are many forms of intelligent behaviour, and that these are influenced by the social context in which people act, is thus now largely accepted by most psychologists. A particularly developed form of this argument is that by Gardner (1985, **Reading, 6.6**) who has suggested that there are 'multiple intelligences'. At the same time though, neurobiologists are documenting differences in the quantity and nature of neural networks in the brain and are controversially attempting to relate these to genetic and social influences. Some form of interaction between the influence of heredity and of environment is therefore certain, but it is doubtful if the nuances of the nature/nurture debate will ever finally be settled. In one sense, this hardly matters, because even if the genetic potential of children is set, teachers and parents can take on the specific, and uncontested, role of acting to enhance the quality of environmental factors.

One important aspect of this role lies in encouraging children to make maximum use of their cognitive skills, to encourage them to think about their reasoning and to draw on their skills, strategies and conceptual understanding in the most appropriate ways for the task in hand. This issue, of meta-cognition, will be considered in detail in section 2.5 of this chapter. However at this point is is worth noting that teachers' assumptions about the nature of intelligence will have a direct impact on these processes. Dweck and Bempechat (1983) have distinguished between teachers who define intelligence as a quality or a trait that a child possesses (an 'entity' perspective); and those who define it as an ever growing quality that is increased through the child's actions (an 'incremental' perspective).

The latter are more likely to facilitate the development of pupils' meta-cognitive strategies (Practical Activity 6.4; see also **Reading, 6.7**).

For reflective teachers, then, it is worth remembering some simple points about intelligence:

1. The use of generalized terms such as intelligence, ability, etc. is imprecise, insecure and unreliable – but is often put to rhetorical use.

2. A teacher can dramatically influence the variable, environmental quality of pupil experience – by providing support which will enhance, broaden and develop each child's inherited potential.

3. There are many kinds of ability and one challenge for teachers is to enhance their pupils' lives by identifying, developing and celebrating the diverse attributes of each child.

Practical activity 6.4

Aim: To monitor the use and abuse of concepts of 'intelligence'.

Method: A simple method is proposed based on noticing, recording and studying any use of language which denotes generalized ability.

This could be done in a school, in discussion with governors, teachers, parents, non-teaching staff or children, from printed articles in newspapers and the educational press, from school or government documents, from the speeches of politicians. It will require active listening – becoming attuned to things which are said which are relevant – and the period of awareness may need to extend over a week or so. Whatever sources are chosen, the statements and the context in which these occur should be recorded in notes as accurately as possible.

When you have a collection of statements, study them. Think about them in their context. For instance: What particular expectations about future attainment are implied? Do they recognize the richness and diversity of children's abilities?

Follow-up: Try to monitor your own use of language. Be explicitly aware of the words and concepts which you use. Distinguish between abilities and attainments. Try to satisfy the criteria of accuracy, discrimination and impartiality in your thinking about children's capacities and potential.

2.2 Culture

The cultures which children experience are significant for their learning. Of course, it has always been thought that home background, peer relationships, the cultures of different schools and, increasingly, the media, do influence how children learn, but the development of social constructivist psychology has led to a much greater understanding of the processes which are at work (Bruner, 1990, **Reading, 6.8**; Mercer, 1992, **Reading, 6.9**).

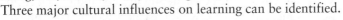

Three major cultural influences on learning can be identified.

Learning framework. Learning is a process of 'making sense' and whatever is taken as being meaningful ('makes sense') will be strongly influenced by the culture, knowledge, values and ideas of social groups which the child has previously experienced. Such cultures provide an initial framework of understanding. Thus, each child's construction (learning) will tend to elaborate and extend the knowledge which is embedded in his or her experienced culture.

Medium of language. Language is the medium of thinking and learning and is created, transmitted and sustained through interaction with other people within the cultures of different social settings. These settings influence the range of 'languages' we use – the register, styles, dialects, etc. Flexibility and appropriateness can enhance communication and thus learning (see Chapter 11 and *Readings*, Chapter 11).

Learning stance. The learning stance adopted by each child is crucial to educational outcomes. Will a child be open or closed to experience and support, will they be confident or fearful, willing to take risks or defensive? This issue, the learning stance of the pupil, is particularly significant regarding schools because of their position as the first formal institution which most children experience in a sustained way.

Four major sources of cultural influence on children can be identified (Pollard with Filer, 1996).

The family: Family background has been recognized as being of crucial significance in educational achievement for many years. This occurs not just in material ways, depending on the wealth and income of families, nor simply because of ownership or otherwise of overt forms of 'cultural capital' (Bourdieu and Passeron, 1977), which is often associated with high status groups in society. The most significant issues for school learning concern what the culture of the family provides in terms of a framework of existing understanding, a language for development and a disposition to adopt a positive stance regarding learning.

Of course, families are themselves part of communities and the rich cultural diversity of modern societies ensures that most schools will provide for children from a variety of cultural backgrounds.

Peers at school: As we saw in Chapter 4, peer group culture is important to children as a way of both enjoying and adapting to school life. As children get older, the culture of boys and girls tends to become more distinctive and the culture of the playground also starts to mirror both academic achievement within school and social factors outside the school, such as social class and ethnicity. Such differentiation is particularly important to pupil motivation and to the learning stance which is routinely adopted. Some peer cultures favour school attainment and are likely to reinforce teacher efforts to engender a positive approach to learning. Other peer cultures derive meaning from alternative values and children who are influenced by such cultures may approach school with minimal or even oppositional expectations. Such children will still be constructing understanding, but it may not to be the type of understanding for which teachers would have aimed.

The school: Schools each have their own unique culture, a point which we shall elaborate in Chapter 14. Such cultures are created by those who work in the school and those who are associated with it.

A school culture must be seen as a learning context which is at least as important as the bricks and mortar, books and equipment which make up the material environment of a school. Again, we have to ask how this culture influences the framework for understanding which is offered to the children, the language in which teaching and learning is transacted and the stance which pupils adopt. For instance, are children encouraged to take risks in their learning? What learning stance is engendered through the symbolic rituals and events of the school, the assemblies and demonstrations of 'good work'? What criteria about standards of schoolwork are communicated? What are the underlying assumptions about learning and knowledge within the school – and how do these impact on the children?

The media: The influence of the media is a controversial topic but it is known that, whilst book reading often seems in relative decline, young children watch many hours of television each week and their play is influenced by advertising. With contradictory research findings abounding, it is impossible to say how this affects children's thinking overall. However, many teachers and parents believe that the influence is noticeable with individuals (see also Bazalgette, 1988, **Reading, 11.11**).

Perhaps it is true to say that television can, with books, 'broaden the mind' by presenting experiences and tapping emotions – albeit only indirectly. The key question is whether the child is passive or active in his or her stance as a viewer. Is the child using television to construct understanding? Of course, the answer to this question is likely to reflect the culture of the home.

Clearly, the nature of these influences on each child will dramatically effect the way in which he or she approaches learning at school. Practical Activity 6.5 focuses on this issue.

Practical activity 6.5

Aim: To map the influence of culture on the learning of a pupil.

Method: Draw up a table, as below, on a large sheet of paper.

	Three influences on learning		
Four sources of cultural influence	Framework of understanding	Language	Learning stance
Family			
Peers			

School			
Media			

Think of one child whom you know well. Consider the way cultures influence the framework of the child's understanding, the language he or she uses and the learning stance he/she adopts. Complete each cell of the table, as far as you can, to map what you know about the cultural influences on that child.

If you have time it would be valuable to talk to the pupil and others – parents, peers and teachers – to improve the quality of your data.

Follow-up: Repeat this exercise with different pupils, or compare the results of similar activities by colleagues. What insights are produced by comparisons of children of different sex, ethnicity, religion, social class, attainment?

Moving to another level of analysis, we also need to consider the different ways in which individual children tackle actual learning tasks. We do this by focusing on the psychological implications of personality on learning style, on motivation and on meta-cognition.

2.3 Personality and learning style

Psychologists' understanding of personality has, according to Hampson (1988), derived from three contributory strands of analysis.

The first is the *lay perspective* – the understandings which are implicit in common-sense thinking of most of us about other people. This is evident in literature and in everyday action. It is a means by which people are able to anticipate the actions of others – ideas about the character and likely actions of others are used for both the prediction and explanation of behaviour.

Such understandings have influenced the second strand of analysis – that of *trait theorists* – although their work also reflects a concerted attempt to identify personality dimensions and to objectively measure the resulting patterns of action. For instance, among the most frequently identified dimensions of personality are:

Impulsivity/reflexivity: (Kagan *et al.*, 1964) from impulsives who rush at a task without stopping to think first; to reflexives who like to chew it over, sometimes endlessly.

Extroversion/introversion: (Eysenck and Cookson, 1969) from extroverts who are outgoing and gregarious; to introverts who are more 'private' and may prefer to keep themselves to themselves.

As the work of trait theorists has become dated, a third strand of personality analysis has become prominent, and Hampson calls this the *self perspective*. This approach sees the development of personality in close association with that of self-image. Crucially, it draws attention to the capacity of humans to reflect on themselves and to take account of the views of others. The social context in which individuals develop, their culture, interaction and experiences with others is thus seen as being very important in influencing views of self and consequent patterns of action.

Of course, this approach has considerable resonance with social constructivist ideas and with our earlier discussion of culture. As Hampson puts it:

> The most important consequence ... is that personality is no longer viewed as residing exclusively within the individual. Instead, personality is viewed as the product of a process involving the conversion of the individual actor's behaviour into socially significant acts by the observer and the self-observer. In this sense, personality should not be located within persons, but between or among persons.

(Hampson, 1988, p. 205)

The concept of 'learning style', though closely associated with trait theorists, has provided a useful vocabulary to describe some common ways in which activities and challenges are typically approached, explored and tackled. Various dimensions have been identified. For instance:

Task involvement/ego involvement. In task involvement the focus is on the task rather than the self; learning is seen as an end in itself and dependent on effort rather than ability. In ego involvement the learner is more self-conscious and more concerned about the way he or she will be perceived by others (e.g. 'bright' or 'stupid'). He or she is more likely to perceive learning as dependent on ability rather than effort (Nicholls, 1983)

Internal control/ external control. The term 'learned helplessness' has been applied to children who never engage in learning tasks on their own initiative but always wait for guidance from an adult or peer. For such children the 'locus of control' of their learning is outside themselves. The internal control leading to autonomy and independent learning is underdeveloped (Lawrence, 1987).

Forthcoming/unforthcoming. Forthcoming children have a positive self-image, are self-assured in learning situations and enjoy challenges. Unforthcoming children have a poor image of themselves as learners and as a result lack confidence, particularly when tackling new learning tasks (Stott, 1976).

Holist/serialist (Pask, 1976; Kagan and Kogan, 1970): from holists who like to get a quick grasp of an overall picture before filling in details; to serialists who prefer methodically and analytically to build up a picture bit by bit.

Divergent/convergent (Torrance, 1962): from divergers who use inspirational flair and imagination; to convergers who wish to find the 'right' answer and prefer closed situations.

In a sense, the three theories of personality which we have reviewed differ in their view of the *source* of personality but reveal considerable overlaps in their descriptions of the personality characteristics. Insights on learning styles can thus be helpful, but such styles should be seen as being amenable to change and development through social and educational processes (Practical Activities 6.6 and 6.7).

Practical activity 6.6

Aim: To analyse individual children's learning styles.

Method:

1. Observe individual children when working in a range of situations – different types of tasks, different time demands, different social contexts. Note their behaviour carefully. Later, review your notes in the light of the dimensions of personality and learning style listed above.

2. Try to monitor yourself in a similar range of situations, and thereby identify aspects of your own styles.

Follow-up: Use this information to review the match between task and child, and to consider the relationship between your teaching and children's learning styles. From these insights, consider the range of teaching strategies which is available to you.

Practical activity 6.7

Aim: To analyse our responses to different learning styles.

Method: Tape-record, take diary notes or ask a colleague to observe your teaching during selected sessions. Monitor the way you help children.

Follow-up: Review the range of help that you offer. Try to distinguish reasons for the variety and assess whether the action taken did enhance the children's learning. Then use the information to analyse your response to others. For example:

1. Do you seem to prefer some pupil learning styles to others, or to respond differently?

2. Do you expect different kinds of learning behaviour from boys and girls? Do you reward them differently?

3. Do you provide different kinds of tasks and opportunities for each of these styles to develop, or do you tend to prepare tasks which suit your own favoured approach?

What are the implications of the answers to such questions?

2.4 Motivation

So far in this chapter we have considered the relationship between learning styles and the task. Whilst this is clearly important it is also essential to consider motivational aspects of learning, for an activity in which children fail to see any purpose or meaning is unlikely to be very productive – however well-intended and carefully planned.

Motivation is highly subjective and is likely to be related to children's perceptions of themselves, teachers and schooling in general (see Chapter 4 and **Reading, 4.7**). It can also be affected by very specific immediate moods and situations which arise in classrooms.

Children's positive motivation towards learning is important not only for maximizing learning outcomes but because of the disruptive effects which children who are poorly motivated can produce. A reflective teacher thus needs to consider the meaning and worthwhileness which an activity is likely to have for children, as well as its potential for developing learning.

Research by Dweck over many years (e.g. 1986, **Reading, 6.7**) has established the importance of how children think about their own capability. Those who adopt an 'entity theory' tend to believe that their personal capability is fixed, and that they either 'can' or 'cannot' succeed at the new challenges that they meet in school. For this reason, they may adopt a form of 'learned helplessness' to accomplish school life. However, those who adopt an 'incremental theory' of their capability believe that they are able to learn and improve. They are thus likely to be more highly motivated, have greater engagement and tend to be more willing to take risks and act independently.

As we saw in Chapter 4, a very common perception of children regarding schools is that they are 'boring'. For this reason, engendering enthusiasm can require a certain amount of imagination, skill and shedding of inhibition on the part of teachers. However, being able to motivate children is basic to the smooth running of a classroom and to effective learning. Yet few teachers can be certain of how children will respond to a particular activity. Developing a motivational match thus requires sensitivity to the children, flexibility, spontaneity and imagination.

The nature of this task is represented in Figure 6.5, which plots the relationship between new learning challenges and existing skills, knowledge and understanding. If too great a challenge is set for a child, then the situation of risk may produce a withdrawal into helplessness. Conversely, if the challenge is too little, then boredom and mischief may ensue. Targeting the effective learning area in which the child will be highly motivated requires considerable skill and knowledge of both the subject matter and the child.

Motivation can stem from a wide range of factors, from positive interest to negative fear. The most commonly identified types of motivation are:

intrinsic – based on a child's personal interest

collective – where pleasure derives from sharing work with friends, the class, school or family

extrinsic – manipulation through the use of such devices as stars and house points

Figure 6.5 *Risk, boredom and motivation*

coerced compliance – where children carry out tasks in order to avoid punishments

A teacher can influence the kinds of motivation children may develop and the attitudes they show towards learning by the ways in which activities are set up and encouraged and by the nature of the activities themselves (Practical Activity 6.8).

> ## Practical activity 6.8
>
> *Aim*: To review the motivational qualities of a series of classroom activities.
>
> *Method*: Consider a teaching/learning session and list the requirements which were made of selected children. This might be done by asking a colleague to observe, or by interpreting a tape recording. From the perspective of each of the selected children, make a judgement of the type of motivation which you feel influenced their actions. Record your judgements. If possible, discuss the session with the children involved and record their accounts.
>
> *Follow-up*: By comparing teacher judgements and children's accounts it should be possible to obtain many insights which could help in developing more appropriate approaches to motivating children in the future.

2.5 Meta-cognitition

We have considered some major factors which are likely to produce patterns in children's approaches to school tasks. The interplay of such factors is, however, extremely complex and will never be entirely predictable. Furthermore, children have the crucial capacity to reflect on their own thinking processes and to develop new strategies. This capacity for self-awareness regarding their own mental powers is called 'meta-cognition' (Flavell, 1970).

Since meta-cognition involves self knowledge and since the self is socially constructed, this form of knowledge involves several factors. Flavell provides a definition of meta-cognitive knowledge which includes psychological factors such as various learning strategies (e.g. self-monitoring, planning, self-evaluating) and the more sociological factors such as beliefs about others and their impact on the learning process. It is a short step from here to seeing meta-cognition in terms of a broader perspective, one which encompasses all social and psychological influences on learning in an institutional context. For instance, pupils' awareness of how they are labelled by teachers or how their self-image is affected by peer relations would count as meta-cognitive knowledge.

Meta-cognition is a particularly important capacity once children start to attend schools. Prior to this, at home, learning is largely self-directed and thinking tends to be embedded in immediate personal experience (Donaldson, 1978). Once at school, the agenda for learning increasingly becomes directed by teachers. Thinking is challenged to become more disciplined and deliberate; tasks are set, problems posed and instructions given; criteria for success and failure become more overt. The result of all this is that a new degree of self-control is required and, in order to achieve this self-control, new forms of reflective self-awareness become essential.

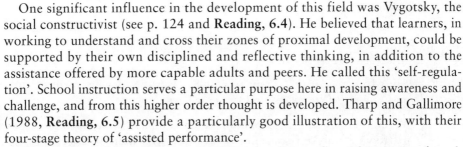

One significant influence in the development of this field was Vygotsky, the social constructivist (see p. 124 and **Reading, 6.4**). He believed that learners, in working to understand and cross their zones of proximal development, could be supported by their own disciplined and reflective thinking, in addition to the assistance offered by more capable adults and peers. He called this 'self-regulation'. School instruction serves a particular purpose here in raising awareness and challenge, and from this higher order thought is developed. Tharp and Gallimore (1988, **Reading, 6.5**) provide a particularly good illustration of this, with their four-stage theory of 'assisted performance'.

The meta-cognitive capacity of children has been a flourishing area of work amongst psychologists in recent years (Robinson, 1983; Yussen, 1985; Wood, 1988), but perhaps the most accessible account is that provided by Nisbet and Shucksmith (1986), who advocate the identification and development of 'learning strategies'.

The most common strategies which Nisbet and Shucksmith identify are listed in Check-list 6.1.

Other development projects, by innovative practitioners, have investigated whether meta-cognitive skills can be developed through teaching (for example, Feuerstein's incremental enrichment programme (1979). The answer to this is a conclusive 'yes' even with very young children. For instance, the High/Scope nursery programme (Hohmann *et al.*, 1979) uses an explicit plan–do–review cycle as the basis of classroom activities. At each stage children are supported in thinking about their own learning. Practice for older primary school children is also well developed (e.g. Fisher, 1990).

These practices reflect the three practical conclusions on fostering meta-cognition in classrooms which were identified by Nisbet and Shucksmith (1986):

1. Set clear cognitive goals
2. Model strategies for learning
3. Encourage meta-cognitive discussion

See also Practical Activity 6.9.

Asking questions:	establishing aims and parameters of a task, discovering audience, relating a task to previous work.
Planning:	deciding on tactics and time-schedules, reduction of task into manageable components, identification of necessary skills.
Monitoring:	continuing attempt to match efforts, solutions and discoveries to intitial purposes.
Checking:	preliminary assessment of performance and results.
Revising:	redrafting or setting revised goals.
Self-testing:	final self-assessment of results and performance on task.

Check-list 6.1 *Common meta-cognitive strategies*

Practical activity 6.9

Aim: To consider the extent to which classroom development of children's meta-cognitive strategies could be enhanced.

Method: Focus on a classroom in which you have some teaching responsibility. Review and self-consciously monitor your own practices. Perhaps you could also ask a colleague to observe you teach a session.

Consider the three simple conclusions suggested by Nisbet and Shucksmith. To what extent do you:

1. Set clear cognitive goals?

2. Model strategies for learning?

3. Encourage meta-cognitive discussion?

How could you further develop the support you offer children in enhancing their meta-cognitive strategies?

Follow-up: Review the children's learning. Has your work on meta-cognition had any impact?

These issues are taken up again in practical ways in Chapter 12, section 1 where we discuss formative assessment and pupil self-assessment.

CONCLUSION

Learning is an immensely complex topic and this chapter has simply touched the surface of the issues which are involved. In one sense, perhaps the provisional nature of our understanding is no bad thing, because, if we knew it all, then one of the greatest sources of fascination and fulfilment in teaching would be diminished. The vocation of teaching will certainly always include this element of intellectual challenge as teachers seek to understand what children understand, and to provide appropriate support.

In this chapter we have reviewed three influential approaches to children's learning and discussed some of the key issues which are involved. As stated in the introduction of the chapter, language provides the crucial medium through which learning takes place and consideration of it has pervaded our discussions here. The issue is taken up again later as the explicit focus of Chapter 11.

We conclude with three key insights on learning derived from the work of Margaret Donaldson (Grieve and Hughes, 1990):

> One needs to consider the whole child, including the social context from which he or she derives meaning and understanding.
>
> One needs to consider any learning situation from the child's point of view.
>
> One needs to remember the overarching difficulty of formal education for children as their thinking develops from being embedded in particular contexts to become capable of more abstraction.

Whatever the strength of their subject knowledge, teachers are likely to be more effective in supporting children's learning if they bear such insights in mind.

Notes for further reading

For a quick insight into the excitement, imagination and creativity of children's thinking, see the regularly reprinted:

De Bono, E. (1972)
Children Solve Problems,
London: Penguin.

For basic psychological introductions to alternative theories of teaching and learning see:

Child, D. (1986)
Psychology and the Teacher,
London: Cassell.

Fontana, D. (1988)
Psychology for Teachers,
London: Macmillan.

Stainthorp, R. (1989)
Practical Psychology for Primary Teachers,
London: Falmer.

A concise and accessible review of approaches to classroom learning is:

Entwistle, N. (1987)
Understanding Classroom Learning,
London: Hodder and Stoughton.

Excellent, but more advanced, overviews on children's learning are:

Wood, D. (1988)
How Children Think and Learn,
Oxford: Blackwell.

Meadows, S. (1992)
*Children's Cognitive Development: The Development
and Acquisition of Cognition in Childhood,*
London: Routledge.

Lee, V. (ed.) (1990)
*Children's Learning in School: Behaviourism,
Piaget and Vygotsky,*
London: Hodder and Stoughton.

A wide-ranging and discursive account is:

Cullingford, C. (1990)
The Nature of Learning,
London: Cassell.

For some classic behaviourist work see:

Skinner, B. F. (1953)
Science and Human Behavior,
New York: Macmillan.   Reading, 6.1

Gagné, R. M. (1965)
The Conditions of Learning,
New York: Holt, Rinehart and Winston.   Reading, 6.2

For Piaget's classic constructivist work see:

Piaget, J. (1926)
The Language and Thought of the Child,
New York: Basic Books.   Reading, 6.3

Piaget, J. (1950)
The Psychology of Intelligence,
London: Routledge & Kegan Paul.

A comprehensive introduction to Piaget's work is:

Ginsberg, H. and Opper, S. (1969)
Piaget's Theory of Intellectual Development,
New York: Prentice Hall.

For a landmark in analysis of children's learning, and in particular a critique of Piagetian theory, see:

Donaldson, M. (1978)
Children's Minds,
London: Fontana.

For classic social constructivist work see:

Vygotsky, L. S. (1962)
Thought and Language,
Cambridge, MA: Massachusetts Institute of Technology.   and Reading, 6.4

Vygotsky, L. S. (1978)
Mind in Society: The Development of Higher Psychological Processes,
Cambridge, MA: Harvard University Press.

The best detailed review of Vygotsky's work is:

Wertsch, J. V. (1985)
Vygotsky and the Social Formation of Mind,
Cambridge, MA: Harvard University Press.

Jerome Bruner is always worth reading. See his beautifully crafted books with brilliant insights into the 'inspiration of Vygotsky':

Bruner, J. S. (1986)
Actual Minds, Possible Worlds,
Cambridge, MA: Harvard University Press.

Bruner, J. S. (1990)
Acts of Meaning,
Cambridge, MA: Harvard University Press.   📖 **Reading, 6.8**

A good collection which draws on some of the best work on children's learning of the last decade is:

Grieve, R. and Hughes, M. (1990)
Understanding Children,
Oxford: Blackwell.

The significance of play and of imagination in learning is becoming seriously underestimated in these days of detailed curriculum planning. For a variety of sources which assert their importance, see:

Moyles, J. R. (ed.) (1994)
The Excellence of Play,
Buckingham: Open University Press.

Garvey, C. (1990)
Play,
Cambridge, MA: Harvard University Press.

For case-studies of children learning through play and imagination, see some of the work of Vivian Paley. For instance:

Paley, V. G. (1981)
Wally's Stories,
Cambridge, MA: Harvard University Press.

Paley, V. G. (1990)
The Boy Who Would Be a Helicopter,
Cambridge, MA: Harvard University Press.

A more analytical account is:

Kelly-Byrne, D. (1989)
A Child's Play Life: An Ethnographic Study,
New York: Teachers' College Press.

And for a fascinating collection of the 'private worlds' of children, see:

Cohen, D. and MacKeith, S. (1991)
The Development of Imagination: The Private Worlds of Childhood,
London: Routledge.

On intelligence, Richardson provides a useful introduction:

Richardson, K. (1991)
Understanding Intelligence,
Buckingham: Open University Press.

For dramatically contrasting views of the nature, origins and study of intelligence see:

Howe, M. J. A. (1990)
The Origins of Exceptional Abilities,
Oxford: Basil Blackwell.

Kline, P. (1991)
Intelligence: The Psychometric View,
London: Routledge.

Gardner, H. (1985)
Frames of Mind: The Theory of Multiple Intelligences,
London: Paladin Books.   📖 **Reading, 6.6**

Two interesting longitudinal studies of 'gifted children' provide case-study material with which to consider the nature/nurture intelligence debates. They are:

Freeman, J. (1991)
Gifted Children Growing Up,
London: Cassell.

Gross, M. (1992)
Exceptionally Gifted Children,
London: Routledge.

For a review of the history and state of work on dyslexia, see:

Miles, T. and Miles, E. (1990)
Dyslexia: A Hundred Years On,
Buckingham: Open University Press.

A great deal of work is now emerging on the influence of culture on children's learning. Two books which make a good start, with a focus on 3 to 5-year-olds and 4 to 7-year-olds respectively, are:

Dunn, J. (1988)
The Beginnings of Social Understanding,
Oxford: Blackwell.

Pollard, A. with Filer, A. (1996)
The Social World of Children's Learning,
London: Cassell.

Three excellent collections of articles are:

Richards, M. and Light, P. (1986)
Children of Social Worlds,
Cambridge: Polity Press.

Light, P., Sheldon, S. and Woodhead, M. (1991)
Learning to Think,
London: Routledge.

Light, P. and Butterworth, G. (eds) (1992)
Context and Cognition: Ways of Learning and Knowing,
Hemel Hempstead: Harvester Wheatsheaf.   📖 **Reading, 6.9**

Family relationships and individual development are discussed in:

White, D. and Woollett, A. (1991)
Families: A Context for Development,
London: Falmer.

There are a lot of books on the relationships between homes, schools and children's learning. Some exceptional ones are:

Grant, D. (1989)
Learning Relations,
London: Routledge.

Athey, C. (1990)
Extending Thought in Young Children:
A Parent–Teacher Partnership,
London: Paul Chapman.

Wells, G. (1986)
The Meaning Makers: Children Learning
Language and Using Language to Learn,
London: Hodder and Stoughton.

Tizard, B. and Hughes, M. (1984)
Young Children Learning,
London: Fontana.

On the influence of the media, see:

Gunter, B. and McAleer, J. L. (1990)
Children and Television: The One Eyed Monster?
London: Routledge.

Messenger Davies, M. (1989)
Television is Good for your Kids,
London: Hilary Shipman.

Eke, R. and Croll, P. (1992)
Television formats and children's classifications of their viewing,
Journal of Educational Television, **18** (1–2), 97–105.

For a good introduction to personality, see:

Hampson, S. E. (1988)
The Construction of Personality: An Introduction,
London: Routledge.

An interesting book which tries to synthesize much previous work into an overarching theoretical framework is:

Kegan, R. (1982)
The Evolving Self: Problem and Process in Human Development,
London: Harvard University Press.

A sustained and accessible account of the development of personality, drawing on the perspectives of children and parents, is:

Wolff, S. (1989)
Childhood and Human Nature: The Development of Personality,
London: Routledge.

The following books contain interesting articles relating to individual differences in learning styles, particularly Section 2 in Entwistle (1985):

Entwistle, N. (ed.) (1985)
New Directions in Educational Psychology: Learning and Teaching,
London: Falmer.

Entwistle, N. (1981)
Styles of Learning and Teaching,
London: Wiley.

On motivation the work of Dweck is best represented by:

Dweck, C. (1986)
Motivational processes affecting learning,
American Psychologist, October.

📖 Reading, 6.7

A classic text which contains much to fire the imagination is:

Holt, J. (1967)
How Children Learn,
London: Penguin.

📖 Reading, 10.3

See also:

Spaulding, C. L. (1992)
Motivation in the Classroom,
New York: McGraw Hill.

Barrett, G. (ed.) (1989)
Dissaffection from School: The Early Years,
London: Falmer.

Docking, J. (ed.) (1990a)
Education and Alienation in the Junior School,
London: Falmer.

Amongst a range of different recent work on meta-cognition, see Chapter 3 of Wood (1988), above, and also:

Robinson, E. (1983)
Meta-cognitive development. In S. Meadows (ed.)
Developing Thinking,
London: Methuen.

Nisbet, J. and Shucksmith, J. (1986)
Learning Strategies,
London: Routledge.

Yussen, S. R. (ed.) (1985)
The Growth of Reflection in Children,
New York: Academic Press.

The two books below are more concerned with the philosophy and practice of thinking critically:

Siegel, H. (1990)
Educating Reason: Rationality, Critical Thinking and Education,
London: Routledge.

Smith, F. (1990)
To Think,
New York: Teachers' College Press.

In the books below, Farnham-Diggory develops a theory of 'cognitive apprenticeship' for pupils, whilst Edwards and Mercer are concerned with the development of classroom understanding between teacher and pupils:

Farnham-Diggory, S. (1990)
Schooling,
Cambridge, MA: Harvard University Press.

Edwards, D. and Mercer, N. (1987)
Common Knowledge: The Development of Understanding in Classrooms,
London: Methuen.

Two sensitive and insightful books by primary school teachers on pupil learning in their classrooms are:

Armstrong, M. (1981)
Closely Observed Children,
London: Writers and Readers.   📖 Reading, 6.10

Rowland, S. (1984)
The Enquiring Classroom,
London: Falmer.   📖 Reading, 6.11

CHAPTER 7

What are the aims, structure and content of the curriculum?

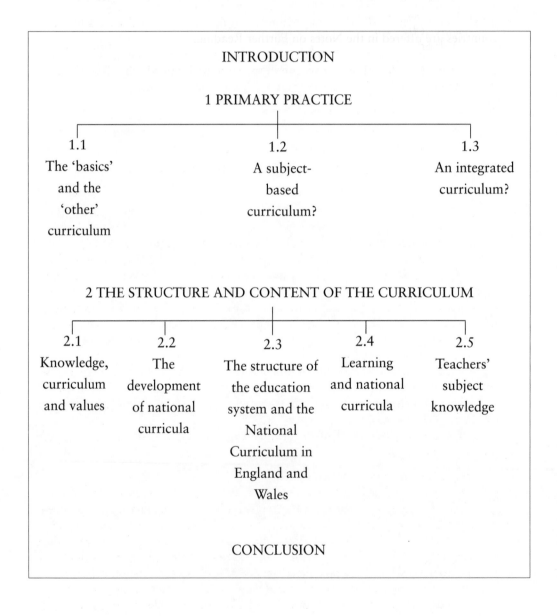

INTRODUCTION

1 PRIMARY PRACTICE

1.1
The 'basics' and the 'other' curriculum

1.2
A subject-based curriculum?

1.3
An integrated curriculum?

2 THE STRUCTURE AND CONTENT OF THE CURRICULUM

2.1
Knowledge, curriculum and values

2.2
The development of national curricula

2.3
The structure of the education system and the National Curriculum in England and Wales

2.4
Learning and national curricula

2.5
Teachers' subject knowledge

CONCLUSION

INTRODUCTION

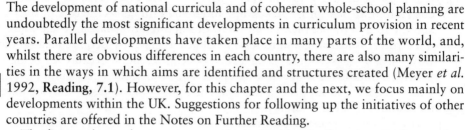

The development of national curricula and of coherent whole-school planning are undoubtedly the most significant developments in curriculum provision in recent years. Parallel developments have taken place in many parts of the world, and, whilst there are obvious differences in each country, there are also many similarities in the ways in which aims are identified and structures created (Meyer *et al.* 1992, **Reading, 7.1**). However, for this chapter and the next, we focus mainly on developments within the UK. Suggestions for following up the initiatives of other countries are offered in the Notes on Further Reading.

The first, and most basic point to make is that, for the first time, Parliament has set out aims for educational provision in the state-maintained schools of the UK. As the Education Reform Act 1988 states, the curriculum must:

- be balanced and broadly based
- promote the spiritual, moral, cultural, mental and physical development of pupils at the school and of society
- prepare pupils for the opportunities, responsibilities and experiences of adult life

Such aims are not exceptional in international terms (Taylor, 1990), though they are certainly the product of an enormous complexity of debate, interest and political activity both within and outside the teaching profession (Proctor, 1990).

For our purposes here, the important point is that aims are now a legal reality, and a curriculum framework, a content specification and forms of assessment logically follow. Teachers and student teachers are thus now required to accommodate their classroom planning within an external and statutory curriculum framework. Hopefully, this will ensure that the learning experience of children is coherent and that they will benefit from curricular progression as they move through their education.

However, high-quality curriculum provision for the classroom will always be enriched by the imagination, knowledge and enthusiasms of individual teachers and both this chapter, and Chapter 8, try to identify how this unique contribution can be made.

We need to be clear too that the term 'curriculum' can be used in a number of different ways.

The official curriculum
This can be defined as 'a planned course of study', i.e. an explicitly stated programme of learning, perhaps incorporating a national curriculum which has been endorsed by government. Such a course of study is likely to have three elements. First, there will be an intended curriculum content. This will have been consciously planned, though it may not always actually be taught nor is it likely to include learning which may take place outside school. Second, the official curriculum will usually structure sequence and progression, thus framing the content and course of activities. Third, the planned course of study will be designed with the intention of challenging children appropriately and matching their learning needs.

The hidden curriculum

The hidden curriculum is rarely explicit and may not be intended. It consists of all that is learnt during school activities which is not a designated part of the official curriculum. It is what is 'picked up' about such things as the role of the teacher and the role of the learner, about the status and relationships of each, about attitudes towards learning and to school. Children may also acquire ideas about the ways boys or girls 'should' behave, or about differences 'because' of being black or white, middle-class or working-class. Thus the hidden curriculum is implicit within regular school procedures and curriculum materials. It may be unrecognized and is often unexamined.

It has been suggested by writers in this field (Jackson, 1968, **Reading, 5.5**; Meighan, 1981) that such implicit messages can have a profound effect on the self-image of children, upon their images of school and on their attitudes to other social groups (see also Chapter 13).

The observed curriculum

This is the curriculum that can be seen to be taking place in the classroom. It may, of course, be different from the intended official curriculum. If so, it may be useful for teachers to identify and evaluate such differences. It must be remembered however, that what can be seen in terms of subject content or activities, is not the same thing as how the children feel about it, or what they learn through it. This leads to the next aspect of 'curriculum'.

The curriculum-as-experienced

This way of conceptualizing the curriculum identifies the parts of the curriculum, both official and hidden, which actually connect meaningfully with children. Arguably, it is only this aspect of curriculum which actually has an educational impact upon children. The rest is often forgotten.

In this chapter we focus mainly on the official curriculum, attending to the hidden, observed and experienced curriculum in many other ways throughout the book. The chapter is in two parts. In the first part, we take stock of common curricular practices in primary schools and consider the strengths and weaknesses of subject-based and integrated forms of curriculum organization. The second part concerns the structure and content of the curriculum including the National Curriculum and the values on which it is based and some of the problems and challenges which it poses. The direct practicalities of planning and implementing a classroom curriculum in the context of the whole school are the subject of Chapter 8.

1 | PRIMARY PRACTICE

Historically, there have been two major alternative strategies for curricular planning within primary schools – by focusing on separate subjects or by planning forms of integration between subjects. The strengths of subject teaching, in terms of curricular progression, are also its weakness regarding overall coherence in pupil learning experiences. Unfortunately, the reverse is also true, in that the coherence of integrated work can lead to fragmentation in understanding of particular subjects.

Whilst subject-based approaches were common in what Blyth (1965) called the 'preparatory school tradition', integrated approaches, using 'topics', have been very significant in primary education ever since the Plowden Report of 1967 (CACE, 1967, **Reading, 7.6**). Indeed, some have argued that topic work became a distinctive feature of primary school ideology (Alexander, *et al.*, 1992, **Reading, 8.4**).

However, the apparent distinctiveness of these approaches conceals a considerable overlap in actual practice.

1.1   The 'basics' and the 'other' curriculum

Whatever is said about the primary curriculum, the evidence from research (e.g. Pollard *et al.*, 1994) and from the prescriptive literature shows that a 'two curriculum syndrome' is in operation. This argument was powerfully made by Alexander (1984) and reinforced by his later work (1989, 1992). The two curricula that he had in mind are those of the 'basics' (reading, writing and mathematics) and those of the rest – the 'other' curriculum. Alexander argued that the rhetoric of child-centred education, which is associated with an integrated form of curriculum organization, has prevented teachers from facing the fact that the basics in the curriculum have usually been taught in a relatively discrete and almost subject-based way. It is only with regard to other, less central, areas of the curriculum that attempts to establish integration have really been made. The following model, Figure 7.1, shows Alexander's analysis of the major dimensions of the 'two curricula'. Some of the concepts in this model are sophisticated and it will be worth revisiting having read other parts of this chapter.

Alexander's model provides both challenges and insights when considering the curriculum. In particular, it shows how actual primary practice often reflects the pragmatism and judgement of 'what works'. The result is something of a necessary compromise, despite the impression which might sometimes be given by rhetoric from either quarter.

1.2   A subject-based curriculum?

A subject-based curriculum is one which maintains high subject boundaries and thus maintains distinctions between subjects. The resulting curriculum, therefore, is a collection of separate subjects, indeed, it has been called a 'collection curriculum' (Bernstein, 1971, **Reading, 7.2**). Progression within each separate subject may be strong, though coherence across subjects is likely to be weak.

A philosophical rationale for a subject-based curriculum is that each element is based on logical structures of knowledge which are believed to be unique to that subject or 'form of knowledge' (Hirst and Peters, 1970; see also Barrow and Woods, 1988, **Reading, 7.3**). Indeed, Alexander, *et al.*, (1992, p. 17) claimed that subjects are 'some of the most powerful tools for making sense of the world which human beings have ever devised.'

However, the approach is one that primarily appeals to traditionalists. Indeed, perhaps the origin of curriculum subjects can be found in the high status which is attributed to the formal, classical education of public and grammar schools and to a belief that this is the only approach which will deliver competencies in basic subjects (Lawlor, 1988, **Reading, 7.9**).

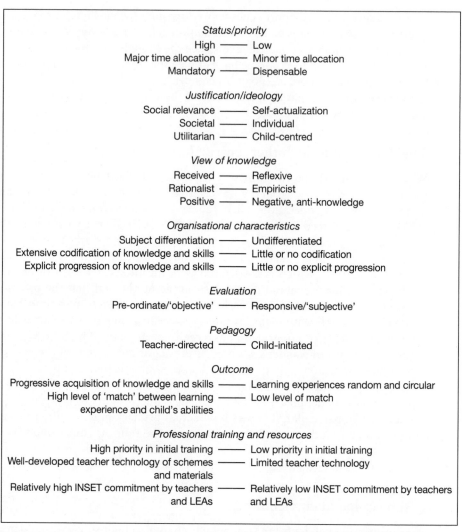

Status/priority
High —— Low
Major time allocation —— Minor time allocation
Mandatory —— Dispensable

Justification/ideology
Social relevance —— Self-actualization
Societal —— Individual
Utilitarian —— Child-centred

View of knowledge
Received —— Reflexive
Rationalist —— Empiricist
Positive —— Negative, anti-knowledge

Organisational characteristics
Subject differentiation —— Undifferentiated
Extensive codification of knowledge and skills —— Little or no codification
Explicit progression of knowledge and skills —— Little or no explicit progression

Evaluation
Pre-ordinate/'objective' —— Responsive/'subjective'

Pedagogy
Teacher-directed —— Child-initiated

Outcome
Progressive acquisition of knowledge and skills —— Learning experiences random and circular
High level of 'match' between learning —— Low level of match
experience and child's abilities

Professional training and resources
High priority in initial training —— Low priority in initial training
Well-developed teacher technology of schemes —— Limited teacher technology
and materials
Relatively high INSET commitment by teachers —— Relatively low INSET commitment by teachers
and LEAs and LEAs

Figure 7.1 *Dimensions for analysing the primary curriculum* (from Alexander (1984), *p.76*)

1.3   An integrated curriculum?

An integrated curriculum is one which draws on several subjects to construct a holistic and, it is hoped, meaningful focus for study (Hunter and Scheirer, 1988, Reading, 8.3).

Many different types of arguments for the desirability of an integrated curriculum have been offered. One suggests that the curriculum should draw on pupil experiences if effective learning is to take place. It is thus considered that the imposition of artificial subject boundaries may inhibit children's understanding.

Another argument is that, in a fast-moving world, new 'subjects' have emerged. These are interdisciplinary and conceptually linked (Pring, 1976), for instance, environmental studies and media studies. Such issues cross 'forms of knowledge'. For example, aspects of health education require us to make responses which are social, moral and economic as well as scientific. This form of integration was highlighted in some Schools Council projects, such as *Place, Time and Society* (Blyth, 1975), and even in the modern subject-based, National Curriculum of England and Wales, cross-curricular themes were prominent in its initial version (see also Chapter 8, section 2.8).

A third argument that underpins integrated curricular planning is that a higher priority can be given to generally applicable processes, skills and attitudes if the emphasis on particular subject knowledge is lessened. The idea here is that knowledge is changing so fast in the world that it is more important for children to learn transferable skills than to concentrate on facts which will rapidly become outdated (Practical Activity 7.1).

Practical activity 7.1

Aim: To consider the use of subject-based and integrated forms of curriculum organization in your school.

Method: Discuss with teachers and colleagues the ways in which the curriculum in your school is planned. Study any relevant documentation. Which elements of subject matter are to be integrated? Which subjects are to be taught separately?

Follow-up: Consider how progression and coherence are being provided. For instance, is progression of a 'step-by-step' nature, a 'spiral' nature (revisiting the same area of knowledge/concepts/skills but at a greater depth), or of a 'spasmodic' nature (with the risk that children's understanding may be fragmentary)? Is the overall pupil experience, day by day, meaningful and coherent – or is it a fragmented exposure to bits and pieces of subject knowledge?

Primary practice then, has been shaped by two differing approaches to curriculum planning, but has, in reality, drawn on both as professional judgement has been exercised. Of course, there may also be some inertia. However, it is the task of the reflective teacher to evaluate the strengths and weaknesses of different approaches for their circumstances, and to work with colleagues to develop the most appropriate strategy for curriculum planning.

In section 2, we consider some of the issues involved in more detail.

2 | THE STRUCTURE AND CONTENT OF THE CURRICULUM

In this part of the chapter we consider the nature of curricular frameworks, with particular reference to the values and views of knowledge which they embody. The case of the UK is documented and we identify some potential problems regarding processes of children's learning and the demands which a broad and detailed curriculum makes on teachers' subject knowledge. See also Barrow and Woods (1988, **Reading, 7.3**)

2.1 Knowledge, curriculum and values

Regarding how knowledge is viewed, we will focus on four positions.

First, as we have seen, there are those who argue that different 'forms of knowledge' exist. Forms of knowledge are thought to be distinguishable, philosophically, by the different ways of thinking and the different kinds of evidence which are employed in investigating them (Hirst, 1965; Peters, 1966). These different 'forms' are thought to be based on *a priori* differences, i.e. logical and inherent differences. Such a view is referred to as 'rationalist' (Blenkin and Kelly, 1981) and is often used to legitimate curriculum subjects.

Second, there are those who argue that knowledge is achieved through individuals interacting with the environment and restructuring their understanding through their experiences. Hence, knowledge is the application of intellect to experience. Proponents of this view are sometimes termed 'empiricists' and it is evidenced in the writings of Dewey and Piaget (see also Chapter 6, section 1.2, and **Reading 6.3**).

Third, a more sociological view suggests that knowledge can be constructed by groups of people, through their interactions with each other. Hence, they share their experiences and their perceptions of those experiences. In such an 'interactionist' approach people are seen as developing a common sense of 'reality' (Berger and Luckman, 1967). This view has some resonance with the work on learning of Vygotsky (see Chapter 6, section 1.3 and **Reading, 6.4**).

Finally, knowledge can be seen in the context of macro-social structures, and of historical forces, as being influenced by powerful social groups which define certain types of knowledge as being important or of high status. They may attempt to control access to certain forms of knowledge, particularly those associated with power (Young, 1971), but they may also try to insist on the exposure of pupils to other forms of knowledge which are deemed to be appropriate. We can call this view of school knowledge 'elitist'.

Of course, these views of knowledge are not discrete and any one person's perspective may draw on several of them, or even on them all. However, the different emphasis which is placed on particular views of knowledge tends to reflect social values.

For instance, during the 1990s the initial and revised National Curriculum of England and Wales was repeatedly criticized for reflecting elitist views. Educationalists, often expressing empiricist or interactionist opinions, were joined by subject professionals, usually with rationalist positions, to contest the influence of so-called 'New Right' pressure groups on government and on the National Curriculum Council and its successor, the School Curriculum and Assessment Authority (see Chapter 2). The outcomes of these debates can particularly be traced within the National Curriculum for history and English, but other subjects were also the subject of considerable discussion.

When a national curriculum for the education of young people and future citizens is being developed, such debates are obviously very significant and may become political (contrast, for instance, **Readings, 7.9** and **7.11**). Indeed, there may even be fears of state indoctrination. The outcome will certainly tend to reflect the balance of political power at the time of decision-making. Thus, for instance, the history curriculum of Jamaica today is very different from that which existed before she achieved independence from Britain in 1962. Practical Activity 7.2 suggests consideration of the influence of views of knowledge, values and power on the national curriculum which exists in your country at this particular point in time.

Practical activity 7.2

Aim: To consider the influence of views of knowledge, values and power on a part of a national curriculum.

Method: This is a potentially huge activity which needs to be scaled down and made specific. We suggest that you study the official, national documentation of a single subject. History or your national language are often good choices.
   Consider three main issues:

First, how is knowledge viewed? Is it seen as an established body of subject content and skills to be transferred or as something to be created?

Second, are particular values and perspectives reflected in the selection of the curriculum which was decided upon?

Third, what values and perspectives do you feel might have been left out?

Follow-up: There may be a national curriculum debate taking place in the media which you could also monitor. Alternatively, if you have a good library available to you and the curriculum you have focused on is reasonably recent, you could trace the debates about it in the press. In the UK, the index of *The Times* newspaper will provide many leads.

A further values-issue concerns how a specified national curriculum framework relates to the continuing commitment of many primary school teachers to child-centred, self-motivated learning. If teachers believe that the curriculum should be based on each individual child's interests and that children should be encouraged to initiate their own learning, does this conflict with the advantages of giving every child access to a similar curriculum? Resolution of this dilemma may revolve around our understanding of the term 'interests': whether we believe that the curriculum should be based on the self-expressed, immediate interests of children, or on areas of learning which are chosen by parents or government agencies as being appropriate. Child or parental influence might result in varied and idiosyncratic learning experiences, whilst the influence of central government could result in a more common curriculum. We would also have to consider whether we believe children are able to express their long-term interests and how much weight we would give to their expression of immediate interests. What criteria should we use to decide which interests to 'allow'? If the curriculum is not to be based on the self-expressed interests of children, on whose interests should the curriculum be based? (Practical Activity 7.3.)

Practical activity 7.3

Aim: To identify our value-position in relation to children's self-expressed interests.

Method: Ask the children what they are interested in studying, and what they would like to do in school-time, or, alternatively, try to think what interests they have shown.

Write down a list. Now consider this list and decide which ones would be acceptable and why, and which ones would not and why. What would you add and why?

Follow up: Having reflected on the lists, preferably with a colleague, what conclusions can we each draw about how children's 'interests' are valued, or not, in the national curriculum?

At the classroom level, the concept of 'negotiation' goes a long way in resolving this dilemma. Children are perfectly capable of accepting that there is a nationally laid down curriculum coverage, but will welcome negotiation with their teacher about how it should be addressed and with what it should be augmented. However, seen from the national level, negotiation produces an unacceptable degree of variation in pupil experience and learning. Hence the development of the National Curriculum.

2.2 The development of national curricula

Taylor's (1990) review of the aims which governments across the world have for primary education shows a considerable emphasis on basic knowledge and skills, intellectual, social and moral development and providing a foundation for subsequent education. The relative priorities given to such aims reflect the circumstances of each country – industrial/agricultural, urban/rural, religious/secular, etc – and their stage of industrial development. However, whatever their priorities, the specification of a national curriculum is commonly seen as an important means of development. The form of such national curricula will reflect the history, culture and circumstances of each country, and perspectives of the political decision-makers who happen to be in power. We focus, below, on the example of the UK.

The 'empiricist' view of knowledge, discussed in section 2.1, was dominant in British primary school rhetoric for much of this century. For example, the Hadow Report (Board of Education, 1931, **Reading, 7.5**) urged that the curriculum should be 'thought of in terms of activity and experience rather than knowledge to be acquired and facts to be stored' (p. 93). Similarly the Plowden Report (CACE, 1967, **Reading, 7.6**) argued that schools should lay stress on 'individual discovery, first hand experience and on opportunities for creative work' (p. 187). It insisted that 'knowledge does not fall into separate compartments', (p. 187). Prior to the 1980s, British primary schools had thus enjoyed considerable autonomy in deciding both what should be taught and how it was to be taught.

Whilst there was considerable overlap in the content of the resulting curriculum, this was combined with much diversity and variation in the quality of the education provided (HMI, 1978; House of Commons, 1986). Many schools were excellent, but the provision was very uneven across the country.

This was a major reason given, in the early 1980s, by educationalists arguing for curriculum reform to raise standards. There was a plethora of curriculum documents, from a number of public bodies. These included *The School Curriculum* (DES, 1981), *A View of the Curriculum* (HMI, 1980), *Better Schools* (DES, 1985b, **Reading, 7.8**) and *The Curriculum from 5–16* (DES, 1985a) and *Primary Practice* (Schools Council, 1983).

Lawton had argued (1975, 1977, 1980) that a national curriculum should be conceived as a selection from Britain's 'common culture', and this idea was developed into a vision of the curriculum as an 'entitlement'. Of course, this idea begs a large number of questions about what our 'common culture' might actually be – particularly if one considers the diversity associated with such realities as ethnicity, gender, religion, geographical region and social class.

Thus, while many agreed in principle with the proposal to create a national curriculum, some important questions were nevertheless raised. What exactly should a framework contain? Who should decide this and how often should it be reviewed? How detailed should the curriculum be and should it be advisory or compulsory? What implications would this have for an increase in central control and the subsequent possible reduction of the professional autonomy of the individual classroom teacher? What would be the likely effects on the balance between individually and socially determined goals, between personal freedom and professional responsibility? Would a national curriculum affect the career structure of the profession and give greater opportunity to the 'subject specialist' or 'consultant' as opposed to the 'generalist' primary teacher?

There was also a harder edge to this debate, with its origins in the Black Papers of the late 1970s, the media critique of 'progressive teaching' and the concerns over the relationship of education to industrial production which had been raised by Prime Minister Callaghan in his 1977 Ruskin Speech (Callaghan, 1977, **Reading, 7.7**). Indeed, eventually the worries of education professionals were swept away by the influence on successive Conservative governments of a number of right-wing pressure groups (Ball,1990; Whitty, 1992). In essence, the message of groups such as the No Turning Back Group of MPs (1986), the Centre for Policy Studies (e.g. Lawlor, 1988, **Reading, 7.9**) and the Hillgate Group (1987) was simple. Educational provision had been captured by the producers, i.e. the teachers, and had to be freed to meet the interests of consumers, i.e. the parents. Specification of a national curriculum, combined with an increase in the local management and autonomy of individual schools, was a strategy for creating a 'market' for education which would both control teachers and raise standards (see Chapter 4, section 1.2).

In due course, the 1988 Education Reform Act was passed and prescribed the subjects of a National Curriculum for England and Wales and, by Orders in Council, for Northern Ireland (Education Reform, Northern Ireland, Order 1990). Scotland, interestingly, remained somewhat outside this structure, with its own distinctive 5–14 curriculum which can be traced back to the Schools (Scotland) Code of 1956.

This movement to establish national curricula drew particularly on rationalist and elitist views of knowledge. Figure 7.2 relates a version of the rationalists 'forms of knowledge' with the 'areas of experience' suggested by HMI and with the curricula of England, Northern Ireland, Wales and Scotland.

There are many continuities between Hirst's forms of knowledge, HMI's areas of learning and experience (DES, 1985a) and the subjects identified by the national curricula. On the other hand, there are also some very significant differences. These particularly concern the way in which subjects are prioritized, and the way in which subjects are compartmentalized.

In Scotland, there are five 'areas of the curriculum', two of which incorporate several subjects. The Scottish Office insist (SOED, 1989) that the primary school curriculum is balanced between these five areas and that three essential features are to be addressed – knowledge and understanding, learning skills and personal and social development. In Northern Ireland the situation is somewhat similar, with subjects being located within 'areas of study' (Education Reform, Northern Ireland, Order 1990).

In England and Wales, priority was given to English, maths, science (and in Wales, Welsh) as 'core' subjects – a structural innovation which was taken to assert their importance as basics. Indeed, this distinction was also used to shape different forms of pupil assessment and reporting to parents. Subjects were then compartmentalized along traditional lines, ignoring (or contesting) the extensive integration of humanities work which was common in primary schools. Most of this structure has existed since 1989, though Information Technology was given subject status only in 1995.

Perhaps the greatest challenge of the introduction of the new curriculum to previous primary school practice was in the use of subjects as the basic planning tool. In the late 1980s this was seen as an attempt to impose an inappropriate 'secondary school' form of curriculum planning and it was thought that the use of subjects would lead to a lack of meaning and coherence in the primary curriculum as an experienced whole (see **Readings, 8.3 and 8.4**). In England when the National Curriculum was initially introduced, the National Curriculum Council was unable to sustain detailed work on the curriculum as a whole and it published a succession of single-subject curriculum orders. Apart from some rather limited exhortations from NCC (NCC, 1989a, b, 1990a), it was left to schools to address the issue of curriculum coherence for pupils.

The Curriculum Council for Wales made somewhat greater progress in producing a 'framework for the whole curriculum' (CCW, 1991) which drew on HMI's areas of learning, statutory and other subjects, and a variety of themes, competencies and dimensions. This framework is reproduced as Figure 7.3 and Practical Activity 7.4 is based on it.

The framework provided by the Curriculum Council for Wales was an exceptional attempt at mapping curricular overlaps and possibilities for providing coherence. However, in doing so it highlighted other features of early national curriculum planning in the UK – that it was both extremely complex and greatly overloaded with content. We will revisit this topic but, suffice it to say that the National Curriculum, in its early 1990's form, turned out to be impossible to deliver in most primary schools (Muschamp et al., 1992, Campbell and Neill,1992; NCC, 1993b; OFSTED, 1993, Pollard et al., 1994). Despite its youth, the initial National Curriculum was eventually 'reviewed' by Sir Ron Dearing and

Forms of Knowledge (Hirst, 1965)	Areas of learning and experience (DES, 1985a)	The areas of curriculum of the 5–14 curriculum of Scotland (SOED, 1989)	The subjects of curriculum of England and Wales (ERA, 1988 and Dearing Revisions, 1995)	The areas of study of the curriculum of Northern Ireland (ER (Northern Ireland) Order 1990)
	Linguistic and literary	Language	English	English
			Welsh in Wales	Irish in Irish-speaking schools
Mathematical	Mathematical	Mathematics	Mathematics	Mathematics
Empirical (physical and social sciences)	Scientific	Environmental studies (encompassing science, place, time and society, healthy and safe living and living with technology)	Science	Science and Technology (encompassing Science, Technology and Design)
	Technological		Design and Technology	
			Information Technology	
	Human and social		Geography	Environment and Society (encompassing History and Geography)
			History	
Aesthetic	Aesthetic and creative	Expressive arts (encompassing art, dance, music and physical education)	Art	Creative and expressive studies (encompassing Art and Design, Music and Physical Education)
			Music	
			Physical education	
Mental (values and intentions)				
Philosophical				
Moral	Moral	Religious and moral education	Religious education	Religious education
Religious	Spiritual			

Figure 7.2 *Forms of knowledge, areas of experience and curricular subjects for primary schools*

 was officially deemed to be 'overloaded and unmanageable' (Dearing, 1993, **Reading, 7.12**) (see also the 1994 Labour Party policy statement, *Opening the Doors to a Learning Society*, indicating how they would have revised the curriculum, **Reading, 7.11**).

ASPECTS OF

	EXPRESSIVE AND AESTHETIC	LINGUISTIC AND LITERARY	MATHEMATICAL	PHYSICAL AND RECREATIONAL
PRINCIPAL FEATURES	*developing:* • the expression of ideas, moods, emothions in a variety of media • emotion and intellectual response to sensory experience • imagination, perception and discrimination • physical control of media *developing understanding of:* • the processes of designing, making and composing • the characteristics of different media • the relationships between arts and society	*developing:* • effective communication in speaking and listening, reading and writing • enjoyment and fascination in the use of language • knowledge of languages and how they work • understanding of and response to literature and the media • the use of language as a tool for learning *developing understanding of:* • the diversity of language • the social and cultural contexts of language use • the relationships between languages	*developing:* • creativity • ability to think logically and analytically • ability to use mathematics to solve problems (theoretical and practical) • ability to handle and communicate mathematical ideas and information using the language of mathematics • positive personal qualities and attitudes • appreciation of the wonder and excitement of mathematics • a sense of the power and limitations of mathematics	*developing:* • knowledge and understanding of the principles of health and well-being and positive attitudes to the development and care of the human body • personal qualities related to perseverance and the pursuit of excellence; coping with success and failure and co-operating with others in individual and team activities • appreciation of the creative qualities in human movement and related skills • skills relating to specific physical and recreational activities as an important contributor to personal and social well-being
STATUTORY SUBJECTS WHICH MAKE MAJOR CONTRIBUTIONS	• art • PE • English • Welsh • music	• English • [modern foreign languages] • Welsh	• mathematics • science • technology	• art • science • music • PE
OTHER SUBJECTS AND ACTIVITIES	• [classics] • dance • drama • media studies	• [classics] • drama • media studies • [other languages]	• [economics/business studies] • life skills	• outdoor education • life skills • rural studies • drama • dance • community work
	[. . .] indicates subjects associated with secondary phase only			
THEMES	SOME ASPECTS OF ALL THEMES careers education & guidance; community understanding; economic & industrial understanding; environmental education; health education			
COMPETENCES	• communication • information technology • problem solving • study	• communication • information technology • problem solving • study	• communication • information technology • numeracy • problem solving • study	• communication • information technology • problem solving • study
DIMENSIONS	• equality of opportunity	• cultural diversity		• special needs

Figure 7.3 *The CCW framework for the whole curriculum: an illustrative description* (from CCW, 1991)

LEARNING

SCIENTIFIC	SOCIAL AND ENVIRONMENTAL	SPIRITUAL AND MORAL	TECHNOLOGICAL
developing: • creativity • ability to use scientific methods of enquiry in an imaginative and disciplined way • understanding of physical, biological and social phenomena in terms of scientific concepts and theories • critical awareness of the role of science in societies and cultures • balanced appreciation of the power and limitations of science as a human activity • positive personal qualities and attitudes	*developing:* • a sense of: place, space and environment, time and context *developing understanding of:* • the physical environment and human influences on it • the past and its influence on the present • the human environment and the inter-relatedness of individuals, groups and societies • the operation of institutions in society • the nature, causes and effects of economic and industrial activity	*developing:* • feelings and convictions about the significance of human life and the world as a whole • a sense of fairness and justice • a respect for different religious convictions *developing understanding of:* • moral and ethical issues • the diversity of religions and relationships between them • the use made by religions of symbol, allegory and analogy • codes of human behaviour	*developing:* • ability to apply knowledge and skills to practical tasks, operating within a range of constraints • ability to think and act imaginatively and creatively • ability to use the products of technological activity sensibly and effectively • ability to evaluate the purposes, processes and products of technology • critical awareness of the role and effects of technology in cultures and societies • positive personal qualities and attitudes
• mathematics • PE • science • RE • technology • geography	• geography • RE • history • MFL • science • English/Welsh	• English/Welsh • music • art • geography • RE • technology • history • science	all statutory subjects
• [social science] • [ecomonics/business studies] • drama • rural studies	• [economics/business studies] • [social science] • rural studies • community work	• [classics] • [social science] • community work	• [economics business studies] • media studies • life skills • community work
SOME ASPECTS OF ALL THEMES careers education & guidance; community understanding; economic & industrial understanding; environmental education; health education			
• communication • information technology • numeracy • problem solving • study	• communication • information technology • numeracy • problem solving • study	• communication • information technology • problem solving • study	• communication • information technology • numeracy • problem solving • study
• the cultural relevance of the curriculum to its Welsh setting – Curriculum Cymreig			

Figure 7.3 continued

Practical activity 7.4

Aim: To consider the value of the CCW Framework for the Whole Curriculum as a planning tool.

Method: Think of a topic or activity which you believe to be appropriate for the children you are going to teach. Brainstorm on the various aspects of the topic, things which you might do and aims which you might have for the children. Then try to map your ideas onto the CCW framework.

How broad and balanced would your curriculum be? How could you develop your ideas?

Follow-up: You could also use the CCW framework as an evaluation tool. Take your records of a programme of work which you have completed. How does it relate to the framework? What does this suggest that you might need to address in future work?

We now move on, to consider some to the new structures in more detail, taking the post-1995 National Curriculum of England and Wales as our example.

2.3 The structure of the education system and the National Curriculum in England and Wales

The Education Reform Act 1988 introduced a clear structure for the education system in England and Wales and there are many important features of this curriculum. We describe these below, for the 5 to 11 age-range. In doing so, we have drawn, in particular, on a joint publication from SCAA, ACAC and the TTA, *A Guide to the National Curriculum* (SCAA, 1996). We have tried to use 'official' language. This is thus a descriptive account of national structures and curriculum as they exist from the 1995/96 school year.

The structures

Key stages denote periods of compulsory schooling which relate to the age of pupils and which, in terms of curriculum and assessment, are administered and provided for in somewhat similar ways. Key Stage 1 relates to the infant school years (5–7), and Key Stage 2 to the junior school years (8–11). (In Northern Ireland Key Stage 1 is from 4 to 8 years old, Key Stage 2 from 9–11.)

Assessment points come at the end of each key stage. In the case of primary schools, this is at the end of the years in which pupils reach the ages of 7 and 11.

Pupil year is a way of describing the year group of pupils.

Figure 7.4 clarifies the relationship between Key Stage, pupil year and pupil age. It also shows the way in which assessment takes place at the end of each Key Stage. We show the extension of the primary years into those of secondary education because one of the most valuable aspects of the National Curriculum is the expectation of continuity in the learning experiences provided between schools at transfer points.

Age of pupils	Pupil year	Key Stage	School	Assessment
5 or under 6 7	Reception (R) Year 1 (Y1) Year 2 (Y2)	Key Stage 1	Infant school	 At age 7
8 9 10 11	Year 3 (Y3) Year 4 (Y4) Year 5 (Y5) Year 6 (Y6)	Key Stage 2	Junior school	 At age 11
12 13 14	Year 7 (Y7) Year 8 (Y8) Year 9 (Y9)	Key Stage 3	Secondary school	 At age 14
15 16	Year 10 (Y10) Year 11 (Y11)	Key Stage 4	Secondary school	 At age 16

Figure 7.4 *Age of pupil, school year and Key Stage*

The subjects

In England, the Education Reform Act 1988 established nine subjects as the basis of the National Curriculum for children aged between 5 and 11, and also required that pupils should receive appropriate religious education. In Wales, Welsh provided an additional subject and in secondary education, pupils must also study a foreign language.

The foundation subjects of the national curriculum are English, mathematics, science, design and technology, information technology (added in 1995), history, geography, art, music and physical education. Welsh is also taught in Wales. These subjects are thought to cover the range of knowledge, skills and understanding commonly accepted as necessary for a broad education.

The core subjects, of English, mathematics and science, are thought to encompass knowledge, skills and understanding without which other learning cannot take place effectively. Competence in language, numeracy and scientific method is regarded as being necessary throughout the curriculum and in all aspects of adult life.

Figure 7.5 sets out the National Curriculum for primary schools in England and Wales.

The statutory framework of the subject orders

'Subject orders' are statutory and consist of 'common requirements', 'Programmes of Study' and 'Attainment Targets'. Pupil attainment for each Attainment Target is described by 'levels of attainment', using either 'level descriptions' or 'end of Key Stage descriptions'.

Core foundation subjects	English Mathematics Science (Welsh, in Welsh-speaking schools)
Other foundation subjects	Design and Technology Information Technology History Geography Art Music Physical Education (Welsh, in non-Welsh-speaking schools in Wales)
Other statutory requirements	Religious Education

Figure 7.5 *The National Curriculum for primary schools in England and Wales*

Common requirements apply to each of the 'subject orders'. They cover issues such as access to the curriculum for all pupils, the use of spoken and written language (including grammatically correct sentences and correct spelling and punctuation), provision of opportunities to use information technology and, in Wales, opportunities to apply knowledge and understanding of Welsh.

Programmes of Study set out essential knowledge, skills and processes which need to be covered in each subject by pupils in each stage of schooling. These are minimum statutory entitlements. Programmes of Study are intended to be used by schools in constructing schemes of work.

Levels of attainment identify points of knowledge, skill and understanding for each subject, against which pupil attainment can be assessed. Most pupils are expected to reach Level 2 at the age of 7, and Level 4 at the age of 11. A helpful representation of this was provided by the Task Group on Assessment and Testing (1988) (See Figure 7.6).

Attainment Targets are defined from within Programmes of Study to represent the knowledge, skills and understanding which pupils are expected to master as they progress through school. Attainment Targets are used in assessment procedures (see Figure 12.1 for detail on the Attainment Targets for England and Wales).

Level descriptions indicate the type, quality and range of work which a child 'characteristically should demonstrate' in a subject to be deemed to have reached a particular level. They are used for English, Welsh, mathematics, science, design and technology, information technology, history and geography (see Figure 12.2 for further details).

End of Key Stage descriptions represent the standard of performance 'expected of the majority of pupils' at the end of a Key Stage. They are used for art, music and physical education.

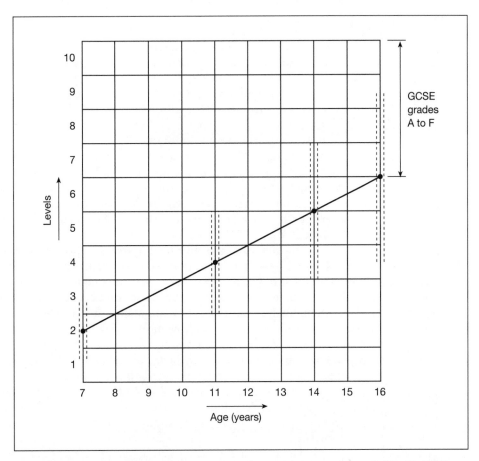

Figure 7.6 *A projected sequence of pupil achievement, ages 7 to 16 (TGAT, 1988)*

Non-statutory Guidance comes in a variety of publications from SCAA and ACAC, and formerly was provided from NCC, SEAC and CCW. It is intended to offer helpful advice on the implementation of the National Curriculum and assessment procedures (e.g. **Reading, 8.5**).

Modifications, disapplications and *exceptions* are terms used for various arrangements for lifting part or all of the National Curriculum requirements to meet the particular circumstances of pupils or schools. These procedures might, for instance, be applied for children with special educational needs, working within the SEN Code of Practice (DFE, 1994).

The documentation associated with the first version of the National Curriculum was immense. However, since 1995 the full primary curriculum has been contained in one volume, with consistent presentation and colour coding.

Those contemplating the structure which we have outlined above for the first time may well feel somewhat daunted by it. However, the National Curriculum structure does provide a carefully delineated framework which has many advantages, some of which we review at the end of the next section. Before this however, we need to consider some of the inherent difficulties which such curriculum structures face.

2.4 Learning and national curricula

There are many dilemmas to be faced in the construction of any national curriculum and some of the most significant concern learning. How can a specified curriculum, at one and the same time address national concerns, set out a national framework for content and progression and yet remain flexible enough to draw on the interests, experiences, learning styles and physical and intellectual capabilities of individual children? The truth, of course, is that no national curriculum can meet all these objectives. There has to be a trade-off.

As we have seen, in the case of the UK, the legislation of recent years has produced a much tighter specification of the curriculum in terms of both content and structure. Topics to be 'delivered' and assessed are specified in the 'Programmes of Study' and 'levels'. To a large extent then, the curriculum for schools has be placed in a linear form within each subject – and this is, of course, backed up by formal assessment procedures.

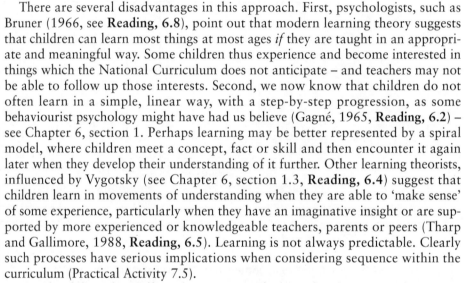

There are several disadvantages in this approach. First, psychologists, such as Bruner (1966, see **Reading, 6.8**), point out that modern learning theory suggests that children can learn most things at most ages *if* they are taught in an appropriate and meaningful way. Some children thus experience and become interested in things which the National Curriculum does not anticipate – and teachers may not be able to follow up those interests. Second, we now know that children do not often learn in a simple, linear way, with a step-by-step progression, as some behaviourist psychology might have had us believe (Gagné, 1965, **Reading, 6.2**) – see Chapter 6, section 1. Perhaps learning may be better represented by a spiral model, where children meet a concept, fact or skill and then encounter it again later when they develop their understanding of it further. Other learning theorists, influenced by Vygotsky (see Chapter 6, section 1.3, **Reading, 6.4**) suggest that children learn in movements of understanding when they are able to 'make sense' of some experience, particularly when they have an imaginative insight or are supported by more experienced or knowledgeable teachers, parents or peers (Tharp and Gallimore, 1988, **Reading, 6.5**). Learning is not always predictable. Clearly such processes have serious implications when considering sequence within the curriculum (Practical Activity 7.5).

Nor do philosophers affirm the existence of a logical and conceptual sequence of national curriculum knowledge. Indeed, their criticisms are combined with those of psychologists and applied even in the case of those subjects which are usually taken to embody progressive logic, such as mathematics (Ernest, 1991a; Noss *et al.*, 1989; Brown, 1989). Ernest's work makes the points particularly clearly. He writes:

> One of the greatest dangers in stipulating a statutory curriculum in mathematics at 10 levels of attainment is that it becomes a barrier which may deny a youngster access to higher concepts and skills when he or she is ready for them. ... The major flaw in this scheme [is] the mistaken assumption that children's learning in mathematics follows a fixed hierarchical pattern. ... This is nonsense. ... Psychological research proves that very few children progress evenly in mathematics. ... By holding children back in some topics, and forcing them ahead in others, this scheme looks set to lower standards in mathematics. There is a very real chance that it will rob children of the chance to develop their gifts.

(Ernest, 1991b, p.50)

Practical activity 7.5

Aim: To experience children's incredible capacity and inclination to search for understanding at young ages.

Method: Play with and talk to a young child with whom you have a good relationship. At an appropriate opportunity, develop a conversation about something in which they are interested. Note down the things which they say and ask, verbatim if you can, and consider what this shows you about their present understanding.

Think hard about some experience which you could offer the child to extend their thinking.

Try it. Again, record and interpret the child's responses.

Continue this process if it seems appropriate.

Follow-up: Consider the knowledge and understanding which the child has revealed and reached. Does this appear in the National Curriculum? If so, where? How appropriate does this seem? (For some examples of such conversations, see Tizard and Hughes, 1987.)

When it comes to many humanities and arts subjects, the sequencing of national curriculum subject matter really comes down to the base point of 'whatever has been agreed'. National curriculum documents, and their selection and allocation of knowledge to levels, are social products, the results of committees, debates or ministerial decisions, rather than being tied to any ultimately sustainable foundation. Perhaps it is only where skill development is involved, that the logic of progression really becomes more sustainable.

However, having identified some disadvantages and weaknesses of a structured national curriculum, we must also point to a large number of advantages which a national curriculum should provide in support of children's learning. These are listed below:

- *Aims and objectives* for each stage of children's education are clearly stated and these provide a helpful clarification of what both children and teachers are expected to do. After all, research has consistently shown that the lack of clarity in teaching and learning aims is a very significant inhibitor on pupil progress.

- *Resources* for the official series of teaching and learning programmes can be developed on a large scale and in an organized, cost-effective way.

- *Parents* have the opportunity to know and understand what is being taught and may be able to support their children more effectively.

- *Curriculum continuity* can be provided between schools.

- *Progression* can be ensured both from class to class and on transfer between schools.

- *Training and professional development* programmes for teachers can be tailored to known national curriculum needs.

As we suggested at the beginning of this section, there are serious dilemmas in having a structured national curriculum, and hard decisions have to be taken. However, the advantages are considerable and clarify the teacher's job in many respects. Indeed, research evidence shows that most primary teachers in the UK welcomed the introduction of the National Curriculum (Pollard *et al.,* 1994) and very few would now want to work without it. However, there are costs in terms of possible constraints and inflexibility regarding children's learning. Tapping children's interests and imagination in such circumstances requires continuing skill and empathy from teachers.

One way of overcoming this problem is to be able to fascinate the children with subject knowledge itself and in this, having sound subject knowledge is a very great asset.

2.5 Teachers' subject knowledge

Some of the most exciting curriculum developments in recent years have come from subject-based initiatives, often resulting from networks of teachers meeting through subject associations. For instance, in the UK we have the Association for Science Education (ASE), the National Association for the Teaching of English (NATE), the Association for the Teaching of Maths (ATM), the Maths Association, the History and Geography Associations, etc. There have also been several very successful and influential subject-based national projects, such as the the National Writing Project, the National Oracy Project (Norman, 1990) and Language in the National Curriculum (Carter, 1990). This vigour and innovation is reflected in a steady stream of subject-related conferences, magazines, journals and books for teachers (see the Notes for Further Reading). A good deal of this developing expertise was also used by working parties in the construction of the National Curriculum. Thus, in terms of innovation, application and specification of appropriate subject knowledge for primary schools, there are rich resources on which to draw.

However, despite these developments, there has been some reluctance among teachers to endorse the use of 'subjects' in primary education. This has been attributed to the commitment to integrated methods of curriculum provision which are associated with 'child-centredness', held, it has been claimed, despite the extensive discussion of subjects in the Plowden Report (CACE, 1967, **Reading, 7.6,** Richards, 1991). Robin Alexander has made a particularly incisive analysis of this commitment to the multifaceted ideal of 'good primary practice' (Alexander, 1992, **Reading, 7.10**). He urges teachers to be open-minded on the issue.

Of course, a commitment to an integrated curriculum is strongly associated with a Piagetian constructivist model of learning which, as we saw in Chapter 6, section 1.2, tends to cast the teacher as a manager of activities and of the learning environment, rather than as a 'teacher' *per se* (**Reading, 6.3**). The development of this position, the social constructivist model deriving from Vygotsky, emphasizes the role of teachers and others in extending and 'scaffolding' children's understanding across their 'zone of proximal development' (see Chapter 6, section 1.3, **Reading, 6.4**). In other words, pupil learning is enhanced by *appropriate* teaching of knowledge, concepts, skills and attitudes. The word 'appropriate' is very important here, for teaching can just as easily lead to pupil boredom as to pupil excitement and interest (see Chapter 6, section 2.4). Reflective teachers thus have to make judgements about appropriateness as they seek to connect with and extend the understanding of the child and, of course, this will be much easier to do if the teacher is confident of his or her own subject knowledge.

Consider Figure 7.7, reproduced from Chapter 6. This shows the crucial role of the teacher in scaffolding children's knowledge and understanding. To act as effective 'reflective agents', teachers need both understanding of how children learn and empathy with them. However, they also need subject knowledge and the skills to apply it.

This view was forcefully expressed by Alexander *et al.,* (1992) when they asserted that:

> Subject knowledge is a critical factor at every point in the teaching process: in planning, assessing and diagnosing, task setting, questioning, explaining and giving feedback. (1992, para. 77)

 The most influential research-based support for this position was provided by Shulman (1986, **Reading, 7.13**) who identified three sorts of subject knowledge:

Content knowledge refers to knowledge of the subject held by the teacher.

Pedagogic subject knowledge refers to knowledge of how to use content knowledge for teaching purposes.

Curricular knowledge refers to knowledge of curriculum structures and materials.

For most teachers, curricular knowledge is much easier to acquire than content knowledge or even pedagogic subject knowledge. Indeed, some would argue that, whilst curricular knowledge can be obtained from textbooks, resources and National Curriculum documentation, content knowledege calls for a type of sustained study which is only available through specialist degree courses.

The scale of the challenge which the breadth and depth of knowledge which the National Curriculum poses for teachers has to be acknowledged, and the demand at the upper end of Key Stage 2 is particularly great. There are very serious

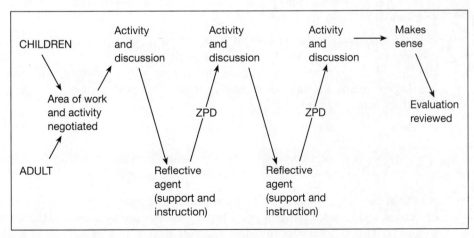

Figure 7.7 *A social constructivist model of roles in the teacher–learning process*

problems here (HMCI, 1996). Indeed, throughout the 1990s, teacher confidence in subject knowledge has been relatively low and perhaps mutual support from 'consultant' systems in schools will always be needed (see Chapter 8, section 4; Practical Activity 7.6).

Practical activity 7.6

Aim: To assess our own feelings of competence in subject knowledge.

Method: Consider the national curriculum of your country, subject by subject. Note which parts you feel competent to teach and about which parts you feel uncertain.

Prioritize your needs for developing subject knowledge and competence.

Share your feelings with a colleague – perhaps you are being too self-critical, or too confident?

Follow up: Consider the implications of your results. If a student teacher, what opportunities are there on your course for you to develop the subject knowledge that you need? If a school teacher, can you devise a practical pro-gramme for professional development and INSET; can you find ways of co-operating with colleagues in reciprocal support?

Of course, one source of curriculum support for teachers who feel that they have relatively weak expertise in a particular subject area lies in published text-books, schemes of work and resource packs of various sorts. Specification of national curricula create huge markets for publishers and there is considerable investment in such materials. However, MacLure and Elliott, in a review of pub-lished texts relating to the English National Curriculum, found that most were traditional and dull. As they put it:

> On the whole, the curriculum portrayed in the textbooks and worksheets is the famil-iar one of knowledge as a closed system of uncontrovertible facts, disconnected from the values and interest of the people who write, teach or read the texts. (MacLure and Elliott, 1993, p.10).

It is not necessarily always so and it may well be that high quality texts and schemes do emerge to join those which already exist. However, experience from the United States is not encouraging and suggests that schemes, with implicit ideologies, gradually take over and control the learning process (Apple and Christian-Smith, 1991; Practical Activity 7.7).

CONCLUSION

National curricula provide a significant means of attempting to fulfil national objectives and of attempting to provide coherence and progression in the learning of pupils. They also clarify the aims and role of teachers. However, as we have seen, the specification of a national curriculum raises the immediate question,

Practical activity 7.7

Aim: To review the strengths and weaknesses of a published curriculum text or scheme.

Method: Identify some materials which are in use in your school or in a school that you know.

Make notes in a matrix like the one below. Consider issues such as:

Does the material provide subject expertise?

Does it enable or constrain teaching?

Does it provide *appropriate* support to learners, when and how they need it?

Does it enhance or undermine pupil motivation?

	For teaching	For learning
Strengths		
Weaknesses		

Follow-up: Your work on this activity should lead you towards being able to identify the model of learning on which the curriculum materials are based. How does this relate to your values and aims? How consistent is it with other parts of your curriculum provision and practice? Do you wish to consolidate or review your use of the curriculum materials?

'Whose curriculum is it?'. Any curriculum reflects values, views of knowledge and of learning. Reflective teachers will accept this and recognize that dominant opinions and influence can change over time.

As we suggested in Chapter 1, it is an appropriate form of professionalism for reflective teachers to provide a constructive critique of curriculum structures if problems arise. In this chapter we have discussed three main issues which seem particularly important in the UK context – the problem of achieving coherence within a subject-based curriculum framework, the issue of learning and development which does not match the implied linearity of the National Curriculum, and the problem of the depth and breadth of subject knowledge which is required of teachers if they are to deliver the curriculum effectively. Such problems are likely to bring about change and development in future years.

Nor should we forget the clarification with which we began this chapter. The official curriculum of any country is a very different thing from the hidden curriculum, the observed curriculum and the curriculum-as-experienced by pupils. There is enormous scope for dilution, distortion, creativity, adaption and extension at every level of an education system. This may or may not be a good thing, depending on the aims and professionalism of those involved and the actual consequences of their actions.

In the next chapter, Chapter 8, we continue the focus on curriculum to attend to three major levels of curriculum planning – the whole school, the class programme and the lesson.

Notes for further reading

An accessible introduction to the historical origins of the primary curriculum and of practice remains:

Blyth, W. A. L. (1965)
English Primary Education,
Vol. II. Background,
London: Routledge.

For an account of the post-war years, see:

Cunningham, P. (1988)
Curriculum Change in the Primary School Since 1945:
Dissemination of the Progressive Ideal,
London: Falmer.

Primary curriculum practice in the 1970s was surveyed by HMI and published in:

DES (1978a)
Primary Education In England: A Survey by HMI,
London: HMSO.

In the 1980s a comprehensive stock-take was provided in:

House of Commons,
Select Committee on Education and the Arts (1986)
Achievement in Primary Schools,
London: HMSO.

An incisive academic account of curriculum practice, distinguishing between the 'basics' and the 'other' curriculum is:

Alexander, R. J. (1984)
Primary Teaching,
London: Holt, Rinehart & Winston.

Alexander has continued to produce challenging analyses of primary education, see:

Alexander R. J., Wilcocks, J., Kinder, K. and Nelson, N. (1995)
Versions of Primary Education,
London: Routledge.

The basic legislation introducing the National Curriculum into England and Wales is the Education Reform Act 1988 (London: HMSO).

Sir Ron Dearing's report, which established the need for immediate revision and 'slimming down' of the original National Curriculum is:

Dearing, R. (1993)
The National Curriculum and its Assessment: Final Report,
London: SCAA.

SCAA is the key government agency regarding curriculum and assessment. For an overview of its activities, see:

School Curriculum and Assessment Authority (1995)
Annual Report, April 1994–March 1995,
London: SCAA.

Subject-based versus integrated curricular arguments are likely to run and run. For principled and aware accounts of the strengths of integrated work, see:

Blenkin, G. M. and Kelly, A. V. (1981)
The Primary Curriculum,
London: Harper & Row.

Hunter, R. and Scheirer, E. A. (1988)
The Organic Curriculum,
London: Falmer.   📖 Reading, 8.3

For brilliant illustrations of the quality of work which can result, see:

Armstrong, M. (1981)
Closely Observed Children,
London: Writers and Readers.   📖 Reading, 6.10

Much has been made of the use of subject-based curricula and whole-class teaching in France. For empirical evidence on this and on the way it influences teachers' views of their role, see:

Sharpe, K. (1992)
Educational homogeneity in French primary education: a double case study,
British Journal of Sociology of Education,
13, (3) 329–48.

Broadfoot, P., Gilly, M., Osborn, M. and Paillet, A. (1993)
Perceptions of Teaching: Primary School Teachers in England and France,
London: Cassell.

The following are examples of writers who are critical of aspects of child-centred approaches and who offer frameworks in which they can be examined.

Anthony, W. (1979)
Progressive learning theories: the evidence,
In G. Bernbaum (ed.) *Schooling in Decline,*
London: Macmillan.

Bantock, G. H. (1980)
Dilemmas of the Curriculum,
Oxford: Martin Robertson.

The most important recent text on 'child-centred ideology' is the report on primary education in Leeds around which a media panic about primary education was mounted in 1991. See:

Alexander, R. (1992)
Policy and Practice in Primary Education,
London: Routledge.   📖 Readings, 7.10 and 8.8

For a sustained critique of 'traditionalist' views of the curriculum and of many recent developments see:

Kelly, A.V. (1986)
Knowledge and the Curriculum,
London: Harper & Row.

For a modern and incisive philosophical overview, see:

Bonnett, M. (1993)
Thinking and Understanding in the Primary School Curriculum,
London: Cassell.

Perhaps the most coherent account of the policy issues involved in the development of the National Curriculum in England and Wales is:

Ball, S. J. (1990)
Politics and Policy Making in Education: Explorations in Policy,
London: Routledge.

The changes had been prefigured in documents such as:

DES (1980)
A View of the Curriculum,
London: HMSO.

DES (1985b)
Better Schools,
London: HMSO.

DES (1985a)
The Curriculum from 5 to 16,
(HMI discussion document),
London: HMSO.   📖 **Reading, 8.2**

The structure of national curricula varies from country to country. Such differences can be traced in:

Meyer, J. W., Kamens, D. H. and Benavot, A. (1992)
*School Knowledge for the Masses: World Models of National
Primary Curricular Categories in the Twentieth Century,*
London: Falmer.   📖 **Reading, 7.1**

Galton, M. and Blyth, A. (1989)
Handbook of Primary Education in Europe,
London: David Fulton.   📖 see **Reading, 2.6**

For England and Wales, by far the most concise and useful official overview of the National Curriculum is:

SCAA (1996)
A Guide to the National Curriculum,
London: SCAA.

For a simple introduction to the revised curriculum, see:

Pring, R. (1995)
The New Curriculum (2nd edn),
London: Cassell.

There are many views on the way in which learning relates to curriculum, many of which form the basis of critiques of national curriculum structures. For a thoughtful book which includes a stimulating discussion of 'an enabling curriculum' see:

Blyth, W. A. L. (1984)
Development, Experience and Curriculum in Primary Education,
London: Croom Helm.

For an analysis that builds on Blyth's argument and relates it to the early stages of the implementation of the National Curriculum in England, see:

Pollard, A. (1993)
Balancing priorities: children and the curriculum in the nineties.
In J. Campbell (ed.)
Breadth and Balance in the Primary Curriculum,
London: Falmer.

In a rather different approach, the books below represent Egan's sustained attempt to link pupil development, imagination, learning and curriculum:

Egan, K. (1979)
Educational Development,
Oxford: Oxford University Press.

Egan, K. (1991a)
Romantic Understanding,
London: Routledge.

Egan, K. (1991b)
Primary Understanding,
London: Routledge.

See also:

Woods, P. and Jeffrey, B. (1996)
Teachable Moments: The Art of Teaching in Primary Schools,
Buckingham: Open University Press.

A key text regarding subject knowledge is:

Shulman, L. S. (1986)
Those who understand: knowledge and growth in teaching,
Educational Researcher, 15, 4–14.   Reading, 7.13

The importance of teachers' subject knowledge is strongly asserted in:

Alexander, R., Rose, J. and Woodhead, C. (1992)
Curriculum Organization and Classroom
Practice in Primary Schools: A Discussion Paper,
London: DES.

Helpful advice on English, science and maths is available in:

Murphy, P., Selijnger, M., Bourne, J. and Briggs, M. (eds) (1995)
Subject Learning in the Primary Curriculum,
London: Routledge.

For interesting studies which follow up the issue of subject knowledge to consider teacher education and classroom practice respectively, see:

Bennett, S. N. and Carré, C. (eds)(1993)
Learning to Teach,
London: Routledge.

McNamara, D. (1994)
Classroom Pedagogy and Primary Practice,
London: Routledge.

For a wonderful supply of subject ideas and innovation, see the regular flow of practical journals on various subjects for teachers in the UK. For instance:

English in Education (National Association for the Teaching of English)
Language and Learning
Books for Keeps
Mathematics in Schools (Mathematics Association)
Micromath (Association of Teachers of Mathematics)
Teaching Geography (Geographical Association)
Strategies
Teaching History (Historical Association)
Primary Science Review (Association for Science Education)
Teaching Science (School Natural Science Society)
Questions: Exploring Science and Technology
The Big Paper (Design Council)
Computer Education (Computer Users Group)
Music Teacher
Arts Education (National Foundation for Arts Education)
RE Today

Most educational publishers also have useful series of books based on curriculum subjects for primary schools. For instance, in the UK see the catalogues of Cassell, Routledge, Falmer Press, David Fulton, Simon & Schuster, Open University Press, Paul Chapman Publishing, etc.

CHAPTER 8

How are we planning and implementing the curriculum?

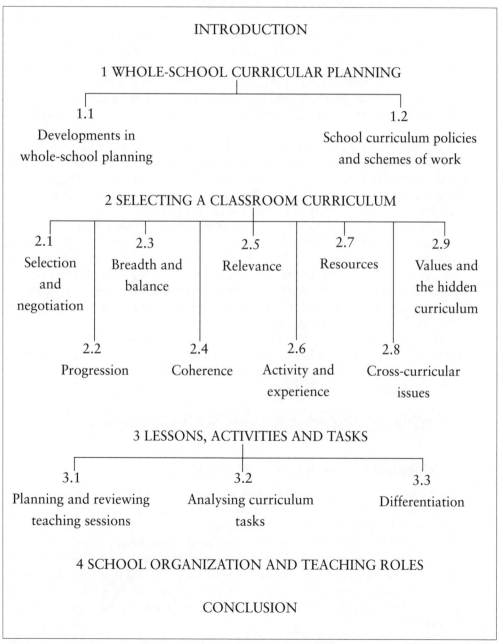

INTRODUCTION

1 WHOLE-SCHOOL CURRICULAR PLANNING

1.1
Developments in
whole-school planning

1.2
School curriculum policies
and schemes of work

2 SELECTING A CLASSROOM CURRICULUM

2.1
Selection
and
negotiation

2.3
Breadth and
balance

2.5
Relevance

2.7
Resources

2.9
Values and
the hidden
curriculum

2.2
Progression

2.4
Coherence

2.6
Activity and
experience

2.8
Cross-curricular
issues

3 LESSONS, ACTIVITIES AND TASKS

3.1
Planning and reviewing
teaching sessions

3.2
Analysing curriculum
tasks

3.3
Differentiation

4 SCHOOL ORGANIZATION AND TEACHING ROLES

CONCLUSION

INTRODUCTION

This chapter has a simple, three-level structure, focusing first on planning and implementing a curriculum for the whole school, then on the curriculum programme of a single class and finally on planning and implementing particular teaching sessions. It thus moves through successive levels of detail, exactly in the way in which a teacher or student teacher must when planning a teaching programme.

Lest this sound overly structured, impersonal and constraining, we must once again affirm the uniquely enriching role of the creativity and imagination of individual teachers in providing high quality, responsive curriculum experiences for the children in their classes (Woods and Jeffrey, 1996). Qualities of experience which may be produced – excitement, surprise, awe, spontaneity, concentration, humour, amazement, curiosity, expression, to name but a few – are enhanced by the dynamic of rapport and interaction between a teacher and his or her class. From the children's point of view, they are often what makes the curriculum 'interesting'.

So, whilst attending to the necessary logic of planning within a national curriculum framework (the *science* of curriculum planning?), we must not lose sight of the unpredictable and uniquely enriching human relationships through which it is manifest (the *art* of teaching?). Chapter 4, on classroom relationships, is very relevant here – as are many other parts of the book.

Reflective teachers are likely to aim to address the structured aspects of curriculum provision carefully, but with a view to this enabling them to interact with the children more empathically and responsively. When it comes to implementation, a *combination* of structure and responsiveness is likely to be most effective (see, for instance, **Reading, 5.2** by Woods). The key judgement, which only the teacher on the spot can make, is what particular combination and form of structure and response is most appropriate.

The chapter concludes with a brief look at the challenges which a broad, entitlement curriculum imposes on the subject expertise of teachers, and at the implications which this could have for school organization and teaching roles.

1   WHOLE-SCHOOL CURRICULAR PLANNING

1.1   Developments in whole-school planning

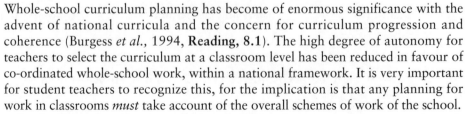

Whole-school curriculum planning has become of enormous significance with the advent of national curricula and the concern for curriculum progression and coherence (Burgess *et al.*, 1994, **Reading, 8.1**). The high degree of autonomy for teachers to select the curriculum at a classroom level has been reduced in favour of co-ordinated whole-school work, within a national framework. It is very important for student teachers to recognize this, for the implication is that any planning for work in classrooms *must* take account of the overall schemes of work of the school.

In the UK, planning at a whole-school level seems to have gone through two phases.

An adaption phase occurred in the early 1990s. When the National Curriculum was new and gradually being set out, there was, necessarily, a considerable amount of pragmatism in the approach of schools. The National Curriculum was initially introduced, it is generally agreed, too fast and in the context of many other changes. It was fragmented, inconsistently presented and subject to controversy at almost every step. The result was an overloaded curriculum and many very exhausted and frustrated teachers (Campbell, 1993; Pollard, 1992). Headteachers acted strategically to try to introduce some order and practical realism into the pace of changes (Wallace 1991, **Reading, 14.4**; Mortimore and Mortimore, 1992). Indeed, one study characterized the key strategy as being that of 'mediation' of the National Curriculum (Croll, 1996). In most cases this meant that existing programmes of work were modified, ordered and codified to accommodate the National Curriculum as it emerged. The Programmes of Study of the National Curriculum were thus grafted on to, and mapped against, existing practices. A common manifestation of this phase was the production of curriculum webs, with each item in the web associated with particular Attainment Targets.

An adoption phase really only become fully possible after 1995 with the availability of the revised National Curriculum as a whole. With a moratorium on further changes until 2000, it is possible for more settled curriculum provision to become established in schools, thus leading to a new phase of whole-school planning. This process starts from the Programmes of Study, as set out in the Statutory Orders for each subject, and judgements are then taken by school staff and governors regarding how the curriculum is to be organized. The School Curriculum and Assessment Authority (1995, **Reading, 8.5**) advises that a key decision concerns the identification of which units of work will be taught in ongoing, subject-specific or cross-subject ways.

1.2 School curriculum policies and schemes of work

Curriculum planning, of whatever sort, is likely to reflect the overall philosophy of the school. Good practice is to tie this in with the process of school development planning (see Chapter 14) and with consultations with school governors, who have legal responsibility for the school curriculum. An initial and structural aspect of policy concerns the basis of curriculum organization in the school as a whole. SCAA have provided very useful advice on curriculum planning across the primary school (SCAA, 1995, **Reading, 8.5**). One of the most important decisions is when to use an integrated or semi-integrated topic-based approach and when to plan by subjects. Indeed, Alexander *et al.*, (1992, **Reading, 8.4**) challenged primary school teams to confront this issue directly.

The next stage will be short *policy statements* on subjects and on other issues, supported by more detailed *schemes of work*. Teacher planning for classroom provision is then selected and elaborated from the school's scheme of work. Finally, there are likely to be procedures for overall *curriculum review* (see Figure 8.1 for a model of these processes; also see Practical Activity 8.1).

Policy statements

Policy statements are intended to act as a simple statement of purpose and framework for action. They need not be long but should be endorsed by school

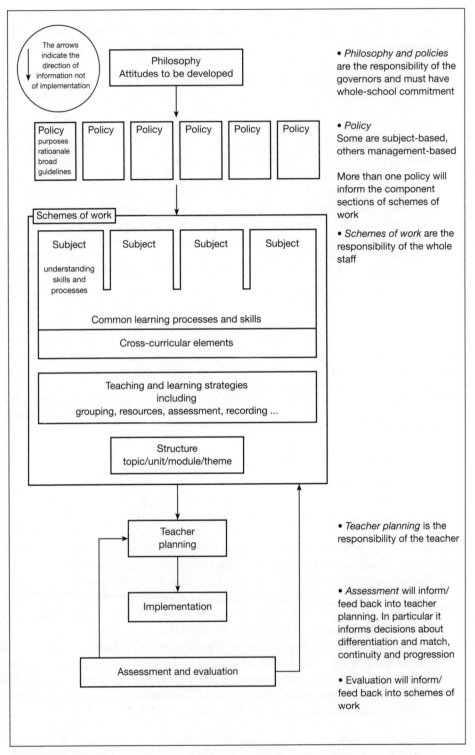

Figure 8.1 *School philosophy, policies, schemes of work and teacher planning* (Avon LEA, 1992)

governors. Obviously they do need to reflect the overall school philosophy. Very often policy statements amount to single A4 sheets with simple, standard headings such as:

Rationale
Purposes
Guidelines

Policy statements provide for an input from governors without involving them in implementation detail.

Schemes of work

Schemes of work should incorporate the Programmes of Study of the National Curriculum but describe how the curriculum should be taught by the staff team of a particular school. Schemes of work may well draw on non-statutory guidelines or other resources. In any event, new curriculum plans and schemes of work should be modified in the light of experience, and should guide teachers in developing their programmes so that continuity and progression through the school is provided.

It is recommended that each scheme of work should address four basic issues:

What do we teach?
To outline knowledge, concepts, skills and attitudes to be developed, links between subjects and cross-curricular elements.

How do we teach?
To cover how the curriculum and learning processes are to be organized, units of work or topics, learning activities and processes, forms of grouping to provide differentiation, resources needed, time allocations and opportunities for assessment.

When do we teach?
To address the issues of curriculum continuity and progression throughout appropriate key stages.

How do we know that children are learning?
Methods and plans for monitoring progress and attainment.

Practical activity 8.1

Aim: To investigate the approach to whole-school curriculum planning in your school.

Method: Insights on this are likely to come from two main sources – documents and discussion. Begin by studying available policy statements, schemes of work and other whole-school curriculum planning documentation. Then ask the headteacher if she or he could talk to you about how whole-school planning has taken the form which it does and how she or he sees it evolving.
    Write a concise summary of the position.

Follow-up: Consider what the implications of the approach to whole-school planning are for you. How does it and will it impact on your plans for classroom teaching?

2 | SELECTING A CLASSROOM CURRICULUM

2.1 Selection and negotiation

Given schemes of work for their school, teachers and student teachers have to make a *selection* of the curriculum which they will actually cover before detailed planning, say for a term or half-term, can begin. This is a key phase in planning and it provides an opportunity for a teacher both to draw on any particular inter·ests or expertise which they have themselves, and to consult with the children in their class. Such consultation with children can lead to what is known as a 'negotiated curriculum'. This is still a curriculum selection but, rather than reflect the judgements of the teacher alone, it builds on the interests and enthusiasms of the class. Obviously, there needs to be clarity in the children's minds about the boundaries of such negotiation and concerning what 'must' be covered in any programme of work (Practical Activity 8.2).

Practical activity 8.2

Aim: To negotiate a classroom curriculum with children.

Method: Do nothing before you are clear in your own mind what you must cover in your programme of work and what areas of activity you can negotiate.

Plan how you are going to explain to the children both the main themes of the curriculum you propose and the constraints they face in making suggestions. Consider how you will elicit and record their ideas, how you will resolve any differences of opinion and how you will act on their views.

Carry out your plan, sharing with, respecting and building on the views of the children. Perhaps you could break this into two phases: eliciting their views and, when you have had time to consider, feeding back a proposal which incorporates their ideas.

Follow-up: Children very rarely fail to rise to the occasion if they are treated seriously. The motivational benefits of such an exercise are considerable. Even so, this is a session which has some risks if it is not carried out with skill and confidence. It would therefore be wise to monitor the reactions of the children and to be prepared to act to settle things down if necessary.

However a classroom programme of work is produced, it will be specific to the teacher and the class and will reflect teacher judgement in the selection of content, activities, teaching strategies and resources and in the balance and sequencing of activities over time. There should also be provision for short-term review and adjustment.

In recent years a degree of consensus has emerged about major issues which should be considered in making judgements about a programme of classroom curriculum work. These originated in some early work by HMI (DES, 1985a, **Reading, 8.2**). Some have been heavily promoted in the UK by the government:

Progression
Breadth and balance
Coherence

Others remain very significant in the judgement of many teachers, but have been less prominent in official documents:

Relevance
Activity and experience
Resources
Cross-curricular issues
Values and the hidden curriculum

We will discuss the selection and organization of a classroom curriculum around each of these concerns.

2.2 Progression

The concept of 'progression' highlights the intended, cumulative outcomes which a planned curriculum is expected to produce: the expectation is that children should make progress in their learning, should build on and integrate their knowledge so that they deepen their understanding and skills.

The sequencing of tasks within the curriculum raises several issues depending, as we saw in Chapter 7, on our view of knowledge and our view of how children learn. At a classroom level, it is possible to be more specific and more flexibly responsive to the evolving understanding of the children we teach. Nevertheless, careful planning is still needed. There are three commonly used techniques for sequencing; the topic web, the flow chart and the curriculum matrix. We illustrate each below.

The topic web

A common practice in primary schools is for teachers to produce a 'topic web' which illustrates ideas and activities to be developed and which can be related to National Curriculum Attainment Targets. This serves as a resource to inform the progression of work during the coming weeks. An elaboration of this is to map out an extended web, which distinguishes between the concepts, knowledge, skills and attitudes that might develop (see Figure 8.2).

The flow chart

Flow charts are a form of constantly evolving planning and recording technique. They can be updated throughout the lifetime of the project. This provides both a record showing the activities anticipated by the teacher and the children's actual activities (see Figure 8.3). Although the whole point is that the teacher does not entirely predetermine the activities, it is important both to ensure National Curriculum coverage and to anticipate other possible avenues for investigation. This is necessary both to prepare resources and because some children are not always sure what they want to do next. Others may tend to opt for the same kinds of activities and sometimes need to be guided into other areas so that their experiences are broadened.

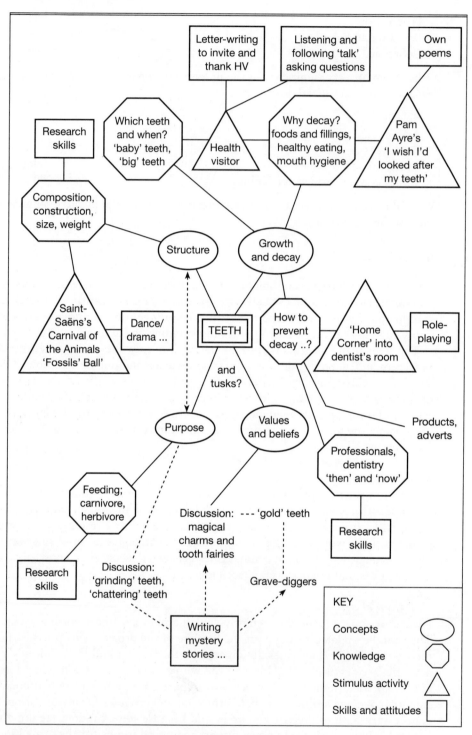

Figure 8.2 *A topic web recording opportunities for developing knowledge, concepts, skills and attitudes. Age: 7–8 years. Focus: teeth*

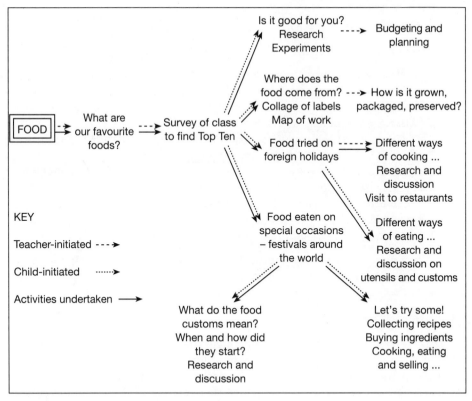

Figure 8.3 *A flow chart recording the development of a class project. Age: 9–10. Focus: Food*

The curriculum matrix

Curriculum matrices are perhaps the 'tightest' form of overall curriculum planning and have a particular advantage of enabling direct consideration of both progression in particular subjects and coherence across them. However, the systematic appearance of such a matrix can sometimes provide a poor representation of the reality of provision, particularly where there are overlaps and connections between subjects.

An illustration of the layout of a subject-based curriculum matrix (to be enlarged and completed for a period of half a term), is provided in Figure 8.4. Practical Activity 8.3 suggests trying out one of these planning methods. It is an important activity, but one which is perhaps best seen as having a provisional and evolving outcome. Indeed, it could be repeated after consideration of each of the issues discussed in this chapter, and it should certainly be refined in the light of the children's responses when curriculum planning is actually implemented. Careful planning is always necessary, but it must also be dynamic and responsive.

Practical activity 8.3

Aim: To make a record to show an intended sequence of tasks.

Method: Plan a curriculum programme for a group or class for which you are responsible, using a topic web, a flow diagram or a curriculum matrix – or develop your own approach. Identify possible tasks and activities, experiment with their scheduling, arrive at your first draft plan.

Think about the way in which your selection should provide for progression in the children's experiences and understanding.

Consider the extent to which the curriculum you have selected will be coherent and meaningful to the children.

Identify the elements of your proposed curriculum which are likely to be seen as highlights by the children. Do they come at appropriate places?

Revise your curriculum programme as necessary.

Follow-up: Could your approach be refined to extend its usefulness as a tool of analysis as well as of planning?

2.3 Breadth and balance

As we saw in Chapter 7, the requirement that the curriculum in the UK should be broad and balanced is set out in the Education Reform Act 1988. This can be interpreted in its widest sense, with reference to 'spiritual, moral, cultural, mental and physical development' and preparing pupils for 'the opportunities, responsibilities and experiences of adult life'. In other words, breadth and balance cannot be simply reduced to a concern about the provision of specified subject matter. This is important, for the requirement for breadth and balance addresses a more holistic question about educational provision, to which the curriculum contributes.

	English	Maths	Science	History	Geography	Technology	Information Technology	Art	Music	PE	RE
Week 1											
Week 2											
Week 3											
Week 4											
Week 5											
Week 6											

Figure 8.4 *A subject-based curriculum matrix*

If you consider the curriculum which you are planning to provide for your class, how broad and balanced does it seem as a learning experience? This is a hard question to answer in the abstract and without the insights of others. Practical Activity 8.4 suggests how to get some help.

Practical activity 8.4

Aim: To consider the breadth and balance of planned curriculum experiences.

Method: Share your curriculum topic web, flow diagram or matrix with a small group of colleagues. Discuss, in turn, the knowledge and experiences which each planned curriculum will provide. Seen as a whole and in conjunction with other, whole-school activities, how does each relate to spiritual, moral, cultural, mental and physical development? To what extent does classroom and school provision prepare pupils for the opportunities, responsibilities and experiences of adult life?

Follow-up: What have you discovered about your planned curriculum? How useful is thinking about children's learning experiences as a whole? What implications may there be there for future curriculum planning?

Gathering actual evidence on curriculum provision is also often revealing and one of the most powerful ways of doing so is to track the experience of a single child. This data on the 'observed curriculum' will bring us far greater awareness of the 'curriculum-as-experienced' than any amount of careful planning can do (Practical Activity 8.5).

Practical activity 8.5

Aim: To evaluate an individual child's curricular experiences over one day or week.

Method: Identify a child for detailed observation. Note down each activity in which he or she engages during this period.

Follow-up: What kind of breadth and balance exists in the observed curriculum of your target child? Is any action or curriculum adjustment necessary?

2.4 Coherence

Coherence refers to the extent to which the various parts of a planned curriculum actually relate meaningfully together. The opposite would be fragmentation.

Clearly this is an important issue if we conceive of learning as a process of 'making sense' (Bruner and Haste, 1987), for that process calls for understanding at overall levels as well as in more detail. Indeed, Gestalt psychologists such as Kohler and Lewin established the enormous significance which developing an overarching understanding and frame of reference has on learning.

Coherence is often sought across subjects and this, of course, is the prime goal of integrating curricula in meaningful ways (see Chapter 7, section 1.3). However, coherence is also necessary, and is not assured, within *single* subjects. In this respect, it is likely to be associated with the extent of subject confidence and expertise of the teacher. Where teacher knowledge and competence is weak, the provision of coherent learning experiences will almost certainly be more difficult.

Coherence is only partially amenable to planning, for it derives its force from the sense, or otherwise, which the children make of the curriculum which is provided. Thus, whilst consideration of the issue at the planning stage is obviously important, Practical Activity 8.6 focuses on the actual *reception* of the curriculum by children. Some research has shown that people tend to enjoy and value learning more when they understand it as a whole. Rather than experience anxiety, overload or bewilderment, they feel more in control and are more willing to think independently and take risks. Whilst feelings of incoherence can lead to feelings of frustration and strategies such as withdrawal, coherence leads to satisfaction and engagement.

Practical activity 8.6

Aim: To investigate the coherence which a planned curriculum has for children.

Method: The technique of concept mapping is ideal for gathering data on this issue (see Chapter 12, section 3.4). You will have to focus the children's thoughts on a small area of the curriculum on which you have worked with your class or group. When they have identified the content, pay particular attention to the connections which they draw, or fail to draw, between the parts. Discuss this with them.

Follow-up: To what extent do you feel curriculum coherence was reflected in the attitudes and learning strategies of the children?

2.5 Relevance

Another important issue in the selection of content is 'relevance'. The term was prominent in the influential discussion paper of HMI (DES,1985a, **Reading, 8.2**) in which it was used to emphasize the importance of the curriculum making connections, in meaningful ways, with children's previous experiences. In a way then, it has resonances with child-centred ideas and this is, perhaps, why it was derided by some right-wing groups (Hillgate Group, 1986) and was absent from government documentation in the early 1990s. However, this is clearly misguided for there is no doubt whatsoever that children learn most effectively when they understand the purposes and context of the tasks and challenges with which they are faced (see also Chapter 6, section 2.4 on motivation). Of course, relevance also refers to that which is 'useful' and has an instrumental, practical function. It can be used in a short-term or a long-term context. However it is used, it relates to meaningfulness and worthwhileness, from the learner's point of view.

When a child complains that an activity is 'pointless', is 'boring' or that they 'don't see what it's for', then the curriculum is failing to satisfy the criterion of relevance. Motivation may fall and with it may go concentration, commitment and quality. The standard of work is thus likely to decrease unless the teacher can justify the activity and bolster motivation. Indeed, even when an activity could have great relevance, this may not have been explained to or appreciated by the children. One long-running finding regarding teaching is that, very often, children do not know why they are doing an activity (Practical Activity 8.7).

Practical activity 8.7

Aim: To investigate the perceived relevance of a classroom programme of work.

Method: The simple method here is to ask the children. If they are capable enough to write, this might be done individually – ask them, say, to write about what they think about working on the particular topic of study. Analyse their writing to see how meaningful they found the topic and how they valued it. Alternatively, explore similar issues through discussions.

Follow-up: Review what you have learned about the children's views. Does this relate to their concentration and to the standard of the work which they are producing or have produced? What are the implications for the future?

2.6   Activity and experience

The value of activity and firsthand experience has been taken to lie in the opportunity it provides for children to interact directly with learning apparatus, real materials and events. Indeed, the very title of this section has a resonance with one of the most famous passages from the Hadow Report of 1931, that 'the curriculum should be thought of in terms of activity and experience rather than as knowledge to be acquired and facts to be stored' (Board of Education, 1931, p. 93, **Reading, 7.5**). As we saw in Chapter 6, such an emphasis is again founded on psychology and on a view of learning as the product of interaction between teaching and experience. For instance, in infant classes an enormous amount of language, mathematics, art and science development can be derived from children's play in media such as sand, water and clay. Older children benefit from more structured direct experiences, such as carrying out 'fair tests' and experiments in science, field work in geography and investigation of artefacts in history (see Hunter and Scheirer, 1988, **Reading, 8.3**).

Use of the children's immediate environment for providing experiences is practical but may need monitoring, for it has been suggested that overdependence on the locality might result in limiting the children to that environment and thus in creating a rather parochial curriculum. On the other hand, it can be argued that children may be able to relate meaningfully to an environment with which they can identify. They can be helped to examine it more closely, to value what they have around them and then be helped to move from the familiar to the unfamiliar.

In any event, the incorporation of activity and direct experience, in proportions and ways which are appropriate to the age of the children, is an essential part of any curriculum provision. If this is ever doubted, try asking the children. One of the most consistent findings in pupil interviews is the liking for 'doing something interesting', which usually means engaging their imagination in some way.

Practical Activity 8.7 suggests doing this for a whole programme of work, but it is just as telling an exercise for a shorter time period, say a day.

Practical activity 8.8

Aim: To review a curriculum plan to analyse the extent of activity and direct experience provided for pupils.

Method: Consider again the curriculum plan which you produced for Practical Activity 8.3. Annotate it to show where children are likely to be most active and obtain direct experience of the topics to be covered.

Follow-up: Review your provision. Is any adjustment appropriate?

2.7 Resources

Resources, in the form of equipment, apparatus, artefacts and media, are a means of deepening, enriching and broadening the curriculum through providing first-hand experiences. For example, artefacts can be brought into the classroom, or children can be taken out on visits. In addition, radio and television can play a role in providing vicarious firsthand experience. This at least allows each child to see and to experience indirectly other environments. In planning a classroom curriculum, then, some attention should be paid to the practical resource implications. Sometimes this requires prior booking, expenditure or preparation and advanced planning is therefore advisable (Practical Activity 8.8).

All resources call for particular skills from children if they are to be used successfully to develop learning. For example, children need to learn how to listen actively to explanations, to look carefully at objects or television, to read books actively and to set up experiments so that they can 'make knowledge their own' and develop strategies for learning. Different resources have particular implications for the curriculum-as-experienced and for the skills, attitudes, knowledge and concepts which are likely to be developed through them. Resources should thus be seen to support a curriculum rather than as a means by which it is selected (see Clegg and Billington 1994, **Reading, 9.5**; Practical Activity 8.9).

Practical activity 8.9

Aim: To consider the resource implications of a planned curriculum programme.

Method: Review the planned curriculum which you developed through Practical Activity 8.8. Make a list, such as the one below, of the resources which are required, and of any preparation or booking which is needed.

Curriculum topics and activities to be covered	Resources available within school	Resources to be made and prepared	Resources to be borrowed or collected

Follow-up: Use your list to check off the necessary jobs as you do them.

2.8 Cross-curricular issues

There are an enormous number of cross-curricular issues which could provide a focus for teacher reflection and provision. For instance, the topic takes us directly back to the debate about the value of focusing a curriculum on transferable skills and attitudes – a 'process-oriented' curriculum. In terms of national curricula, such cross-curricular potential is often narrowed. For example, in England, 'cross-curricular elements' were prominent in the 1989 version of the National Curriculum in terms of 'dimensions' (such as equal opportunities), 'skills' (such as communication, problem-solving, information technology) and 'themes' (such as health education, citizenship, economic and industrial understanding and environmental education).

To take one 'theme' as an example, the National Curriculum Council claimed that 'education for economic and industrial understanding makes an important contribution to the personal and social development of pupils' and will 'prepare them for their future economic roles as producers, consumers and citizens in a democracy' (NCC, 1990b, p.1). NCC, with the help of the Department of Trade and Industry (NCC, 1991), provided copious examples of how the theme can be fed into and derived from work in foundation subjects. Thus, a sample topic for Key Stage 1 (NCC, 1990a) included reading a story about shopping, discussion of shopping, a survey of and visit to local shops, art work, map making and graph-work on local shops, visits to school by shopworkers and descriptive writing on the theme of shops. Links with subjects of the National Curriculum are explicated at each point.

Such work has exciting potential, for children are very often interested by cross-curricular themes (see, for example, Siraj-Blatchford and Siraj-Blatchford, 1995; Webb, 1996). Indeed, this has been the foundation of 'topic work' approaches. To continue with our example, children are interested by and have all sorts of ideas about the world of work which are worth extending (Blatchford, 1992). However, there are problems as well as possibilities in such work (Holden and Smith, 1992) particularly if inappropriate concerns are imposed on the education of young children and if the necessity of covering cross-curricular themes produces an impractical and overcrowded curriculum (Campbell, 1992; Practical Activity 8.10).

> ### Practical activity 8.10
>
> *Aim*: To enquire into the teaching of cross-curricular themes in your school.
>
> *Method*: Ask a teacher if they will explain to you, frankly, about their class-room work on each of the cross-curricular themes for your country. Make notes.
>
> Consider, in the context of the whole-school curriculum planning framework, the strategies which the teacher has used – incorporating, avoiding, focusing, skimming...?
>
> *Follow-up*: What approach to cross-curricular themes will you adopt in your future plans?

2.9 Values and the hidden curriculum

At a very simple level, values may be reflected in the selection of curriculum content and resources. For example, the way in which a local environment is used in a programme of work could convey teacher attitudes towards the value of children's environment. The artefacts, visits, programmes or books which are selected may also indicate to children that certain things are legitimate objects of learning whereas others are not. For many years, attention has been drawn to the books used in school with regard to the implicit values that they contain. Thus analyses of the illustrations of children's reading schemes used to show considerable sex, class and ethnic stereotyping: the girls help Mummy in the kitchen, the boys help Daddy wash the car, they mostly live in neat detached houses and the characters are predominantly white (Lobban, 1975). History books have often been found to be highly Anglophile and some geography books may give an impression of non-European countries as poor and the inhabitants as simple peasants. Few references may be made to the development of their economies, the sophistication of their cultures, the impact of interaction between different civilizations or, indeed, to the fact that European countries may have their own economic problems. Practical Activity 8.11 suggests that you investigate this yourself. Whilst the difficulties in finding appropriate resources are diminishing as publishers address such problems, in England and Wales the issue is not helped by the relative insularity of some National Curriculum orders. Certainly those for history and geography generated fierce debate, as did requirements for promoting standard English.

A second way in which values may be conveyed is through the interaction and language which are associated with teaching and learning processes. This is a particular focus of Chapter 13. However, we may note here that the work of post-structuralist researchers provides an unusually sophisticated analysis of such processes. For them, rather than discrimination or social differentiation being overt, they are embedded in the very structure of social relations as classroom events are played out and are integral elements of classroom discourse (see, for instance, Davies, 1993, **Reading 11.5**; and Epstein, 1993, **Reading 13.5**).

Practical activity 8.11

Aim: To identify the aspects of the hidden curriculum in a selection of books for use in a primary school.

Method: Select a number of books which you might use to support a series of planned lessons (or a number of texts in your own specialist subject). Analyse the illustrations and then the text in terms of the values which are implicitly, and explicitly, conveyed. You might wish to identify values which relate to gender, class, ethnicity, religion or disability.

Follow-up: What conclusions can you draw about the hidden curriculum as evidenced in these books? How would you use such books? What could a reflective teacher do about any particular bias in books?

In summary, then, the major task in planning and reviewing any course of class-room study is to identify, select and justify the curriculum which is actually provided. Much of this can be done at the planning stage; some of it requires continuous review during the process of implementation. The reflective teacher must take account of:

Whole-school policies and schemes of work
Progression
Breadth and balance
Coherence
Relevance
Activity and experience
Resources
Cross-curricular issues
Values and the hidden curriculum

This is far from easy, but the most important thing for a reflective teacher is to be aware of the issues, to accept the difficulties and to work progressively and constructively to develop their competence at curriculum planning, as suggested by the cyclical model in Chapter 1.

Of course, there is another important level of planning too, that of each actual lesson, task or activity, and this is the focus of the next major part of this chapter.

3   LESSONS, ACTIVITIES AND TASKS

3.1   Planning and reviewing teaching sessions

Classroom learning sessions are central activities for teachers and learners. They have to be planned carefully and put into action sensitively and skilfully. Reflective teachers are likely to have already considered their general aims and curriculum plans in the light of the National Curriculum, school schemes of work and their classroom organizational strategies. They may also have been able to review their overall curriculum plan in the light of experience and have some formative assessment information about their children so that specific objectives can be identified. Against this background, a particular learning session can be planned effectively.

Of course, such plans provide a teacher with structure and security and it should not be forgotten that the resulting confidence can be used to be responsive to the children during the session. Good planning underpins flexibility (Practical Activity 8.12).

The classic approach to planning a learning session is that a number of questions need to be considered:

Context
1. What are the present capabilities and knowledge of the children?
2. How and when will planning be done by a teacher before the session; with a group/whole-class at the start of a session?
3. Are there any constraints imposed by simultaneous demands from other teachers or events (e.g. timetabling of hall)?
4. With which audiences will the learning be shared: a teacher, other adults, the class, the school during Assembly, or parents at an 'open evening'?

Objectives
What are the specific objectives, in terms of learning elements (skills, attitudes, concepts and knowledge in relation to the National Curriculum) and learning domains (intellectual, social, moral, physical–motor and aesthetic)?

Action
1. What learning opportunities will be provided for the selected objectives to be developed?
2. What organizational strategies will be required in terms of people, time, space and resources?
3. How will the session start, develop and end?
4. What will the teacher be doing at each of these stages and what range of things will the children be doing?

Assessment of learning
1. How will the progress of the children be monitored, assessed and recorded?
2. How will such information be analysed and used?

Evaluation of teaching
1. How will the quality of the session be evaluated?
2. How will such information be analysed and used?

Having analysed one learning session in this way, it is of course important to review it in the context of other sessions so that the links between them can be considered. A somewhat daunting check-list might include:

- appropriate curricular breadth and coverage of the scheme of work
- appropriate levels and types of task demand
- appropriate quality of experiences and activities
- appropriate task differentiation

- appropriate curriculum progression
- appropriate curriculum coherence
- appropriate classroom organization
- appropriate language (including the needs of bilingual children)

Needless to say, all these checks require the application of reflective, professional judgements to decide what is, and is not, 'appropriate'. Perhaps such a review will support consideration of the ways in which good planning and preparation before a teaching session underpin flexibility and responsiveness to the children during learning activities. Certainly, as Calderhead (1984, **Reading, 8.6**) makes clear, the realities of planning by experienced teachers are more intuitive than the structured approach outlined above.

Practical activity 8.12

Aim: To manage a learning session, through consideration of context, objectives, action, assessment of learning and evaluation of teaching

Method:

1. Prepare responses to the first three sections listed below. In this way you should be able to produce an outline sketch of what will happen during the session.

   CONTEXT...

   OBJECTIVES...

   ACTION...

2. Teach the session. Keep some notes or some examples of children's work to refer to later.

3. Now use your evidence and your judgement to assess the children's learning and to evaluate the quality of your teaching. Refer back to the objectives you set.

   ASSESSMENT OF LEARNING ...

   EVALUATION OF TEACHING ...

Follow-up: This process should help you to anticipate potential management problems so that you can avoid many of them. By being prepared you will be more likely to be able to encourage and extend the children's learning by appropriate questioning and explaining. With the careful assessment and evaluation which is suggested, it should also be possible to diagnose difficulties and spot opportunities for both pupil and personal development.

3.2 Analysing curriculum tasks

So far we have focused on the overall issues of structure and content in the curriculum. More detailed analysis is sometimes valuable to identify the various learning elements contained within the tasks set by teachers or initiated by children. This is a particularly useful in planning and monitoring a sequence of teaching–learning experiences.

First it is necessary to decide how we wish to analyse learning experiences. One common way of doing this is to distinguish between knowledge, concepts, skills and attitudes – all of which may be considered as 'elements of learning' across the whole curriculum:

Knowledge: selections of that which is worth knowing and of interest.

Concepts: generalizations which enable pupils to classify, organize and predict – to understand patterns, relationships and meanings, e.g. continuity/change, cause/consequence, interdependence/adaptation, sequence/duration, nature/purpose, authenticity, power, energy.

Skills: the capacity or competence to perform a task, e.g. personal/social (turn-taking, sharing), physical/practical (fine/gross motor skills), intellectual (observing, identifying, sorting /classifying, hypothesizing, reasoning, testing, imagining and evaluating), communication (oracy, literacy, numeracy, graphicacy), etc.

Attitudes: the overt expression of values and personal qualities, e.g. curiosity, perseverance, initiative, open-mindedness, trust, honesty, responsibility, respect, confidence, etc.

The items listed above provide a very useful analytic framework but they are not without problems. In particular, the concept of a 'skill' has some ambiguities of meaning. First, it can be used in the sense of analysis of the component skills of a task. Skill analysis can thus provide a way of diagnosing difficulties and can assist in planning new learning provision. In such instances, the word 'skill' is associated with the mechanistic breakdown of activities into the basic components which are believed to contribute to mastery. On the other hand, the concept of 'skills' is also used to denote key elements in learning to learn, attributes which are heralded as being flexible and transferable rather than specific and mechanistic. In this context it is argued that skills are especially useful in a time of rapid change when particular knowledge may rapidly become obsolete. This sense of the term is used to encourage a consideration of what are considered as key elements in learning to learn, indeed, in meta-cognition (see Chapter 6, section 2.5).

The attempt to define 'attitudes' and to distinguish them from 'skills' has raised further conceptual issues. This is particularly evident when considering social skills and attitudes. For example, what is the relationship between social behaviour and attitudes? Does it require skill to be able to behave in a chosen way?

There is also an important relationship between attitudes and intellectual skills, for learners are likely to have feelings and attitudes towards what they are trying to learn. A reflective teacher may therefore want to ask to what extent positive attitudes can foster intellectual development and to consider the role which motivation might play in learning (see Chapter 6, section 2.4, and **Readings** such as 6.7, 10.2 and 10.3).

Despite these complexities, the analytic power of the distinction between skills, attitudes, knowledge and concepts is very useful in gauging what it is that we are actually asking children to do when we present them with new challenges (see Practical Activity 8.13).

Practical activity 8.13

Aim: To identify and select knowledge, concepts, skills and attitudes in planned teaching sessions.

Method: First, identify an intended teaching group and a series of teaching sessions. Select an appropriate curriculum topic, such as subtraction, or road safety, and list the knowledge, concepts, skills and attitudes which you aim to develop.

Then, using a grid similar to the one below, fill in the activities session by session, so that you can plan what opportunities for which elements of learning will occur.

	Knowledge	Concepts	Skills	Attitudes
Session 1				
Session 2				
Session 3				
Session 4, etc.				

Follow-up: How easy was it to identify and select elements in the four categories? Was it easier to think of an activity and then analyse it? How might this approach be refined to improve its usefulness as a tool of planning and analysis? What relationship between knowledge, concepts, skills and attitudes did you arrive at?

The purpose of analysing activities in this way is threefold. In the first place, it allows us to examine the breadth and balance of the provision we are planning, across the curriculum as well as in terms of subjects. Second, it encourages us to think more precisely about what we are trying to do. This should help to guide us in the questions we pose to the children. Third, it provides a detailed framework which we can use to monitor the children's learning. The overall framework, from which we might select different items on different occasions, provides a fine-grain analysis of tasks and assists us in enacting the reflective cycle which was described in Chapter 1.

3.3 Differentiation

The concept of differentiation highlights the nature of the demands which a curriculum or an activity makes of the learner. Awareness of differentiation should help teachers to match tasks and children as appropriately as possible, in the expectation that greater progress will be achieved.

Differentiation can be seen at a general or specific level. At a general level it relates to the appropriateness or otherwise for children with particular needs. Thus, for instance, the needs of young children are significantly different from those of older pupils and, where 4 year-olds are have been admitted to primary schools, their whole curriculum must be planned with this in mind (DES, 1990a; Hurst, 1992; Anning, 1995). Similarly, the needs of children with special educational needs, or those who are deemed 'gifted', are very significant. Delivering a full National Curriculum in some circumstances is extremely difficult (Jones and Charlton, 1992) and it may be necessary to 'disapply' parts of the curriculum where they are inappropriate.

At a more specific level, differentiation relates to the appropriateness, or otherwise, of particular tasks and activities. In investigating this match between pupil and learning task, four stages of analysis are implied:

1. Understanding the perceptions and intentions of the teacher and the child.
2. Identifying the child's existing knowledge, concepts, skills and attitudes.
3. Observing the process by which the task is tackled.
4. Analysing and evaluating the product, or final outcome, of the task, so that future plans can be made.

A mismatch could occur at any (or all) of the stages. To take an example at the first stage, a teacher could set a task for a particular purpose, but, if it were not explained adequately then the child might misunderstand. Any task might be done 'wrongly', or it may be done 'blindly' i.e. without seeing the point of it.

There could also be a mismatch at the second stage. The task may be too hard for a child because it requires certain knowledge or skill which the child does not have.

A mismatch at the third stage can be illustrated by a task which may be set with an instruction to use certain apparatus, or to present the outcome in a certain way. However, the apparatus may not be necessary and may actually confuse the child, or the style of presentation may assume some skill which the child has not yet acquired.

Additional problems could also arise from a mismatch at the fourth stage. For instance, teachers often 'mark' the end-product of children's learning. However, a high percentage of 'errors' cannot necessarily be assumed to relate to 'bad' work or 'poor' learning. Indeed, the 'errors' can be very important clues as to the learning that has taken place. In this respect they can be regarded as 'miscues' which indicate where misunderstandings may have occurred.

On the other hand, miscues can themselves be misinterpreted. For instance, an absence of miscues could be taken to indicate a good cognitive match, but it could also hide the fact that the task was too easy and that no cognitive learning had taken place. This could have resulted in two contrasting affective outcomes: either that the children had gained in confidence in their abilities, or that they had become bored. Conversely, the existence of many miscues might be interpreted as a poor match where the task had been too hard and thereby frustrating. However, a large number of miscues could also indicate that the task had been too easy, uninteresting or unchallenging, and that the children either had not followed the instructions or had not wanted to be bothered with it.

Many opportunities thus exist where mismatch can occur and conflicting interpretations are possible. For these reasons, monitoring learning processes carefully requires both observation, analysing information and judgement. Nevertheless, it is a powerful way in which a reflective teacher can gain a better understanding of the learning experiences of the children.

A research report based on interview, observation and testing in infant schools has demonstrated the value of such a detailed monitoring procedure (Bennett *et al.*, 1984). The researchers distinguished between five types of task demands:

1. *Incremental.* Introduces new ideas/procedures/skills which are acquired during a task.
2. *Restructuring.* Requires children to invent/discover for themselves, thus learning is advanced.
3. *Enrichment.* By using familiar ideas/procedures/skills on new problems, learning is applied.
4. *Practice.* This reinforces ideas/procedures/skills which are assumed to be already known.
5. *Revision.* This reactivates ideas/procedures/skills which have not been used for some time.

The study found that 60 per cent of tasks set in Language and Maths were intended as short-term practice, 25 per cent were 'incremental', 6 per cent were enrichment, 6 per cent were intended as long-term revision and only 1 per cent were intended as restructuring.

The very high figure of tasks set for practice needs to be considered carefully. What were these children learning, cognitively or affectively? Practice tasks may be useful in confirming knowledge or skills, but one would have to consider at what point might such tasks cease to increase confidence but cause frustration? Interestingly, the percentage of practice tasks was even higher when examined in terms of how the tasks were perceived and performed by the children. This was particularly so for high ability children, who were often set tasks intended as incremental or enrichment, but which, in fact, involved yet more practice. Three reasons were suggested for this: that the children were already familiar with the knowledge or skills demanded by the tasks, that tasks were not well planned to meet the teacher's aims and that tasks were not clearly explained with the result that children misunderstood them.

In describing each of these types of task, a reflective teacher should consider that tasks of each type are probably necessary if learning is to develop positively and surely. As we saw in Chapter 6 and Chapter 7, section 2.4, increases in learning do not necessarily occur in a smooth, ever-upward fashion. If learning develops in somewhat unpredictable developments of insight and understanding then occasional plateaux may also be experienced and needed (Practical Activity 8.14).

Practical activity 8.14

Aim: To examine tasks in terms of their learning demands.

Method: Analyse the demands of each task set during the day by using the grid below.

TASK TYPE

Incremental	Restructuring	Enrichment	Practice	Revision
(new skills acquired in task)	(known skills advanced in task)	(known skills applied in task)	(known skills assumed in task)	(known skills reactivated in task)

TASK NO.

1

2

3

4

5

Having analysed the tasks, then ask the children for their views (using terms which they would recognize) as to which kind of tasks they thought they were doing.

Follow-up: From this evidence, what can you deduce about the match or mismatch in the classroom? Can you identify the reasons for it? What can you do about it?

A reflective teacher needs to monitor the match closely to try to ensure the best balance between boredom with too easy tasks, frustration with tasks that are too hard, comfort from consolidation tasks and excitement from a task that is challenging but not too daunting.

4 | SCHOOL ORGANIZATION AND TEACHING ROLES

The established image of the primary school classroom is that of the teacher working, across the whole curriculum, with her class. It is only amongst the 'prep schools' of the private sector and at the top end of the junior school that significant amounts of timetabling to take advantage of the subject expertise of particular teachers is to be found. Most primary school teachers have, therefore, expectations of acting as 'generalists' and of working with their class on a close and continuous basis. The strength of this is the closeness of teacher–pupil relationships which can develop. This provides security for pupils and enables the teacher to get to know them holistically, as people, and to make curricular provision accordingly.

However, the increasing emphasis on the importance of subject knowledge in recent years, culminating in the National Curriculum, has posed very significant problems for generalist teachers, particularly in Key Stage 2 (Webb and Vulliamy, 1996). Indeed, the curriculum is so detailed and so broad that it is almost impossible to conceive of any one person being capable of doing justice to all of it. The problem is compounded by the mixed year groups which make up many primary school classes. This phenomenon is caused by the size of school intakes and will exist whenever the enrolment is other than a neat and tidy whole class for each school year – in other words, in *most* primary schools. In small schools, despite accumulative advantages of relationships and knowledge of pupils (Bell and Sigsworth, 1987) the curriculum delivery problems may be particularly acute.

In response to this insistent problem, the possibility of using teachers who have particular subject expertise more imaginatively within primary schools has been advocated more and more in recent years (e.g. House of Commons, 1986). Such teachers, it was suggested, could add a consultancy role to their generalist responsibilities and thus help to develop curricular provision in their identified area. They would offer advice and give support to colleagues. Such generalist-consultants might be able to develop greater continuity of curriculum experiences and ensure progression throughout the school (Campbell, 1985).

This consultancy model has proved to be quite difficult to implement in practice, for there are problems both in the availability of appropriate staff in schools and in the inadequate amounts of non-contact time available to primary school teachers to support each other. For such reasons, Alexander *et al.*, (1992, para. 141) asserted that staff deployment in primary schools needs to be re-examined and that two principles should be applied. First,

> every primary school, regardless of size, needs access to subject knowledge in all nine National Curriculum subjects and religious education.

> this expertise needs to inform curriculum planning and teaching, directly and meaningfully, for every year group, class and pupil.

In addition to the role of generalist and generalist-consultants, Alexander *et al.*, suggested that both specialist and semi-specialist roles need to be considered. Elsewhere, Alexander has argued that we may eventually see an 'end of the classteacher system' (1992, **Reading, 8.8**). There is, as they say, no simple answer and schools will have to work out their particular combination in the light of their own circumstances.

Beyond teacher roles, there is also a trend towards reconsidering class arrangements in the upper end of Key Stage 2. Types of 'setting', and 'targeting' are increasingly used to group pupils by attainment for particular subjects (this is often termed 'ability grouping' – a term which unfortunately implies an absolute capacity; see Chapter 6, section 2.1). Of course, this constitutes a form of social differentiation (see Chapter 13, **Reading, 13.8**) as well as academic differentiation and could have unfortunate social consequences. However, there is awareness of the divisive effects of the fixed 'streaming' systems which were common in the 1950s and 1960s (Jackson, 1964, **Reading, 8.9**).

Nevertheless, the form of primary school organization and teaching roles is likely to be a continuing area of change and development. More use may be made of non-teaching classroom assistants (Audit Commission, 1991), there may be more clustering of small schools for curriculum delivery, there may be more use of subject specialists within schools and new forms of school organization. Reflective teachers can play a role here in contributing to discussion of an almost intractable set of dilemmas. In the end, judgements will have to be made about what is best for the particular school (Practical Activity 8.15)

Practical activity 8.15

Aim: To consider possible forms of organization and staff deployment in a primary school.

Method: It is essential to think about a real school for this activity, since the dilemmas and problems emerge when confronting realities. However, it should be done sensitively and preferably with the help of a senior teacher who can advise.

First, gather some basic information about the school:

- The number on roll and their distribution among year groups.

- The number of teaching staff, their curriculum expertise and age-phase strengths.

- The present school organization and staff deployment.

Second, consider the two principles suggested by Alexander *et al.*, (1992)

That every primary school, regardless of size, needs access to subject knowledge in all ten national curriculum subjects and religious education.

That this expertise needs to inform curriculum planning and teaching, directly and meaningfully, for every year group, class and pupil.

To what extent do you feel the two principles are achieved at present?

Can you think of ways in which the two principles could be implemented, given the real circumstances of the school and the needs of the pupils? If so, what are the costs and benefits of such implementation?

Follow-up: There are unlikely to be any easy answers to these questions, but you might like to consider what forms of school organization you might create if you had different aims and priories.

CONCLUSION

Curriculum planning is a highly skilled activity. It requires awareness of curriculum requirements at national level, of whole-school team decisions and, not least, of the needs and interests of children. Subject expertise must then be combined with sound practical organization to deliver an interesting and appropriately challenging set of learning experiences. In the hands of a skilled and sensitive teacher, structure and purpose will be tempered by flexibility, excitement and intuition.

Notes for further reading

On developments in whole-school curriculum planning see:

Hargreaves, D. H. and Hopkins, D. (1991)
The Empowered School: The Management
and Practice of Development Planning,
London: Cassell.   Reading, 14.3

Nias, J., Southworth, G. and Campbell, P. (1992)
Whole-School Curriculum Development in the Primary School,
London: Falmer.   Reading, 8.1

For comprehensive whole-curriculum frameworks, which can be used as a basis for classroom planning and which make constructive use of concepts such as breadth, balance, coherence, progression and continuity, see:

Department of Education and Science (1985a)
The Curriculum from 5 to 16,
HMI, Curriculum Matters Series,
London: HMSO.   Reading, 8.2

Curriculum Council for Wales (1991)
The Whole Curriculum in Wales,
Cardiff: CCW.

Curriculum planning in the context of national curricula has become an important issue for debate. See:

Alexander, R., Rose, J. and Woodhead, C. (1992)
Curriculum Organisation and Classroom
Practice in Primary Schools: A Discussion Paper,
London: DES.   Reading, 8.4

However, sound practical advice has also been offered:

School Curriculum and Assessment Authority (1995)
Planning the Curriculum at Key Stages 1 and 2,
London: SCAA.   Reading, 8.5

Topic-based curricula can be developed through careful analysis and planning. The first two books below provide general theoretical frameworks and the remainder offer many practical suggestions:

Tann, S. (ed.) (1988)
Developing Topic Work in the Primary School,
London: Falmer.

Hunter, R. and Scheirer, E. A. (1988)
The Organic Classroom: Organising for Learning 7–12,
London: Falmer.

📖 **Reading, 8.3**

Arnold, R. (ed.) (1991)
Topic Planning and the National Curriculum,
London: Longman.

Kerry, T. and Eggleston, J. (1988)
Topic Work in the Primary School,
London: Routledge.

Avann, P. (ed.) (1985)
Teaching Information Skills in the Primary School,
London: Edward Arnold.

'Curriculum-led staffing' is a way of relating staff resources in primary schools to an assessment of curriculum needs. Where there is a national curriculum, this can be quantified and used as a planning guide and as an argument for more equitable resourcing. See:

Simpson, E. (1988)
Review of Curriculum-Led Staffing,
Windsor: NFER.

Coopers & Lybrand Deloitte (1991)
Costs of the National Curriculum in Primary Schools,
London: National Union of Teachers.

Cross-curricular themes were introduced in:

National Curriculum Council (1990)
The Whole Curriculum.
Curriculum Guidance 3,
York: NCC.

A critique of the National Curriculum in England and Wales and argument in favour of cross-curricular themes is provided in the first book below and the others elaborate their importance:

Hall, G. (ed.) (1992)
Themes and Dimensions of the National Curriculum:
Implications for Policy and Practice,
London: Kogan Page.

Siraj-Blatchford, J. and Siraj-Blatchford, I. (1995)
Educating the Whole Child,
Buckingham: Open University Press.

Webb, R. (ed.) (1996)
Cross-Curricular Primary Practice,
London: Falmer Press.

For a review of work on the hidden curriculum, see:

Meighan, R. (1981)
The Sociology of Educating,
London: Holt, Rinehart & Winston.

Awareness about bias in classroom materials has been increased by considerable public discussion of the issues. Evidence of this can be found in:

Dixon, B. (1977)
*Catching Them Young: Sex, Race and
Class in Children's Fiction,*
London: Pluto Press.

Stinton, J. (1979)
Racism and Sexism in Children's Books,
London: Writers and Readers.

Zimmet, S. G., and Hoffman, M. (1980)
Print and Prejudice,
London: Hodder and Stoughton.

Tutchell, E. (ed.) (1990)
Dolls and Dungarees: Gender Issues in the Primary School Curriculum,
Buckingham: Open University Press.

Myers, K. (1992)
Genderwatch,
Cambridge: Cambridge University Press.

The analysis of curriculum tasks is well illustrated in the cases of science education and of group work:

Harlen, W. (1985)
Primary Science: Taking the Plunge,
London: Heinemann.

Bennett, N. and Kell, J. (1989)
A Good Start? Four Year Olds in Infant Schools,
Oxford: Blackwell.

Bennett, N. and Dunne, E. (1992)
Managing Classroom Groups,
London: Simon & Schuster.

📖 Reading, 11.6

Differentiation is not at all easy to provide in classrooms with large numbers of pupils. An important source of evidence on this is:

Bennett, N., Desforges, C., Cockburn, A. and Wilkinson, B. (1984)
The Quality of Pupil Learning Experiences,
London: Lawence Erlbaum Associates.

📖 Reading, 8.7

See also:

Simpson, M. (1989)
*A Study of Differentiation and
Learning in Primary Schools,*
Aberdeen: Northern College of Education.

The very young age of some children within primary schools can easily be ignored when schools are anxious to implement the National Curriculum, despite the importance of approprately differentiated provision:

Department of Education and Science (1990)
*Starting with Quality: Report of the Committee
of Enquiry into the Quality of Educational
Provision for Under Fives,* (Rumbold Report),
London: HMSO.

Hurst, V. (1992)
Planning for Early Learning: The First Five Years,
London: Paul Chapman.

Anning, A. (ed.) (1995)
A National Curriculum for the Early Years,
Buckingham: Open University Press.

Attainment and the specifics of educational need also pose enormous challenges. See, for instance:

Ashdown, R., Carpenter, B. and Bovair, K. (1991)
*The Curriculum Challenge: Access to the National
Curriculum for Pupils with Learning Difficulties,*
London: Falmer.

Lewis, A. (1991)
Primary Special Needs and the National Curriculum,
London: Routledge.

Jones, K. and Charlton, T. (1992)
Learning Difficulties in the Primary Classroom,
London: Routledge.

SCAA (1996)
*Planning the Curriculum for Pupils with Profound
and Multiple Learning Difficulties,*
London: SCAA.

On school organization and teaching roles, the following book contains a useful review of curricular issues, in particular the role of postholders in 'collegiate primary schools':

Campbell, R. J. (1985)
Developing the Primary School Curriculum,
London: Holt, Rinehart & Winston.

This approach was affirmed in:

House of Commons, Select Committee on Education, Science and the Arts (1986)
Achievement in Primary Schools,
London: HMSO.

The most comprehensive research on the issue is:

Webb, R. and Vulliamy, G. (1996)
*Roles and Responsibilities in the Primary School:
Changing Demands, Changing Practices,*
Buckingham: Open University Press.

The need for review of existing conventions regarding internal school organization is argued in:

Alexander, R. (1992)
Policy and Practice in Primary Education,
London: Routledge.

📖 Reading, 8.8

CHAPTER 9

How are we organizing the classroom?

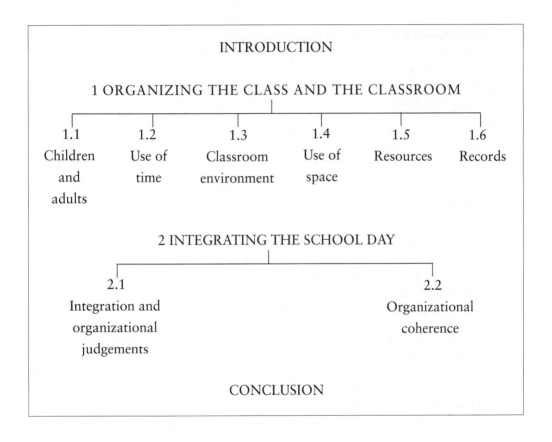

INTRODUCTION

Organization is vital in implementing values, aims, and curriculum plans for learning. It is the last of the main factors which contribute to the 'planning and provision' section of the reflective cycle outlined in Chapter 1.

By organization, it is meant the way in which the class and classroom is structured in order to facilitate teaching and learning. For such teaching and learning to succeed, classroom organization must relate to values, aims and curriculum plans as a whole and also to practical circumstances.

A vital factor is class size – despite what policy-makers tend to think (except when considering the education of their own children). However, the views of headteachers, governors, teachers and parents is consistent (Bennett, 1994) and there have been many research studies which support their point of view (Glass, 1982; Pate-Bain *et al.*, 1992, **Reading, 9.1**). However, there are other contradictory findings and further research is needed. A key issue is the extent to which teaching methods are adapted to suit a particular class size, rather than simply extended from one situation to another.

If an appropriate organizational coherence can be achieved, then the teacher and the children should benefit from having a common framework within which to work. The strength of such a framework will derive from its internal consistency: the mutual reinforcement of its elements and its legitimacy (the reciprocated agreement between the teacher and the children). Because of the interdependent nature of organizational elements it is important to remember that change made in one aspect is likely to affect other aspects.

However, organizational structure does not mean rigidity, for if the rules and routines of the classroom are clear and agreed, good organization can free the teacher to teach and the learner to learn (Bennett *et al.*, 1984). In particular, it should give the teacher more time to diagnose children's learning difficulties; to design an appropriate match of task to child; and to teach rather than having to spend time on 'housekeeping' aspects of routine classroom life (Hilsum and Cane, 1970; Galton *et al.*, 1980; Pollard *et al.*, 1994, **Reading, 9.6**). One particularly memorable image of this has been offered by Campbell and Neill (1992) with their concept of 'evaporated time'. They found that it took up about 10 per cent of all classroom time: the equivalent of one afternoon a week.

Six key organizational issues are listed below and each will be discussed in the first section of this chapter:

1. The way in which children and adults are organized

2. The use of time

3. The use of the classroom environment

4. The use of classroom space

5. The use of resources

6. The use of records for monitoring classroom organization

Section 2 will examine additional issues related to integrated forms of school organization and the 'integrated' day (Brown and Precious, 1968, **Reading, 9.8**). We will use this for two purposes. First, it will provide a case study to illustrate the importance of coherence between organizational strategies and values, aims and curriculum plans. Second, it is important to try to clarify some of the misconceptions about the integrated day as a form of classroom practice. It is commonly referred to in the rhetoric of primary ideology, but is variously employed in reality and can still make a worthwhile contribution to a repertoire of strategies.

1. ORGANIZING THE CLASS AND THE CLASSROOM

1.1 Children and adults

The people in a classroom need to be organized in ways which are most appropriate for supporting the learning activities which have been planned. Obviously this involves children but, in many classes, it also involves adults such as ancilliary staff. There is also an increasing degree of involvement by parents in classrooms. However, we will begin by focusing on the children.

The first basic decision to be made regarding the children concerns the appropriate balance between individual work, classwork and group work. This must be made with regard to both pedagogical and practical considerations but, whatever decisions are made, the form of organization must be 'fit for its purpose' (Alexander, *et al.*, 1992).

Pedagogical considerations include the general aims of the teacher as well as any particular objectives for the task and children. Practical factors include the number of children, the size of the room and the availability of resources – factors which will be discussed in more detail below. The basic ways of organizing pupils for teaching purposes are:

Individual work. This is thought to be particularly useful for developing children's ability to work independently and autonomously.

Classwork. This is useful for starting and ending the day, for giving out administrative instructions, introducing, teaching, extending and reviewing work, and for many activities which build a feeling of belonging to a class (e.g. through discussions, story, singing, music, dance and games).

Group work. This is often recommended for developing social and language skills and as a means by which pupils can support, challenge and extend their learning together (e.g. through problem-solving or work on a creative task).

Each of these ways of organizing the children has its advantages and rationale, but each also has its particular limitations. For example, a teacher who relies heavily on setting individual work may find that similar teaching points have to be explained on many separate occasions to different children. Individual work also often results in a lot of movement in the classroom, with either the teacher moving around the classroom seeing each child in turn, or the children moving from their chairs and queueing at the teacher's desk. This emphasis on working with each individual separately inevitably means that only a limited amount of time can be spent with any one child. Even then, it has been shown that most of this time is spent in monitoring each child's work, rather than in developing their understanding (Galton *et al.*, 1980, **Reading, 9.2**).

Teachers using whole-class organizational procedures tend to spend more time in discussion with the class. Such opportunities may give the teacher a chance to instruct the class more directly and economically and to stimulate children's thinking by exploring ideas, asking more 'probing' questions, sharing common problems and encouraging children to join in trying to solve them. However, if classwork is used too extensively it may pose a severe strain on both the teacher and the listener, for it is very difficult to match the instruction appropriately to each child's different needs without sufficient individual consultation.

 'Groups' are likely to exist in some form in every classroom. However, their form and function may vary considerably (McNamara, 1994, **Reading 9.4**; Reason, 1993, **Reading, 9.3**). Four main types of groups can be identified:

Task allocation. The teacher may have a group of children in mind when setting or allocating a task, though the group may not sit or work together.

Teaching groups. Groups can also be used for 'group teaching' purposes, where the teacher instructs children who are at the same stage, doing the same task, at the same time. This may be followed by the children working individually. Such a system can be an economical use of teacher instruction time and, possibly, of resources.

Seating groups. This is a very common form of grouping, where a number of children sit together around a table, usually in a four or six. Such an arrangement is flexible. It allows children to work individually, to socialize when appropriate, and can be used as the basis for other forms of group work.

Collaborative groups. This is a more developed form of group work, where there is a shared group aim, work is done together and the outcome is a combined product – perhaps in the form of a model, play or problem solved.

Although groups are very commonly found for task allocation, seating purposes and teaching purposes, relatively little collaborative group work has been found by observers (DES, 1978a; Galton *et al.*, 1980; Pollard *et al.*, 1994). Teachers have identified a number of problems which they associate with group work and, therefore, consider to be disadvantages (Tann, 1981). First, many teachers appear concerned about motivating the children and helping them to recognize that being in a group is for the purposes of work rather than a chance to chat and just 'have fun'. Second, the monitoring of group work can pose problems, especially if the group is intended to work collaboratively on their own without a teacher. Third, the management of groups, in terms of such issues as who should be in the group, how many children and where they should work, may pose difficult dilemmas which have to be resolved. Research by Galton and Williamson (1992), Bennett and Dunne (1992, **Reading, 11.6**) and Biott and Easen (1994, **Reading, 10.4**) is providing new insights in this area.

Identifying criteria by which groups may be formed may help to clarify some of the key issues (Kerry and Sands, 1982). Possible criteria may include:

Age-groups. These are occasionally used as a convenient way of grouping for some activities. They are much less useful as a basis for specific teaching points because of the inevitable spread of attainment interests and needs.

Attainment groups. Groups based on attainment levels are useful for setting up specific and well matched tasks. They are divisive if used as a permanent way of grouping.

Interest groups. It is important to enable children with shared interests to work together from time to time. There may be particular advantages for the social cohesion of the class when children are of different attainment, sex, race, social class.

Friendship groups. These are popular with children and provide opportunities for social development. Awareness of the needs of any isolate and marginal children is necessary, as is some attention to the possibility that friendship groups can set up divisive status hierarchies among the children, or reinforce stereotypes about gender, race or abilities.

As with decisions concerning the balance between different general strategies for organizing the children, if group work is to be used, professional judgement is necessary to achieve an appropriate balance in the use of particular types of groups. Each has a different purpose and specific potential and, therefore, each has its own justifiable place in the primary classroom (Practical Activity 9.1).

The second very important category of people who are increasingly to be found in primary school classrooms are adults, particularly parents. Whilst this is a developing trend, it is still the case that less than half of British primary schools involve parents in the classroom (Stierer, 1985) and of course, the Parent's Charter, introduced by a Conservative government in 1992, implies a more distant relationship with the parent simply as a 'consumer' of educational services.

A wide range of patterns of parental involvement thus exist (Hughes *et al.*, 1995, **Reading, 14.6**). Three basic types can be distinguished:

Parents as consumers: receiving the services of the school but maintaining a discrete separation of parent and teacher responsibilities (e.g. where involvement is through formal parents' evenings and other 'managed' school events).

Parents as resources: providing a range of help, for example: parental activity in support of the school, as in PTA fund-raising schemes, outside school time; parents working in school on non-educational activities, as in helping to duplicate, or mend books; parents involved with educational activities, as in helping children in the library, hearing reading; parents teaching with small groups (often withdrawn), as in cooking and sewing; parents teaching in the classroom, as in the art area, or with general learning activities.

Parents as partners: recognized as partner in each child's all-round development (e.g. discussing the curriculum and each child's response); supporting curriculum (e.g. reading), learning at home; supporting skill development (e.g. writing and other skills) at home; contributing as parent governors; having open access to the classroom and regular informal contacts with teachers.

It seems that both parents and teachers, and perhaps the children, have mixed feelings on the question of parental involvement in classrooms (Cullingford, 1985). For instance, some parents may feel anxious and uneasy about working in a school. This may be because of their own 'bad' experiences of school, or because they do not feel they have anything to offer the 'expert' teacher. Parents may be unsure about how to relate to children in the school situation, particularly if their

Practical activity 9.1

Aim: To decide the most appropriate type and size of grouping for the activities planned.

Method: We suggest that notes on the size of groupings are made on the most appropriate cell of a matrix of types such as the one given below:

Activity	Individual work	Whole-class work	Group work				
			Random grouping	Age grouping	Attainment grouping	Interest grouping	Friendship grouping
Story-time							
Measuring activities							
Dismissal							
Topic work							
Clay-work							
Drama							

Follow-up: The benefit of this sort of analysis is in the increased sensitivity to the unique potential of each type of learning situation. It will support the development of professional judgement and should help in ensuring coherence between learning aims, social context and organizational strategies.

own child is in the class to which they are attached. Because of this, parents are unlikely to take initiatives in the classroom unless these are suggested and endorsed by the teacher. Further, parents are often only available for short and specific periods of the day. They are volunteers and have many other responsibilities and do not always find it easy to fit into school routines. However, other parents feel unwilling to participate in classroom activities for quite different reasons. Some would maintain that it is the teacher's job to do the teaching and that they should therefore be allowed to get on with it. Others may feel that if they tried to help the child, at home or at school, they may do things in different ways to the teacher's approach which might only confuse the child.

Although we have talked of 'parents' we are, in general, referring to fathers or mothers who are not in paid full-time employment, for despite the interest of many, very few parents with full-time jobs have the opportunity to participate in classroom life. In practice, the vast majority of parental participants are mothers who are concentrating their efforts on bringing up a family.

There are also mixed feelings amongst teachers about parental involvement. Some welcome the opportunity to create a stronger partnership between home and school so that both can work together in the interests of the children. Others, however, feel vulnerable in case something goes wrong which could undermine their status in the eyes of the parents. Teachers are also aware that parental help can become a socially divisive factor, giving still greater advantages to the already advantaged middle-class children whose parents are most likely to participate in such schemes.

Despite some well-documented educational benefits of the involvement of parents in classrooms (e.g. Wolfendale, 1989), there is also considerable scope for the wastage of their time and their talents. In addition, there is considerable scope for misunderstandings and anxieties to emerge. Perhaps three basic things need to be done. The first is to find time for adequate discussion with parents to find out what they have to offer and to help them relax in the school environment. The second is to think carefully about how parents can be most educationally productive when they are in the classroom. The third is to negotiate clear ground rules on issues such as classroom roles, confidentiality and access to the staff-room.

In studies of 'room management' it is suggested that the quality of classroom teaching is very greatly enhanced if all the adults in a classroom plan together so that they understand and carry out specific activities in a co-ordinated and coherent fashion (Thomas, 1992, **Reading 9.7**). Parental partnership in the classroom means making careful organizational provision to use the time and talents of parents to the full. A related range of organization issues could be applied to ancillary assistants (Practical Activity 9.2).

1.2   Use of time

The way in which time is used in a classroom is very important. Studies such as those of Campbell and Neill (1992) have updated an influential, but dated study of the issue by (Hilsum and Cane, 1971) to show that the notion of the time available for teaching needs careful analysis. The average hours of work of the infant school teachers whom Campbell and Neill studied in 1992 were as given in Table 9.1.

Table 9.1 *Hours of work per week by Key Stage 1 teachers*

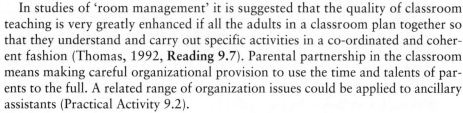

Category	Hours per week	Percentage of total time
Teaching	18.0	34
Preparation	14.5	28
Administration	13.6	26
Professional development	7.2	14
Other activities	3.8	7
Total	52.4	100

Note: The sum of hours is slightly smaller than the parts because of overlapping of categories

Practical activity 9.2

Aim: To prepare for having parents or ancillary staff working in the classroom.

Method: A pro forma, such as the one below, could be used to prepare for a session with parental or ancillary involvement, to monitor it and to get the parents' feedback.

Initial discussion with parent/ancillary

Parent/ancillary's feeling about involvement ....

Parent/ancillary's contribution on offer ....

Parent/ancillary availability ....

Any anticipated problems ....

Planning activities and objectives for sessions

1) ....

2) ....

3) ....

4) ....

Agreed contribution for parent/ancillary ....

The session in action

Notes ....

Follow-up discussions

Notes ....

Follow-up: It is unlikely that this activity would be carried out for every session involving parents or ancillary assistants but it is very valuable when starting off a new partnership for classroom work. It is also useful on an occasional basis to heighten awareness and to check that benefits are being maximized.

A great deal of effort thus goes into the creation of 'teaching time'. However, of that, Campbell and Neill show that almost 10 per cent is lost as 'evaporated time' in the classroom management activities which are necessary to create teaching and learning opportunities. Children thus have to get books out, change, move locations, tidy up, etc. Other findings on the use of teacher time, based on systematic observation, are very similar (Pollard *et al.*, 1994).

Looking at this issue in terms of pupil time, Bennett (1979) has related pupil progress not only to the time which is actually made available for 'curriculum activity' but also to the pupil time spent in 'active learning'. 'Active learning', as opposed to just 'busy work', is a qualitative category not just a quantitative one. 'Active learning' is linked to further factors such as motivation, stimulus and concentration. There is evidence to suggest that, in order to maintain 'active' learning, appropriate variety in activities is needed (e.g. Kounin, 1970, **Reading, 10.6**). However, even quantitatively, findings from the PACE study (Pollard *et al.*, 1994, **Reading, 9.6**) showed considerable variations between different classrooms in the proportions of pupil time with high levels of engagement. Overall, Key Stage 1 children were task-engaged for about 60 per cent of classroom time, distracted for about 20 per cent of the time and organizing themselves or being organized for the remaining 20 per cent. We thus have three aspects to consider in the use of time:

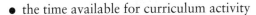

- the time available for curriculum activity
- the time spent in active learning
- the stimulus and variety in activities over time

The first of these, time available for curriculum activity, is relatively easy to document (see Practical Activity 9.3).

The second of the issues identified above was the time spent on active learning. This is affected by a wide range of factors. Thus, whilst the time spent on active learning can be assessed at any point (see Practical Activity 9.4), it may also be seen as providing summative information: a product of the overall organization, relationships and teaching which are provided for the children. However, the time in a classroom which is spent on active learning is clearly related to a number of organizational strategies. The most obvious of these concerns are the routine procedures which are developed: for example, those which help to avoid queues and bottle-necks. These help to manage the pressure which might otherwise be placed on the teacher by the children and they contribute to producing a positive, structured classroom environment. Check-list 9.1 may be helpful in considering these.

Practical activity 9.3

Aim: To record the time available for curriculum activity.

Method: The time available for curriculum activity is the remaining time in each teaching/learning session, once it has properly started, excluding interruptions and up to 'tidying up' time. All that is necessary here is to use a notebook and a watch to record the actual time available for activity throughout a school day.

Follow-up: Assuming that a fairly representative day has been chosen, it may provide a salutary experience to multiply the total for the day by the total number of school days in the year excluding days set aside for professional development work, and election days if the school will be closed, etc.

Check-list 9.1

Purpose of procedure	Procedure	Evaluation of procedure	Possible improvement
Entering in the morning			
Completing the register			
Collecting dinner money			
Introducing activities and tasks			
Managing playtime			
Managing dinner-time			
Moving to and from assembly			
Changing for PE			
Going to the toilet			
Getting help in class			
Using classroom resources			
Getting work marked			
Knowing which task to move on to			
Tidying up			
Exiting at the end of the day			

Practical activity 9.4

Aim: To monitor an individual child to estimate active learning time.

Method: Watch a chosen child during a teaching/learning session. Judge the times at which:

1. The child is 'on task' (i.e. actively engaged in the given task).
2. The child is doing other necessary activities related to the task (e.g. sharpening pencils, fetching equipment).
3. The child is 'off task'.

Calculate the total amounts of learning time in each category:

'On task' time	[ ]
Task management time	[ ]
'Off task' time	[ ]

Follow-up: Are there any changes in classroom organization or management strategies which could help to maximize active learning time?

The third aspect of time, the stimulus and variety of tasks over time, is an organizational issue to which Kounin (1970, **Reading, 10.6**) drew attention when arguing that teachers should avoid 'satiation' (i.e. letting the children get bored by monotonous activities). It is very easy to fall into this trap through an overreliance on published materials, such as maths schemes, reading and spelling workshops, or through the setting of repetitive individualized activities. Resources in the form of schemes are convenient. They appear to offer a secure basis for implementing the curriculum in which progression has been systematically considered and they are often strongly marketed by publishers. However, overreliance on schemes can have a narrowing effect on the curriculum and lead to satiation and boredom. Considerable amounts of child activity will inevitably be directed through print, there is a tendency to require written recording and a remorseless, hierarchical structure is often in-built. All these aspects impose a relatively depersonalized and technical control on children. Indeed, it has been argued that the preponderance of such routine activities in some schools may have consequences in terms of the reproduction of a docile workforce, rather than develop children whose creativity and critical thinking have been stirred (Bowles and Gintis, 1976, **Reading, 13.1**; Apple, 1982; see Practical Activity 9.5).

1.3 Classroom environment

Research by ecological psychologists (e.g. Barker, 1978; Bronfenbrenner, 1979) has suggested the importance of the quality of the environment and the fact that it can influence behaviour. Such research reinforces the view, which is commonly expressed by practitioners, that the environment in a primary school classroom should be aesthetically pleasing; should stimulate children's interest; should set high standards in

Practical activity 9.5

Aim: To evaluate the stimulus and variety of tasks and activities.

Method: This evaluation could be carried out by an observer who focuses on a particular child for a day. All activities should be recorded in terms of their motivational appeal, explicit purpose and in terms of what the child was required to do (write, draw, listen, watch, move, sing, etc.). Alternatively, tasks could be monitored, by the teacher, for a longer period.

Some questions which might be asked could include:

a. Is there a planned highlight for each day?

b. Are there long sequences of seatwork and or writing?

c. Is there a reasonable degree of variety between active and passive tasks?

d. Is there a reasonable degree of variety between children working alone, in small groups, as a whole class?

Follow-up: Consider the findings from this exercise and, preferably with a colleague, try to deduce the reasons for any patterns you identify. How do you evaluate the results? If you judge it appropriate, what could you do to increase the stimulus and variety of tasks and activities?

the display and presentation of children's work; and should be created in such a way that it is practical to maintain (Clegg and Billington, 1994, **Reading, 9.5**).

Reflective teachers may also aim to structure the environment so that opportunities are taken to reinforce their overall purposes. They should be able to develop their classroom environment by considering the questions in Check-list 9.2.

1.4   Use of space

Space in a classroom is always limited; yet what space there is must be utilized in such a way that the wide-ranging activities which form essential elements of the primary school curriculum can occur without major disruptions. This requires a considerable amount of thought. A first step is to produce a planning tool, such as a classroom plan (see Practical Activity 9.6), with which the existing constraints and the possibilities of the room and furniture can be explored.

1.5   Resources

A good supply of appropriate resources is essential, given the importance of direct experience and practical work to children's learning. In some ways, this aspect of organization is a straightforward matter, but it, too, requires careful thought and attention to detail. For instance, it is all too easy to discover that the clay has dried out or the paint is not mixed, when a group of children come to use them. Practical Activity 9.7 suggests a method for planning resources.

Check-list 9.2

Aim: To examine the classroom environment.

1. *Design.* What are the main design features of the room and how do they affect its aesthetic feel?

2. *Possibilities.* What are the possibilities for display (in two and in three dimensions?) on walls, on windows, on flat surfaces, off the ceiling? What are the possibilities for plants or animals? Is work displayed in a variety of media? Is it mobile or static?

3. *Purposes.* Do the displays stimulate and inform? Do they provide opportunities for children to interact with them, for example, by posing questions; inviting their participation in a quiz or problem-solving challenge; offering alternative viewpoints to consider; encouraging the children to touch/smell/taste as well as look and listen? Further, do displays only show finished products or do they also reveal processes, which might be used for discussion, sharing problems, giving mutual support and advice?

4. *Quality.* Is the standard of mounting, writing and display such that it shows that the children's work is valued? Does it provide a model which children may apply to their own work?

5. *Practicality.* Is the classroom environment as practical as it can be to maintain? How often is it necessary to change displays? Do the children mount their own displays? Can children help with classroom jobs such as watering plants and feeding pets?

Practical activity 9.6

Aim: To produce a classroom plan.

Method: A simple plan should be made of the fixed points in the classroom – walls, windows, doors, sinks, pegs, etc. If squared paper is used, it is relatively easy to produce a plan to scale.

Major existing items of furniture should be represented on card and to the same scale as the classroom plan. The 'furniture cards' can be moved around on the plan to experiment with different classroom layouts.

Follow-up: Careful analysis is needed of the space requirements of each classroom activity and of each activity in relation to the others. So, for example, it is important to note if creative artwork or relatively noisy activities will interfere with quieter ones. Also, consider the relationship of activity areas and the accessibility of the resources for each activity. Finally, it is necessary to relate the location of the activities to the likely movement of the children, so that crowding or bottle-necks can be anticipated. This may need to be done on a session-by-session basis, and by first considering the most commonly occurring sessions. The children can help in this activity, and thereby become more aware of the need for careful use of space.

Practical activity 9.7

Aim: To plan the resources to support learning activities.

Method: Identify the aim for each activity, then consider the resources which are required, using the four criteria listed in section 1.5 as a starting-point:

Activity:

Aim:

Resources required:

    Appropriateness:

    Availability:

    Storage:

    Maintenance:

Follow-up: Analysing the need and use of resources in this fashion could lead to their more rational and practical deployment. Can you produce a programme for immediate action and another for further development?

Four possible criteria which might be considered when organizing resources are:

Appropriateness.	What resources are needed to support the learning processes which are expected to take place?
Availability.	What resources are available? What is in the classroom, the school, the community, businesses, libraries, museums, resource centres? Are there cost, time or transport factors to be considered?
Storage.	How are classroom resources stored? Which should be under teacher control? Which should be openly available to the children? Are they clearly labelled and safely stored.
Maintenance.	What maintenance is required? Is there a system for seeing that this is done?

1.6 Records

There are two basic types of record which teachers have to keep: those relating to class and school organization and those relating to the assessment of pupil progress. We deal with organizational records here and with assessment records in Chapter 12.

By organizational records we simply mean those records which are necessary to ensure the smooth running of the school and classroom. These range from the attendance and dinner registers, which are extremely important to the administration of the school, to such things as records of group membership for various activities, timetables for use of shared school facilities such as the hall, and records of resource maintenance or loan periods (Practical Activity 9.8).

Practical activity 9.8

Aim: To trace procedures relating to the registers.

Method: Try to follow the administrative chain in a school. This typically takes a form as suggested below:

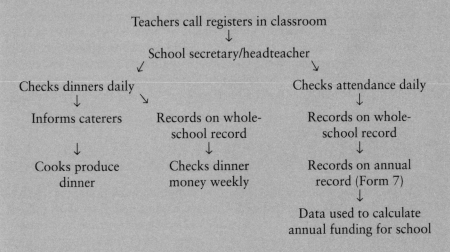

Teachers call registers in classroom
↓
School secretary/headteacher
↙   ↘

Checks dinners daily   Checks attendance daily
↓   ↘   ↓
Informs caterers   Records on whole-   Records on whole-
↓   school record   school record
Cooks produce   ↓   ↓
dinner   Checks dinner   Records on annual
                money weekly   record (Form 7)
                                         ↓
                                    Data used to calculate
                                    annual funding for school

Ask the school secretary, the cook and the headteacher to explain the importance of accurate and promptly available registers.

Follow-up: This activity may be helpful in understanding the tension that can sometimes be created when registers are kept poorly and in grasping the significance of the information which derives from them. It has even been suggested that rates of attendance can be used as an indicator of the performance of a school. If they are used this way, accurate completion of registers will become even more important.

Records of classroom organization are also essential for smooth day-to-day operation. The nature of these records – and whether the children or the teacher will be responsible for keeping them – depends on the extent of teacher or pupil control over the timing and selection of tasks and activities. A teacher may keep a simple list to show which children are expected to do what activity and in which order. This information may be kept in a teacher's record book, be written on the blackboard or displayed on a wall chart indicating children's names and tasks. Some teachers use a 'wheel' to show the activities to which a child or group should move on to next. Alternatively, it may be the child who plans the task or who draws up a 'contract' with the teacher indicating the work intended to be covered. Whatever system is chosen, it is most important that a record system should be quick and easy for the teacher to refer to, and for anyone else who may have to take over the class in an emergency.

Teacher care and ingenuity has been enormous, over many years, in attempts to develop smoothly operating and manageable ways of resolving the fundamental dilemma: how do you motivate and develop individual children whilst managing a class of many children? How then, are tasks and activities delivered to, or chosen by, children? There are many systems.

For instance, a teacher may devise a number of tasks which the children may do on a rotation basis. Or children may be given tasks to complete during a day, in the order of their own choice, on a quota basis. The tasks may be displayed as a constant reminder in either pictorial codes or writing. Older children may extend this and negotiate with the teacher on a range of tasks that need to be completed over the period of a whole week, and which can be chosen in an order which is most satisfactory and meaningful to them. Even very young children can be encouraged to take some responsibility in deciding the tasks and in planning when and how they should be completed. This has been demonstrated by the High/Scope nursery project (Hohmann *et al.*, 1979), where children are asked to 'plan', 'do' and then 'review' their activities.

2 | INTEGRATING THE SCHOOL DAY

In this chapter we have focused so far on the organizational means by which we could put our plans into practice. Clearly, to implement such plans fully we have to develop organizational strategies which are coherent with each other and with our aims. We noted in Chapter 7 that the concept of 'integration' is important in analysing curriculum coherence. A similar situation exists with regard to the analysis of organizational flexibility and coherence. This particularly applies to primary schools because of their relatively small size and because of the enormous diversity in their circumstances. The result is that it is almost impossible to generalize about optimal forms of organization for primary schools. Professional judgement needs to be applied in each particular case and is likely to require continuous flexibility over time. One common outcome of this is the use of various forms of interlinking and integration regarding teaching groups, teachers, resources and learning activities.

We consider below the main organizational issues about which integration and flexible grouping of people and use of resources are often likely to be advantageous.

2.1 Integration and organizational judgements

1. Organizational issues across the school
(a) *Integration of age groups*: for example, organizing children into 'vertically grouped' classes – the practice of combining more than one year group into a single class. For instance, a group of 5–7, or 7–9-year-olds may be grouped together. This is sometimes done out of necessity in small schools, but is it also deliberately chosen by teachers who believe that there are positive advantages in such integration. The possible advantages include:

● older children can help the younger ones to settle;
● opportunities exist for children to develop responsibility;
● stable, long-term learning situations provide greater continuity for the children;
● the teacher has a better chance to understand the children, which could lead to a better match of tasks to abilities and attainment.

Possible disadvantages include:

- the wider range of ages may make whole-class activities difficult, e.g. PE, story-time;
- the need for a wide range of resources and tasks may pose storage and planning difficulties;
- younger and less-able children could feel overawed by the older or brighter children;
- the wide range of age and attainment demands very careful monitoring by the teacher to ensure an adequate matching of task and child.

 (b) *Co-ordination*: for example, of the teaching staff to provide subject specialist teaching – a school staff, perhaps in response to the challenges of teaching a full national curriculum, wish to teach to their subject strengths across the whole school. Flexible consideration of this was strongly advocated by an influential report on classroom organization in England (Alexander *et al.*, 1992, **Reading, 8.4**).

Advantages could include:

- being able to use teacher subject knowledge to the full;
- being more able to challenge each class in the specifics of each subject;
- being able to ensure curricular progression in each subject from class to class.

Disadvantages could include:

- a weakening of classroom relationships between teachers and children;
- a lack of coherence across the whole curriculum;
- insecurity amongst some pupils, e.g. children with special educational needs.

(c) *The integration of teaching responsibilities*: for example, in open-plan schools where team-teaching is used. This is a form of organization where more than one class, or home/base unit, works in large shared areas with more than one teacher. In such open situations, co-operation is essential to co-ordinate activities and to avoid simultaneous demands on resources. Teachers may also plan their curriculum jointly and, in this sense, integrate their planning and provision. Again, advantages and disadvantages co-exist in such a system.

Advantages could include:

- being able to give each other greater support;
- being able to pool and develop ideas;
- being able to make use of each other's specialisms;
- being able to share tasks (e.g. story-time) and give each other time to do other jobs (e.g. mounting children's work).

Disadvantages could include:

- extra time may be needed to have the necessary meetings to plan and co-ordinate planning and provision;
- the possibility that teachers have different values or aims;
- reduced opportunities may exist for flexibility in tasks to match individual children or to introduce changes in activities spontaneously.

2. *Organizational issues in the classroom*

(a) *The integration of space and curriculum resources*: specialist areas of space, such as those for art, sand/water, library/reading, maths, English or science, are usually incorporated into one classroom area.

Advantages could include:

- a considerable breadth of curriculum subjects and experiences can be offered simultaneously for which the teacher can conveniently oversee the children across all curriculum activities;
- the children can be self-directing in moving between the curriculum activities without waiting for set times.

Disadvantages could be:

- the wide range of demands on the teacher's expertise, the possible hazards and distractions;
- particularly the challenge of managing complex provision and the time which this takes from the 'noisy' or 'messy' activities.

(b) *The integration of teaching sessions*: that is, the minimal use of timetabling. This is perhaps the main hallmark of the 'integrated day', a form of classroom organization which is intended to be particularly responsive to children's interests. Such an approach was particularly prominent in the 1970s (Brown and Precious, 1968, **Reading, 9.8**). However, there have been many modern developments of it.

Advantages are seen as:

- flexibility for the children to choose how much time to spend on an activity, and in which order;
- encouraging children to accept greater responsibility for their own work;
- increase in the children's intrinsic motivation to learn resulting from the greater control over and involvement in their own learning.

Disadvantages relate to:

- the difficulty of monitoring who is doing what in a busy classroom;
- the considerable range of resources required;
- the demands on teachers to manage a relatively complex form of organization.

The key rationale for having integrated teaching sessions is that they allow children to follow their own interests and to be in control of their own learning (see Rowland, 1984). Hence, it can serve as a motivational device by freeing children from the constraints of starting and finishing tasks according to teacher-imposed, organizational requirements, and by allowing them to follow their own patterns of learning. It allows both for intense individualization of learning, and for flexible grouping as and when it seems appropriate.

An alternative rationale for having several simultaneous activities (group or individual) is thus that it is a managerial device for making maximum use of minimal resources.

In fact, whatever organizational approach is chosen, there will have to be compromises. High-quality provision will thus be flexible provision. It will reflect the use of a variety of forms of classroom organization, drawn on by teachers because of their appropriateness for the educational purposes which are judged to be most important.

Open-plan classrooms, where more than one teacher and one class share a work area, can facilitate further opportunities for flexibility of activities and use of resources. This may include the shared use of teachers and other adults.

Notwithstanding all these possibilities, in the early 1990s there was a considerable challenge of integrated organizational approaches combined with advocacy of the merits of whole-class teaching, particularly in the context of the National Curriculum. Whole-class teaching certainly has strengths in making it easier for the teacher to challenge more children at any one point of time. However, there are serious problems in meeting the needs of the high and low-achieving extremes of the class and of providing children with appropriate learning *experiences*. This can be very hard to do in a whole-class situation because of the demands on resources (for which textbooks are likely to provide only a partial solution).

There is thus no one best method – but we would suggest that there are two crucial criteria for judging all organizational approaches, appropriateness and coherence. Is the form of organization fit for its purpose? Do all aspects of the classroom organization mesh consistently together?

2.2 Organizational coherence

As reflective teachers we need to analyse the degree of coherence between the aims and values underlying our curriculum planning and the organizational strategies which are adopted when we try to implement those plans.

As an example of this we can consider the relationship between the basic possible forms of classroom organization. For analytical purposes, a number of key dimensions can be distinguished which may help in analysing the learning contexts which children experience (see Figure 9.1). Two of these dimensions relate to the curriculum and the remaining five relate to its organizational implementation. The table in Figure 9.1 can be used to examine the degree of coherence between our curriculum, organization and aims. It does not represent polar opposites, but dimensions of the range of forms of organization from which a reflective teacher might draw.

For example, if a child is working on an individual project, the context allows for developing autonomy and independence. Conversely, if children are working in a group or whole-class situation, the context allows for the development of a wide range of collaborative social skills. On the other hand, a teacher-directed context may be more suitable for children who have not yet learned the necessary skills and attitudes for working independently. However, the learning opportunities are immense if children are placed in a position where they can plan collaboratively and take responsibility not just for their own efforts but for the whole class. Further, using a variety of resources is valuable, if feasible. Each kind of resource imposes its own organizational demands. The same applies to the different prime audiences. Finally, recording can provide valuable evidence to help us monitor the continuity, cohesion and coherence of the learning and teaching experiences of the class (Practical Activity 9.9 and 9.10).

Some teachers always implement their curriculum plans in a similar way (e.g. at the extreme left of each dimension, or the extreme right). Others may adopt positions at different points of each of the seven dimensions, but always remain with

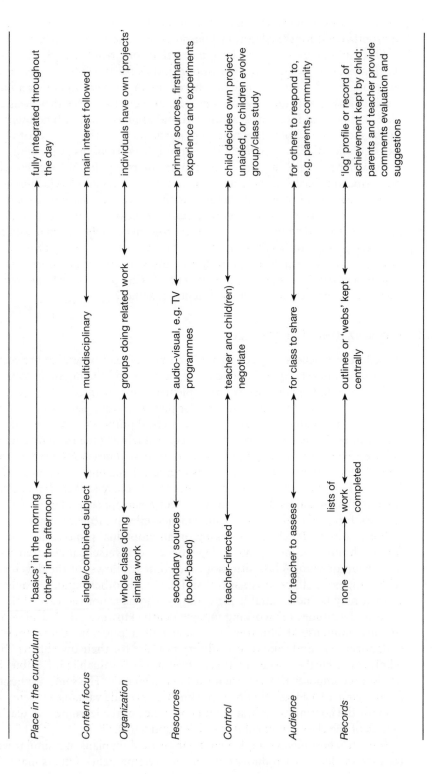

Figure 9.1 *Characteristics of integrated curriculum practice*

Practical activity 9.9

Aim: To identify learning objectives which are coherent with each of the positions on the seven dimensions in Figure 9.1.

Method: Using Figure 9.1, identify the possible learning aims which could be associated with each of the suggested positions on each dimension.

Follow-up: Which of these learning aims are consistant with your own aims as identified in Practical Activity 4.4? Which organizational practices would therefore be most coherent with your own aims?

Practical activity 9.10

Aim: To analyse 'topic' work in terms of the seven dimensions in Figure 9.1.

Method: Review the activities contributing to current topic work.

Follow-up: How much variety of approaches is experienced by the children? Is there comprehensive and coherent coverage of alternative approaches so that the strengths of each can be exploited? In the light of this examination what decisions need to be made regarding the next topic?

that same combination. Yet others may deliberately vary the combinations to exploit the strengths and minimize the weaknesses of each different combination.

There is no single 'best way'. In order to provide opportunities for teaching and learning a wide range of skills, attitudes, knowledge and concepts, organizational practice must vary appropriately. Only then can a full coherence between aims and methods be achieved.

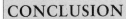

CONCLUSION

In this chapter we have discussed some of the key aspects of organizational planning and the need for consistency between them. We have also emphasized the importance of coherence between classroom organization and educational aims and values. This can only be achieved through the exercise of professional judgement by reflective teachers who have the knowledge, skill and confidence to draw on a range of forms of classroom organization and thus maximize 'fitness for purpose'.

In the next chapter we turn to the issue of managing the implementation of those plans in action.

Notes on further reading

Classroom organization is a very complex area and one which has been the subject of both research and controversy in recent years.

For a review of research, and one of the best overviews of pedagogy in primary education currently available, see:

Galton, M. (1989)
Teaching in the Primary School,
London: David Fulton.   📖 **Reading, 10.2**

For the book dealing with the Leeds project, which generated the controversy which led to the 'Three Wise Men' report (Alexander *et al.*, 1992), which in turn led to the Secretary of State for Education to call for 'an end to trendy teaching methods', see:

Alexander, R. J.(1992)
Policy and Practice in Primary Education,
London: Routledge   📖 **Readings, 7.10 and 8.8**

As all practising educationalists know, circumstances vary in different classrooms and professional judgement has to be applied to select appropriate forms of classroom organization for the purposes which the teacher has in mind. Some general books with sound practical advice are listed below. The last book is particularly relevant to younger children.

Moyles, J. (1992)
Organising for Learning in the Primary Classroom:
A Balanced Approach to Classroom Organisation,
Buckingham: Open University Press.

Bassey, M. (1978)
Practical Classroom Organization,
London: Ward Lock Educational.

Waterhouse, P. (1983)
Managing the Learning Process,
London: McGraw-Hill.

Dean, J. (1991)
Organizing Learning in the Primary School Classroom,
London: Routledge.

Hohmann, M., Banet, B. and Weikart, D. (1979)
Young Children in Action,
Ypsilanti, MI: High Scope Educational Research Foundation.

For innovative books on classroom group work which draw on research and relate it to practice, see:

Dunne, E. and Bennett, N. (1990)
Talking and Learning in Groups,
London: Routledge.

Galton, M. and Williamson, J. (1992)
Groupwork in the Primary Classroom,
London: Routledge.

Bennett, N. and Dunne, E. (1992)
Managing Classroom Groups,
London: Simon & Schuster.   📖 **Reading, 11.6**

The question of 'how to group?' is contentious. For an overview of research on 'ability-based' grouping, see:

Slavin, R. E. (1987)
Ability grouping and student achievement in elementary schools: a best-evidence synthesis, *Review of Educational Research*,
57(3), 293–336.

Reason, R. (1993)
Primary special needs and National Curriculum assessment. In S. Wolfendale, (ed.) *Assessing Special Educational Needs*,
London: Cassell.   📖 Reading, 9.3

McNamara, D. (1994)
Classroom Pedagogy and Primary Practice,
London: Routledge.   📖 Reading, 9.4

Two excellent books are now available on teachers and others working together in classroom teams. See:

Biott, C. (1990)
Semi-detached Teachers: Building Support and Advisory Relationships in Classrooms,
London: Falmer.

Thomas, G. (1992)
Effective Classroom Teamwork: Support or Intrusion?
London: Routledge.   📖 Reading, 9.7

The following books focus on issues relating to parents in the classroom, many of which are relevant to working with other adults. The first book contains an excellent case-study of development of parental involvement in one school over seven years.

Edwards, V. and Redfern, A. (1988)
Parental Participation in Primary Education,
London: Routledge.

Lang, R. (1986)
Developing Parental Involvement in Primary Schools,
London: Macmillan.

Topping, K. and Wolfendale, S. (1985)
Parental Involvement in Children's Reading,
London: Croom Helm.

Classroom display is a somewhat neglected topic for publications, but see:

Clegg, D. and Billington, S. (1994)
The Effective Primary Classroom,
London: David Fulton.   📖 Reading, 9.5

Hodgson, N. (1988)
Classroom Display,
Diss: Tarquin Publications.

Dean, J. (1973)
Display,
London: Evans.

Phelps, R. (1969)
Display in the Classroom,
Oxford: Blackwell.

Ideas for record-keeping appear in many different 'subject'-based books and are increasingly being influenced by the assessment requirements of the National Curriculum. However, for a wide range of suggested ways for 'keeping track' see:

Clift, P., Weiner, G. and Wilson, E. (1981)
Record Keeping in the Primary School,
London: Macmillan.

Johnson, G., Hill, B. and Tunstall, P. (1992)
Primary Records of Achievement,
London: Hodder and Stoughton.

The following books focus on the concept on an integrated day and discuss some of the practicalities.

Brown, M. E. and Precious, G. N. (1968)
The Integrated Day,
London: Ward Lock.

☐ Reading, 9.8

Allen, I. *et al.,* (1975)
Working an Integrated Day,
London: Ward Lock.

Walton, J. (ed.) (1971)
The Integrated Day: Theory and Practice,
London: Ward Lock.

CHAPTER 10

How are we managing learning and coping with behaviour?

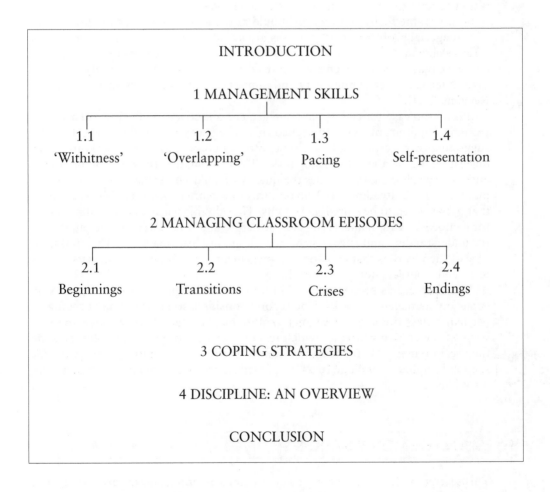

INTRODUCTION

1 MANAGEMENT SKILLS

| 1.1 | 1.2 | 1.3 | 1.4 |
| 'Withitness' | 'Overlapping' | Pacing | Self-presentation |

2 MANAGING CLASSROOM EPISODES

| 2.1 | 2.2 | 2.3 | 2.4 |
| Beginnings | Transitions | Crises | Endings |

3 COPING STRATEGIES

4 DISCIPLINE: AN OVERVIEW

CONCLUSION

INTRODUCTION

Having considered the issues involved in organizing a class, we now move it into the 'action' part of the reflective teaching cycle. This chapter begins with a consideration of classroom management. This includes reflecting on how to manage and cope with learning situations.

These are issues of perennial concern to teachers because of the numbers of children in a typical classroom (Pate-Bain *et al.,* 1992, **Reading, 9.1**). As Jackson (1968, **Reading, 5.5**) indicated, this means that, in a sense, the teacher is always dealing with a 'crowd'. Control of that crowd must, therefore, be a priority. It is a well-documented finding that for many student teachers in particular, this concern initially displaces almost all other aims as they take on the challenge of coping with the class. Nevertheless, it is a legitimate concern and is an issue about which it is important to develop both skills and judgement.

However, the focus of attention should arguably be directed at the prevention of managerial problems, so that crises are avoided, and to the maintenance of a positive climate for learning. This is by no means easy, since classrooms are such complex places, where events can unfold very quickly. Doyle's analysis of the 'multidimensionality, simultaneity and unpredictability' of this is excellent (1977, **Reading, 10.1**).

It is all too easy for classroom management objectives to take precedence over learning requirements. Galton argued this in one way (1989, **Reading, 10.2**), by suggesting that, despite high teacher control of classrooms, pupils are often very unclear about the aims of learning tasks. The combination is a sense of ambiguity and risk, which then undermines the quality of children's engagement with learning. Holt (1982, **Reading, 10.3**) makes this idea more controversial by suggesting that pupils 'learn to be stupid' in schools. They do this when teacher requirements for conformity with managerial rules, structure and order override the pupil need for understanding and engagement in high quality learning tasks. The vital message of such work is that classroom management is an absolutely necessary means to an end – but it is not the end itself.

This chapter has been structured in four sections. The first section focuses on some key management skills. The second considers some of the most regularly occurring classroom episodes which require management. Section three analyses some of the coping strategies which teachers and children may develop and the final section uses a United Kingdom report, the Elton Committee of Enquiry into school discipline (**Reading, 10.9**), to provide an overview of classroom management issues.

1 MANAGEMENT SKILLS

This section builds on the work on curriculum planning and on preparing for a teaching session which was discussed in Chapter 8. Having considered how a learning session might be planned (Chapter 8, section 3.1, **Reading, 8.6**), we will now look at four important management skills which relate to the maintenance and development of such sessions in action: 'withitness', 'overlapping', pacing and self-presentation. Many of the issues in this and the following section on 'Managing Classroom Episodes' are also addressed in **Readings, 10.5** and **10.6**.

1.1 'Withitness'

This is a term coined by Kounin (1970, **Reading, 10.6**) to describe the capacity to be aware of the wide variety of things which are simultaneously going on in a classroom. This is a constant challenge for any teacher and can be a particular strain for a new teacher until this skill is acquired.

Teachers who are 'withit' are said to 'have eyes in the back of their head'. They are able to anticipate and to see where help is needed. They are able to nip trouble in the bud. They are skilful at scanning the class whilst helping individuals and they position themselves accordingly. They are alert; they can pre-empt disturbance; and they can act fast. They can sense the way a class is responding and can act to maintain a positive atmosphere.

1.2 'Overlapping'

This is another of Kounin's terms and describes the skill of being able to do more than one thing at the same time. This can be related to withitness if, for example, a problem emerges concerning occasions when giving sustained help to a particular child results in relatively neglecting the rest of the class. In addition, overlapping is also an important and separate skill in its own right. Most teachers work under such pressure that they have to think about and do more than one thing at a time. Decisions have to be made very rapidly. Jackson (1968) calculated that over a thousand interpersonal exchanges a day typically take place between each teacher and the children in their care. For these reasons, reflecting, anticipating and making rapid judgements are very much a necessary part of any teacher's skills.

1.3 Pacing

Pacing a teaching–learning session is another important skill. It involves making appropriate judgements about the timing and phasing of the various activities and parts of a session and then taking suitable actions. At the simplest level, there is the practical judgement to be made at the end of a session about when to switch into a 'tidying up phase' – it is very easy to get involved in activities, forget about the clock and suddenly to find that it is playtime. More complex educational judgements are necessary in relation to learning activities and the various phases of a typical session. For instance, the activities have to be introduced: this is often an initial 'motivational phase' where the children's interest is stimulated. This motivation also has to be maintained. Sessions then often enter an 'incubation and development phase' in which children think about the activities, explore ideas and then tackle tasks. From time to time there may be a need for a 'restructuring phase' where objectives and procedures may need to be clarified further. Finally, there may be a 'review phase' for reinforcing good effort or for reflecting on overall progress.

Judgements about pacing – about when to make a new initiative – depend crucially on being sensitive to how children are responding to activities. If they are immersed and productively engaged then one might decide to extend a phase or run the activity into the next session. If the children seem to be becoming bored, frustrated or listless then it is usually wise to retain the initiative, to restructure or review the activity or to move on to something new. If the children are becoming too 'high', excited and distracted, then it may be useful to review and maybe redirect them into an activity which calms them down by rechannelling their energies.

1.4 Self-presentation

The last of the four management skills which we have identified is self-presentation, for how to 'present' oneself to children is also a matter for skill and judgement. Teachers who are able to project themselves so that children expect them to be 'in charge' have a valuable ability. There is a very large element of self-confidence in this and student teachers, in particular, may sometimes find it difficult to enact the change from the student role to the teacher role. Perhaps this is not surprising, for a huge change in rights and responsibilities is involved. The first essential, then, is to believe in oneself as a teacher.

A second range of issues concerned with self-presentation is more skill-based. Here non-verbal cues are important. Self-presentation relates to such things as gesture, posture, movement, position in the room, facial expression, etc. These will be actively interpreted by children. The intended impression might be one of sureness, of confidence and competence. The reflective teacher will need to consider how non-verbal cues can help to convey such attributes.

A further very important skill is voice control. A teacher's use of voice can be highly sophisticated and effective. Changing the pitch, volume, projection and the intensity of meaning can communicate different aspects about self. If anyone's voice is to be used in this way then it will require some training and time to develop. Teachers, like singers and actors, can learn to use their diaphragm to project a 'chest voice', to breathe more deeply and speak more slowly so that their voice and their message is carried more effectively. Developing voice control is also an important asset in telling and reading stories, which may involve having to present many different characters. In the first instance it may be a good idea to try out different 'voices' – privately, and far enough away from others that a 'big' voice does not disturb anyone else! Although tape recorders never seem flattering, recording a practice story-telling can be a useful way of seeing how much appropriate voice variety is developing.

A fourth and more general area of skill which is involved in how teachers present and project themselves is that of 'acting' – as though on a stage. In this sense it is the ability to convey what we mean by 'being a teacher', so that expectations are clear and relationships can be negotiated. Acting is also an enormous strength for teachers for one other particular reason. When one is acting one is partially detached from the role. It is possible to observe oneself, to analyse, reflect and plan. Acting, in other words, is controlled behaviour which is partially distanced from self. In the situations of vulnerability which sometimes arise in classrooms this can be a great asset.

The skills which we have been reviewing above need to be put in a context. They are simply skills and have no substantive content or merit in their own right. A self-confident performer who lacks purpose and gets practical matters wrong (for example has ill-defined objectives, mixes up children's names, plans sessions

> ### *Practical activity 10.1*
>
> *Aim:* To gather data about one's management skills and judgement.
>
> *Method:*
>
> 1. Ask a colleague to observe a session which you take and to make notes on the way in which you manage the children. They could watch out for examples of appropriate withitness, overlapping, pacing and self-presentation (or chances missed). Discuss the session together afterwards.
>
> 2. Set up a video camera to record a session which you take. Analyse the play-back in terms of the criteria above.
>
> *Follow-up:* Such analysis should increase self-awareness of management skills. Try to identify possible improvements which could be made. These can be practised and worked on.

badly, loses books, acts unfairly, etc.) will not be able to manage a class. A teacher has to be competent as well as skilled and must understand the ends of education as well as the means (see Practical Activity 10.1).

2   MANAGING CLASSROOM EPISODES

'Flow' is an important summary criterion which can be used to describe classroom management. By 'flow' what is meant is the degree of continuity and coherence which is achieved in a learning session. It implies a steady, continuous movement in a particular direction. The suggestion is thus that we should work with the children to develop a coherent sense of purpose within our classes; should organize our classrooms in ways which are consistent with those purposes; and should manage the children, phases and events so that educational objectives are cumulatively reinforced. If this can be done then energy, interest and enthusiasm for learning is likely to be focused productively.

Achieving such a flow of activities requires a high degree of awareness, sensitivity and skill and it is sometimes the case that events seem to conspire to produce jerky, fragmented incoherent sequences of activities which lack momentum.

There are four classroom episodes which pose particular management challenges to the flow of sessions. These are 'beginnings' of sessions; 'transitions' between phases of sessions or between sessions themselves; 'crises', and 'endings' of sessions. We can consider each in turn.

2.1   Beginnings

The beginning of a session is often seen as important because of the way in which it sets a tone. The aim is usually to introduce and interest the children in the planned activities; to provide them with a clear indication of what they are expected to do; and to structure the activity in practical, organizational terms. See Check-lists 10.1, 10.2 and 10.3.

2.2   Transitions

Transitions are a regular cause of control difficulties, particularly for student teachers. This often arises when expectations about behaviour concerning one activity are left behind and those of the new one have yet to be established. In

---

Check-list 10.1

Aim: To consider how we get the children's attention and keep it.

1. How do we call for attention? Is a recognized signal used (e.g. standing in the front, clapping hands)?

2. How do we know if we have got their attention?
Have they stopped what they were doing?
Are they looking?
Are they listening?

3. Has the speaker maximized conditions for listening?
Are the listeners facing the speaker (so those who hear little can see facial expressions)?
Is it quiet (so those who hear 'too much' have fewer distractions)?

Check-list 10.2

Aim: To consider how the children are stimulated at the start of a session.

Some possibilities are:

- Capitalizing on children's interests and their own experiences (e.g. someone who has a wobbly tooth or a filling)

- Challenging them to investigate, interpret (e.g. survey of number of new teeth or fillings in the class)

- Channelling their curiosity – artefacts, models, posters, stories, videos (e.g. dentist leaflets, jaw bones)

1. Which kind of stimulation is used most?

2. How often are alternatives tried?

3. What has been most/least successful – why and when?

Check-list 10.3

Aim: To consider how the children are orientated to know exactly what is expected of them.

1. Do they know why they are doing this activity?

2. Do they know what they are going to learn from it?

3. Do they know if any follow-up is expected?

4. Do they know on what criteria it is to be assessed?

5. Do they know what they are going to do with completed work?

6. Do they know which activity they are to go on to next?

---

these circumstances, a skilled teacher is likely to take an initiative early and to structure the transition carefully.

For example, it would be a challenging prospect if a whole range of creative, English and maths activities were in full flow when physical education in the hall was timetabled and the children had to get changed suddenly. It is important to break down a transition such as this into discrete stages. The skill lies in anticipating problems before they arise; in prestructuring the next phase; and in interesting the children in the next phase so that they are drawn through to it. These principles apply to any transition (see Check-list 10.4).

2.3 Crises

A classroom 'crisis' is obviously an immediate source of disruption to the flow of a session. Crises can come in many forms, from a child being sick or cutting a finger, to children or perhaps a parent challenging the teacher's authority and judgement. Despite the wide-ranging issues which are raised, there are three fairly simple principles which can be applied from the classroom-management point of view.

Check-list 10.4

Aim: To monitor a transition.

1. Did I give an early warning of the transition?

2. Did I give clear instructions for leaving existing work?

3. Did I give the children clear instructions for the transition and for any movement that was necessary?

4. Did I arouse the children's interest in the next phase?

The first principle is to minimize the disturbance. Neither a child who is ill or hurt, nor a parent or child who is upset, can be given the attention which they require by a teacher who has continuing classroom responsibilities. Help from the school secretary, an ancillary helper or the headteacher should be called in either to deal with the problem or to relieve the classteacher so that he or she can deal with it. In this way disturbance to the classroom flow can be minimized and those in need of undivided attention can receive it. Of course, a student teacher usually has a full-time teacher upon whom to call.

The second principle for handling a crisis is to maximize reassurance. Children can be upset when something unexpected happens and it may well be appropriate to reassert the security of their classroom routines and expectations. A degree of caution in the choice of activities for a suitable period might therefore be wise.

The third principle which is appropriate when a crisis arises concerns oneself with pausing for sufficient thought before making a judgement on how to act. Obviously, this depends on what has happened and some events require immediate action. However, if it is possible to gain time to think about the issues outside the heat of the moment, then it may produce more authoritative and constructive decisions (see Practical Activity 10.2).

Although, hopefully, crises will be rare, there may be other sorts of behavioural problems which can upset the 'flow' of a session. However, by constant monitoring and being 'withit', it is usually possible to anticipate undesirable behaviour which threatens the working consensus (see Chapter 5) and to 'nip it in the bud'. Nevertheless, difficulties are bound to occur from time to time, and a prudent teacher is likely to want to think through possible strategies in advance so that he or she can act confidently in managing such situations. A range of strategies exist which might be used to meet possible incidents:

Practical activity 10.2

Aim: To monitor responses to a classroom crisis.

Method: After a crisis has arisen, a diary-type account of it and of how it was handled could be written. This might describe the event, and also reflect the feelings which were experienced as the events unfolded. It might be valuable to encourage children to make a similar description and reflection after the event, so that you can gain an insight into why they behaved as they did.

The following questions might be asked:

1. Did I minimize disturbance?

2. Did I maximize reassurance?

3. Did I make appropriate judgements on how to act?

Follow up: Having examined your actions and the children's responses to the crisis, it would probably be helpful to discuss the event and the accounts with a friend or colleague.

Strategies to pre-empt general misbehaviour

1. Make sure each child knows what to do and how to do it.

2. Show approval of appropriate work or behaviour.

3. Be supportive of any problems encountered.

Strategies to respond to misbehaviour

1. Ignore it if it only occurs once.

2. If repeated:

    2.1 Make eye contact.

    2.2 Move towards the child.

    2.3 Invite the child to participate – ask a question or encourage a comment.

3. If persistent, in addition to the responses above:

    3.1 Name the child firmly and positively.

    3.2 Move to the child.

    3.3 Stop the action.

    3.4 Briefly identify the inappropriate behaviour.

    3.5 Clearly state the desired behaviour.

    3.7 If necessary, isolate the child – avoid a contagious spread, a public clash and an 'audience' which can provoke 'showing-off'.

4. After the event:

    4.1 Encourage the child to identify what had been wrong, thus sharing responsibility with the child.

    4.2 Invite the child to draw up a 'contract' of what the child and the teacher will do and with which tangible rewards.

    4.3 Modify behaviour by withdrawal of privileges and by providing opportunities to earn praise.

Other, major ongoing problems can also exist in any classroom. These may be associated with an individual child who has particular difficulties. In such instances, it is important to analyse the behaviour and try to identify the possible causes before any positive action can be taken. One might consider the conditions, characteristics and consequences of the behaviour:

Conditions. When exactly does the disruption occur?

- Is it random or regular?
- Is it always the same child?
- Is it always regarding the same task?
- Is it always with the same teacher?

Characteristics. What exactly happens?

- Is it a verbal reaction?
- Is it a physical reaction?

Consequences. What are the effects?

- On the child, the teacher?
- On the class, the school?
- Do they join in, ignore, retaliate?

Such major, persistent problems are best discussed with other colleagues and a common strategy worked out. This might also involve the parents and the whole class, if necessary, so that a consistent approach can be adopted.

Whether a problem is associated with an individual child or most of the class, a consistent approach is essential and would, hopefully, provide security for the children as well as support for the teacher. It must be remembered that children respond to situations and experiences. We, as teachers, structure such experiences. Thus, if children respond problematically, we must reflect on the experiences which we provide rather than simply trying to apportion blame elsewhere.

A final regularly occurring type of event or phase which influences the flow of classroom life concerns the endings of sessions.

2.4 Endings

Ending a session is a further management issue and four aspects will be reviewed. The first is a very practical one. At the end of any session equipment must be put away and the classroom must be tidied up ready for future sessions. The second aspect relates to discipline and control. Children can sometimes get a little 'high' at the end of a session when they look forward excitedly to whatever follows. This, combined with the chores of tidying up, can require a degree of awareness and firmness from the teacher. The procedures which are called for here are similar to those for transitions. The two other aspects involved in ending sessions have more explicit and positive educational potential. One of these concerns the excellent opportunities which arise for reviewing educational progress and achievements, for reinforcing good work and for contextualizing activities which have been completed. This is complemented by the opportunities which also arise for asserting the membership of the class as a communal group. Shared experiences, teamwork and co-operation can be celebrated and reinforced through enjoying poetry, singing, games, stories, etc. There are thus lots of very productive opportunities at the ends of sessions and even an odd space of unexpected time, perhaps waiting for a bell, can be used constructively.

Overall, a carefully thought-out and well-executed ending to a session will contribute to the flow of activities by providing an ordered exit, by reinforcing learning and by building up the sense of 'belonging' within the class as a whole (Check-list 10.5).

Check-list 10.5

Aim: To monitor the end of a session.

1. Did I give early warning of the end of the session?

2. Did I give clear instructions for tidying up?

3. Did I reinforce those instructions and monitor the tidying up?

4. Did I take opportunities to reinforce the educational achievements, efforts and progress made?

5. Did I take opportunities to build up the sense of the class as a community?

6. Did I praise the children for what they did well?

7. Did I provide for an ordered exit from the room?

---

3 COPING STRATEGIES

The previous sections of this chapter have considered classroom management exclusively from the point of view of the teacher's judgements and actions. However, classroom management is a more complex issue than this implies for the obvious reason that it applies to an interactive situation between the teacher and children. The process of managing and coping is thus one of active judgement and decision-making on both sides.

 The concept of a coping strategy is useful here (Woods, 1977; Hargreaves, 1978; Pollard, 1982, **Reading, 10.8**). It refers to the strategies which people adopt in response to their circumstances, as a means of sustaining their sense of self. The issues of classroom management, control and survival are all included in this concept. For a teacher, a major question might be 'How do I cope in my classroom with large numbers of children, limited space and resources and a wide range of expectations bearing on me?' For a child, a prominent question might be 'How do I cope in the classroom when I am on my own among so many other children, having to do certain things, with the teacher judging my work and when my parents and friends expect certain things of me?'

The answer, to both questions, is that action is likely to be tactical (i.e. based on judgements which are made about actions which will best serve each person's immediate interests). A great many different examples of teacher and child strategies have been identified. Among these are the child strategies listed below:

Open negotiation – collaborative participation

- discussing, reasoning, initiating
- sharing a joke

Seeking recognition/reassurance

- fake involvement
- acting

Drifting – relying on routines for cover

- pleasing the teacher
- docility/resignation
- right answerism

Evasion – apathy

- time-stealing
- redoing work

Withdrawal – avoidance

- minimizing effort

Rebellion – aggression

- messing around
- 'winding up' the teacher

Such strategies can be identified by observation and interviews with children. They may well strike a chord with personal experiences of being a pupil, or indeed cause reflection concerning children who have been taught. Such strategies are a means by which children 'manage' in the classroom (see Practical Activity 10.3).

Some common types of teaching strategies which have been identified include the following (see Practical Activity 10.4):

Practical activity 10.3

Aim: To reflect on the range of coping strategies which children use in the classroom.

Method: Observe a small group of children in a classroom (either in your own class, or a colleague's). Try and work out the meaning and purpose behind what they are doing. Are they trying to demonstrate their 'best work' to the teacher? Are they evading and playing for time? Are they having a laugh? Afterwards you could discuss some of the events with the children to gain insights into their interpretation of events, rather than just to rely on your own.

Follow-up: Understanding children's coping strategies can help us to be more sensitive to their needs when we make managerial decisions.

Practical activity 10.4

Aim: To reflect on the coping strategies which we use when teaching.

Method: This issue can be tackled by a combination of personal diary records together with the comments and observations of a colleague. Alternatively, a video recording of a session followed by analysis could be a way of collecting information about our own coping strategies.

Follow-up: Having identified the range of strategies and the types most frequently used, the question of their appropriateness and educational effectiveness can begin to be answered.

Open negotiation – mutual collaboration

- discussion and explaining
- sharing a joke

Distancing – avoiding confrontation

- enforcing rigid routines
- ritualizing
- 'routinization' – keeping them busy
- repetition
- moderating demands

Manipulation

- using reward/punishment
- flattery
- personal appeals

Domination/charisma

- relying on personal charisma
- intellectual 'showing off'

Coercion

- sarcasm
- threatening
- hitting (which is, of course, illegal in the UK and many other countries)

It is important to note the interactive context of the classroom (see Chapter 5 and *Readings*, Chapter 5). Since the actions of teachers and children have an immediate effect on each other, a mesh of teacher and child strategies tends to develop. This, of course, is closely related to the form of relationships and to the 'working consensus' which has been negotiated (see Chapter 5; **Reading, 5.3**).

One way of conceptualizing this mesh of strategies is indicated in Figure 10.1.

Teacher strategies			Child strategies
Unilateral strategies	Strategies within the working consensus		Unilateral strategies

Open negotiation

distancing ←——————→ seeking recognition
routinization ←——————→ drifting
manipulation ←——————→ evasion

domination ←——————————————————————→ withdrawal
coercion ←——————————————————————→ rebellion

Figure 10.1 *The interrelationships between teacher and child strategies*

The significant implication of this model of interaction is that the actions of the children are clearly related to the actions of the teacher. It suggests that, if difficulties arise in connection with classroom management, it is not sufficient just to review the 'awkward characteristics' of the children – for this simply passes all responsibility on to them and generates negative ideas about them. It is also necessary to analyse the situation interactively and to consider our responsibilities as teachers.

4 | DISCIPLINE: AN OVERVIEW

Good discipline and order in classrooms and schools are the products of a great many factors and influences. When they break down, there tends to be an almost instinctive, but oversimplified, response to 'sort out the trouble-makers'. This can even occur at a national level. For instance, in March 1988 a Committee of Enquiry, chaired by Lord Elton, was set up in the United Kingdom following a media outcry over reports of teachers being physically attacked by pupils and about 'indiscipline in schools today'. Wisely, however, the Elton Committee took a balanced and wide-ranging view of the issues involved and this is reflected in their report (DES, 1989b, **Reading, 10.9**). As the Elton Report stated:

> The behaviour of pupils in a school is influenced by every aspect of the way in which it is run and how it relates to the community it serves. It is the combination of all these factors which give a school its character and identity. Together, they can produce an orderly and successful school in a difficult catchment area; equally, they can produce an unsuccessful school in what should be much easier circumstances.
>
> (DES, 1989b, p.8).

The report went on to emphasize the importance of having clearly stated boundaries of acceptable behaviour, of teachers responding promptly and firmly to those who test boundaries, of motivating pupils to learn, of providing a stimulating and appropriately differentiated curriculum, of managing groups skilfully, of creating a positive school atmosphere based on a sense of community and shared values, of achieving the highest possible degree of consensus about standards of behaviour among staff, pupils and parents, of promoting values of mutual respect, self-discipline and social responsibility. Furthermore, it drew attention to the role of governors, local education authorities, training organizations and government in supporting teachers.

The holistic approach of the Elton Committee is well founded and the issues to which they drew attention are considered thoroughly in the chapters of this book. School and classroom discipline should, above all, be pre-empted where purposeful communities of people exist; with teachers acting sensitively, skilfully and authoritatively to maintain the values, rules, expectations and activities which provide an infrastructure for order and meaning.

Of course, primary schools are generally seen as being relatively successful in developing and maintaining discipline and in providing a constructive atmosphere for learning. Certainly, only 11 per cent of the primary teachers questioned by researchers for the Elton Committee (Gray and Sime, 1989) thought that there were any 'serious' discipline problems in their schools and parental confidence is also generally high (Hughes *et al.*, 1994, **Reading, 14.6**).

However, there is no place for complacency and it must be recognized, in particular, that many of the skills which lead to competence in classroom management can only be developed through extensive practice with children in classrooms. In doing this it is advisable to move gradually from small groups, to larger groups and on, to taking the whole class. The support and advice of an experienced teacher or colleague is likely to be invaluable.

The Elton Report includes a statement of 11 'principles of classroom management' (DES, 1989b, p. 71, **Reading, 10.9**) which reflect much good sense and experience. They are included in Check-list 10.6 in the form of questions for use in planning, undertaking and reflecting on classroom practice.

Check-list 10.6

Aim: To reflect on classroom management and discipline using the Elton Report's 'principles of classroom management'.

Do I:

1. Know my pupils as individuals – names, personalities, interests, friends?

2. Plan and organize both the classroom and the lesson to keep pupils interested and minimize the opportunities for disruption – furniture layout, pupil grouping, matching of work, pacing lessons, enthusiasm, humour?

3. Involve pupils in establishing the rules for classroom behaviour and routinely reinforce why they are necessary?

4. Act flexibly to take advantage of unexpected events rather than being thrown by them?

5. Continually observe or 'scan' the behaviour of the class?

6. Remain aware of, and control, my own behaviour, including stance and tone of voice?

7. Model the standards of courtesy that I expect from pupils?

8. Emphasize the positive, including praise for good behaviour as well as good work?

9. Make sparing and consistent use of reprimands – being firm not aggressive, targeting the right pupil, using private not public reprimands, being fair and consistent, avoiding sarcasm and idle threats?

10. Make sparing and consistent use of punishments – avoiding whole group punishment and pupil humiliation which breed resentment?

11. Analyse my own classroom management performance and learn from it?

As the Elton Committee concluded, Item 11 is 'the most important message of all'.

CONCLUSION

This chapter has examined aspects of management and discipline which help to establish and sustain conditions for successful learning. These questions of management are matters of great concern to teachers, as are the questions of teachers and children learning to cope with each other and with learning situations. Managing collaborative group work can be particularly challenging, though Biott and Easen (1994, **Reading, 10.4**) provide some excellent advice. Most of us soon become more familiar and gradually grow in confidence and competence with such challenges. Direct experience is irreplaceable in developing competence, but there is also much to be said for sharing ideas, problems and successes through discussion with colleagues.

Many of the issues considered in this chapter relate closely to the content of Chapter 5, on classroom relationships and discipline. For instance, there is specific discussion there on bullying.

Notes on further reading

For a book which provides many insights on classroom management, and which has become a classic, see:

Kounin, J. S. (1970)
Discipline and Group Management in Classrooms,
New York: Holt, Rinehart & Winston   📖 **Reading, 10.6**

It is crucial to hold on to management issues in the context of broader education objectives. On this, see:

Putnam, J. and Burke, J. B. (1992)
Organising and Managing Classroom Learning Communities,
New York: McGraw Hill.

For a philosophical account see:

Straughan, R. (1988)
Can We Teach Children to be Good? Basic Issues in Moral, Personal and Social Education,
Milton Keynes: Open University Press.

A book which provides a wide ranging review of issues and approaches to classroom management in primary schools is:

Roberts, T. (1983)
Child Management in the Primary School,
London: Allen & Unwin.

and also:

Good, T. and Brophy, J. (1978)
Looking in Classrooms,
New York: Harper & Row.

Docking, J. M. (1980)
Control and Discipline in Schools,
London: Harper & Row.

Sound advice deriving from a recent empirical study of the issues may be found in:

Wragg, E. C. (1993b)
Class Management,
London: Routledge.

Wragg, E. C. (1993a)
Primary Teaching Skills,
London: Routledge.

Another concise discussion of the major issues, and with a good section on teacher stress and how to cope with it, is provided by:

Laslett, R. and Smith, C. (1992)
Effective Classroom Management: A Teacher's Guide, (2nd edn)
London: Routledge.   Reading, 10.5

For an account of alternative ways of analysing disruptive behaviour see:

Tattum, D. P. (ed.) (1986)
The Management of Disruptive Pupil Behaviour in Schools,
Chichester: Wiley.

For more practical advice on managing classroom behaviour, see:

Fontana, D. (1986)
Classroom Control: Understanding and Guiding Classroom Behaviour,
London: Routledge.

McManus, M. (1989)
Troublesome Behaviour in the Classroom: A Teacher's Survival Guide,
London: Routledge.

Haigh, G. (1990)
Classroom Problems in the Primary School,
London: Paul Chapman.

McNamara, S. and Moreton, G. (1995)
Changing Behaviour: Teaching Children with Emotional and Behavioural Difficulties in Primary and Secondary Classrooms,
London: David Fulton.

Merrett, F. (1993)
Encouragement Works Best: Positive Approaches to Classroom Management,
London: David Fulton.

An analysis of teacher and child coping strategies in the primary school can be found in:

Pollard, A. (1985)
The Social World of the Primary School,
London: Cassell.   Reading, 5.3

The Elton Report is well worth consulting, together with some of the work which has derived directly from it.

DES (1989b)
Discipline in Schools,
Report of the Committee of Enquiry chaired by Lord Elton.
London: HMSO.   Reading, 10.9

Wheldall, K. (1991)
Discipline in Schools: Psychological Perspectives on the Elton Report,
London: Routledge.

Docking, J. (1990b)
Managing Behaviour in the Primary School,
London: David Fulton.

For two books which approach disciplinary issues more explicitly at a whole-school level see:

Farmer, A., Cowin, M., Freeman, L., James, M., Drent, A. and Arthur, R. (1991)
Positive School Discipline: A Practical Guide to Developing Policy,
London: Longman.

Munn, P., Johnstone, M. and Chalmers, V. (1992)
Effective Discipline in Primary Schools and Classrooms,
London: Paul Chapman.

A constructive programme of activities for whole-school development is provided by:

Maines, B. (1991)
Challenging Behaviour in the Primary School: A School Development Programme,
Bristol: Redland Centre for Professional Development, University of the West of England.

CHAPTER 11

How are we communicating in the classroom?

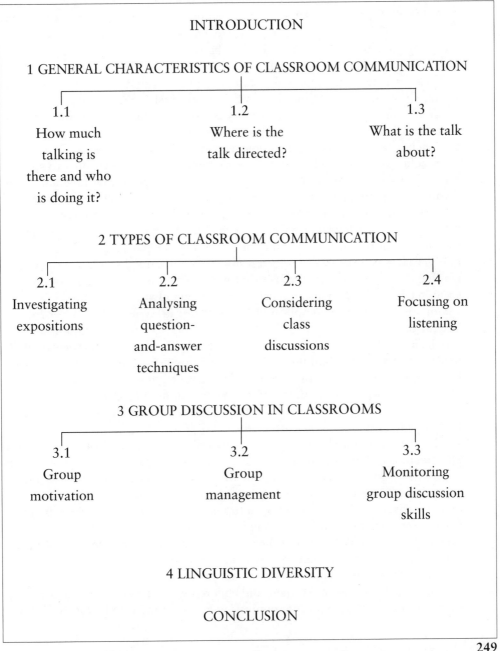

INTRODUCTION

1 GENERAL CHARACTERISTICS OF CLASSROOM COMMUNICATION

1.1
How much talking is there and who is doing it?

1.2
Where is the talk directed?

1.3
What is the talk about?

2 TYPES OF CLASSROOM COMMUNICATION

2.1
Investigating expositions

2.2
Analysing question-and-answer techniques

2.3
Considering class discussions

2.4
Focusing on listening

3 GROUP DISCUSSION IN CLASSROOMS

3.1
Group motivation

3.2
Group management

3.3
Monitoring group discussion skills

4 LINGUISTIC DIVERSITY

CONCLUSION

INTRODUCTION

So far in Part Two, we have examined the perspectives and expectations of children and teachers, their relationships, the ways in which knowledge, concepts, skills and attitudes are planned and presented through the curriculum and the manner in which classrooms can be organized and managed. All of these aspects facilitate the learning which we hope will be taking place in the classroom. It is now time to turn directly to teaching and learning processes. Fundamental to these processes is the language through which teaching and learning is mediated. The Bullock Report (DES, 1975) emphasized the crucial role of language to learning and suggested the notion that all teachers were 'language teachers'. In accepting the centrality of language, this chapter focuses on the nature of spoken communication, and on how it might affect teachers, children and learning.

Three basic teaching approaches can be identified. First, teachers can demonstrate, show or tell children how to do certain tasks. Second, they can leave children to discover and examine experiences for themselves. Finally, they can discuss the task to clarify what should be done, why it is important, how it might be approached, and to explore any problems that might be experienced. Often, these approaches are combined, with different emphasis to each according to specific activities, particular individuals and special circumstances at that time. However, discussion is particularly important because it is central to exchanging views and understandings. It is at the heart of a reflective teaching–learning process.

Most of our teaching and learning is achieved through some form of communication. In schools, although communication may be partially accomplished in non-verbal ways, the most important media are talking, listening, writing and reading. However, despite the fact that most of the time spent in classrooms is spent in trying to communicate, such efforts are not always successful.

Communicating is a complicated business, for it involves three sets of skills. Language skills are, of course, fundamental but, since communication involves people, it requires social skills as well. In addition, since communication is usually focused on some meaningful topic, it calls for appropriate cognitive capacities – knowing something about the subject under consideration and being able to think about and process what others are trying to communicate to us. Nor can we forget the attitudes of the participants and the context itself, for these are also likely to add meanings to the encounter.

Para-verbal and and non-verbal features of oral language contribute to the effectiveness of how we communicate. Apart from what we say, a great deal is conveyed by how we say it. Thus, tone of voice, pace, pitch and how we project our voice are all part of the communication process. Meanings which we convey by these para-verbal features are open to misinterpretation, particularly by those from different cultures and backgrounds. In addition, there are non-verbal aspects such as looks and gestures, and the ways in which we move, which accompany what we say. These can sometimes extend our meanings but they can also sometimes confuse or even contradict what we say.

In classroom situations, teachers and children will act as both speakers and listeners. Hence, if classroom communication and learning is to be assured, all the participants need to have knowledge, skills and attitudes which are appropriate to both talking and listening in schools. This cannot be assumed.

The National Curriculum gives due prominence to Speaking and Listening within English. However, the 'overloading' and breadth of the curriculum, felt initially at Key Stage 1 but remaining at Key Stage 2, may have made it difficult for teachers to have given this issue the attention which it merits. In a review of teaching and learning processes, Sammons *et al.,* (1994, **Reading, 11.1**) highlight the links between language and learning and consider the impact of new curriculum requirements for pupil participation in talk, for the adoption of active roles, for group work and other teaching methods, for the entitlements of bilingual pupils and in respect of the promotion of 'standard English'. This chapter addresses such issues in the following way.

Having identified the importance of oral communication in this introduction, the chapter moves on to a general review of the characteristics of classroom communication. This is followed by a focus on particular types of classroom 'talk' and then by a consideration of the demands made on 'listening'. A section on group discussion follows and the chapter concludes by addressing linguistic diversity.

1 GENERAL CHARACTERISTICS OF CLASSROOM COMMUNICATION

Any observer in a primary classroom cannot fail to notice the amount of talking – and listening – that occurs. If we examine this talk closely a number of characteristics can be identified. These can provide important clues regarding the quality of the teaching–learning process.

1.1 How much talking is there and who is doing it?

Classic research in America suggested that two-thirds of the teaching sessions studied were usually spent in talk and two-thirds of that talking was done by the teacher (Flanders, 1970). Since then investigations in British primary schools have shown similar figures (Galton *et al.,* 1980; Bennett *et al.,* 1984).

1.2 Where is the talk directed?

The findings of one large investigation into classroom talk, the ORACLE research, showed that approximately 80 per cent of teachers' time, in junior school classrooms, was spent in talk between the teacher and children – 56 per cent with individuals, 15 per cent with the whole class, 7 per cent with groups (Galton *et al.,* 1980, **Reading, 9.2**). Interestingly, a similar large project a decade later, the PACE research, found that in infant classrooms, the proportion of whole-class work was twice as high, with a lower figure for individual work (Pollard *et al.,* 1994).

Apart from the size of the 'audience' with whom a teacher is communicating, it is also significant to consider how the teacher's time is distributed between the children; between girls and boys, and between children of different abilities or different needs. Some research suggests that boys often receive a greater share of a teachers' attention – both positive and negative (Clarricoates, 1981; Serbin *et al.,*

1993, Spender and Sarah, 1980), and that children of different ethnic origins receive different types of attention (Galton, 1986). The impact of integrating children with special needs has also been studied (Croll and Moses, 1985).

1.3 What is the talk about?

The ORACLE study showed that the highest percentage of teacher talk in junior school classrooms was generally devoted to supervising tasks set – rather than to talking about the substantive content of those tasks (Galton *et al.*, 1980). Most of this talk was in the form of statements of fact. Very little time indeed was spent in asking questions which required children to think for themselves in any kind of open-ended, problem-solving capacity. In general, teacher talk seemed to be largely concerned with the smooth running and management of the classroom, and the practice of engaging the children in challenging discussion was rare. In infant classrooms such talk is also likely to concern the shaping of pupil behaviour as the children learn various aspects of the pupil role (Willes, 1983).

As reflective teachers it is important to review these findings and consider their significance – processes which have been begun in excellent development work through the National Oracy Project and the Language In the National Curriculum Project (see Notes for Further Reading). For example, what might be the effects on the children? What impressions might children gain about learning and about their own role in the learning process? What kinds of attitudes towards learning might children acquire? What types of learning are likely to take place?

To begin to answer such questions, a reflective teacher is likely to want to collect data rather than rely on impressions. Tape-recording can be a useful technique for collecting certain kinds of data on classroom talk, though an alternative way of collecting information about particular aspects of teacher talk is to devise appropriate check-lists. These can be helpful both as a guide when preparing a session, or as a framework within which to reflect afterwards. A third approach is to devise a schedule of specific categories of behaviour. For example, three categories could be used, such as when the teacher asks a question, explains a task, or tells a child off. Each time one of the listed behaviours is noted it can be 'marked up' using a tally system (Practical Activity 11.1).

2 | TYPES OF CLASSROOM COMMUNICATION

There are four particularly common types of classroom communication. These are:

Expositions: where the speaker describes, informs, instructs, or explains.

Question-and-answer exchanges: frequently for testing and checking purposes, where there is often one right answer, (i.e. a 'closed' situation).

Discussions: where the participants (whole class or small group) explore ideas and feelings together (i.e. an 'open' situation).

Listening: where the receiver hears and responds to the speech of other people.

Practical activity 11.1

Aim: To investigate time spent in talking and listening, in a classroom-based group activity.

Method: Tape-record (or better still video record) part of a teaching session (e.g. 15 minutes). Remember that unless a relatively quiet room is used, it may be difficult to hear what is said against background noise. In a whole class situation the teacher's voice often dominates. In a small group situation all the participants can usually be heard on the average cassette recorder.

Focal Points for consideration:

1. How much talking is there and who is doing it?

    - Calculate total amount of time spent on teacher talk.
    - Calculate time spent by children talking to teacher, and to each other. Are there any differences between boys/girls, high/low attainers, etc.?

2. Where is the talk directed?

    - Calculate the number of times the teacher is spoken to, by whom, why.
    - Calculate the number of times different children are spoken to, by whom, why.

3. What is the talk about?

    - Calculate the amount of time spent on social/personal discussion.
    - Calculate the amount of talk spent setting the task up, and supervising the work.
    - Calculate the amount of time spent on discussing the main points, or substantive content, of the task.

Follow-up: Information of this kind can highlight the pattern of talk in our own classroom. It can often reveal aspects which surprise us, because it is so difficult to be aware of how much we talk, to whom and why, whilst we are engrossed in the process of teaching itself. Having identified the pattern of talk we need to decide whether what we do is consistent with our aims.

Each of these situations has features in common as well as features which are unique to itself. For example, since every communicative situation is at least a two-way process, we need to consider the speakers as well as the listeners. In an 'exposition' situation the listeners are not likely to participate verbally very much. Nevertheless, the speaker should be aware of the listeners and watch the listeners for signs of understanding or otherwise, so that adjustments can be made. The listeners must listen, must be able to react and show if understanding has taken place, or, if not, must be able to ask for clarification. In addition, the listeners may also want to respond more actively. Hence 'expositions' can sometimes become 'discussions'. In such situations the roles of speaker and listener may change rapidly. The listeners will have to respond to the speaker and hold on to their own ideas, wait their turn so that their ideas can be added later. Hence, in a discussion situation of this kind, considerable linguistic, social and cognitive demands are made.

Each situation, in fact, calls for particular types of awareness about the rules of communication. In order to participate productively, the rules must be clear and each participant must understand and accept those rules. Learning to speak and to listen are thus very important skills. Neither skill can be considered 'passive', for they both take place in an interactive situation.

We now turn to examine the first of the four main types of communication that we find in the classroom – exposition.

2.1 Investigating expositions

Often the first task in each teaching session is to stimulate the children and to structure activities. This is just as pertinent to whole-class sessions as to group or individual work. Expositions, therefore, are a common aspect of any teacher's talk. They are less regular tasks for the children, though they do occur when children 'report back' on an activity, or 'tell their news'. In any such situation the opening 'moves' are very important in setting the tone of the session.

A number of different aspects of exposition might be considered:

1. Getting attention.

2. Motivating the listeners.

3. Orientating, so that expectations about the session are clear.

4. Constructing and delivering the exposition itself.

The first three of these aspects have already been discussed in Chapter 10, as part of our discussion of classroom management. Here therefore, we suggest some check-lists to help to focus our attention on the fourth aspect of expositions – constructing and delivering the exposition itself (see Check-lists 11.1 and 11.2).

2.2 Analysing question-and-answer techniques

Teachers, and children, use questions for a wide range of purposes and they can be seen as a vital tool for teaching and learning (Perrot, 1982; see also **Reading, 11.8**). Asking questions provides immediate feedback on how participants are thinking and on what they know and it accounts for a high proportion of teacher talk. Question-and-answer techniques are therefore seen as an essential means of helping us to understand learning processes. Listening to the 'answers' and not prejudging them is an important way of learning about a learner.

Particular aspects concerning questions which might be reviewed are:

1. The purpose, or function, of questions.

2. The form in which questions are asked.

3. The ways in which responses are handled.

Each of these aspects is now considered in further detail.

Check-list 11.1

Aim: To investigate aspects in the delivery of expositions.

When the speaker delivers the exposition:

- is eye contact sustained, to hold attention and give interim feedback?
- is an interesting, lively tone of voice used?
- is the pace varied for emphasis and interest?
- is the exposition varied by encouraging orderly participation?
- are pauses used to structure each part of the exposition?
- are appropriate examples, objects or pictures used to illustrate the main points?
- are appropriate judgements made regarding the level of cognitive demand, size of conceptual steps and length of the concentration span required?
- is a written or illustrated record of key points provided as a guide, if listeners need memory aids?

Check-list 11.2

Aim: To examine how an exposition is constructed. Are the instructions, directions, descriptions and explanations clear, concise and coherent? Has the speaker:

1. planned what is going to be said?

2. stated the outline structure of the exposition? (by means of advance organizers' e.g. 'We are going to find out...').

3. selected the key points: identified and made explicit the relevance of each and their relationship to each other? ('There are four things we need to think about ... because ...')

4. sequenced key points appropriately?

5. used short, simple sentences: explained specialist vocabulary if it needs to be used, given concrete examples or asked the listeners to generate their own?

6. signalled when a new point is made? ('Now let's look at..'. 'The third thing to look out for is...')

7. summarized key points (or got the listeners to summarize)?

8. sought feedback to check understanding (at each point if necessary)?

The purpose, or function, of questions

Questions can be grouped in many different ways. However, two main categories commonly occur. The first is psycho-social questions: those which centre on relationships between children or between a teacher and the children. The second category is 'pedagogic' questions: those which relate to more specifically educational concerns, and to the teaching and learning of skills, attitudes, concepts and knowledge (see Check-list 11.3).

The form of questions

Among the most important issues associated with classroom questioning techniques is the form in which the question is posed in relation to its purpose.

The form of a question can have very diverse effects. For example, a question can be posed in such a way as to invite a monosyllabic answer, for instance,

Q. 'Did you like the book?'
A. 'Yes.'/'No.'

What effects would such a question have if the aim was to develop a discussion?

Conversely, would this be any more appropriate in a testing situation? For instance,

Q. 'Has potato got starch in it?'
A. 'Yes.'/'No.'

Another form is the 'direct' question, which is short and simple in construction and has a single specified focus. For instance,

Q. 'How did the Vikings make their boats?'

to which the answer may be lengthy though straightforward and factual, or,

Q. 'What makes a good book?'

to which the answer may also be lengthy but consisting of opinions and ideas which may be complex to articulate.

Very different effects might result from using a 'direct' question compared to one which invites a monosyllabic response. A reflective teacher would need to consider whether such a form would be appropriate if the aim was to encourage exploration, evaluation or to focus contributions on a particular suggestion.

A third form of question is the 'indirect' question. This is a long, composite, question which may include a number of different leads. Again, such a question can be very useful in some situations but inappropriate in others. For example, 'indirect' questions can offer a number of different suggestions which might help in opening out a discussion and in providing a range of possible leads to explore. It would be less suitable in a testing situation, as the focus of the question would be relatively unclear. It could also be confusing to a child who found it hard to take everything in and who therefore got lost.

The ways in which responses are handled

A third aspect of questioning, that of handling responses, is also important to consider. A key issue is how long to pause and wait for an answer. It has been found that, on average, a classroom teacher waits only two seconds before either repeating the question, rephrasing it, redirecting it to another child or extending it.

Check-list 11.3

Aim: To provide a framework for analysing classroom questions. See how many uses of classroom questions you can spot in your school.

Purposes of psycho-social questions:

- *to encourage* shy members to integrate by participating (e.g. 'Jan, you've got a little kitten too, haven't you?')
- *to show interest* in and value for group members (e.g. 'You had a good idea, Norita. Will you tell us?')
- *to develop respect* for each others' views (e.g. 'What do you think you would have done?')
- *to assert control* (e.g. 'Wayne, what are you up to?')
- *to implement routines and procedures* (e.g. 'Ahmed, what did I tell you to do next?')

Purposes of pedagogical questions:

1. Closed questions (low-level cognitive demand)

   - *to recall information* – for testing, consideration or feedback (e.g. 'Where is Ethiopia?')
   - *to give an on-the-spot solution* (application of known rule to new variables) (e.g. 'What is 28 divided by 4?')
   - *to encourage analysis* – by describing, comparing or classifying (e.g. 'What's the difference between...?')

2. Open questions (high-level cognitive demand)

   - *to explore information and ideas* with no set 'answer' (reasoning/interpreting, hypothesizing/speculating, imagining/inventing) (e.g. 'How do you think the hero would feel if...?')
   - *to encourage synthesis* of information and ideas by focusing on contradictions, discrepancies, different sources of evidence (e.g. 'What do you think really happened...?')
   - *to encourage evaluations, decision-making and judgements* (e.g. 'Would it be fair if...?')
   - *to encourage the transfer of ideas* and application of knowledge, (e.g. 'How is what we've found out useful...?')

Having got a response, teachers have many alternative strategies which can be used. We can reject the response, modify, ignore, pass over, correct or accept it. We can also hold it with others for general consideration when many suggestions have been given, offer it for others to comment upon, extend it, invite a child to develop it or respond with praise. With such a range of options a reflective teacher might usefully consider what the effects would be for different children in different situations.

Practical Activities 11.2 and 11.3 suggest ways of examining question-and-answer sessions with regard first to asking questions and second to handling responses.

Apart from monitoring the level and variety of types of questions, it is also important to remember that a listener may not perceive a question in the same way as the person who asks it. For example, a teacher may ask an apparently closed question, intended to check understanding, but, to a child who does not know the answer, the question may seem very open. In addition, there are rules

Practical activity 11.2

Aim: To investigate teacher questions within 'question-and-answer' exchange.

Method: Either tape-record a teaching session, or, by agreement, observe a colleague. Choose three 5-minute periods in the teaching session (e.g. beginning/middle/end) and write down the questions the teacher asks during each period.

It may also be possible to code the audience to whom the questions were addressed, (e.g. B= boy, Bb = group of boys, G =girl, Gg = group of girls, Mg = mixed group, C = class).

The questions could be classified using the pedagogic or psycho-social categories from Check-list 11.3.

Follow-up: Classifying questions should highlight the variety and level of the cognitive demands that were made. It is then possible to consider whether what we do matches our intentions and, if not, what changes could be made.

If the audience has been noted, it is also possible to analyse the distribution of questions and to consider any implications.

The activity could be repeated to analyse children's questions.

Practical activity 11.3

Aim: To investigate teachers' handling of children's responses within 'question-and-answer' exchanges.

Method: Choose three 5-minute periods during a teaching session (beginning/middle/end) and record how the teacher handles pupil responses during each period. The responses can be related to the list of teacher purposes discussed in Check-list 11.3.

Follow-up: Analysing the data may help reflection upon the teacher's intentions, and whether they were fulfilled. It may also illuminate the extent to which pupil responses are 'heard' and engaged with by teachers. What effects can be identified resulting from the ways in which pupil responses were handled?

and conventions which guide this kind of classroom interaction. For example, a question directed to a child which may appear perfectly acceptable, may, if directed to the teacher without altering para-verbal and non-verbal features, be regarded as 'cheeky'.

Such discrepancies between how a question is intended and how it is received raise some important issues concerning the classification of questions. This is a difficulty which is both theoretical – in terms of identifying and defining 'types' of questions, as well as practical – in terms of recognizing and interpreting intention and therefore responding appropriately.

2.3   Considering class discussions

Discussion makes an absolutely fundamental contribution to learning. Its import- ance is well established for the development of very young children and Wells (1986, **Reading, 11.3**) coined the attractive image of 'conversation as the reinven- tion of knowledge'. This nicely conveys the element of exchange, construction and interpretation which is involved. However, as the evidence reviewed in section 1 showed, much so-called 'discussion' in schools takes the form of teacher-dominated transmission of pre-established knowledge (see Barnes, 1975, **Reading, 11.2**, for a classic analysis of this distinction). One common result of such tight teacher control is that pupils' engagement may become relatively routinized and ritualistic. According to Edwards and Mercer (1987, **Reading, 11.4**), classroom discussions certainly function to 'establish joint understandings' and 'common knowledge' between teachers and pupils. However, as they put it:

> The basic process is one of introducing pupils into the conceptual world of the teacher .... It is essentially a process of cognitive socialization through language.

Whilst such teacher instruction is appropriate for some purposes, a genuine class discussion must start with some attempt to elicit opinions and knowledge from the pupils, to treat them seriously and to explore their consequences.

Such distinctions between the varied forms and purposes of discussion are often useful. At the beginning of a session a teacher may wish to find out what the chil- dren already know about the topic on which she wishes to focus. This 'elicitation' may be achieved through open questioning. The elicitation may call for factual knowledge or opinions. If, however, the information that is elicited is also exam- ined, interrogated and reinterpreted then the episode becomes a more open-ended 'exploration'. It is the latter, exploratory, situation which can be identified as a discussion. The content of what is discussed may vary considerably and may include what is believed to be factual knowledge, opinions, hypotheses, etc. It is the manner in which the content is treated rather than the content itself which is the distinguishing factor between elicitation and exploration. For a useful set of ideas on how to structure discussion and debates, see Phillips (1985, **Reading, 11.7**) (Practical Activity 11.4).

Discussion can also be distinguished from debate in terms of both aims and style. Discussion aims to explore and is relatively loose and informal in style, whilst debate aims to persuade and is more tightly and formally structured. The recognition of the importance of such oral forms is given, for example, in the National Curriculum in England and Wales which encourage these forms to be

259

Practical activity 11.4

Aim: To analyse the dynamics of group discussion.

Method: Tape-record (or video) a group discussion. General features can be monitored on the following schedule. Additional detailed analysis can be carried out using Check-lists 11.1 and 11.2 above.

Group characteristics	Comments
1. Composition of the group (e.g. size, sex, ability)	
2. Seating arrangement (draw diagram)	
3. Was there a leader, or scribe?	
4. Was this challenged?	
5. Did anyone not participate? (How did the others respond?)	
6. In what ways did the group collaborate?	
7. Was help needed/requested?	
8. What intervention was given?	
9. In what ways was the task successful?	
10. Did the group feel satisfied?	

Follow-up: Information gained from such schedules can help in the analysis of group interaction. It can help in understanding the roles of the members and whether these change if the composition of the group changes. Devising our own schedule can make us more aware of what we are aiming at. It also provides a framework for action to develop the potential of the group.

developed: it refers to discussion skills as well as to argumentation in both oral and written form (Check-list 11.4).

Check-list 11.4

Aim: To examine discussion skills.

A reflective teacher may find it useful to consider some of the following questions:

1. Do the participants take turns or do they frequently talk over each other or interrupt?

   Do they invite contributions, redirect contributions for further comments, give encouragement?

   Do they listen to each other? Are they willing to learn from each other (i.e. respond and react to each other's contributions)?

   Do they indulge in 'parallel' talk (i.e. continue their own line of thinking)?

   Does conflict emerge or is harmony maintained?

   Is conflict positively handled?

   - by modifying statements, rather than just reasserting them?
   - by examining assumptions, rather than leaving them implicit?
   - by explaining/accounting for claims?

2. Do participants elaborate their contributions?

   - by giving details of events, people, feelings?
   - by providing reasons, explanations, examples?

   Do they extend ideas?

   - by asking for specific information?
   - by asking for clarification?

   Do they explore suggestions?

   - by asking for alternatives?
   - by speculating, imagining and hypothesizing?

   Do they evaluate?

   - by pooling ideas and suspending judgement before making choices?

2.4 Focusing on listening

If communication is a two-way process, we have dwelt long enough on the speaker, or 'initiator'. It is also necessary for teachers and children to be competent listeners, or 'receivers'. However, we have already noted how the position of 'initiator' is usually taken by the teacher and that the role of 'receiver' is more often than not assigned to the children. Estimates of the amount of time children spend listening are difficult to establish. However, a comparison between ORACLE findings (Galton *et al.*, 1980) and PACE findings (Pollard *et al.*, 1994) suggests that the amount of time children spend interacting with, and listening to, their teacher may be rising. PACE showed infant children interacting with their teacher for about 40 per cent of the working day, of which almost 35 per cent was as part of a whole class. For most of the latter the pupils were listening. ORACLE showed junior children interacting with the teacher for only 12 per cent of the day, most of which was again spent in listening. The remainder was spent in interacting with peers – both listening, talking and sharing activities. The average teacher, however, still spends about 80 per cent of each day interacting with children, and doing most of the talking!

It is possible to identify different types of listening situations within classrooms, which serve specific purposes and impose particular demands. These purposes can be categorized in the following way:

Interactive listening such as during a discussion, where the role of speaker and listener changes rapidly. In such circumstances participants need to exercise 'bidding' skills, for example, by raising a hand; sitting more upright and forwards; or by starting to move their lips. Some individuals will not have acquired any such skills and thus find it very hard to draw attention to the fact that they want to join in. Others may find it hard to notice tentative moves by group members and therefore may not 'let others in'.

Reactive listening where listeners follow an exposition. For example, a set of instructions may be given which children are then expected to act upon, or an extended input of information may be provided, which the listeners are expected to be able to 'take in', possibly 'take notes' on, and then respond to. In reactive and interactive listening, the emphasis is on following the meaning of the speakers. Differences are often in the degree of formality and the status of the speaker *vis-à-vis* listeners.

Discriminative listening where listeners have to discriminate between and identify sounds rather than meaning – for example, phonic sounds for spelling or reading purposes, or environmental/musical sounds.

Appreciative listening where listeners listen for aesthetic pleasure, perhaps to musical or environmental sounds – for example, to the rhythm or sounds of words in poems and fairy stories; or to other languages or accents.

It is useful to distinguish between these different types of listening so that we can be aware of the demands we make upon ourselves and the children. For example, how often do we allow appreciative listening, requiring perhaps a receptive level of listening? Do we convey how we want the children to listen actively in such a situation? How often do we demand extended attention, in a reactive situation, so that we hear someone out, follow a line of argument, consider a large amount of information, before moving into discussions?

As reflective teachers, we may want to be aware of the different demands that each type of listening makes. We also need to consider how many different listening contexts are experienced and how this might affect our listening and that of children (Dickson, 1981) (see Practical Activity 11.5).

Practical activity 11.5

Aim: To analyse listening demands in the classroom.

Method: During a session, a day or a week, try to note down how much time a teacher or children spend:

1. on each of the four types of listening mentioned above
2. in each of the four contexts indicated below

The results could be recorded on a matrix for each session/day.

Types of listening (purposes)	Contexts of listening			
	Where (informal to formal)	To whom (known to unknown)	What (familiar to unfamiliar)	For how long
Interactive				
Reactive				
Discriminative				
Appreciative				

Follow-up: Having collected the data, it is then possible to estimate how different a teacher's experience is from the children's (and whether the children's experiences are very different). It is also possible to reflect upon the range and balance of experiences and to decide on their implications.

3 | GROUP DISCUSSION IN CLASSROOMS

In recent years a great deal of emphasis has been placed on the use of group work in classrooms based on the knowledge that it is a very common means of working in the adult world. Indeed, the success of the human species itself has been attributed to the capacity to co-operate (Schmuck, 1985). Group work also, of course, fits well within the social constructivist model of learning, which we considered in Chapter 6, and this potential has been exploited in two excellent studies of classroom group work (Galton and Williamson, 1992; Bennett and Dunne, 1992, **Reading, 11.6**). Vygotskian ideas emphasize the importance and meaningfulness of the social context in which the learner acts and this is exactly what co-operative classroom group work, at its best, can provide. However, clarity of goals, the appropriateness of the task and the composition of the group have been found to be particularly significant. Bennett and Dunne (1992) for instance, offer an

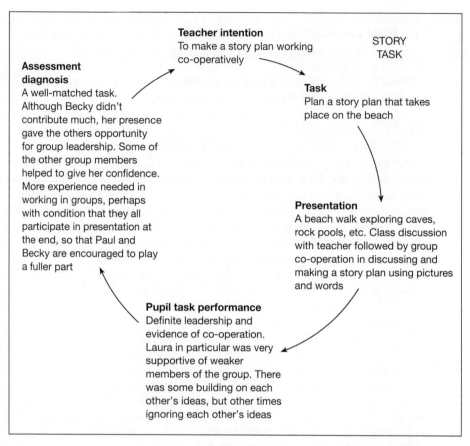

Figure 11.1 *A teaching cycle for an illustrative group task* (Bennett and Dunne, 1992)

illustration of a teaching cycle for a group task on co-operatively producing a plan for a story (Figure 11.1). This is based on the five key elements, or phases, in the teaching cycle which had been identified in Bennett and Dunne's research.

Considerable interest in learning from British and American experience is being demonstrated by many European countries, from France and Spain to the new, post-Communist states of central Europe, in which co-operative forms of learning may be seen as 'democratic'. Despite many of the positive outcomes which can emerge from such collaborative, learner-centred contexts, large classes with a wide range of pupil abilities, personalities, aptitudes and experiences pose severe challenges to any teacher. Indeed, the most consistent finding from the research is that, despite the commitment to this form of classroom practice, it is very difficult to implement consistently. From the point of view of a reflective teacher, three main issues arise. These relate to the motivation, management and monitoring of groups.

3.1 Group motivation

Perhaps the most important contributory factor to successful group work is the nature of the task itself (Tann, 1988), including both social and cognitive aspects

(Bennett and Dunne, 1992, **Reading, 11.6**). It is important to decide whether a task could just as effectively be done by an individual or whether there is a genuine need for a group. This, of course, depends on the purpose of the task and on the way it is presented.

Early work in this field demonstrated that the teacher's presence often inhibited pupils and prevented them from putting the issues in their own language and focusing on questions which they wanted to raise. Instead, participants were found to be engaged in a game of 'guess what's in the teacher's mind': they therefore tried to anticipate correct answers rather than raise questions or explore issues (Barnes *et al.*, 1969). Without a teacher present, pupils could learn to take responsibility for their own learning. However, without a clear perception of the nature of the task and the purpose of the activity, teacher-less small group activity can become a time for 'chat and mucking about', rather than for 'discussion and work' (Tann, 1981). Research has shown how, with appropriate guidance, infant and junior pupils can become very skilled discussants in collaborative group work situations (Ede and Wilkinson, 1980; Tann and Armitage, 1986; Prisk, 1987). Many further examples of classroom initiatives can also be found in the documents produced by the National Oracy Project (Norman, 1990).

Understanding the social skills which can contribute to effective group work, can help to structure group processes. Helping the participants understand and develop these skills can be valuable (see Check-list 11.4). It is also useful for a teacher (and pupils) to recognize the kinds of group roles which participants might adopt which affect the dynamics of the group: leaders and followers, or jokers, inquisitors, non-participants, obstructionists and many other 'characters' might emerge. These roles often result from the participants' insecurities in the social context. If they can be helped to identify with the purpose of the task some of the insecurities may gradually dissolve.

Collaborative group work provides a unique context for pupils in which they can learn and demonstrate new social skills. The composition of such groups is critical. Compatibility is more important than just attainment. Sometimes friendship groupings can be successful, but not if friendship is more highly prized by the members than critical exploration which might reveal friendship differences. Interest groupings might be useful, but not where personalities might clash destructively. A teacher therefore needs to be very alert to the social groupings within the class, to the placement of shy or less popular children and with regard to the possible interaction of different personalities.

3.2 Group management

Group size and type are particularly important factors in management, but so too is the overall classroom context in which groups work. Bennett and Dunne (1992), for instance, advocate that co-operative groups are also involved in whole class activities and that they report back to the whole class. This provides a sense of purpose and accountability within the culture of the class as a whole.

Several sorts of group are possible, as the following examples show:

Buzz groups: various sizes of buzz group can be used to stimulate ideas and generate alternative approaches to initiate follow-up action. Larger groups may cause more reticent children to remain silent. As an alternative, a pyramid group process could be used. Individuals think of their views or contribution; they share it with another child; each pair talks to another pair and agrees the ideas which they want to offer to the whole group; all the ideas are then pooled.

Problem-solving groups: these are used where a single outcome is required from member collaboration. It is often successful in small to medium-sized groups of four or five. This is particularly common in drama, technology, science and maths.

Forum work: when carefully structured, this works well for large groups, such as the whole class, debating ideas or controversial issues (e.g. Troyna and Carrington, 1988).

Sharing groups: where teachers want to encourage a positive interchange of views in a mutually trusting atmosphere, they can often succeed by using smaller, more intimate groups. Expecting the group to provide feedback on the processes of their discussion and/or the outcome is useful in helping to focus the participants' views. The end-product, in such instances, could be a list of feelings or a poster depicting group conclusions for action.

Whatever size, type or composition of group is chosen, the success or otherwise of the activities which follow cannot be absolutely predicted. There are no consistent research findings but teachers are wise to attend carefully to the personalities and capacities of the children whom they select to work together. It is also crucial that the task, and its parameters, is clearly presented.

3.3 Monitoring group discussion skills

Several phases have been identified in successful group work which can be used as a framework in monitoring progress. First, children need to be encouraged to spend time orientating themselves to the other members of the group. They need time to listen to each other and to explore the demands and boundaries of the particular task (Practical Activity 11.6). Second, during the development phase, the participants must learn to share ideas and extend suggestions and give time for the ideas to incubate. Although the number of contributions at this stage may be an indication of exploration and collaboration, it is the nature of the interactions which is of greatest importance to the quality of discussion. In the third, conclusion phase, the quality of group interaction, together with the quality of the ideas themselves, should be evident. This should be apparent if a final 'product' is shared with the rest of the class.

A major component of developing discussion skills is encouraging the participants to monitor themselves. While the more socially and linguistically competent children may well 'pick things up', and therefore learn to discuss by discussing, children with less meta-cognitive awareness (see Chapter 6, section 2.5) may benefit from more specific support. Hence, discussion about discussing can make an important contribution to developing co-operation. At the end of a discussion, a group can be asked if it thought it had been a 'good' discussion and if so, what had made it good. The children could be encouraged to consider their discussion and identify useful strategies using their own terms. These can then be compared to those in Check-list 11.4.

Teachers can do a number of things to help develop constructive group work and discussion – for example, by praising those strategies which children use. They can

Practical activity 11.6

Aim: To appraise the listening skills of individuals.

Method: Record, or observe, a range of individuals (including the teacher) during a normal teaching–learning session in a classroom.

Note the types of listening called for and the contexts. Also, note any child's behaviour that might indicate that they heard, understood or responded. For example, did they: look at the speaker, or look around; appear to agree, answer questions, offer suggestions; show awareness of others' needs, take turns?

Follow-up: By watching individuals closely, it may be possible to pin-point more precisely any difficulty a child might have, and whether it is specific to certain types of listening or contexts.

motivate children to want to contribute. Also, they need to manage the classroom so that opportunities for discussion can be supported. Finally, teachers need to monitor discussions with the children and to record their progress and problems.

4 | LINGUISTIC DIVERSITY

Attitudes to oral language have changed dramatically in the last twenty years. For instance, there is much less consensus about *the* way to talk or write, as is evident from broadcasters and the diversity of written styles in use in modern society. This has occurred partly because of changes in two separate spheres. First, there has been a change in our understanding of the efficiency, as means of communication, of different styles of language. Early work by Labov (1973) identified the grammars of black teenagers in New York and argued that their language was not 'deficient', 'sloppy' or substandard. He suggested that their grammars were 'different' and just as regularly rule-bound as more socially accepted forms of standard English. Secondly, there has been a change in the social acceptability of a wider range of different styles of language. This has meant that the notion of 'appropriateness' has increasingly come to be used (i.e. that different kinds of language are suitable for different purposes, audiences and situations). This is a contrast to the notion of 'accuracy' as an absolute standard to be used to judge all language situations (see Stubbs, 1983, **Reading, 11.9**, for further discussion of this issue).

Within classroom contexts, this led to two further developments. The first of these was support for the importance of accepting a child's language because it is part of accepting the child and thereby strengthens a positive self-image. This, in turn, led into the broader issue of the acceptability of language varieties. The use of non-standard English has for long had negative social consequences, of a discriminatory nature. Now, however, there is greater acceptance among educationalists that, whilst speaking in standard English should be part of the linguistic repertoire of each child, variation in language style should not be equated with language deficit, intellectual deficiency or social disadvantage (Edwards, 1983; Stubbs and Hillier, 1983).

The necessity for a constructive and appreciative approach of this sort is most obvious when considering the extent of linguistic diversity in modern societies. For instance, a 1987 language census in London (ILEA, 1987) found that no less that 172 different languages were spoken by school children. Some of such languages have been mapped in terms of the geolinguistic areas from which they are derived (Alladina and Edwards, 1991) and this is shown in Figure 11.2.

Language varieties used within a society with a single dominant language, such as English, reflect far more than simply an alternative means of communication (Pinsent, 1992). Language is intimately connected to cultural identity and is thus closely associated with the life experiences of minority ethnic groups in diverse societies. Often, of course, such groups are both economically and socially disadvantaged. As Pattanayak has so clearly expressed it, countries such as the UK have a poor record of affirming and working with different social groups, and yet the opportunity remains. He writes:

> As the identity of the various oppressed groups is threatened, identity assertion movements ensue. ... Ethnicity, which in the literature is variously expressed as assertion of cultures, communal upsurges, revival of religions, voices and movements of marginalised peoples ... hurts the power elites. ... Britain is on the crossroads. It can take an isolationist stance in relation to its internal cultural environment. ... The second road would be working together with cultural harmony for the betterment of the country. The choice is between mediocrity and creativity.

(Pattanayak, 1991, p. x).

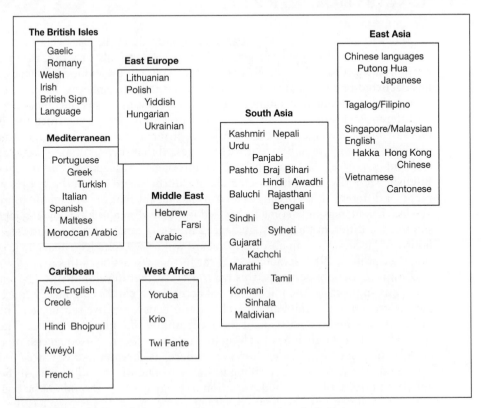

Figure 11.2 *Geolinguistic areas of languages spoken in Britain*

Practical activity 11.7

Aim: To highlight some of our own responses to language varieties.

Method: Use the results of this provocative rating scale for comparison with the results that colleagues obtain. Discuss the results of the comparison.

	I tend to agree		I tend to disagree		
1. Dialects are ungrammatical forms of English	1	2	3	4	5
2. In general middle-class children speak better than working-class children	1	2	3	4	5
3. Children should speak standard English at all times in school, including in the playground	1	2	3	4	5
4. The first task for all children in Britain is to learn good English	1	2	3	4	5
5. Dropping your 'Hs' is sloppy, and creates a bad impression	1	2	3	4	5
6. Poor grammar and spelling should be corrected	1	2	3	4	5
7. All primary school children should learn to appreciate some Shakespeare	1	2	3	4	5
8. It is confusing for young children to speak two languages in school	1	2	3	4	5
9. We should not use expressions like 'black mark' as they illustrate racist language	1	2	3	4	5
10. We should always try to use books which show different people as equals.	1	2	3	4	5
11. Books with class or race stereotypes can be used with care.	1	2	3	4	5

Follow-up: The exercise above should produce some interesting discussion, but actual knowledge and understanding of these issues is another thing. Among speakers of majority languages, the most common state is one of relative ignorance regarding language varieties and the cultures and social circumstances of different social groups. The Notes on Further Reading may provide some ideas.

Teachers have a particularly important and sensitive role to play here. The danger is that 'educational' concerns become overly framed by dominant monolingual conceptions of traditional English culture and language. Indeed, they may also become structured by socially unaware requirements of national curricula and assessment procedures. Whatever the circumstances, we would suggest that reflective teachers should work to affirm the positive value of minority languages and cultures, wherever they teach. This is likely to mean affirming and building on the bilingual capacities of many children (Bourne, 1989; Levine, 1990; Miller, 1983, **Reading, 11.10**). (Practical Activity 11.7).

Changes have also occurred in attitudes to reading and writing in terms of what is acceptable in content and style. For instance the English component of the National Curriculum of England and Wales identified the entitlement of pupils as one where they should be taught to read, to understand and to respond to a wide variety of reading matter, including novels, magazines, information books, as well as material relating to the 'real world' (labels, notices, menus, maps, manuals, computer printouts and visual displays). The inclusion of 'response' to books is embodied in the requirement that pupils should be able not just to read books but to talk about them in terms of structure, content and language style. Similarly pupils should talk about and evaluate their own writing in discussion with their teacher or peers at drafting and final 'publishing' stages. Communication skills in the oracy mode are thus seen as integral to developing communication skills in a literacy mode.

Further, there is the expectation that pupils will be encouraged to 'be aware' of their own use of language in speaking and listening, reading and writing and be aware of the linguistic, cognitive and social processes involved in using language. This broader conceptualization of what it means 'to be literate' is very much in line with current work in Australia as well as the USA. The Kingman Report (1988) and the subsequent LINC project (Language In the National Curriculum) (Carter, 1990) gave teachers rich insights into what was meant by 'awareness' and how such awareness might be developed. However, the English curriculum has been something of a political football in the 1990s and there is still pressure from some right-wing groups to narrow it to focus more exclusively on the basic skills required to produce standard English.

CONCLUSION

This chapter has raised a large number of issues relating to communication which takes place within teaching–learning situations. Communication has been viewed as a key component of classroom life and therefore as an important influence on the learning which might take place. It is now time to consider the assessment of that learning and how reflective teachers might analyse and respond to it. This is the subject of Chapter 12.

Notes for further reading

For general introductions to the importance and use of language in the primary classroom see:

Tann, S. (1991)
Developing Language in the Primary Classroom,
London: Cassell.

Wray, D. and Medwell, J. (1991)
Literacy and Language in the Primary Years,
London: Routledge.

Jackson, M. (1993)
Literacy,
London: David Fulton.   Reading, 11.1

To make the points about the centrality of language in a different, and very engaging way, see:

Paley, V. G. (1981)
Wally's Stories,
Cambridge, MA: Harvard University Press.

A classic text on language and curriculum is:

Barnes, D. (1975)
From Communication to Curriculum
London: Penguin Books   Reading, 11.2

There have been three excellent development projects on language in the UK, with publications which are practical, imaginative and firmly rooted in an understanding of children's learning. Some of their valuable publications are in the form of pamphlets, booklets or newsletters but are worth a search.

However, on the National Writing Project see, for instance:

National Writing Project (1989a)
A Question of Writing,
Walton-on-Thames: Nelson.

National Writing Project (1989b)
Becoming a Writer,
Walton-on-Thames: Nelson.

National Writing Project (1989c)
Writing and Learning,
Walton-on-Thames: Nelson.

On the National Oracy Project see:

Norman, K. (1990)
Teaching, Talking and Learning in Key Stage One,
York: National Curriculum Council.

Baddeley, G. *et al.* (1991)
Teaching, Talking and Learning in Key Stage Two,
York: National Curriculum Council.

On the Language In the National Curriculum Project (LINC Project), see:

Carter, R. (ed.) (1990)
Knowledge about Language and the National Curriculum,
London: Hodder and Stoughton.

Department of Education and Science (1990–1)
Language in the National Curriculum (LINC): Materials for Professional Development,
London: HMSO.

National Curriculum Council and National Oracy Project (1991)
Assessing Talk in Key Stages One and Two,
Occasional Papers in Oracy No. 5,
York: National Curriculum Council/National Oracy Project.

Clear overviews of classroom talk are provided by:

Richards, J. (1979)
Classroom Language: What Sort?
London: George Allen and Unwin.

Graddul, D., Cheshire, J. and Swann, J. (1987)
Describing Language,
Milton Keynes: Open University Press.

Perera, K. (1987)
Understanding Language,
London: National Association of Advisers in English.

Excellent guides to methods of investigating classroom language are:

Edwards, A. D. and Westgate, D. P. G. (1987)
Investigating Classroom Talk,
London: Falmer.

Bennett, K. and Kastor, T. (1988)
Analysing Children's Language,
Oxford: Blackwell.

Research evidence on the language used in primary schools is very wide-ranging. See, for instance:

Wells, G. (1986)
*The Meaning Makers: Children Learning Language
and Using Language to Learn,*
London: Hodder and Stoughton.　　　　　　　　　　　📖 Reading, 11.3

Galton, M., Simon, B. and Croll, P. (1980)
Inside the Primary Classroom,
London: Routledge & Kegan Paul.　　　　　　　　　　📖 Reading, 9.2

Barr, M., D'Arcy, P. and Healy, M. K. (eds) (1982)
*What's Going On? Language/Learning Episodes in British and American Classrooms,
Grades 4–13.*
Montclair, NJ: Boynton/Cook.

Stubbs, M. and Hillier, H. (eds) (1983)
Readings on Language and Classrooms,
London: Methuen.

Edwards, D. and Mercer, N. (1987)
*Common Knowledge: The Development of
Understanding in Classrooms,*
London: Methuen.　　　　　　　　　　　　　　　　📖 Reading, 11.4

Davies, B. (1993)
Shards of Glass: Children Reading and Writing Beyond Gendered Identities
Sydney: Allen and Unwin　　　　　　　　　　　　　📖 Reading, 11.5

For work on explaining and questioning skills, see:

Wragg, T. and Brown, G. (1993)
Explaining,
London: Routledge.

Brown, G. (1978)
Lecturing and Explaining,
London: Methuen.

Kerry, T. (1982)
Effective Questioning,
London: Macmillan.

Brown, G. and Wragg, T. (1993)
Questioning,
London: Routledge.   📖 Reading, 11.8

On developing discussion, see work from the National Oracy Project referred to above. See also the classic, and salutary:

Barnes, D., Britton, J. and Rosen, H. (1969)
Language, the Learner and the School,
Harmonsworth: Penguin.

See also:

Ede, J. and Wilkinson, J. (1980)
Talking, Listening and Learning,
London: Longman.   📖 Reading, 11.7

MacLure, M., Phillips, T. and Wilkinson, A. (1988)
Oracy Matters: The Development of Talking and Listening in Education,
Milton Keynes: Open University Press.

For some interesting case-studies of the use of debate and discussion, see:

Troyna, B. and Carrington, B. (1988)
Children and Controversial Issues: Strategies for the Early and Middle Years of Schooling,
London: Falmer.

For communication in classroom group work two recent books have drawn on research and related it to practice, see:

Bennett, N. and Dunne, E. (1992)
Managing Classroom Groups,
Hemel Hempstead: Simon & Schuster.   📖 Reading, 11.6

Galton, M. and Williamson, J. (1992)
Groupwork in the Primary Classroom,
London: Routledge.

See also:

Tann, S. (1981) Grouping and group-work,
in B. Simon and J. Willcocks (eds)
Research and Practice in the Primary School,
London: Routledge & Kegan Paul.

For a very practical workbook on implementing many of these research insights, see:

Dunne, E. and Bennett, N. (1990)
Talking and Learning in Groups,
London: Routledge.

It is important to be aware of linguistic diversity in our culturally rich modern societies. See, for instance:

Alladina, S. and Edwards, V. (eds) (1991)
Multilingualism in the British Isles (2 vols),
London: Longman.

Linguistic Minorities Project (1985)
The Other Languages of England,
London: Routledge & Kegan Paul.

For constructive work which recognizes the opportunities and challenges presented by linguistic diversity, see:

Pinsent, P. (1992)
Language, Culture and Young Children,
London: David Fulton.   Reading, 11.9

On providing for bilingual children, see:

Verma, M. K., Corrigan, K. P. and Firth, S. (1995)
Working with Bilingual Pupils,
Clevedon: Multilingual Matters.

Levine, J. (ed.) (1990)
Bilingual Learners and the Mainstream Curriculum,
London: Falmer.

Miller, J. (1983)
Many Voices: Bilingualism, Culture and Education,
London: Routledge.   Reading, 11.10

CHAPTER 12

How are we assessing children's learning?

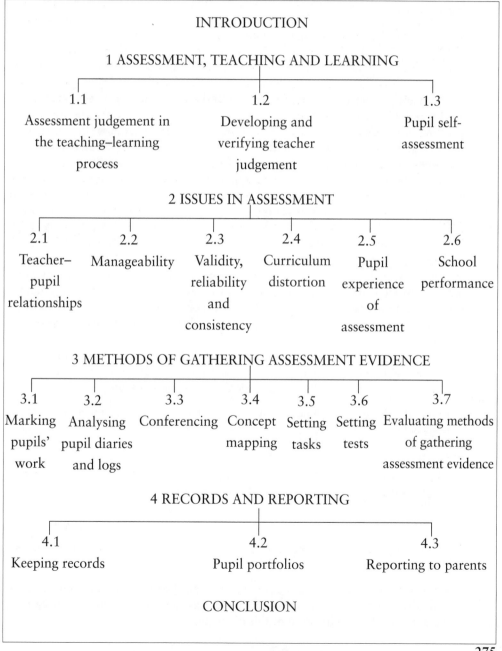

INTRODUCTION

1 ASSESSMENT, TEACHING AND LEARNING

1.1
Assessment judgement in the teaching–learning process

1.2
Developing and verifying teacher judgement

1.3
Pupil self-assessment

2 ISSUES IN ASSESSMENT

2.1
Teacher–pupil relationships

2.2
Manageability

2.3
Validity, reliability and consistency

2.4
Curriculum distortion

2.5
Pupil experience of assessment

2.6
School performance

3 METHODS OF GATHERING ASSESSMENT EVIDENCE

3.1
Marking pupils' work

3.2
Analysing pupil diaries and logs

3.3
Conferencing

3.4
Concept mapping

3.5
Setting tasks

3.6
Setting tests

3.7
Evaluating methods of gathering assessment evidence

4 RECORDS AND REPORTING

4.1
Keeping records

4.2
Pupil portfolios

4.3
Reporting to parents

CONCLUSION

INTRODUCTION

In recent years and in most parts of the world, assessment has become more and more important in education. This has occurred for two reasons.

The first, and by far the most significant, has been the concern of governments to introduce ways of 'measuring' educational outputs. In the United Kingdom, this has been seen as a means of informing parents about the progress of their children and as a way of comparing school performance to inform an educational market based on choice and diversity (e.g. Major, 1991; DES, 1992c). In this scenario, assessment is expected to raise standards of pupil achievement. Output assessment data, of the sort required by these arguments, is known as 'summative'.

The second reason for the growth in interest in assessment derives from teachers, who have increasingly come to realize the value of continuous assessment in informing the process of their teaching. Thus, as a course of study or a lesson progresses, a teacher gathers evidence of pupil responses and adjusts the learning programme to meet pupil needs. Teachers are thus able to engage more directly and accurately with the development of the learner's thinking and understanding. Process assessment data, of the sort required by these arguments, is known as 'formative'.

The basic difference in purpose produces serious tensions between these two forms of assessment – for instance, comparison vs. support, product vs. process, government vs. professional control. Many assessment experts suggest that the effectiveness of one form of assessment is likely to have the unfortunate effect of undermining the effectiveness of the other (see Harlen *et al.*, 1992, **Reading, 12.1,** for an important discussion of the purposes of assessment). In particular, when summative testing is emphasized, there is a tendency for teaching to be narrowly directed towards whatever the tests measure. A broad and balanced curriculum is thus distorted (e.g. Gipps, 1990; Broadfoot *et al.*, 1991). Other commentators feel that the two major forms of assessment can be mutually supportive – formative assessment supports the process of learning, summative assessment measures the result.

The latter view was strongly endorsed by the Task Group on Assessment and Testing (TGAT) which produced the report from which assessment in the UK was initially derived (TGAT, 1988). The Task Group suggested that:

> Promoting children's learning is the principle aim of schools. Assessment lies at the heart of this process

but...

> The assessment process should not determine what is to be taught and learned. It should be the servant, not the master, of the curriculum.

(TGAT, 1988, para. 3/4)

With this overall commitment in mind, TGAT set out four criteria for the assessment system. It should be:

Criterion-referenced – relate directly to what children can do, rather than to how they compare with others (norm-referenced) (see Croll, 1995, **Reading, 12.2,** for further explanation of this distinction).

276

Formative – provide a basis for teacher decisions about further learning needs.

Moderated – be made consistent and fair across schools.

Relate to progression – reflect expected routes of pupils' development and learning.

What followed, as the assessment structures and procedures of the National Curriculum, was the identification of ten levels of attainment for each subject (as described in Chapter 7, section 2.3). Each of these was specified with Attainment Targets and Statements of Attainment, against which both formative and summative assessments could be made. For primary schools, assessments were to take place at the ages of 7 and 11, the end of Key Stages 1 and 2. Aggregated results from schools were to be published so that information was available for parents.

Formative assessment was to be called 'Teacher Assessment' (TA) and was to be incorporated into classroom routines. Summative assessment was to be carried out using 'Standard Assessment Tasks' (SATs) – nationally devised, structured activities and tasks to be carried out at set periods during the year.

The implementation of these assessment plans was not straightforward. Parents in Scotland protested so much at the testing of 7 year-olds that SATs were withdrawn, whilst the use of SATs in England and Wales produced severe problems of manageability and comparability (Pollard *et al.*, 1994). Teachers protested against the priority which had legally be given to SATs in reports to parents and in the aggregated results for each school. In Northern Ireland there was an effort to avoid the problems found in England and Wales by using Externally Assessed Resources (EARs) and Common Assessment Instruments (CAIs).

In 1993, Sir Ron Dearing was appointed to conduct a review of the arrangements in England, and parallel work took place in Wales (Dearing, 1993, **Reading, 7.12**). The result was the production of the new National Curriculum and revised assessment procedures which took effect in September 1995.

A major change was that the number of Attainment Targets was considerably reduced. Those for the revised curriculum for England and Wales are set out in Figure 12.1.

A second innovation was that Statements of Attainment were replaced by 'level descriptions' and 'end of key stage statements'. An official definition of these is provided in Figure 12.2. The introduction of level descriptions and end of key stage descriptions was very important since it represented both a reduction of the complexity of the previous arrangements and a decision to trust teachers' overall judgements about pupil attainments. As the Secretary of State at the time put it, it was decided to 'go with the grain of teacher professionalism' (Shephard, 1994).

However, standard, externally set, national assessment continued. The use of relatively conventional statutory 'testing' for the core curriculum subjects developed (see Figure 12.3 for the position in 1996), although formal assessment of science was dropped from Key Stage 1. Assessment by 'tasks' became focused on the youngest and lower attaining pupils only and other subjects continued to be assessed by teacher assessment alone.

A further important recommendation of the Dearing Review was that teacher assessment should have parity with the results of nationally set tests. However, this has been extremely difficult to bring about since, in discussion of 'results', the media tend to focus almost exclusively on the test results alone. For instance, the Key Stage 2 results for 1995 (DFEE, 1996) showed positive teacher assessment

Subject	Attainment Targets in England	Attainment Targets in Wales
English	Speaking and Listening Reading Writing	Speaking and Listening Reading Writing
Welsh	Not applicable	Oral (speaking, listening and viewing) Reading Writing
Mathematics	Using and applying mathematics Number Shape, space and Measures (and Handling data in Key Stage 2 only)	Using and applying mathematics Number Shape, space and Measures (and Handling data in Key Stage 2 only)
Science	Experimental and investigative science Life processes and living things Materials and their properties Physical processes	Experimental and investigative science Life processes and living things Materials and their properties Physical processes
Design and Technology	Designing Making	Designing Making
Information Technology	Information technology capability	Information technology capability
History	History	History
Geography	Geography	Geography
Art	Investigating and making Knowledge and understanding	Understanding Making Investigating
Music	Performing and composing Listening and appraising	Performing Composing Appraising
Physical Education	Physical education	Physical education

Figure 12.1 *Attainment Targets within each National Curriculum subject as they apply to primary education in England and Wales*

Level descriptions

Level descriptions indicate the types and range of performance that a pupil working at a particular level characteristically should demonstrate over a period of time.

There are eight per attainment target.

Teachers should exercise their professional judgement to weigh up the pupil's strengths and weaknesses to decide what description best fits the pupil's performance, using as the basis a range of the pupil's work.

By the end of Key Stage 1, the performance of the great majority of pupils should be within the range of Levels 1 to 3. By the end of Key Stage 2, it should be within the range 3 to 5.

End of key stage descriptions

End of key stage descriptions set out the standard of performance expected of the majority of pupils at the end of each key stage.

They apply to Art, Music and Physical Education only.

Teachers should use their professional judgement to decide the extent to which a Pupil attainment relates to the expected standard of performance at each key stage

The statements are broadly equivalent to Level 2 at Key Stage 1 and Level 4 at Key Stage 2.

Figure 12.2 *Level descriptions and end of key stage description (SCAA, 1996)*

	Statutory tasks or tests in England	Statutory tasks or tests in Wales
End of Key Stage 1	English Mathematics	English (but Welsh in Welsh-speaking schools) Mathematics
End of Key Stage 2	English Mathematics Science	English (but Welsh in Welsh-speaking schools) Mathematics Science

Figure 12.3 *Statutory tasks or tests in England and Wales 1996*

outcomes but, with lower test scores for English and maths, they produced banner headlines about 'failing schools'.

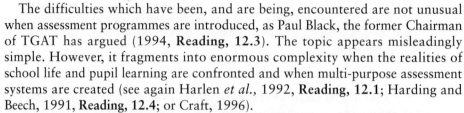

The difficulties which have been, and are being, encountered are not unusual when assessment programmes are introduced, as Paul Black, the former Chairman of TGAT has argued (1994, **Reading, 12.3**). The topic appears misleadingly simple. However, it fragments into enormous complexity when the realities of school life and pupil learning are confronted and when multi-purpose assessment systems are created (see again Harlen *et al.*, 1992, **Reading, 12.1**; Harding and Beech, 1991, **Reading, 12.4**; or Craft, 1996).

This chapter is organized in four parts. We begin by considering the very positive forms of support to learning which can, in principle, derive from assessment. In section 2 we review some of the difficult issues which may also emerge. Section 3 provides an account of various ways of gathering evidence and conducting both teacher-controlled and externally set assessment. Section 4 concerns records and reporting.

1 ASSESSMENT, TEACHING AND LEARNING

Attention has repeatedly been drawn in this book to the role of judgement in determining appropriate teacher actions, and this is of paramount importance in the flow of teaching–learning processes.

1.1 Assessment judgement in the teaching–learning process

The social constructivist model reviewed in Chapter 6, section 1.3, conceives of teachers analysing pupil skill and understanding, in the course of an activity or task, so that appropriate information, questions, explanations or advice can be offered. A teacher acts, we suggested, as a 'reflective agent' who makes accurate judgements, provides an appropriate teaching input and thereby scaffolds the child's understanding across what Vygotsky called the 'zone of proximal development' (**Reading, 6.4**). Children's knowledge and understanding is thus extended, by appropriate teaching, to levels which could not have been attained without the teacher intervention.

Notwithstanding the need for subject knowledge and a repertoire of teaching skills, this process is fundamentally dependent on the quality of the teacher's formative assessment. Without that, an intervention could easily be inappropriate and confuse the child's attempt to construct a meaningful understanding – and evidence from Bennett *et al.*, (1984) has shown just how common this is. This, then, is the direct link between assessment and learning in modern primary school practice. Without it, no teacher can hope to support children's learning appropriately.

It is worth looking at the various stages of this process in more detail and we represent it, schematically, in Figure 12.4 (derived from National Primary Centre (SW), 1991a). Five phases of a teaching programme are distinguished in this model. They build, progressively, from children's existing knowledge, understanding and skill and, at each point, the role of teacher assessment is emphasized.

	PURPOSES		POSSIBLE PROCESSES
ORIENTATION	Arousing children's interest and curiosity	Ensures that the children are focused on the topic and are motivated	Introducing Explaining Discussing
ELICITATION/ STRUCTURING	Helping children to find out and clarify what they think	Enables the teacher to **assess** pupil understanding in order to plan appropriate next steps	Questioning Discussing Predicting
INTERVENTION/ RESTRUCTURING	Encouraging children to test, develop, extend or replace their ideas or skills	Provides opportunities for children to engage, actively, in learning tasks Enables the teacher to observe pupil behaviour and, by **assessing** their skill and understanding, to make appropriate teaching interventions	Practising Observing Measuring Recording Speculating
REVIEW	Helping children to evaluate the significance and value of what they have done	Offers a chance for pupils to take stock of their learning and for the teacher to guide them in consolidating their understanding Provides an opportunity for the teacher to **assess** new learning and to consider next steps	Recording Discussing Explaining Hypothesizing Reporting Evaluating
APPLICATION	Helping children to relate what they have learned to their everyday lives	Enables the children to locate new learning meaningfully in the wider context of their lives Provides an opportunity for the teacher to reinforce and consolidate key points	Relating to experience Discussing Interpreting

Figure 12.4 *Phases of teaching, learning and assessment*

Such a model is helpful in highlighting the significance of formative assessment. Continuous assessment is the crucial means through which a teacher 'connects' with the pupils' thinking, and is thus able to extend, challenge and reinforce it as appropriate (Practical Activity 12.1).

1.2 Developing and verifying teacher judgement

Of course, the correctness of teacher judgement in constructive interventions in the learning process cannot be assumed. Indeed, high-quality judgement is something which has to be worked at and maintained.

The most commonly advocated way of doing this is through gathering actual evidence of children's skill, knowledge and understanding. As we illustrate in section 3 of this chapter, there are many ways of doing this, with observation, listening, questioning, viewing products and setting tasks and tests being commonly used in one way or another. Of course, these are used routinely by all teachers. However, they are not routinely used in the systematic ways which are appropriate for informing assessment judgement.

The means which is used to break into routinized judgement is the collection and analysis of *evidence*. In itself, this sounds very simple, and in one sense it is. However, if collection is undertaken rigorously and analysis is approached with an open mind, the results are invariably interesting, are often surprising and may be challenging. Investigating children's learning in detail has shown, time after time, how little we know as teachers and how fascinating it is to find out, even when we may think that we can sum up a child accurately.

Practical activity 12.1

Aim: To study key phases of a teaching session.

Method: Plan to teach a session involving some new learning to a group of children. As you plan, think about the five phases which were identified in Figure 12.4 and about the role of assessment. Consider how best to orientate the children, how to elicit and then make use of what they already know, etc. Having thought about the possibilities, be prepared to respond to their input.

Prepare for obtaining a record of what happens. For instance, you could set up a video or ask a colleague to observe you. In the case of the latter, try to get your colleague to make detailed notes on what is said by both you and the children.

Teach the session.

Analyse what happened. Were the five phases apparent and helpful? What opportunities for assessment occurred? Were they used to maximize the quality and appropriateness of the teacher input?

Follow-up: This is primarily an activity for awareness raising. We suggest you try it from time to time, mulling over the results and considering ways in which you could apply the insights about your teaching which you obtain.

Interestingly, a recent study of teacher assessment in England (McCallam *et al.*, 1993, see **Reading, 12.5**) has suggested that there are three basic teacher approaches to teacher assessment. 'Critical intuitives' view national assessment schemes as interrupting their intuitive action, knowledge and skill – be that grounded in long experience or particular beliefs such as child-centredness. 'Evidence gatherers' use assessment in relatively limited ways to monitor and check that children have absorbed what has been taught. Only 'systematic planners' really draw on the formative power of teacher assessment and integrate it as a form of feedback and feedforward for curriculum planning. According to McCallum *et al.*, such teachers tend to adopt social constructivist models of teaching and learning (see Chapter 7; Practical Activity 12.2).

Of course, the collection of evidence is vital in refining judgement, but we must also note its impracticality on a large scale. Indeed, it is simply not possible to collect evidence about everyone and everything in a primary school classroom. In our view, then, use of more intuitive teacher judgements is inevitable. However, gathering evidence makes three vital contributions.

First, it is a means of developing and verifying the quality of teacher judgement. Wise and reflective teachers will not trust their opinions without some form of regular check. Gathering evidence on pupil attainment for assessment purposes is thus a form of staff development. It attunes teacher thinking and it provides a professional justification for the use of more intuitive judgements.

Second, the gathering of evidence should be undertaken when problem-solving is necessary, when the performance of a child is causing concern, or perhaps when a very new curriculum topic is taught. On such occasions, systematic consideration of evidence can take teacher thinking forward considerably, as well as delivering attainment data.

Third, evidence collected in each classroom can contribute to the process of achieving *consistency* of teacher judgements concerning the official 'levels' of attainment which children have reached – 'Teacher Assessment' (see section 2.3).

Practical activity 12.2

Aim: To test the value of collecting evidence in informing teacher judgement.

Method: Select a child whose attainment you think you know well. Identify an area of the curriculum on which to focus. Review any relevant Attainment Targets and level descriptions. Write down your present view of the child's knowledge, skill and understanding.

Then select, from section 3 of this chapter, some appropriate ways of gathering evidence of the child's attainment. Phase these into a practical teaching programme and *record* the evidence in some way.

Assemble and analyse your evidence.

To what extent have your presuppositions been reinforced or amended?

Follow-up: If detailed consideration of evidence brings insights which you might not otherwise have had, how could you incorporate such procedures into your routine classroom activity?

1.3   Pupil self-assessment

Self-assessment is a process through which people learn to monitor and evaluate their own learning strategies and achievements. In psychological terms, self-assessment contributes to processes of 'meta-cognition', as discussed in Chapter 6, section 2.5. The key capacity is that of being able to stand back from a learning experience and to make an open, personal evaluation so that future actions can be adjusted. This is, as Vygotsky put it, a form of 'self-regulation' and for pupils it heralds the development of independence as external support for learning provided by teachers, parents and others becomes less necessary.

When developing pupil self-assessment with a primary school class, it is helpful to think of three stages of work (Muschamp, 1991, **Reading, 12.7**):

Stage one: share aims and plan targets

This is the vital first step and foundation for everything else. Learning objectives and criteria must be discussed fully and be clearly understood by the children. It is likely that aims will have to be focused and discrete – hence the term 'targets'. However, they are still likely to cover the basic distinction of skills, knowledge and understanding.

When learning a skill, a child may clarify her target by asking herself: 'What will I be able to do?' When the target concerns learning or finding out new knowledge, a child may ask himself: 'What will I know about?'. When focusing on the development of understanding, a child may ask: 'What will I explain?'

Such targets may be recorded on 'planning sheets', placed in a personal record, shared and discussed with a group or the class or treated in any other way which will establish the clear priority for the future efforts of each child.

Stage two: review and record achievements

At an appropriate point after the setting of targets for pupil self-assessment, a review is necessary. In the first place this may be fairly general, but it is then useful to make it quite specific by selecting and discussing examples of work which illustrate the achievement of the targets. As with the development of teacher judgement, reviewed in section 1.2 of this chapter, the point of this is to develop understanding by challenging subjective impressions with actual evidence. For instance, a child who had targeted 'using full-stops properly' might look at examples of his or her writing; a child who targeted 'doing more interesting paintings' would study these. Review might take place in pairs, small groups and with or without the teacher. Notes could be made or the work annotated.

The outcome of the review should be recorded and may result in revised targets. Examples of work may be placed in a pupil portfolio of work.

Stage three: help report progress

This is another powerful phase in which it is possible to gain an enormous amount from pupil involvement. The basic idea is that the children themselves take a leading role in reporting their progress to parents. Children can produce part of a report, play host to the parent visit and participate in the interview.

The outcome of these stages in the development of pupil self-assessment cannot be assured, but, even when the learning targets are very specific, pupils' sense of ownership of their learning progress tends to increase and they become more active learners as they see how they can, themselves, achieve objectives. They begin, as Vygotsky said, to become 'self-regulated' (Vygotsky, 1978, **Readings, 6.4** and **6.5**).

2 | ISSUES IN ASSESSMENT

The introduction of assessment procedures tends to cause anxiety. For instance, in the United Kingdom, of all the diverse features of the recent educational reforms, the assessment requirements have been of particular concern to teachers of young children.

Of course, we should not forget that assessment happens informally, and quite naturally, all the time in relationships with people. Whenever people meet, judgements are made and expectations developed. When people part, knowledge of each other may be reinforced, refined or changed. These new understandings are then brought to the next encounter. Such processes enable people to build reciprocal expectations, to develop close relationships and to become aware of needs. Sensitivity to others, empathy and understanding are thus founded, one way or another, on naturally occurring forms of assessment.

However, there is a world of difference between this naturally occurring interpersonal awareness and assessment procedures which are required by the state and are intended to be formally institutionalized in schools, detailed in league tables and made available to the press. The potential destructive power of such a system is immense, and in this section we consider some of the main issues which are raised.

2.1 Teacher–pupil relationships

There is concern that assessment procedures, particularly SATs, may intrude upon or even destroy the warm interpersonal relationships which have characterized primary practice for so many years (see Chapter 5). As a teacher explained recently:

> Relationships with the children is the key. If you get on well with them, discipline problems don't emerge and you get more done. I also think they learn better in a secure environment and I certainly get more personal satisfaction from being with them – in fact, for me, it's what is really rewarding about teaching.

The fear, of course, is that formal assessment will introduce tension and suspicion into teacher–child relationships, for few people feel comfortable when being assessed. More common is a sense of vulnerability, of exposure, of scrutiny and of threat (Practical Activity 12.3).

Early research on the impact of assessment in England and Wales (Gipps *et al.*, 1991; Pollard *et al.*, 1994) suggested that teacher skill and commitment can minimize this potentially divisive effect. Nevertheless, the issue of how children feel about assessment and how this influences their relationships with their teacher is so important that it must be kept under review (see Practical Activity 12.4).

Practical activity 12.3

Aim: To consider people's feelings when experiencing assessment.

Method: Join with a colleague and talk in pairs, each person taking it in turns to talk. First, each shares a personal experience from their childhood about which they felt positively. Second, each shares a personal childhood experience of being assessed about which they felt negatively. We suggest that each person talks, without interruption, for about five minutes.

When each person has shared their experiences, work together to identify the issues which were involved. Did any of the following come up: dignity, self-esteem, anxiety, humiliation, unfairness, pleasure, pride, recognition, affirmation?

Follow-up: Do you think the children with whom you work in school have feelings now which are similar to those which you had?

Practical activity 12.4

Aim: To obtain direct evidence of children's feelings about routine assessment.

Method: Work with a group of children from your class and discuss with them some examples of some assessments which you have made. Perhaps you could use some written work that has been produced and look at any comments and corrections which you made. How do the children feel about your responses?

You could also self-consciously monitor your verbal feedback to children during a teaching session. Listen to your comments, observe the children's faces. How do they seem to respond? Are they: delighted, wary, confused, anxious, angry, resigned?

Follow-up: What ways of protecting children's dignity can you develop, whilst still providing appropriate assessment feedback to them? Could you negotiate with the children to establish criteria by which their work will be evaluated?

2.2 Manageability

This brings us to a practical question – the issue of whether it is physically possible to gather, record, analyse and report assessment evidence on the scale and of the detail that may be required. In the UK of the early 1990s, there were over 400 individual 'Statements Of Attainment' for 7-year-old children, each of which had to be assessed within the National Curriculum. Assessment of all pupils against these statements became a huge task, and, in 1993, resulted in a teacher boycott because of the excessive workload.

If assessment data is to be collected, the implications for classroom management and practice at peak assessment points must be considered. Time for actual teaching could be compromised unless priorities are set (Practical Activity 12.5).

Practical activity 12.5

Aim: To monitor the time and resources used to sustain assessment.

Method: We recommend using the same form of self-report schedule as that developed by Campbell *et al.*, (1992). To do this, you will need to keep a log of your use of time – jotting down, at convenient moments, what you have been doing.

The easiest way to do this is to replicate the record sheet used by Campbell. This divides the day into 10-minute blocks and is used to record predominant activities during these time periods. We suggest that you use the same categories to classify your activities:

T: Teaching (direct contact with children)
P: Preparation or marking (not in direct contact with children)
I: In-service training (all formal and informal activities designed for professional development)
A: Administration (all activities concerned with the routines of school work)
O: Other (anything else related to school work)

Follow-up: Compare your results to those found by Campbell and his colleagues. How does your pattern of use of time compare with that of the teachers they studied? How have you developed your classroom practice to accommodate assessment requirements?

2.3   Validity, reliability and consistency

Validity and reliability are technical terms of immense importance. Do assessments actually represent what they purport to measure (validity)? Can the procedures be implemented in ways which ensure consistency in assessments across the country and from year to year (reliability)? In addressing the latter question regarding teacher assessment, SCAA (1995) prefer to use the term 'consistency'.

Opinions and evidence about the validity and reliability of any assessment system are crucial to its long-term credibility. If high standards on both criteria are not met, then criticism is likely to follow. Where validity is low, assessments will be regarded as partial, limited and crude because of the factors which they ignore or cannot measure. Where reliability is low, assessments will be regarded as inconsistent, unfair and unreliable because of the variation in the procedures by which the assessment results were produced.

The technical problems in constructing and implementing a national system of assessment are considerable and, unfortunately, there is an element of tension between validity and reliability. The quest for validity tends to lead in the direction of assessment procedures which are designed for normal classroom circumstances, covering a wide curriculum and using a range of assessment techniques. In the specialist literature, this is known as 'authentic assessment'. However, the drive for reliability tends to suggest simplification in both assessment procedures and in the range of the curriculum to be assessed, so that there is more chance of comparability being attained. The result of this is likely to be greater use of methods which can be tightly controlled, such as pencil-and-paper testing.

This dilemma has been played out in the development of national standard assessment requirements for 7- and 11-year-olds in England and Wales during the 1990s. In 1991, the assessment round for Key Stage 1 was broadly based and used a variety of assessment methods, including setting of authentic classroom tasks. However, it was found to be both unmanageable and to have considerable problems of reliability (Shorrocks *et al.*, 1991; Whetton *et al.*, 1991). In 1992, the assessment procedures were simplified and tightened, to introduce a greater element of testing. Although many teachers protested at the more limited view of the curriculum which these narrow procedures implied, evaluative evidence again showed that there were reliability problems across schools and LEAs (Pollard *et al.*, 1994). After the Dearing Review, assessment procedures for English and mathematics were simplified and tightened further, an external 'audit' procedure was introduced and attempts to introduce standard assessment in science were dropped. At Key Stage 2, when national assessment was introduced in 1994, pencil-and-paper tests were used immediately, and these have since been further refined.

There is a similar story regarding teacher assessment (TA). In the early 1990s, the role of teacher assessment in informing the teaching–learning process was emphasized. As TGAT put it, such assessment evidence was to 'feed forward' and enable teachers to meet pupil needs more precisely. The profession endorsed this view wholeheartedly, and a great deal of work was done in schools and LEAs to develop the approach (see also **Readings, 12.5, 12.8** and **12.9**). By 1995, however, the School Curriculum and Assessment Authority were presenting teacher assessment almost exclusively as a means of assessing and reporting pupil attainment against National Curriculum levels. Rather than draw out the potential contribution to teaching and learning, SCAA emphasized the need to 'define the standard' of National Curriculum levels and 'the benefits of consistency' for reporting purposes (SCAA, 1995). For instance:

> Consistency in assessment helps to ensure that, when judgements are made against the standards in the revised National Curriculum, there is fairness for pupils across classes, schools and key stages.

> Effective approaches to consistency can enhance teachers' knowledge and increase confidence in their own assessments. It can establish a basis for trust in the judgement of other teachers. This, in turn, results in a greater willingness to value and build on prior assessments of pupils.

> Properly planned and coordinated assessment activity ... helps to develop a collective view of assessment, a shared expertise in the planning of teaching and assessment, and an agreed understanding of standards, expectations and pupils' achievements throughout the school. These can provide helpful support to teachers when they make the judgements at the end of a key stage.

> (SCAA, 1995, p.5)

To increase consistency, SCAA recommend the development of school portfolios containing samples of work which are agreed to represent each level.

The trend during the 1990s has thus been in the same direction for both standard and teacher assessment, with the formative role of assessment in informing teaching being gradually eroded by the priority given to the production of summative assessment information.

Assessment arrangements may be tightened still further during the late 1990s in a drive to improve reliability so that the performance of pupils and schools can be monitored (see section 2.6). However, this is likely to continue to reduce validity. The results may become more precise and comparable, but they may also become more narrow, less meaningful and less helpful to teachers in informing future teaching (Practical Activity 12.6).

2.4 Curriculum distortion

The tension between validity and reliability is so endemic that it is unlikely that a complete solution to it will ever be found. Where assessment is used formatively, to inform the teaching–learning process, this is of less significance because the information can still be used constructively within each school. However, where assessment is used summatively, and published with the claim that it reflects pupil and school performance, then the stakes become high both for pupils and schools. In these circumstances there is a well-documented tendency for teachers and pupils to 'work to the test' (Broadfoot *et al.*, 1991). The result is likely to be a narrow curriculum and, whilst standards in the tested areas of the curriculum may rise, a reduction in overall standards across the broader curriculum may occur.

Concern is justified by the experience of the United States of America, where a great deal of testing has been used for many years (Shepard, 1987; Corbett and Wilson, 1991; Rottenberg and Smith, 1990; Romberg and Zavinnia, 1989). As Rottenberg and Smith comment:

> As the stakes become higher, in that more hangs on the results, teaching becomes more 'test-like', such that testing tends to result in the substitution of means for ends.

It is interesting to note the determined moves in the United States to move away from 'high-stakes testing' (such as SATs with league tables) towards formative, authentic testing (Resnick and Resnick, 1991; Practical Activity 12.7).

Practical activity 12.6

Aim: To highlight the dilemma between validity and reliability.

Method: Focus on a specific target for pupil attainment, for instance, one of those associated with children's mathematical understanding and computational competence with number. Consider how the competence and understanding of pupils across the country could be assessed with regard to the selected Attainment Target. Focus this, perhaps by imagining some individual children whom you know in different schools.

Do you think your assessment method could reflect what is really involved in understanding and competence (validity), and yet be administered in standard and consistent ways by teachers wherever or whoever they are (reliability)?

Follow-up: Consider any test materials with which you are familiar. How do you feel that test designers have tried to resolve the validity/reliability dilemma? What compromises have they made? Do you think it is possible to devise assessment with high validity and high reliability for all subjects?

Practical activity 12.7

Aim: To investigate the danger that high-stakes assessment distorts curriculum provision.

Method: Talk to several teachers about the assessments which they carry out and, in particular, about those which have to be reported publicly. Ask them about any concerns which they may have. Enquire if it has been necessary to change curriculum provision to ensure that the children can perform respectably on publicly reported tests. Ask if public reporting of assessment results broadens, narrows or makes no difference to the curriculum which they provide.

Follow-up: You could reflect on a potentially very significant dilemma here. The National Curriculum sets broad curriculum targets, whilst national assessment procedures test only a narrow range. Does one undermine the other?

2.5 Pupil experience of assessment

We have already discussed the potential threat which increased assessment activity could pose to the quality of teacher–pupil relationships, the dangers of stress and of a narrowing curriculum as teachers 'teach to the test'. Many teachers have feared that such effects will eventually be felt by children in a worsening of the quality of their education experiences and an undermining of the self-confidence of less successful pupils.

Evidence on the short-term impact of new assessment procedures in the United Kingdom is somewhat inconsistent. The early phases of the introduction of assessment procedures in England and Wales brought enormous protests from teachers, many of whom provided illustrations of distressed children (Torrance, 1991). However, more representative samples of teacher opinion did not show the same level of concern (Pollard *et al.*, 1994). Worries from parents were very strong in Scotland, but were relatively small in England and Wales (Hughes *et al.*, 1994). Evidence from children themselves on their experience of SAT testing mostly shows that many of them enjoyed it (Pollard *et al.*, 1994). Indeed, in many classrooms the *early* testing procedures seem to have broadened the curriculum and been well received by children.

The longer-term picture may change as testing procedures are narrowed and tightened by government agencies. Evidence of classroom practice shows that teaching programmes are being attuned more closely to assessment requirements and this will limit the scope for some children to demonstrate their capabilities. Similarly, there are signs of stigma emerging from the overt way in which some assessment procedures 'test' most children, whilst lower attainers are set less challenging 'tasks'. The ways in which assessment results influence the expectations which teachers have of pupils, pupils have of each other and pupils have of themselves is not yet fully documented (but see the discussion of differentiation and polarization in Chapter 13 and, for instance, **Reading, 13.8.** See also interim results of the PACE project; Pollard *et al.*, 1994; Croll, 1996; and, for the wider implications, see Dale, 1996, **Reading, 15.5**).

There is little doubt that national assessment procedures will have long-term effects on pupils. Perhaps these will be all positive, in that the quality of teaching and learning will be enhanced. Reflective teachers, however, will be mindful of the extent of comparative experience of assessment systems which shows the curriculum narrowing to the tests (e.g. Corbett and Wilson, 1991; Rottenberg and Smith, 1990; Romberg and Zavinnia, 1989). They will want, prudently, to watch for effects which could both damage the self-image and self-confidence of pupils and have other divisive effects (see Practical Activity 12.8).

2.6 School performance

National assessment results have increasingly been used as an indicator of school performance. This began in the summer of 1992 when a number of newspapers published unofficial 'league tables' of secondary schools, based on GCSE results. Official data on secondary schools was issued from 1993 and it has been a government intention to publish similar primary school data. For Key Stage 2, this was introduced, against much professional opposition, in 1996.

It is important to note that summative assessment results, such as those produced in the UK by SATs and used for league table purposes, show measured attainment levels only. They do not show the *progress* of pupils, or the circumstances of the families, schools and communities which influence attainment. If data on pupil attainment on entry and data on social circumstances is available, it is possible, by statistical methods, to measure the value added by schools (the *progress* of pupils from entry to exit) (Mortimore *et al.*, 1988; Sammons and Nuttall, 1992).

Practical activity 12.8

Aim: To investigate the impact of assessment activity on children.

Method: One simple method here is to ask the children what they think about being assessed, or tested. Their comments can then be analysed for patterns. For instance, are there any differences between high achievers and lower achievers, between boys and girls? However, asking the children directly may not be appropriate if they are not aware of assessment activity.

Observation is an alternative source of data. Watch the children carefully when assessment activity is going on. This may occur as part of routine activities of praise, encouragement, direction or correction. How do they respond? Are some children blasé? Are others tense or anxious? Make some notes on your observations and let these accumulate over a week or so. Then review what you have found. Can you see any patterns?

Follow-up: Assessment is, necessarily, a means of differentiating between children (see Pollard, 1987d, **Reading, 13.8**). Despite the fact that assessment may be undertaken so that pupil needs can be identified and met, it is nevertheless somewhat threatening.

Consider how you can both maintain constructive assessment activity and sustain the self-confidence of all the children in your class (see Thorne, 1993, **Reading, 13. 9**, for some suggestions).

The policies of the major political parties in the UK illustrate different approaches to the use of raw data and value-added calculations. For most of the early 1990s, the Conservative government advocated the simple use of raw data. This practice was criticized for failing to take account of pupil and school circumstances, and for fuelling a 'market' in education as parents interpreted raw results when choosing schools. In 1995 the Department for Education announced that value added measures would be developed to compare raw scores gains of pupils from school entry. The Labour Party however, has suggested that performance tables should 'allow sensible comparisons to be made' and supports the development of value added measures that take account of social circumstances and 'measure progress'. Further, they state that:

> This process should not be used to develop a competitive market in education. The information should be used to lift and support schools, rather than to embarrass or denigrate them. The key way to raise standards is to set targets for pupils and schools and then set out the steps to achieve them.

(Labour Party, 1995, p. 26–7)

Of course, whatever approach is adopted, early assessment data, such as that collected on entry to school, becomes essential as a basis for later comparisons. Such 'baseline assessment' is supported by both political parties. National baseline assessment may be introduced following the publication of a pre-school curriculum statement, *Desirable Outcomes* (DFEE, 1995). However, the issues concerning validity and reliability (section 2.3) are particularly intractable in the assessment of very young children. For instance, given what we know about young children's learning, the Labour Party's very narrow description of baseline assessment as 'assessing whether a child has learnt the basics of the alphabet and how to count' (Labour Party, 1995, p. 23) does not inspire confidence in the procedure.

The use of pupil assessment data to indicate school performance clearly poses many difficulties. As the introduction to this chapter made clear, assessment can be used for such purposes, but to do so weakens its use in other ways (see also Harlen *et al.*, 1992, **Reading, 12.1**).

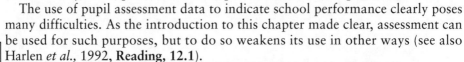

3 │ METHODS OF GATHERING ASSESSMENT EVIDENCE

As we commented in Chapter 3, there is a vast range of data-gathering methods which could be drawn on in selecting appropriate ways of gathering assessment evidence. We reproduce Figure 3.1 as Figure 12.5, to summarize the techniques which are specifically introduced in this book. All *italicised* methods are particularly appropriate for the assessment of pupil learning. Those in ***bold italic*** are discussed in detail in Chapter 11; those in *plain italic* are discussed in this chapter. All other methods are considered in Chapter 3. Comprehensive Notes for Further Reading on data gathering are also provided at the end of Chapter 3.

3.1 Marking pupils' work

The most common way for teachers to monitor children's learning is to 'mark' work which has been completed. This can be anything from a verbal comment

	LOOKING	LISTENING	ASKING
ROUTINELY OCCURRING	Participant observation (C3, 3.1) Document analysis (C3, 3.2) *Marking pupils' work (C12, 3.1) Analysis of pupil diaries or logs (C12, 3.2)*	***Active listening*** *(C11, 2.4)* *Discussing (C11, 2.3) Conferencing (C12, 3.3)*	***Questioning*** *(C11, 2.2) Setting tasks (C12, 3.5) Testing (C12, 3.6)*
SPECIALLY UNDERTAKEN	Systematic observation (C3, 3.3) Photography (C3, 3.4)	Audio recording (C3, 3.6)	Interviewing (C3, 3.7) *Concept mapping (C12, 3.4)* Questionnaires (C3, 3.8) Sociometry (C3, 3.9) Personal constructs (C3, 3.10) Curriculum matrices (C3, 3.11) Check-lists (C3, 3.12)
	Video recording (C3, 3.5)		

Figure 12.5 *A typology of data-gathering methods and their locations in the book*

(e.g. What an exciting story!), to setting spelling corrections at the end of an exercise, or giving a grade/mark. This form of monitoring is often done by the teacher in the absence of the children concerned, so that there is no opportunity to talk with them and find out more about how they set about the task. Such monitoring is more evaluative than diagnostic in contrast to the examples of monitoring which we have discussed earlier. It focuses exclusively on the product and is, primarily, a monitoring technique.

Marking can, of course, be used in conjunction with other forms of monitoring. For instance, diagnosis of a process of learning, though discussion, could have taken place earlier. It is often used in conjunction with observations – as when the teacher circulates around the room – and, also, with discussions.

When marking, it is important to consider each piece of work as part of a sequence. It is only by comparing each example with previous work that it is possible to assess whether any learning has taken place and what significance to attach to any mistakes. If such mistakes, or 'miscues', are analysed carefully they can provide valuable clues to possible learning difficulties. For instance, it is revealing to note whether errors are consistent or one-off. If a pattern emerges then a future teaching–learning point has been identified. Such diagnostic marking can provide useful information upon which to base subsequent discussion, or be used when making judgements about matching future tasks (Practical Activity 12.9).

3.2 Analysing pupil diaries or logs

When diaries or logs are kept, children of appropriate writing capability write down their reflections of their learning experiences. This is particularly useful, for example, when children are doing self-directed work. They can use their diary or logbook to comment on their ongoing progress, to keep the teacher 'in touch' without posing undue management problems.

A diary or log can take many forms. It might include the child's original plan of intended work, and the reason for doing it. It might also include a description of what was done, whether any changes were made and why. It could include an analysis of what knowledge or skills had been employed, which were reinforced, which were acquired and which extended. The child could then go on to comment on what had been enjoyed – or not enjoyed – and what had been worthwhile – or not. Finally, a log could include the children's view of what they would like to move on to next. Such self-analysis requires considerable sophisticated self-reflection from a child – the meta-cognitive skills which were discussed in Chapter 6. It may be something which at first is found difficult, but, by attempting such an analysis a child may become more aware of their progress and of their strengths and weaknesses (Practical activity 12.10).

Practical activity 12.9

Aim: To mark a child's work to identify his or her achievements and weaknesses.

Method: Collect examples of a child's work which form a sequence. Contrast the early and later work and note the major developments. Then list and prioritize continuing weaknesses. Talk with the child and affirm his or her progress. Negotiate with the child to agree targets for future development.

Follow-up: This is a way to use marking formatively for an individual. Marking the work of the whole class on a particular piece of work is also helpful in identifying teaching which several children may need or for gauging understanding and competence in the class as a whole. Look back through your marking though. How often is it encouraging? How often do your comments engage with what the child was trying to do?

> *Practical activity 12.10*
>
> *Aim:* To use learning diaries with a class of pupils.
>
> *Method:* Before approaching the children, it is important to be clear about the purpose of introducing a learning log and to think through the practicalities. Having a clear and agreed focus is particularly significant and children should certainly not be asked to write too much, nor required to 'cover' everything.
>
> *Follow-up:* Learning diaries can facilitate a type of private communication between each pupil and the teacher but, reviewed as a whole, they also make it possible for a teacher to review the learning needs of the class. This may be particularly helpful in developing insights into pupil self-confidence, study skills and learning strategies.

An important extension of the use of pupil diaries or logs is the opportunity they also provide for parents and teachers to add comments and respond to issues which are raised. The children receive such support very tangibly, and on their own terms, so that there may be a growth in mutual understanding.

3.3 Conferencing

This is a term used to describe an extended discussion between teacher and child. Conferencing is similar to conducting an informal interview. Such a session offers an opportunity for a teacher and child to come to a mutual understanding of the nature of work in progress and to discuss what has been found to be enjoyable/not enjoyable or easy/challenging/hard. It also provides a chance to discuss any difficulties which are being experienced and to plan future activities.

Such discussions should allow a teacher and child to talk about the activities and their feelings about them, for conferencing can contribute to an openly negotiated working consensus. Such in-depth discussions could pose management problems for a teacher: the problem of how to fit in all the necessary discussions, and what the rest of the class does whilst the teacher is thus engaged. The length of the discussions will, of course, vary with the needs of the child. However, the teacher will need to plan to set aside a certain amount of time, perhaps at a set period each day, when the class know that the teacher must not be disturbed, if at all possible. In many situations discussions with a group would be appropriate, though it is important that the group context does not inhibit some individuals within the group. It is often an advantage if there are some activities in which the whole class is taking part, as then some issues can be discussed collectively (Practical Activity 12.11).

3.4 Concept mapping

The term mapping denotes a procedure which requires children to 'map' out what they have learnt and how it appears to 'fit' together (see, for instance, *Junior Education*, October, 1992; examples are given in Figure 12.6). Children might be

Practical activity 12.11

Aim: To experiment with conferencing.

Method: Conferencing should initially be tried on a relatively small scale, with a few identified pupils, so that it does not take too much time.

Who: Begin, then, by thinking which pupils you wish to engage with through conferencing. Perhaps you will identify individuals with particular learning needs, or children with whom you wish to negotiate some changes in behaviour.
When: The question of timing is crucial for the practicality of this one-to-one activity. Decide how you will make time for it, with particular attention to what the other children will be doing.
What: Be clear what you wish to conference about, and, if possible, agree this with the pupil. If at all possible, define your focus so that you can reach a target and an agreement together. Building small success on small success is often a safer way to make progress than trying a 'great leap forward'.
How: Consider how you are going to discuss the issue with the child. What will be the most appropriate strategy?

Follow-up: Review the practicality and value of your conferencing experience. Was it valuable? Does it have a place in your repertoire of teaching methods?

helped to draw a web or flow chart to show what they have been learning about. Such a chart would, eventually, represent the ideas, concepts and knowledge that the children have been working with during a particular unit of work, as perceived by the child. The procedure might begin by listing aspects of the topic which were covered (e.g. baby teeth and big teeth, dentist, wobbly teeth, bad teeth, fluoride, healthy food, toothbrush, etc.). The children can then map the relationships between the different items – explaining how they see any links. This provides a way of seeing what they have understood. It could then provide a basis for teacher and child to talk over understandings and misunderstandings (see Practical Activity 12.12).

3.5   Setting tasks

Perhaps the most routinely available source of evidence of pupil learning is that which arises, lesson by lesson, as children engage in the activities and tasks which the teacher has prepared for them. Something will inevitably happen. The important questions are 'what happens?' and 'is anyone paying attention?'

Teachers who are aware of the need for formative assessment and of the potential for gathering evidence from routine classroom activities should be able to focus tasks so that the pupil actions and performance reveal what they know, can do and understand. The skill, then, lies in providing tasks which are appropriate and accessible for all the children but which also enable you to discriminate constructively in terms of what particular children know and learn. This is a form of 'differentiation by outcome' – the development of understanding about the needs and capacities of the child by evaluating 'how they got on' (Practical Activity 12.13).

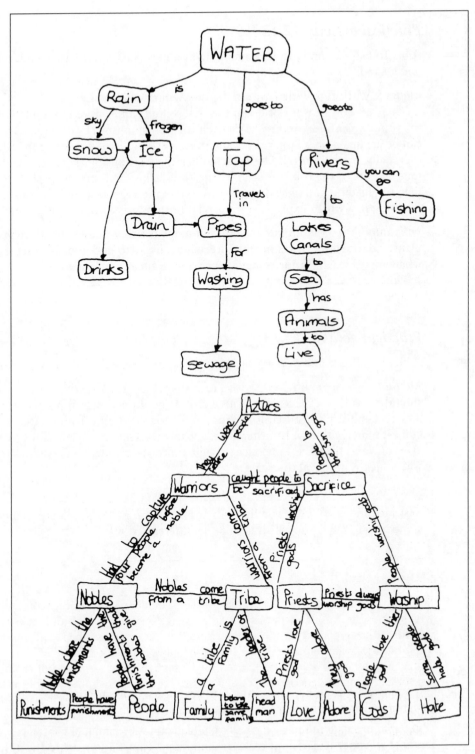

Figure 12.6 *Children's concept maps* (from Johnson, 1992).

Practical activity 12.12

Aim: To practice and evaluate mapping as a means of investigating children's understanding.

Method: Work first with a group, then try with a whole class.

There are lots of ways of doing this. Each child can be asked to think 'what the topic was about' and to write each item on small pieces of paper. These can be arranged on a larger sheet and moved around experimentally to reflect eventually, by their proximity to each other, the relationships between the various aspects of the topic as seen by the child. The small pieces of paper can then be glued on and lines drawn between them to represent the relationships. Finally, a few words expressing these relationships are written on each line.

Follow-up: You could relate the concept maps which you create both to your plans and to relevant Attainment Targets. It is likely to underline the fact that, whatever we teach, children make sense of it in their own ways.

Practical activity 12.13

Aim: To evaluate and develop the use of tasks as a means of pupil assessment.

Method: A review and comparison of tasks which are already routinely set should provide initial insights. Three criteria could be used: appropriateness and accessibility for all children; potential for yielding differentiated outcomes; manageability. In other words, can the tasks involve and motivate everyone and produce some clear insights into the children's capacities in a way which is practical to use?

Tasks for comparison	Accessibility for all children	Potential for differentiation of outcomes	Manageability
1.			
2.			
3.			
etc.			

If some tasks are more useful than others for assessment purposes, can you identify what it is about the best ones that makes them so useful?

Follow-up: Think about some specific learning targets which you have for the children. What tasks could you devise to help you assess their progress and attainment?

Bennett (1992) has developed a model (see Figure 12.7) of the teaching phases which are involved in setting and using tasks . It is clear from the research evidence that the role of the teacher is particularly significant. Over time, it should be the aim of every teacher to develop a repertoire of tasks, suitable for assessment, which can be drawn on as appropriate.

The strengths of using tasks for assessment purposes derive both from the frequency and routine nature of the opportunities which are available and from the high validity which this form of assessment is likely to have. After all, it is embedded in everyday classroom processes. It should provide a rich source of insights about pupil learning strategies and attainments.

3.6   Setting tests

Tests can also be used for a range of different purpose and are distinguishable by a number of criteria:

Teacher tests/published tests

Those which teachers devise themselves and are directly related to what has been taught, compared with published tests which are intended to be generally applicable to a wide range of situations.

Criterion-referenced/norm-referenced tests

Those tests which use specific items to identify aspects of individual children's work, compared to tests which are used to compare individuals in terms of 'normal' expectations of achievement.

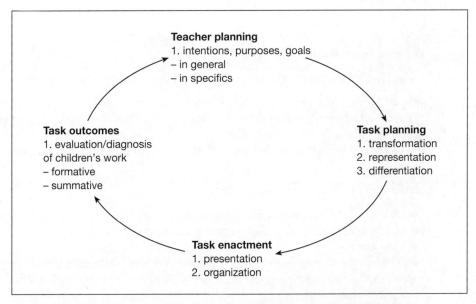

Figure 12.7 *A cycle for classroom tasks* (from Bennett, 1992)

Diagnostic/prognostic

Those which aim to identify what the child can/cannot do now, compared with tests designed to highlight future potential (e.g. IQ/11+ tests)

Open/closed

Those which have questions to which there is room for imagination and creativity, compared with tests to which there is one right answer.

Teachers often devise their own tests for particular diagnostic purposes in order to help them achieve the best cognitive match which is possible. Such tests could be used to discriminate between children's achievements, or used to assess a teacher's effectiveness in implementing specified learning objectives. Criterion-referenced, mastery tests, in carefully graded series, are popular in many sports award schemes, such as those for swimming, athletics and gymnastics.

Criterion-referenced testing is supposed to underly all assessment activity in the UK (TGAT, 1988) and is the specific rationale for the creation of the structure of levels, Attainment Targets and Statements of Attainment. However, research has shown that normative assumptions tend to creep back into the judgements which teachers and others make when carrying out both teacher and standardized assessment procedures (McCallum *et al.*, 1992; Croll, 1995, **Reading, 12.2**).

There is no doubt that appropriate comparative scores for children can be helpful in any review of the attainments of children, teachers or schools. However, whatever type of test is used it is most important for a reflective teacher to try to identify its strengths, weaknesses and its underlying assumptions about learning. For example, what does a reading test actually test to indicate 'reading'. Upon which theory of learning to read is it based? Is it successful in what it aims to do? Is the test based on valid data so that it really measures what it is supposed to? Can the test be reliably used so that data collected are consistent? (See Practical Activity 12.14.)

Practical activity 12.14

Aim: To practise and evaluate the use of tests as a means of assessment.

Method: Decide on a worthwhile topic for testing, consider the type of test you require (see above) and devise a short test. Plan how you are going to manage the test in the classroom.

Carry it out with some children. Make notes on how it went. Evaluate the results.

Follow-up: Consider questions such as:

- Did your test provide useful information?
- Can you use the information in future teaching?
- How did the less successful children respond to the test?
- Was the test a valid indicator of what you wanted to find out about?
- Was the test completed reliably? (Any children distracted, interrupted, tired, disturbed?)

Practical activity 12.15

Aim: To evaluate different techniques for gathering assessment evidence.

Method: Draw up a three-column table, with some chosen techniques for gathering assessment evidence listed on the left, and two adjacent columns for the advantages and disadvantages of each.

Fill in the table bearing in mind the following:

- Why gather evidence in this way?
- For whom is this assessment being done?
- What can be most appropriately monitored in this way?
- How often might this technique be used?
- In what situations can this technique be used?
- How can the results be interpreted?
- Are there any unforeseen effects of such assessment?
- Are the techniques valid and free from cultural bias?

Follow-up: Having made your own decisions about the 'pros' and 'cons' of different techniques for gathering assessment evidence, you should now be in a position to choose which techniques you will use for various purposes, and in which contexts. This should help you to devise a flexible and powerful set of techniques to assess processes and products within your classroom.

3.7 Evaluating methods of gathering assessment evidence

Within this book, as Figure 12.5 summarized, we have reviewed a very large array of different ways of gathering evidence of pupil learning for assessment purposes. Nor is this an exclusive coverage. In addition, creative teachers will, we hope, develop other methods which meet their needs and circumstances.

However, all methods of gathering data, whatever their origin, can be evaluated against criteria such as worthwhileness, validity, reliability and practicality (see Chapter 3). Those that seem effective should pass into the repertoire of teachers so that they can be drawn on when needed. Practical Activity 12.15 suggests conducting an evaluative review.

4 | RECORDS AND REPORTING

4.1 Keeping records

Records are important for many reasons. Among them are:

To inform future teaching

As classroom teachers, we need accurate and relevant information about the children in our classes on which we can base our pastoral care, our curriculum planning and our ongoing teaching judgements. Such records should make it easier to achieve an appropriate match between children and tasks.

To support personal reflection

The review of records of pupil achievements can provide a partial mirror on our own teaching which, for the self-aware teacher, can provide a constructive spur to further pedagogic or curricular development.

To underpin continuity and progression

Records exchanged between teachers provide the crucial means of ensuring that there is continuity and progression in the children's learning experiences from year to year (see Broadfoot, 1996, **Reading, 12.6**).

To contribute to assessment and accountability processes

Records and evidence of child attainments are increasingly needed for assessment purposes – particularly when teacher judgement is drawn on in conjunction with more standardized summative assessments. Such records are also directly helpful when reporting to parents. However, where 'league tables' are published such data may also be used to compile indicators of teacher, school or local education authority performance. Records can thus contribute to both assessment and accountability processes.

Keeping accurate and consistent records is thus of major significance for schools and is likely to be structured by whole-school policies. Individual classroom teachers, and student teachers, can certainly keep whatever personal records they wish, but they are likely to be required to contribute to the official whole-school system. Obviously it is vital that information is collected in manageable ways and that it is possible to organize it, analyse it and use it effectively (Practical Activity 12.16). Inappropriately elaborate and time-consuming systems are likely to be discarded. In England and Wales, the basic legal requirement is that individualized records of attainment in each National Curriculum subject must be kept for each pupil. Of course, this is likely to be time-consuming but there may be elements of record systems – perhaps to do with curriculum activities – that children could maintain for themselves.

It should be remembered that in most countries there are moves towards increasing access to records. For instance, in England and Wales teachers can keep personal records of their own, but any official record which may be transferred to other teachers or other professionals must be made available to parents on request. The issue reflects more general ethical concerns about the central accumulation and recording of information about individuals – whether it is medical information, financial, criminal or anything else. Indeed, most of us would probably want to know what was being kept on us and many people take the view that this should be a right. Continuous awareness of the possible audiences for teacher-created records is thus necessary.

It is useful to think of the range of alternative forms in which records could be kept. For example, personal teacher records may simply be jotted in an exercise book. More formal records for whole-school systems are likely to be recorded with a standardized pro forma or layout employed by all staff. Certain local education authorities have devised sheets or profiles with a given set of criteria for all schools to use. A more elaborate method is to put pupil information on to a computer

Practical activity 12.16

Aim: To identify information about the children which it is important for you, as their teacher, to know and record.

Method: Make notes, under the following headings, of:

1. What information do you think is important for you to know about children in your class?

2. Why is it important?

3. How you would use it?

4. How would you record it?

5. How would you check on the objectivity and fairness of your records?

6. Who has a right of access to your records?

Follow-up: Asking such basic questions could provide a check on the keeping of records. Any information should be reviewed which is not demonstrably useful to teaching, manageable, consistent with school policy and ethically sound.

database, where it can be easily updated and quickly accessible. In addition to providing normal access to parents, such databases must be registered appropriately – in England, under the terms of the Data Protection Act 1985.

4.2 Pupil portfolios

A portfolio is simply a durable file which can act a method of retaining and recording *evidence* of a child's learning. To maximize the educational value, each child should be closely involved in the selection of evidence for inclusion in his or her portfolio, and in review of the contents. Portfolios should thus be accessible to pupils in the classroom and, in that the portfolio is an attempt to represent their achievements, the pupils should have a sense of ownership of the contents. Portfolios can move with the children as they progress through school, thus providing information for successive teachers and facilitating continuity and progression.

The use of portfolios in primary schools has been common for many years, but it has recently evolved in more structured forms as a constructive way of contextualizing and broadening legal assessment procedures (CCW, 1993). The principles on which use of portfolios are based are influenced by the use of 'records of achievement' and 'profiling' in secondary schools (DES, 1984; Broadfoot, 1986; Hitchcock, 1986; Broadfoot, *et al.*, 1988). According the the DES paper, such approaches were intended to:

- recognize, acknowledge and give credit for what pupils have achieved
- contribute to pupils' personal development and progress by improving their motivation, providing encouragement and increase awareness of strengths, weaknesses and opportunities

- help schools identify the all-round potential of their pupils and to consider how well their curriculum, teaching and organization enable pupils to develop
- provide a record and summary document for reporting to others

A recent development project has found four important processes in the constructive use of portfolios with primary school pupils (National Primary Centre (South West), 1991a–c).

First, each child, with their teacher, must *select* examples of work and evidence of learning to be included. Clearly, not everything can be kept but the selection should be negotiated to reflect the breadth of curriculum activity, progress over time, significant highlights, national curriculum attainments and other personal achievements.

Second, the items in the portfolio should be *dated and annotated*. Whilst dating evidence simply locates it in sequence for future reference, annotation provides an opportunity to record the significance of any item. The criteria for selection will thus emerge. These are likely to reflect targets for learning and development which have been negotiated between the child and the teacher. The portfolio thus records progress.

Third, the portfolio should be *reviewed* from time to time. This is a wonderful opportunity for teachers to conference with individual pupils to take stock of their achievements, set new targets and update or edit the contents of the portfolio.

Fourth, the portfolio should be used to *report* the range of each child's achievements. One obvious use for this is with parents (see section 4.3 below), and the National Primary Centre (South West) project (1991a–c) documented some excellent work when children used their portfolios to contribute directly to teacher–parent discussions. Of course, portfolios can also be shared with other children.

There is nothing complicated about any of these stages and procedures, but they each achieve the central objectives of supporting children in reflecting on their own work, in affirming it, evolving future targets and harnessing the support of appropriate others. Of course, the strength of these procedures derives from the way in which they support the development of self-assessment and meta-cognition in children (see section 1.3 of this chapter and Chapter 6, section 2.5). At the same time, the active participation of the children will provide evidence of pupil responses for the teacher – and reflective teachers will use this feedback to review their curriculum provision (Practical Activity 12.17).

4.3 Reporting to parents

The ways in which primary school teachers report children's progress to parents are influenced by two seemingly contradictory sets of expectations.

The first makes the assumption that parents are *partners*, with teachers, in supporting the learning of each child (Wolfendale, 1992a). Parents may thus be routinely invited into school, parent–teacher discussions are likely to be wide-ranging and include consideration of the processes and progress of the pupil – perhaps by focusing on a portfolio of evidence.

The second expectation is based on an image of parents as *consumers* of education, having contracted with the school for the provision of educational services to their child (Chubb and Moe, 1990; Johnson, 1990). They thus require a report of outcomes, through which the school can be held accountable for pupil progress.

Practical activity 12.17

Aim: To experiment with the use of portfolios.

Method: We assume here that portfolios are not in use in your school, and that you will be wanting to take some initial steps to develop or evaluate their use in your classroom.

We suggest that a scaled-down use of portfolios is used for piloting purposes. The four stages of selection, annotation, review and reporting, as outlined above, could be used within a short time period – perhaps a term – or in respect of a curriculum topic only. If necessary, rather than start with the whole class, a small group of children, whom it is judged would benefit, could also be selected.

Follow-up: Consider the outcomes of your experiment. Can you evaluate it in terms of the four concerns set by the DES (1984) (see above): recognition of achievement, motivation and personal development, all-round development and document of record?

Above all, ask yourself two questions. Did the children learn about themselves from the experience? Did I learn things about the children which I would not have learned in any other way?

Needless to say, most schools make provision which reflects elements of both these approaches. This is not surprising, for, whilst the partnership model is professionally acknowledged as contributing very constructively to pupil learning, the consumer model is increasingly underwritten by legal requirements.

For instance, in England and Wales DFE Circular No. 1/95 requires that annual pupil reports include:

- comments on general progress and on attendance record
- details of arrangements for a parent–teacher discussion of the report
- particulars of progress on each National Curriculum subject
- results of statutory assessments

However, more detail is required in reporting the achievements of 7-year-olds and 11-year-olds at the end of each key stage, including

- specified information about National Curriculum levels of attainment, particularly regarding English and mathematics
- comparative information about the attainment of all other pupils in the school at the end of the key stage
- national comparative information (as supplied by the DFEE)

Such specification reflects an emphasis on standards in basic numeracy and literacy skills. However, in the requirement for comparative information to be provided, national requirements feed the 'consumer' model of education.

It is by no means certain how this tension between partnership and consumerist models of parent–school relationships will develop. Whilst the consumer model is projected centrally, local influences on primary schools seem very resilient. For instance, a recent research project (Hughes *et al.,* 1994, **Reading, 14.6**) reported that the proximity of the local school was the most important factor in influencing parental choice of primary school. In characterizing a 'good school', the first ten factors which parents looked for were, in order of frequency: relationships between parents, teachers and children; the staff; the atmosphere; the ethos of the school; good discipline; wide-ranging education offered; the headteacher; development of the whole child; academic results; good resources. This is an instructive list, with academic results listed in ninth position. It may be that many parents of young children understand the importance of the conditions in which pupil learning takes place and are concerned about the wider social and developmental aims of primary education. Perhaps potential in the partnership model remains? If this is so, one of the most explicit ways of manifesting it will be through the processes which a school adopts in reporting pupil achievements to parents (see Practical Activity 12.18).

CONCLUSION

Assessment has been, and remains, a controversial issue in education. It is a fast moving area in policy arenas and, as we have seen, professional practice tends to be shaped by the assessment purposes which have been given priority. In recent years, summative performance measures for pupils and schools have been emphasized extremely strongly. However, the direct contribution of formative assessment, at the heart of the teaching–learning process, should never be forgotten. Ultimately, it may be more important in achieving educational quality.

Practical activity 12.18

Aim: To develop an informative and constructive procedure for reporting to parents.

Method: Again, this activity must be tailored to circumstances. Discuss with appropriate colleagues the aims and scope of a reporting exercise. If you are a student teacher, you might want to limit it to reflect a project which you have completed, or build it into an end-of-term open day.

Consider the following questions:

● How can you best provide information to parents?
● How can you involve the children?
● How can you elicit information and support from parents?

Follow-up: Evaluate your reporting procedure. Did you find consumerist or partnership expectations from parents? How did the children benefit? What will you do when your next opportunity arises?

Notes for further reading

Assessment in schools is a crucial issue of social policy and various responses have historically been adopted in different parts of the world. In most cases, however, assessment processes have been becoming more prominent. A contradiction between assessment as a means of enabling learning and assessment as a means of certificating and measuring learning continues. Such issues are explored in three wide-ranging books:

Murphy, P. and Moon, B. (eds) (1989)
Developments in Learning and Assessment,
London: Hodder and Stoughton.

Broadfoot, P. (ed.) (1984)
Selection, Certification and Control: Social Issues in Educational Assessment,
London: Falmer.

Hargreaves, A. (1989)
Curriculum and Assessment Reform,
Milton Keynes: Open University Press.

For an excellent overview of issues to do with equity and assessment, drawing on research from across the world, see:

Gipps, C. and Murphy, P. (1994)
A Fair Test? Assessment, Achievement and Equity,
Buckingham, Open University Press.

For a review of school practices in England prior to the Education Reform Act 1988, see:

Gipps, C., Steadman, S. Blackstone, T. and Stierer, B. (1983)
Testing Children: Standardised Testing in LEAs and Schools,
London: Heinemann.

A concise account of the assessment issues facing primary schools in the 1990s is provided in the paper below, whilst the two books which follow provide excellent introductory resources for engaging with the issues:

Broadfoot, P., Abbott, D., Croll, P., Osborn, M., Pollard, A. and Towler, L. (1991)
Implementing national assessment: issues for primary teachers,
Cambridge Journal of Education 21 (2), 153–68.

Gipps, C. (1990)
Assessment: A Teachers' Guide to the Issues,
London: Hodder and Stoughton.

Craft, A. (ed.) (1996)
Primary Education: Assessing and Planning Learning,
London: Routledge.

For concise introductions to the technical aspects of assessment and much more besides, see:

Desforges, C. (1989)
Testing and Assessment,
London: Cassell.

Harding, L. and Beech, J. (eds) (1991)
Educational Assessment of the Primary School Child,
London: Routledge.

Reading, 12.4

The best analysis of Teacher Assessment and of the ways in which SATs were introduced in England is:

Gipps, C., Brown, M., McCallum, B. and McAlister, S. (1995)
Intuition or Evidence?
Buckingham: Open University Press.   Reading, 12.5

Constructive and critical accounts of national assessment procedures in the UK are:

Blenkin, G. M. and Kelly, A. V. (eds) (1992)
Assessment in Early Childhood Education,
London: Paul Chapman.

Drummond, M. (1993)
Assessing Children's Learning,
London: David Fulton.   Reading, 12.9

Conner, C. (1990)
Assessment and Testing in the Primary School,
London: Falmer.

For practical support on assessment see:

Sutton, R. (1991)
Assessment: A Framework for Teachers,
London: Routledge.

Merttens, R. and Vass, J. (1990)
How to Plan and Assess the National Curriculum in the Primary Classroom,
London: Heinemann.

McMullen, H. (1992)
Assessment in the Primary School,
London: Cassell.

National Primary Centre (South West) (1991a)
Constructive Teacher Assessment: Progression in Children's Understanding, PIPE No. 6.
Bristol: NPC (SW).

National Primary Centre (SW) (1991b)
Strategies for Classroom Assessment, INSET Pack.
Bristol: National Primary Centre (SW).   Reading, 12.7

An interesting book on techniques of assessment is:

White, R. T. and Gunstone, R. F. (1992)
Probing Understanding,
London: Falmer.

The most comprehensive collection, though a bit dated, of advice and ideas on keeping records about children is:

Clift, P., Weiner, G.,and Wilson, E.(1981)
Record Keeping in Primary Schools,
London: Macmillian.

A simple, and more recent, introduction is:

Johnson, G., Hill, B. and Tunstall, P. (1992)
Primary Records of Achievement,
London: Hodder and Stoughton.

A specific book, but with many generalizable ideas, is:

Lawson, H. (1992)
Practical Record Keeping for Special Schools,
London: David Fulton.

National recording and reporting requirements vary in different countries. In England, see:

Department of Education and Science (1990b)
Records of Achievement, Circular 8/90,
London: DES.

Department of Education and Science (1993)
Reporting on Pupils' Achievements to Parents, Circular 16/93,
London: DES.

On profiling and constructive attempts to involve parents through reporting assessments of their children's learning, see:

Ritchie, R. (ed.) (1991)
Profiling in Primary Schools,
London: Cassell.

Wolfendale, S. (1992a)
Involving Parents in Schools,
London: Cassell.

Jowett, S. and Baginsky, M. (1991)
Building Bridges: Parental Involvement in Schools,
London: Routledge.

Stacey, M. (1991)
Parents and Teachers Together: Partnership in Primary and Nursery Education,
Buckingham: Open University Press.

Johnson, D. (1990)
Parental Choice in Education,
London: Routledge.

CHAPTER 13

What are the social consequences of classroom practices?

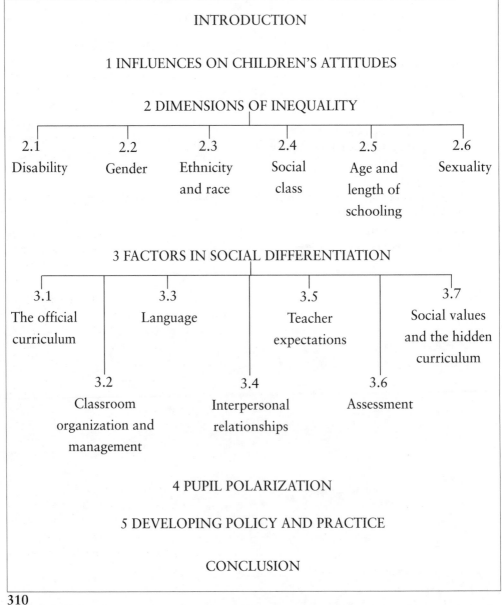

INTRODUCTION

1 INFLUENCES ON CHILDREN'S ATTITUDES

2 DIMENSIONS OF INEQUALITY

| 2.1 | 2.2 | 2.3 | 2.4 | 2.5 | 2.6 |
| Disability | Gender | Ethnicity and race | Social class | Age and length of schooling | Sexuality |

3 FACTORS IN SOCIAL DIFFERENTIATION

| 3.1 | 3.3 | 3.5 | 3.7 |
| The official curriculum | Language | Teacher expectations | Social values and the hidden curriculum |

| 3.2 | 3.4 | 3.6 |
| Classroom organization and management | Interpersonal relationships | Assessment |

4 PUPIL POLARIZATION

5 DEVELOPING POLICY AND PRACTICE

CONCLUSION

INTRODUCTION

The concept of reflective teaching encompasses a concern with the social consequences of educational processes. It also involves us in identifying our degree of
responsibility for their consequences (see Chapter 1, section 2.1).

In Chapter 2 we considered a model of the relationships between individuals
and society which was based on the notion of a dialectical process. This suggested
the existence of a continuous interplay between social forces and individual
actions (Mills, 1959, **Reading, 2.1**). This conception of the dialectical process of
social change should cause us to look at our daily actions in the classroom and to
consider their possible social implications. In this view, 'society' does not develop
exclusively 'somewhere else' controlled by indeterminate powers – by 'them'.
Future developments are partially in our own hands and we can make our own
small, but unique, contribution.

To the credit of the teaching profession, awareness of how opportunities can be
unequal for some groups of children, and how such inequalities can be tackled, is
considerable. It is recognized that the provision of equal opportunities requires
both careful reflection on the social consequences of routine classroom practices
and the development of constructive whole-school policies. Concerned teachers
will want to consider how to provide the best possible educational experiences for
all children, including any groups that are particularly vulnerable to inequalities in
provision, how to enable children to learn about important issues of equality and
rights through the curriculum and how to promote equal opportunities through
staffing policies and practices.

These are perennial issues. For instance, even in the 1960s, the Plowden Report
(CACE, 1967, **Reading, 7.6**) recognized the particular needs of children living in
disadvantaged socio-economic conditions. In the intervening years, equal opportunities issues have become more clearly understood and, as a result, concern has
become more specifically focused. There was legislation, including a Race Relations Act (1976), a Sex Discrimination Act (1975) and the Education Act (1981)
on Special Education. The Commission for Racial Equality and the Equal Opportunities Commission were created. Major reports have been published on the
education of children from ethnic minority groups (DES, 1981b; DES, 1985d) and
on children with special educational needs (DES, 1978b). More recently, the Education Act (1993), the Children Act (1989) and the Education Reform Act (1988)
all had implications for the provision of equal opportunities.

The UK government affirmed its commitment to the provision of equal opportunities in the context of the implementation of the Education Reform Act (1988).
For instance, their explanatory document, *National Curriculum – From Policy to
Practice* (DES, 1989a, para. 3.8) stated that: 'The whole curriculum, for all pupils,
will certainly need to include ... coverage, across the curriculum, of gender and
multi-cultural issues. ... They are clearly required in the curriculum to which all
pupils are entitled.' This theme recurred in the revised National Curriculum,
introduced in 1995, which has a 'common requirement' that all children should
have access to the National Curriculum. OFSTED inspections also focus on the
issue, and inspectors are required to evaluate how each school complies with relevant legislation and 'promotes equal access by all pupils to the full range of
opportunities for achievement that the school provides' (OFSTED, 1995, p. 106).

Reflecting their own commitments and as a result of national requirements, most Local Education Authorities have developed policy or position statements on equal opportunities. Some policies address both curriculum and employment practices; others address particular aspects, such as racial or gender equality, multicultural or anti-racist education. Some LEAs even embrace 'equality assurance'(Runnymede Trust, 1993). However, since the legislation of the late 1980s, the curricular and strategic planning powers of LEAs have been considerably reduced. Parental rights to select schools in an 'education market' can create spirals of success and failure for schools, with tendencies for pupils to be moved out of inner city schools to those in 'leafy suburbs' or out of town locations. The social consequence and equality aspects of such quasi-markets are raised in Chapters 14 and 15 (see particularly **Readings, 15.5** and **14.5**).

However, within schools, facing issues of social consequences and opportunities remains a challenging process and, to be successful, it almost always requires a spirit of co-operation, support and collective openness. Notwithstanding this, the issues remain just as real at the level of the individual classroom and there is much that a reflective teacher can do to ensure that all the children have an equal opportunity to fulfil their potential.

This chapter is structured in five parts, beginning with consideration of factors which influence children's attitudes towards others. We then consider major dimensions of equal opportunities, factors which contribute to differentiation of pupils by teachers and further polarization by pupils themselves and, finally, how to develop constructive classroom policies.

1 | INFLUENCES ON CHILDREN'S ATTITUDES

Categorization is used by people to help them make sense of their lives. It is thus a natural, and necessary process. However, a problem emerges if such categorization develops to a point where people are seen in ways which reduce their opportunities. For example, in most societies there are commonplace assumptions about parenting and the nature of the 'normal' family which may, in fact, be stereotypical. Such ideas are reproduced and perpetuated through the socialization of children, and children thus often develop attitudes and prejudices very early in their lives. For instance, research has shown that such attitudes can develop by the age of 4 (e.g. Goodman, 1952; Bellotti, 1975).

Of course, no child is born innately racist or sexist, but all children certainly have the instinct to learn and to gather ideas from people and influences within their environment. The problem arises because children often develop attitudes which perpetuate the inequalities which already divide society. What factors may contribute to such attitudinal formation? We review some of these below, but see also Chapter 6, section 2.2.

The family: Adults' actions, words and deeds are living examples for young children. Through interpreting the actions of significant others in their families, young children begin to assimilate the norms and values of society. Of course, children may not understand what they are learning, but they behave in particular ways in order to please parents, adults and peers. The behaviour may display attitudes that are sexist and/or racist which, amongst other things, perpetuate inequalities. Practical Activity 13.1 may help in exploring this issue by considering families and roles within families.

Practical activity 13.1

Aim: To explore children's understanding of families and roles within families.

Method: Ask the children to draw a house with a family in the house 'doing things that people in families do'.

Discuss with the children, individually or in groups, the variations in their drawings. Encourage them to explain their drawings. Have they drawn their own family? If not, how did they decide what to draw? What are different members of the family doing in the drawing? Why were those particular activities chosen for the picture?

Analyse the differences that emerge in the children's understandings of what constitutes a family. Perhaps you could discuss your conclusions with a colleague who has also done this activity.

Follow-up: You might like to consider ways of discussing and exploring with the children the variety of families and family lifestyles in this country. You could start with the families of the children in the class, encouraging a positive view of variety and difference.

The community: Each child, like the family, is a member of the wider community, and from the community children also assimilate attitudes which may perpetuate myths and stereotypes. If, for instance, the language that is used about black people and/or women is derogatory, then children will unwittingly absorb such prejudices as they conform to the community within which they live. If a child sees black people only in menial jobs or as sports people, dancers or musicians, then, unless they are shown otherwise, the child may think that these are the limits of the capabilities of black people. If a child sees women only as mothers and in domestic roles, rather than in external positions of responsibility, then that is the expectation which the child may form of women. If people with a disability are always treated as being in need of help, then that is what a child is likely to believe.

The school: Of course, the school is within the community and is also likely to influence a child's attitude formation. For instance, a modelling of possibilities is provided by the presence, absence and roles of black and white people, able-bodied and disabled people, women and men on the staff. Children will be also be directly influenced by the information, values and attitudes which are conveyed through the curriculum and by the experiences which are provided within the school. Of particular importance are the values which are projected regarding diversity and the uniqueness of individuals. This is likely to be expressed most powerfully through symbolic events, such as assemblies, when the school community comes together as a whole under the leadership of the headteacher. The ways in which school and classroom life act as forms of 'social differentiation' is the subject of section 3.

Peer culture is also of enormous influence at school. As children work and play together they create a type of child society which mirrors many of the features of the adult world (see Chapter 4, section 2.3). There are patterns in the friendship groups and status hierarchies which tend to evolve, and these often reflect the influence of gender, ethnicity, social class, age, attainment and physical abilities. The social structure which emerges within child culture has been found to reflect the initial differentiation by adults so that, put crudely, 'pro-school' and 'anti-school' pupil subcultures may form. Processes within peer culture can thus reinforce and multiply the effect of school-initiated differentiation. This process is known as 'polarization' and is the subject of section 4 of this chapter.

The media: Until the advent of film and TV, books were the most influential carriers of culture. Their influence may have diminished, but they inevitably reflect attitudes of the dominant culture towards ethnic groups, gender, social class, disability, etc. While older children can be more objective and critical of the content, a young child has little on which to discriminate. We must therefore look closely at the reading material which is provided for children and at the messages which it conveys (see also Chapter 8, section 2.9).

There is now considerable evidence of the long television viewing hours of children and of the growing impact of computer games and activities. As a result, concern has been raised over the power of electronic media to influence people to be violent or to develop sexist or racist views. More cogent opinion, however, stresses the way in which the media throw certain features into sharp relief whilst obliterating others, and point to the ways in which users are active in processing information. However, while such media may not determine attitudes, they do structure and select the information that colours them. Indeed, it is interesting to note research which shows that, while younger children depend upon their parents for views and attitudes, older children place greater dependence on TV, computers and reading materials. A tendency also grows to recall those items that support opinions which have already formed. The power of the media, especially TV, to influence children in forming unhealthy concepts related to race, gender, class, sexuality and disability thus needs to be recognized. However, it has similar potential for forming positive concepts and attitudes.

Practical Activity 13.2 suggests one way of investigating children's ideas about adult roles.

2 | DIMENSION OF INEQUALITY

In this section we consider six dimensions in terms of which social differences and inequalities have often been documented: disability, gender, ethnicity and race, social class, age and length of schooling and sexuality.

2.1 Disability

Understanding of disability as an equal opportunities issue has grown in recent years as a result of people with disabilities articulating a strong voice and rejecting society's traditional views of the disabled as 'inadequate' or 'less than whole'.

Practical activity 13.2

Aim: To explore children's perceptions of adult roles.

Method: Ask the children to draw and colour pictures of members of various occupations, such as:

a teacher

a doctor

an athlete

a nurse

a scientist

a shopkeeper

a bus driver

a television news-reader

a cook

a dentist

It is important to make sure you have available a full range of crayons or paints for different skin colours.

Display the pictures and consider the gender and racial characteristics of different representations.

Discuss them with individual children and as a class. Try to ascertain why the children drew what they did. Do their pictures match their direct experience of specific doctors, athletes, shopkeepers, etc.? Is there any evidence of stereotypical views of who does what?

Follow-up: You might like to continue the activity by collecting pictures of people in the occupations which the children have drawn. You could include examples of women, black people and disabled people and encourage children to review their ideas of who can do what sort of job.

Such views have deep roots in our history and culture, drawing initially on pagan and religious superstitions, later to be unwittingly validated by the rise of the medical profession with its power to diagnose, treat and cure the 'sick' disabled person. Under the enormous influence of the medical model, people have been defined by their physical or mental impairments as 'abnormal', placed in institutions, segregated into separate schools and often denied access to a full family life, to employment and to a voice. Disabled people have challenged this:

> Disabled people's own view of the situation is that whilst we may have medical conditions which hamper us and which may or may not need medical treatment, human knowledge, technology and collective resources are already such that our physical or mental impairments need not prevent us from being able to live perfectly good lives. It is society's unwillingness to employ these means to altering *itself* rather than *us*, which causes our disabilities.
>
> (Rieser and Mason, 1990)

315

Both the Warnock Report (DES, 1978b) and the 1981 Education Act recommended that children with disabilities be integrated into mainstream schools, whenever possible. The 1981 Act, however, was 'enabling' legislation rather than being compulsory. Local Education Authorities were thus encouraged, but not legally obliged, to implement integration and no extra resources were made available by government to help achieve this. The Children Act of 1989 requires co-ordination of services and establishes children's interests as the top priority – but again no further resources are guaranteed.

When thinking of children in schools, a key question is whether any child who has a disability is restricted in access – physically or psychologically – to the education which is enjoyed by other children. If access is restricted then the disabled child has been handicapped and the *right* of access to the National Curriculum has not been fulfilled (see Roaf and Bines, 1989, **Reading, 13.7**).

2.2 Gender

There are some similar problems with defining gender and the term 'sexism', which is connected to it. Certainly there is a readily accepted scientific basis for recognizing two sexes. Nevertheless, a large number of differences which are conventionally associated with sex have been shown to be socially constructed through such processes as socialization and the pressure of expectation. It is all too easy to think of occupations where the workforce is predominantly of one sex or the other, but in fact there are few occupations which cannot be carried out equally by women and by men. For this reason, the term 'gender' is an important one because it describes the *social definition of sex-roles* rather than the simple distinction of sex itself. 'Sexism' can then be seen to be the operation of forces in society by which members of one sex get advantages over the other, because of and through their gender. It is most commonly evident in the advantages men acquire over women. For instance, in primary teaching itself it is difficult, if not impossible, to explain the disproportionate number of men in headships and deputy headships without reference to processes of sexual discrimination (see De Lyon and Migniuolo, 1989; Weiner, 1990, **Reading, 13.3**). However, it is also pertinent to note how few men are teachers in nursery and reception classes, and to reflect on the attitudes encountered by those men who do choose to work with this age-range.

Considering pupils, enduring questions have been whether boys and girls are treated equally at school, how school life contributes to gender socialization and why it is that girls tend to perform slightly better than boys when in primary school (e.g. Delamont, 1990; Davies, 1993, **Reading, 11.5**; Walkerdine, 1988, **Reading, 13.4**).

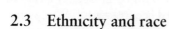

2.3 Ethnicity and race

The word 'race' has a strong common-sense meaning in society. However, biologists have shown that differences of external physical features, which are most commonly associated with the idea of race, are relatively insignificant in terms of fundamental capacities. People within the human race are essentially enormously alike. However, cultures and social structures, compounded by differences of historical development such as the effect of colonization and geographical setting, can make a considerable difference to people's experience, thus leading to much variation amongst ethnic groups. This has produced a confusion, in some cases distortion, whereby race is wrongly understood to be a determining factor in intelligence and behaviour. From the belief in people having distinct racial origins, strongly felt ideas sometimes follow which separate people into 'us' and 'them'. It is then an easily taken, but false, step to define one set of people as 'superior' and another as 'inferior'.

To challenge the validity of ethnicity and race as factors in determining human capacities is not to deny the significance of racism as a cause of the unequal opportunities accorded to some children. Racism is the term which describes processes in society which affect people according to their identification as members of one ethnic group or another. Racism has a long history in the UK going back to the imperial past and beyond, and it has taken root in the discourse and structure of society. It has led to the development of fairly widespread racial prejudice, which sometimes takes hold in the minds of certain individual or groups, and is even embedded within child culture (Troyna and Hatcher, 1992, **Reading, 13.6**). Such prejudices may be further amplified by the social, cultural, legal and political structures that have developed over time (see Epstein, 1993, **Reading, 13.5** for further discussion of these issues).

The development of racism, and the prejudiced behaviour associated with it, can be seen as a cause of the relative inequality which is experienced by black people in society. Most black people, for example of Caribbean origin, gain less in society in terms of employment, education, income, housing and wealth than their white peers.

2.4 Social class

The claim has sometimes been made that, 'Great Britain is now a classless society'. Underlying this assertion are suggestions that real standards of living have risen and that every individual has the opportunity to be successful regardless of his or her social origins. The research evidence is strongly against such propositions. For instance, since 1977 there has been a consistent trend for the gap between the highest and lowest incomes in the UK to widen. This has been caused by developments such as the shift to indirect taxation policies that disadvantage those who must spend a large proportion of their income, changes in the labour market which have adversely affected job security, the introduction of new technologies and competition from cheap labour sources overseas. One consequence is the fact that in 1995 there were 3.5 million children living in families on or below the 'poverty line' (Institute for Fiscal Studies, 1995). However, at the same time, many families were very well-off and approximately 7 per cent of school-age children still attended private schools.

Most teachers are aware of the effects of social context on children's learning and development. Indeed, pupil achievement tends to be closely related to social class factors, as is particularly apparent from the publication of raw score league tables of school results. However, although there are always exceptions even within the same school, children from poor homes tend not to do as well as children from wealthy homes.

Not all definitions of class are based on income or wealth as such. For example, most teachers are not particularly wealthy, but the occupation is certainly considered to be 'middle class'. Some definitions thus relate more to occupation than to earnings.

A social class judgement may also be affected by a person's lifestyle – taste in clothes, food, music and art for example. However, this is a dangerous thing to do given the enormous diversity of cultural forms in modern society. Where traditional forms of culture have high status, a powerful analytic concept is that of 'cultural capital' (Bourdieu and Passeron, 1977). This denotes knowledge, attitudes and experiences which socialization within a 'higher-class' family can offer, and which can be used in later life to maintain such advantages and secure them for the next generation. Such a process is termed 'social reproduction'.

2.5 Age and length of schooling

Children in the UK are required to begin formal education in the school year in which they become 5 years old, but there is wide local variation in admission policies. Thus some full cohorts start at the beginning of the year, other children are admitted at the beginning of the term in which their birthday falls, whilst some must wait until after their fifth birthday.

The accident of birthdate, when combined with the start of the school year in September each year, thus produces children who are significantly 'older' or 'younger' within each year group. A child born in mid-August will be almost a year younger than his or her classmates throughout his or her education. Conversely, a child born in mid-September will have the benefit of being amongst the oldest within their cohort. This is a significant point, particularly in the formative years of Key Stage 1, and studies have shown that age effects can be traced to attainment in secondary school.

Variations in admission policies introduce another factor concerning the length of schooling. A child in one part of the country may be offered a Reception year of one term, whilst a child in another area may attend for three terms. Of course, length of schooling is not necessarily a positive benefit and there has been concern about inappropriate provision for 4-year-olds in schools. However, the fact remains that the availability of formal education is not equal.

 Adverse effects of age and length of schooling are by no means inevitable. Indeed, Tizard *et al.* (1988, **Reading, 13.2**) demonstrated that other in-school factors could have a significant effect. The two most important factors in her study of 33 infant schools were 'the range of the 3R curriculum offered' and 'the nature of teacher expectations' of the children. Where teacher expectations were high, a wide curriculum was introduced and the pupils tended to make more progress. Whilst we might want to think carefully about the extent to which it is appropriate to present formal curriculum challenges to very young children, there is little doubt that children who are young in their year can suffer from low teacher expectations when immaturity is misinterpreted as a lack of ability.

2.6 Sexuality

There is still considerable stigma associated with open expressions of sexuality and most teachers are understandably hesitant about addressing such issues, especially with young children. Yet the recognition and acceptance of such differences may be extremely important to the provision of equal opportunities for some pupils – and also for some teachers and others in the school community. Indeed, the increasing openness of members of the lesbian and gay communities has resulted in some local authorities recognizing them as minority groups deserving of support. However, such developments have met with opposition from national government, and this was expressed most clearly in the controversial Section 28 of the 1988 Local Government Act. This prohibited local authorities from intentionally 'promoting' homosexuality.

With regard to education, there are several important issues to consider. First, what is the school experience of teachers who are lesbian or gay? Discrimination has been common in the past, obliging many to work under the continual stress of pretence and secrecy. Second, what provision should be made for children who come from families where one or more members are lesbian or gay? The relationship may be just as stable, loving or prone to breakdown as any heterosexual partnership. Does the ethos and curriculum of the school offer appropriate support to such children? Third, should primary school pupils be introduced to sexuality as an issue or not? There is likely to be awareness among many. For instance, we know that accusations of homosexuality are sometimes used among surprisingly young children to reinforce conformity to sex roles. An independent girl may be accused of being a 'lessie', or an affectionate, gentle boy may be labelled 'queer' or a 'poof'. What place should discussion of sexuality have in a sex education programme?

In this section above, we have briefly introduced six dimensions which research shows may be associated with unequal experiences and life chances. These are enormously complex issues, and no teacher can shoulder full responsibility for them. However, we do have a responsibility to consider how our daily practice may affect such issues, and this could partially be achieved though a review of our expectations of particular children. This is suggested in Practical Activity 13.3.

3 | FACTORS IN SOCIAL DIFFERENTIATION

We use 'differentiation' here to refer to social processes which increase distinctions between children and which are largely under teacher or school control. At a whole-school level, a classic form of differentiation is 'streaming' which was commonplace in the 1960s but was found to be extremely divisive (Jackson, 1964, **Reading, 5.5**; Barker Lunn, 1970). In the 1990s new forms of 'setting' for particular subjects are developing and it remains to be seen if these will have unintended social effects, as seems likely. Within classroom settings, differentiation arises from such practices as the use of 'ability-based' groups, hierarchically organized schemes of work, 'star' systems for rewarding good behaviour, imbalances in the display of children's work and from variations in teacher's perceptions of and relationships with children. We discussed several factors similar to these when considering the concept of the 'incorporative classroom' in Chapter 5, section 3.2.

However, differentiation for educational purposes is likely to be unavoidable. Indeed, the emphasis which we have placed on matching learning tasks to the needs of individual children makes it clear that elements of such differentiation are essential if teachers are to help each child to maximize his or her full potential. And yet educational differentiation also has social consequences. Most immediately it can affect self-esteem and social status (see Chapter 5; section 2.1; Lawrence, 1987,

Practical activity 13.3

Aim: To review the possible influence of common dimensions of inequality on our expectations of a class of children.

Method: Taking each applicable dimension in turn, think of two children in your class, one of whom may be likely to be 'advantaged' in terms of the dimension and the other who may be 'disadvantaged'.

	'Advantaged'	'Disadvantaged'
Disability		
Gender		
Race		
Social class		
Age and length of schooling		
Sexuality		

Think hard about the capabilities and potential of each of the children. Consider how your expectations are influenced by:

- established images and stereotypes within our culture
- the pressures of school and classroom life
- your own biography

Follow-up: Consider the implications of this activity. For instance, a very exciting and worthwhile thing to do is to identify and gradually build on the particular strengths and potential of children who may have been performing relatively poorly at school.

Reading, 5.6; Maylor, 1995, **Reading, 4.8**). This impacts on self-confidence and identity, and then on the ways in which the child engages with new learning challenges. Ultimately, it can affect performance which may reinforce the cycle again (see Pollard with Filer, 1996, for detailed case-studies of pupils). Such spirals can be positive or negative, which is why promoting the self-belief of young children makes an important contribution to increasing standards of educational attainment.

Almost all classroom practices may touch on issues of social differentiation, so it is not surprising that this section reaches out across the book as a whole. The section is elaborated from the discussion in Pollard (1987d, **Reading, 13.8**) which it would be helpful to read at this point.

3.1 The official curriculum

The content of the curriculum, and the focus of books, resources and school activities, places value on what is taught and learned (see Chapter 4, section 1.2 and Chapter 7, section 2.1). The curriculum is thus a vital issue in the social reproduction of culture and values, as well as knowledge, skills and attitudes. As an aspect of differentiation, where the curriculum fails to affirm the experiences of particular social groups, then this very omission devalues them, just as inclusion could contribute to the development of self-confidence (see Practical Activity 13.4).

Practical activity 13.4

Aim: To consider the content of the National Curriculum in terms of inclusion, exclusion and equal opportunities.

Method: Review official documents related to the National Curriculum: Statutory Orders, Non-statutory Guidance, reports or consultative documents. Examine the documents closely for direct (or implied) references to social groups and to equal opportunities issues. To what extent do you feel the National Curriculum reflects the diversity of modern society?

Follow-up: Consider the National Curriculum in relation to international commitments to Human Rights. For this purpose, see the Introduction of this book, Chapter 15, section 1 and **Reading, 15.4**)

At the classroom level, to what extent do you feel that your planned curriculum provides an inclusive experience for all your pupils?

3.2   Classroom organization and management

This is a very important topic, an adequate treatment of which must recognize the classroom necessity for practical and effective systems, rules and strategies for managing the class and maintaining order. Such issues are the subject of Chapters 9 and 10 in both this book and in *Readings*.

However, the reality is that management and organization of the 'crowd' of children (Jackson, 1968, **Reading, 5.5**) almost invariably rests on forms of social differentiation (see Chapter 3, section 3.2). Thus we have grouping systems, procedures for reward and punishment, routines for particular phases of the school day and a myriad of classroom rules (of both explicit and tacit types). Maintenance of such structures is a necessary part of a teacher's repertoire, but we must also recognize that they do tend to suit some children more than others. Thus we get different patterns of pupil response, ranging from forms of conformity through to negotiation and deviance.

From here it is not far to the introduction of classroom management strategies based on comparison and competition: 'The Red Group is sitting up well. I wonder if the rest of you could do that too?' 'Who is ready to go out now?' 'Let's see who got that right.' In one sense, such interactions simply introduce the children to the realities of the modern world, but in another sense they can be seen as a form of the classic tactic of 'divide and rule' which the powerful have used to further their positions throughout history. Teachers are certainly in positions of power, and classrooms must be organized and managed effectively. The responsibility and challenge, however, is in using that power wisely and with social awareness, in ways which do not undermine the confidence and opportunities of children who are less advantaged in school situations.

Practical Activity 5.9 suggests ways of reviewing the ways in which all children can identify with class activities within an incorporative classroom.

3.3 Language

Language is a primary medium of social interaction and learning. It is thus of enormous importance, as we saw in Chapter 11. In section 4 of that chapter we raised the issue of linguistic diversity in all its forms. How do issues such as dialect, accent, vocabulary, grammar, bilingualism and the use of standard English affect classroom processes (see also **Readings 11.9** and **11.10**)? Many years ago Bernstein (1971) suggested that there were two language codes – 'restricted' and 'elaborated'. Since schools use forms of elaborated code, pupils who were reliant on more restricted codes, predominantly from working-class communities, were disadvantaged. However, many linguists, following Labov (1973) have shown the sophistication of the diverse forms of language use which we have in modern societies, so that it is not possible to say that one is 'better' than another. A professional consensus has thus settled on the proposition that children should be prepared to use language appropriately, in relation to particular audiences and contexts. However, it is certainly the case that standard English is the highest status form of language in the UK and being taught to speak in this way has been enshrined as an entitlement in the National Curriculum.

Within any classroom there will be children with very different levels of linguistic capability in relation to the four basic skills of speaking, listening, reading and writing in English. Attainment in most school subjects is likely to be closely related to these capabilities, but a reflective teacher would wish to monitor the extent to which the form of language used in the classroom helped, or hindered, fulfilment of the capabilities of each individual.

Language is particularly important as a way of making sense of experience, and one way in which this is done regarding people and relationships is through naming. In the playground domain of peer culture, names are often used to assert inclusion or exclusion between groups of children. This can be quite divisive, as the example of racist name calling illustrates (Troyna and Hatcher, 1992, **Reading, 13.6**). However, we as adults can also learn something from considering colloquial uses of language to name people, as is suggested in Practical Activity 13.5.

An innovative way of analysing language is as a form of 'discourse'. Influenced by the work of Foucault (1977), this approach attempts to penetrate beneath the surface features of social interaction to demonstrate how relationships are regulated in terms of power and control. Thus 'post-structuralist' psychologists and sociologists highlight the ways in which personal and political issues are embedded within the 'discursive practices' of very ordinary, routine interaction. Thus we have analyses of classroom events which highlight the ways in which characteristic scripts are played out and in which patterns of discursive practice 'position' participating subjects in particular ways. The exercise of control, with its attendant social consequences for the experiences, learning and identities of children, is thus revealed. For examples of this approach to classroom analysis regarding gender, see Davies (1993, **Reading, 11.5**) and Walkerdine (1988 and **Reading, 13.4**); regarding race, see Epstein (1993, **Reading, 13.5**).

Practical activity 13.5

Aim: To consider the significance of names and naming.

Method: Working with at least one colleague, select one of the following groups of words and create a dictionary entry for each word. Try to encompass all the meanings you can think of, including slang. As you do so, discuss when these words might be used, what they describe, what associations they have for individuals in the group.

- Asians, immigrants, blacks, negro, spastic, queer, Jew, Hun
- hunk, bitch, stag, cow, tart, he-man, blonde, housewife
- gossip, nag, talk, natter, discuss, yak, heart-to-heart
- secretary, novelist, gardener, barrister, nurse, doctor, chef, cook

Look at your definitions. Do any of them have negative/pejorative meanings? Which have positive connotations? Would you classify any as 'neutral'? Are any obsolete? Are any relatively recent? Why do you think they came into use?

Follow-up: Use your findings to discuss the implications of naming for the provision of equal opportunities. This quotation might make a starting-point.

> In order to live in the world, we must name it. Names are essential for the construction of reality for without a name it is difficult to accept the existence of an object, an event, a feeling ... By assigning names we impose a pattern and a meaning which allows us to manipulate the world ... Naming, however is not a neutral or random process ... All naming is, of necessity, biased and the process of naming is one of encoding that bias ... difficulty arises when one group holds a monopoly on naming and is able to enforce its own particular bias on everyone, including those who do not share its view of the world.
>
> (Spender, 1980, p. 163)

3.4 Interpersonal relationships

We discussed classroom relationships at length in Chapter 5 and suggested that teachers and children usually negotiate a 'working consensus' (see also **Reading, 5.3**). This represents ways of getting along together and from it emerges a range of tacit rules about behaviour and a sense of what is and is not 'fair'. We suggested that children's actions might range from conforming to rules, to engaging in routine deviance or, by stepping outside the bounds of the 'working consensus', to acting in unilateral and disorderly ways. One study (Pollard, 1985) identified three types of friendship groups among 11-year-olds. 'Goodies' were very conformist, fairly able but considered rather dull. 'Jokers' liked to 'have a laugh', were very able and got on well with their teachers. 'Gang' group members were willing to disrupt classes, had low levels of academic achievement and were thought of as a nuisance.

If we relate characteristic pupil actions to types of child friendship group, then we get a range of parameters as indicated in Figure 13.1. This figure simplifies great complexities, but it does highlight some important social consequences of classroom

	Actions within the understanding of the working consensus		Actions outside the understandings of the working consensus
	Conformity	Routine deviance	Disorder
Goodies	——————————————→		
Jokers	——————————————————————→		
Gangs	——————————————————————————————————→		

Figure 13.1 *Parameters of child behaviour*

relationships. In particular, it draws attention to the issues of being fair and offering interesting learning opportunities. If the quality of both interpersonal relationships and curriculum provision is high, then the parameters of children's actions are likely to move to the left of the diagram and differentiation may decrease. If interpersonal relationships are poor and curriculum provision is inappropriate, then the parameters are likely to move to the right of the diagram. The result is likely to be an increase in disruption, a decrease in learning and the growth of dissatisfaction with school. Overall, differentiation is likely to increase, as the teacher acts to deal with disruptive children.

It is very easy and common to see causes of disruption as being exclusively to do with particular children. Reflection on the quality and pattern of relationships and of teacher actions in respect of the working consensus may provide another set of issues for consideration – issues , furthermore, which, to a great extent, are within our own control as teachers (Practical Activity 13.6).

Practical activity 13.6

Aim: To reflect on the quality and consequences of relationships between teacher and children, over several weeks.

Method: We suggest that a diary is kept. In this diary feelings and observations can be recorded regarding the responses and behaviour of children who have different dispositions to school. Perhaps 'goodies', 'jokers' or 'gang' children might be tentatively identified.

The diary might be analysed to see how our own feelings, provision and actions affected the children.

Follow-up: Perhaps the children's behaviour and application to work varies with the quality of educational provision and our own energy and commitment. If this happens, then a reflective teacher may want to consider such things as the nature of deviance and his or her own responsibility for them.

3.5 Teacher expectations

The expectations of teachers for the children in their charge have long been recognized as contributing to children's achievements in school. The classic study of this, by Rosenthal and Jacobsen (1968), suggested that a 'self-fulfilling prophecy' could be set up, in which children who were believed to be 'bright' would do well, but, where negative expectations existed, then children's school performance would fall. Indeed, although the ways in which teacher expectations influence pupil behaviour and attainment is highly complex, there is a broad consensus that high expectations can have a very positive effect. For instance, it is often emphasized by HMI (e.g. HMCI, 1995).

However, other research has shown differences in teachers' expectations of children from different social class backgrounds (e.g. Sharp and Green, 1975; King, 1978; Hartley, 1985). Similar issues have been raised in relation to gender (see Delamont, 1990) and race (see Wright, 1992). This raises a very important issue for reflective teachers who will want to ensure that they do not, unwittingly, favour some children over others. Two particularly comprehensive studies of links between expectations, behaviour and performance were carried out in London and considered differences in terms of gender, social class, race, etc. (Mortimore *et al.*, 1988, **Reading, 5.7**; Tizard *et al.*, 1988, **Reading, 13.2**).

Whilst teachers should aim to raise their expectations and look for positive points for potential development in their pupils, there are also dangers from the existence of negative expectations. For instance, stereotyping is the attribution of particular characteristics to members of a group, and is often used negatively. Thus sex role stereotyping might be found, say, in an infant classroom with girls being encouraged to become 'teacher helpers'. Perhaps they might also play domestic roles in the 'home corner' while boys engage in more active play, such as using construction equipment. And yet, as Walkerdine and other feminists have shown, girls in such situations can assert power through the adoption of an appropriate discourse (Walkerdine, 1981, **Reading, 13.4**). Stereotyping should be avoided, but it is never absolute in its effects.

Bias is a further source of unequal treatment of pupils. It might refer to images and ideas in books and in other resources which suggest the superiority or inferiority of certain groups of people (Chapter 8, section 2.9). However, educational procedures can also be biased in themselves. For example, there has been a long-standing debate about bias in intelligence tests and such questions are recurring with regard to aspects of national assessment procedures. This debate has focused on class, gender and cultural bias at various times and is closely associated with the ways in which disadvantages can be 'institutionalized'. The institutionalization of disadvantage refers to situations in which social arrangements and procedures are established and taken for granted, despite the fact that they may systematically disadvantage a particular social group. Epstein has provided a particularly clear analysis of this with regard to racism (Epstein, 1993, **Reading, 13.5**; see Practical Activity 13.7).

3.6 Assessment

The evaluation of pupils has always been an endemic feature of classroom and school life (Jackson, 1968, **Reading, 5.5**). After all, children attend school to learn

Practical activity 13.7

Aim: To explore teachers' perceptions of children in class.

Method: List the names of all the children in your class from memory. Then quickly choose a single word or short phrase to describe key characteristics of each of the children.

Consider any patterns that emerge. Is there any significance in the order in which you recalled the names? Were any hard to remember? Are there any similarities or differences in your descriptions or thoughts that were based on gender, race, ability? Which children (if any) received negative comments? Which attracted positive comments? Could any of your choices of words or phrases be classed as stereotypical?

Consider the implications of your findings for classroom relationships and the provision of equal opportunities.

Follow-up: Consider the policies, procedures and practices of your school with regard to the needs of different social groups. Do any aspects of school provision represent forms of institutionalized disadvantage?

and teachers to teach. However, following the 1988 Education Reform Act, the significance of assessment in primary education has grown considerably (see Chapter 12). Whilst it once took place relatively informally using intuitive criteria, assessment has become increasingly 'categoric' and formal (Broadfoot, 1996).

Children are aware of teacher judgements in many ways, and indeed of where they personally stand in relation to them. Even in routine classroom life there are often relatively overt indicators of attainment, such as position in reading book systems, maths schemes or grouping systems. Pupils are also very aware of more subtle indicators of teacher assessment and disposition, for these are revealed through the quality of rapport or interaction which develops between the teacher and particular individuals.

Two types of more formal assessments are now required in England and Wales for the core subjects, Teacher Assessment (TA) and Standard Assessment Tasks and Tests (SATs) (see Chapter 12, introduction and section 2.3). In both cases children's capabilities must be assessed against 'levels' which are set out in the Statutory Orders for the subject. Whilst the SATs are assessed by a child's capability against specific criteria, teacher assessment for this purpose is based on judgements of which official 'level description' provides a 'best fit' with the pupil's attainment. This judgement is obviously vulnerable to the unintended influence of teacher expectations, stereotyping, etc. In addition, despite considerable efforts to achieve consistency through moderation processes, there is some evidence of teachers developing varying notions of 'levelness' for key levels such as Level 2 and Level 4 (see also **Reading, 12.2**) and there are also significant disparities in the ways in which SATs are managed (SCAA, 1996). How reliable, therefore, can the formal assessments be?

A related issue concerns the range of pupil capabilities which are assessed. Most emphasis is on the core curriculum, and this is particularly 'high stakes'

because of reporting and publication requirements. However, this bias makes it hard for teachers and schools to provide parity of esteem for the achievements of children whose talents may lie elsewhere, in art, music, physical education, etc. This is an issue of the validity of the forms of assessment, but it also has implications for equal opportunities and the social differentiation of pupils.

Social differentiation is connected to assessment processes because of the use which is made of assessment information, and also because of the social messages which are conveyed. For instance, assessments in reading or number work are often used as a basis for the allocation of pupils to groups. At a whole-school level, other methods of setting or targeting to match the intellectual challenge to each child are also developing rapidly. Placement of a child in a particular group or set will certainly be noted by parents and by other pupils, and the latter may well identify the 'bright ones' and 'thickos', with consequent implications for the self-image and social status of both groups.

Encouraging pupils to become involved in self-assessment is a constructive way of guiding all children to recognize their own capacities and to understand what is needed for future development. The involvement of each pupil in self-assessment is likely to make its implications less socially divisive (see Chapter 12, section 1.3 and **Reading, 12.7**; Practical Activity 13.8).

Practical activity 13.8

Aim: To investigate assessment results, their use and implications.

Method: Consider a set of SAT and TA results for one subject, say English, for a year group. Are there any patterns in the scores in relation to gender, ethnicity, social class, age, special needs, etc.? Do you feel that the results provide a valid indicator of the full capabilities of the children? What use is made of such results within the school? What meanings are inferred by other teachers and parents? How do pupils interpret the results when thinking about others, and when thinking about themselves?

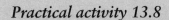

Follow-up: Try reading Armstrong (1989, **Reading, 12.8**) and Drummond (1993, **Reading, 12.9**) for suggestions of how important it is to use *valid* forms of assessment and to relate outcomes to children's learning needs.

3.7   Social values and the hidden curriculum

As teachers, the consequences of our actions may show in the perspectives, attitudes and behaviour of children whom we may influence. Indeed, to 'socialize' children into the 'values of society' has often been seen as part of a teacher's role (Parsons, 1959; Dreeben, 1968; see also Chapter 4, section 1.2; Chapter 14, section 1; and Tate, 1995, **Reading, 15.3**).

Another way of conceptualizing the social consequences of teachers' actions is to see them as being part of the 'hidden curriculum'. As we saw in Chapter 7, section 2.9, the hidden curriculum is formed from tacit assumptions and practices which nevertheless convey messages and expectations to children.

Some sociologists have suggested that the hidden curriculum is directly concerned with producing social conformity. For instance, Bowles and Gintis (1976, **Reading, 13.1**) argued that schools tend to induce passivity and the acceptance of authority in combination with concern for the quantity and quality of work irrespective of its purpose or meaningfulness. There was said to be a 'correspondence' between the social relationships of workplaces and those of schools. The suggestion which follows is that children who attend such schools may come to accept future positions in society which 'seem appropriate' to their social class, gender, race, etc. Their future opportunities and rights as individuals might thus be narrowed by school practices. Dale (1977) suggested that such processes of social reproduction have always existed within the education system. However, whereas they were once relatively explicit in the official curriculum, in modern societies it is the 'form' of schooling which is important. This is part of the 'hidden curriculum'.

An example of this may be helpful. Pollard (1985) collected examples of teacher talk – instructions, comments, questions. They were analysed to reveal three clusters of values:

1. *Relating to productivity and efficiency at school-work.*
   Effort (e.g. 'Let's make a really big effort today.').
   Perseverance (e.g. 'Try a bit longer.').
   Neatness (e.g. 'That's a nice page.').
   Regularity (e.g. 'Is that your best work?').
   Speed (e.g. 'Has anyone finished yet?').

2. *Relating to behaviour and social relationships.*
   Self-control (e.g. 'Stop being silly.').
   Obedience (e.g. 'Did you hear what I said?')
   Politeness (e.g. 'That's not a very nice thing to do.').
   Quietness (e.g. 'Silence, now.').
   Truth (e.g. 'Let's have it straight now.').
   Respect for authority (e.g. 'Hands up if you want something.').

3. *Relating to individualism and competitiveness.*
   Achievement (e.g. 'Have you got that right?').
   Individualism (e.g. 'Do it yourself.').
   Hierarchy (e.g. 'Who got ten out of ten?')
   Self-reliance (e.g. 'Go and find out.').

The existence of such values in schools may seem appropriate to some and serve to support the current social and economic system which sets out to achieve high levels of both economic productivity and of individual competition. Simultaneously, at the classroom level, such values may also support teachers' concerns with discipline and control. They thus may seem to 'make sense' at two levels – the macro and micro.

The projection of values is inevitable in a classroom, but these should be carefully monitored as a necessary part of reflective teaching. A procedure is suggested in Practical Activity 13.9.

Practical activity 13.9

Aim: To gather indications of the social values which form part of the hidden curriculum.

Method: Make a tape recording, or ask a colleague to take detailed field notes. Identify the instructions, guidance, exhortations, reinforcements, reprimands and condemnations which are used when working with children.

These could be sorted into those to do with 'work' and those to do with 'behaviour'. An analysis of the underlying values could be carried out.

A further development would be to sort statements by the characteristics of the people to whom they were directed – by sex, race, social class, etc.

Follow-up: Reflective teachers might consider how results from evidence or this kind relates to their own educational values (see Practical Activity 4.3).

4 | PUPIL POLARIZATION

When children who share a similar position in relation to school success or failure come together as a group, they begin to develop subcultures. Such processes are termed 'polarization', for they involve a reinforcement of the initial differentiation as the children themselves respond to it. In a sense, it is a form of cultural coping strategy, developed in response to experience and circumstances.

There has been a series of studies of the internal workings of secondary schools (e.g. Hargreaves, 1967; Lacey, 1970; Ball, 1981b) which has shown how children interpret their experiences of differentiation. There are tendencies for them to identify with or against school, with children who feel that they are 'educational failures' who reject school values in order to protect their own pride and self-esteem.

Primary schools are very different from secondary schools but similar processes may be found. Indeed as we have seen, Pollard (1985) identified three types of friendship groups among 11-year-olds: 'goodies', 'jokers' and 'gangs'. The origins of these types of groups were related to processes of differentiation within the school and classrooms and seemed to be leading to further polarization. In later work Pollard and Filer (forthcoming) have traced the 'school careers' of individual pupils and have recorded the social influence of peer, family and teacher relationships as they form increasingly differentiated and unique identities.

Perhaps differentiation and polarization processes are almost inevitable in schools, but this cannot diminish our responsibility as teachers for monitoring them and for acting to minimize any unnecessary divisive effects. In Practical Activities 13.10 and 13.11 we suggest two ways of gaining some insights into the polarization of pupils within peer culture.

A key connection is to try to relate the differentiating effect of teachers and schools to the polarizing processes that occur within child culture. Practical Activity 13.12 is designed to assist in this and suggests bringing together the results

Practical activity 13.10

Aim: To explore children's perceptions of the playground.

Method: Watch the children at your school in the playground. Notice particularly how children use and occupy playground spaces and any significant actions or verbal exchanges between different groups of children. Make quick notes of your observations.

In the classroom, talk with the children about their use of the playground. Ask them to draw a plan of the playground, marking areas where they or others can go or play, what activities take place, how they feel about different parts of the playground, such as where they feel safe. Discuss their plans with the children in groups.

Make a note of the points that emerge. Do you begin to get a sense of the friendship groups which exist within the pupil culture of your school? Are equal opportunity issues raised?

Follow-up: Share your response to the activity with a colleague who has also done the activity.

Practical activity 13.11

Aim: To obtain indications of children's aspirations and expectations regarding their future lives.

Method: The essential element here is to ask children to compare aspirations and expectations. First, they should be asked to say what they would like to be or do as adults. Second, they should be asked to say what they actually expect to do or be. If there are differences, they can be asked to consider the reasons for them.

Drawings, discussion, or writing may be appropriate depending on the age of the children.

Follow-up: Such an exercise could not actually 'prove' anything but it could provide vivid and indicative data on children's perception of their futures. Are there signs of peer culture influencing the aspirations of the children? Are there signs of polarization in the choices they make?

from several practical activities. The key processes, which may be evident, lie in a chain from classroom differentiation being reinforced by polarization and then beginning to affect self-image and self-esteem. The next effect is likely to be felt on attainment and, in due course, life chances.

Lest readers feel overawed by the responsibilities outlined above, we should reassert two realities. First, that all children have different prior experiences and capabilities on entry to classrooms. Teachers cannot wave magic wands and make them all be equal in what they can achieve, though pupils do have equal rights to be supported in fulfilling their potential. Second, that differentiation is

Practical activity 13.12

Aim: To highlight the possible influence of classroom differentiation and polarization processes.

Method: Simple indicators for both differentiation and polarization are required.

1. For differentiation: positions in ability-based groups, on reading/maths schemes or from national assessment procedures can be used to rank individuals or group children into ability quartiles.

2. For polarization: patterns revealed by a sociogram can be used (see Practical Activity 4.15) and these can be combined with findings from Practical Activities 13.10 or 13.11.

These indicators then have to be examined together, for example, by setting out friendship groups and aspirations, and recording the differentiation indicators beside each child's name. Do you begin to see a pattern?

Follow-up: This exercise may suggest ways in which classroom practices by teachers and children's responses interact together to create or reinforce social and individual differences. If this is so, a reflective teacher needs to consider what if any action should be taken.

necessarily inevitable in classrooms. It is part of helping each child to fulfil his or her potential. And yet, that prime responsibility also brings a second responsibility, which is, wherever possible, to mitigate adverse social effects.

5 | DEVELOPING POLICY AND PRACTICE

In this chapter we have suggested a number of ways in which reflective teachers might monitor their practices in terms of social consequences and the provision of equal opportunities. Such monitoring may facilitate our own learning and professional development because of the increase in our understandings of classroom life.

Any of the forms of social differentiation, described in section 3 above, could harm children's sense of self-esteem and thus their learning. They influence self-confidence and engagement with educational experiences. Where children are affected by more than one of the factors, adverse effects are likely to be multiplied. A review of these possibilities is suggested in Practical Activity 13.13. However, there can be difficulties here, for classroom life make complex demands on teachers. Indeed, Doyle (1977, **Reading, 10.1**) has suggested that, for student teachers, the complexity and need for rapid decision-making in classrooms can often be overwhelming. Ways of simplifying such complexities need to be found.

We would suggest that one way of doing this is to try consciously to develop classroom policies. As long-term targets, such policies could inform specific actions and support continuous development. Reflective teachers who have engaged in the

Practical activity 13.13

Aim: To reflect on common forms of social differentiation and polarization.

Method: Review the issues raised in sections 3 and 4, and read Andrew Pollard's article on 'social differentiation' in **Reading, 13.8.** Seven aspects of classroom differentiation are raised, as is the multiplying effect of pupil polarization. Consider each in turn as they may apply to your own classroom.

- The official curriculum
- Classroom organization and management
- Language
- Interpersonal relationships
- Teacher expectations
- Assessment
- Social values
- Pupil polarization

Choose *one* issue for particular attention, and target developments in your practice which you think will provide more help to ensure equal opportunities for your pupils. Try out your ideas for, say, a week. As you do this, identify the things which go well and consider how you were successful. Think about the things which did not go so well. Consider the difficulties you encounter and alternative approaches you could try.

Follow-up: You might like to consider the ways in which various forms of differentiation and polarization may interconnect. A specific focus helps to make development work manageable, but is likely to highlight other issues for further exploration. Pace classroom development work, reviewing and planning as you go.

activities in this book should be in a very good position to think through such policies and to take control of their own classroom actions. It is one more way of ensuring that the cyclical process of reflection, discussed in Chapter 1, moves forward positively.

We will give some examples of issues about which long-term policies might be framed, though obviously many others could be identified (see also Practical Activity 13.14).

1. *Listening to children.* As part of the search for understanding the interactive nature of the teaching–learning process it is clearly important to gain access to children's perceptions. This requires that we are open and receptive listeners and it may change our relationship with the children. Also, in encouraging children to explain their views they are also likely to begin to reflect themselves. This process may help the children to become more aware as learners and perhaps help them to develop independence and self-confidence. However, such developments are unlikely unless we consciously and consistently provide the conditions for children to talk and explain their points of view.

2. *Being positive.* It is very easy to respond negatively to children when under pressure. Perhaps taking a policy-decision to try to be encouraging, and to seek out good work and reinforce creativity, would provide a check and a guide when responding in potentially difficult situations.

3. *Encouraging co-operative relationships among children.* This is particularly important because of the effects which pupil culture can have. Barrie Thorne (1993, **Reading, 13.9**) suggests a range of teacher strategies including using particular forms of grouping and task setting, facilitating equal access to activities and intervening to challenge stereotyping or inappropriate use of power.

4. *Acting 'fairly'.* This is a very suitable issue for a policy-decision, bearing in mind the power of teachers as seen by children. It is a very important issue to children and simply calls for awareness of how they are likely to view a teacher's action *before* it is made. The role model offered by a teacher as she exercises her authority is certainly a very significant social consequence of classroom life.

Practical activity 13.14

Aim: To identify important issues on which to focus classroom policies.

Method: Consider and list the major issues of social consequence and equal opportunities that arise in your classroom. As a way of doing this, you could review each section of this chapter, treating it as a check-list. Record the issues which seem to be of relevance. At a deeper level, you could consider the outcomes of the Practical Activities which you have carried out.

Select a few of the most important issues and consider how you could improve the classroom situation. Rather than thinking of one-off actions, try to formulate 'classroom policies' that you can sustain over time.

Follow-up: Pupils have a strong sense of fairness and appropriateness. Perhaps you could enlist their support in enacting your classroom policies.

CONCLUSION

Whatever forms of school or classroom practices are developed, there will be social consequences, because processes of social differentiation and polarization are probably impossible to avoid in school settings. A crucial issue thus concerns how to manage these social processes so that their most divisive effects are mitigated. At the same time, the promotion of equal opportunities should be actively pursued through school policies, teaching of the curriculum and other classroom practices. It is a difficult goal, but it nevertheless remains a continuing responsibility to work towards. Indeed, there can be little doubt that the provision of equal opportunities will always be a major concern in education.

Despite a comprehensive awareness of equal opportunities issues and positive commitments regarding constructive classroom policies, it is clear that classroom teachers cannot act in isolation from the school in which they work and the society in which they live. For this reason we conclude the book by moving beyond the classroom and by considering the reflective teacher in the context of schools and society.

Notes for further reading

Regarding the social consequences of classroom practices in primary schools, the following books provide case-study illustrations:

Lubeck, S. (1985)
Sandbox Society,
London: Falmer Press.

Pollard, A. (1985)
The Social World of the Primary School,
London: Cassell.   📖 **Readings, 4.7 and 5.3**

Hartley, D. (1985)
Understanding the Primary School,
London: Croom Helm.

For more general reviews of common processes of interaction within schools and classrooms which can lead to social differentiation, see:

Woods, P. (1983)
Sociology and the School,
London: Routledge & Kegan Paul.

Pollard, A. (1987d)
Social differentiation in primary schools,
Cambridge Journal of Education,
17 (3), 158–61.   📖 **Reading, 13.8**

A very insightful practical account of developing equal opportunities practices in primary school classrooms is:

Griffiths, M. and Davies, B. (1995)
In Fairness to Children,
London: David Fulton.

Specific treatment of particular issues is provided in books such as:

1. Gender

Golombok, S. and Fivush, R. (1994)
Gender Development,
Cambridge: Cambridge University Press.

Lloyd, B. and Duveen, G. (1992)
Gender Identities and Education:
The Impact of Starting School,
London: Harvester Wheatsheaf.

Evans, T. (1988)
A Gender Agenda: A Sociological Study of Teachers,
Parents and Pupils in their Primary Schools,
Sydney: Allen and Unwin.

Browne, N. and France, P. (1986)
Untying the Apron Strings,
Milton Keynes: Open University Press.

Delamont, S. (1980)
Sex Roles and the School,
London: Routledge.

Davies, B. (1993)
*Shards of Glass: Children Reading and
Writing beyond Gendered Identities*,
Sydney: Allen and Unwin.   📖 Reading, 11.5

Walkerdine, V. (1988)
The Mastery of Reason,
London: Routledge.   📖 Readings, 13.3 and 13.4

2. Race

Troyna, B. and Hatcher, R. (1992)
*Racism in Children's Lives: A Study
of Mainly White Primary Schools*,
London: Routledge.   📖 Reading, 13.6

Wright, C. (1992)
Race Relations in the Primary School,
London: David Fulton.

Grugeon, E. and Woods, P. (1990)
Educating All: Multicultural Perspectives in the Primary School,
London: Routledge.

Massey, I. (1991)
More Than Skin Deep: Developing Multicultural Education in Schools,
London: Hodder and Stoughton.

Epstein, D. (1993)
Changing Classroom Cultures: Anti-Racism, Politics and Schools,
Stoke-on-Trent: Trentham Books.   📖 Reading, 13.5

3. Special educational needs

Wolfendale, S. (1992b)
Primary Schools and Special Needs,
London: Cassell.

Croll, P. and Moses, D. (1985)
*One in Five: The Assessment and
Incidence of Special Educational Needs*,
London: Routledge & Kegan Paul.

Ainscow, M. (1991)
Effective Schools for All,
London: David Fulton.

Evans, J., Lunt, I. and Wedell, K. (1992)
Special Needs and the 1988 Act,
London: Cassell.

Vulliamy, G. and Webb. R. (1992)
Teacher Research and Special Educational Needs,
London: David Fulton.   📖 Reading, 13.7

4. Social class

Jackson, B. (1964)
Streaming: An Education System in Minature,
London: Routledge & Kegan Paul.

Sharp, R. and Green, A. (1975)
Education and Social Control,
London: Routledge & Kegan Paul.

King, R. (1978)
All Things Bright and Beautiful,
Chichester: Wiley.

Lareau, A. (1989)
*Home Advantage: Social Class and Parental
Intervention in Elementary Education,*
London: Falmer.

Reid, I. (1989)
*Social Class Differences in Britain:
Life Chances and Life-Styles,*
London: Fontana.

Reading, 8.9

Reading, 13.1

PART 3

BEYOND CLASSROOM REFLECTION

CHAPTER 14

Reflective teaching and the school

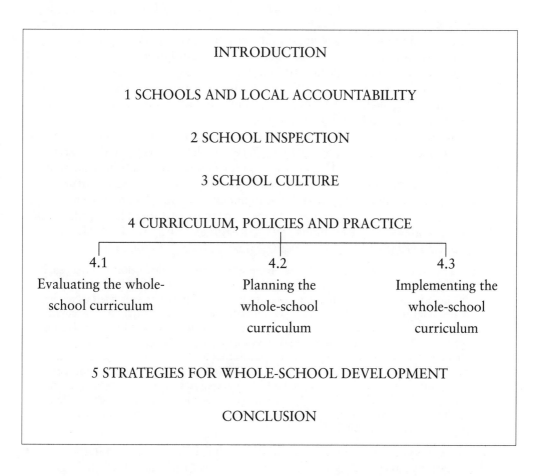

INTRODUCTION

1 SCHOOLS AND LOCAL ACCOUNTABILITY

2 SCHOOL INSPECTION

3 SCHOOL CULTURE

4 CURRICULUM, POLICIES AND PRACTICE

4.1	4.2	4.3
Evaluating the whole-school curriculum	Planning the whole-school curriculum	Implementing the whole-school curriculum

5 STRATEGIES FOR WHOLE-SCHOOL DEVELOPMENT

CONCLUSION

INTRODUCTION

In this chapter we focus on the context of the whole school. During the 1990s there was an enormous increase in the significance of schools as free-standing and self-managed organizations. Legislation gradually moved state schools from the shelter of local education authority support structures and associated lines of accountability, and even created a type of school funded directly by a national grant. By the late 1990s almost all schools had control of their budgets, policies and practices and were formally accountable to governors and parents. Nevertheless, LEAs continued to have important roles in providing advice (through policy frameworks and modest Advisory Services), co-ordination (such as for special educational needs) and some central services (such as payroll). The autonomy of schools is relative, for it must still be exercised within the legislative framework which prescribes such vital issues as curriculum and assessment, and this is backed by a national system for school inspection.

From the professional perspective, too, the importance of schools as organizations is being reasserted. For instance, there is gathering evidence that variations in the internal policies and practices of schools does influence educational effectiveness, (Mortimore *et al.*, 1988; Sammons and Nutall, 1992), and we have evidence that positive educational developments are almost impossible to sustain without teamwork and coherent planning at an institutional level (Nias *et al.*, 1992; Hargreaves and Hopkins, 1991, **Readings, 14.2** and **14.3**). Roger and Richardson (1985) characterize a 'self-evaluating school' as follows:

> It is the school which is aware of the pressures of accountability being experienced in education yet is concerned to maintain and advance its professionalism, not least in the area of autonomy of decision-making. It is a school which sees itself as having many relationships with its employers, its community and particularly its clients. These relationships... are susceptible to improvement. It is a school in which the staff see themselves as part of a collaborative venture aimed at the purposeful education of children.... It is a school which also recognizes that it may lack experience and expertise in particular areas and is therefore prepared to be open to advice and information from outside agencies. It is a school which is prepared to devote precious time and energy to reflective activities .... Above all, it is the school which has a genuine desire to find out about itself and by so doing to make itself a better place for young children to develop. (pp. 20–1).

This view is consistent with the position which is being advocated in the present book but we have to recognize that not all schools fit the model which Roger and Richardson suggest. In fact, in many cases the schools in which reflective teachers find themselves may be far more static, 'routinized' and locked into 'taken-for-granted' conventions. This chapter and its associated practical activities are intended to clarify the accountability context in which primary schools now find themselves, to assist reflective teachers to gather and analyse information about their school and, finally, to consider appropriate strategies for action.

Some sharp ethical and professional issues may be raised by this focus, for it represents a move outside the classroom which has been the traditional boundary of many teachers' responsibilities. However, modern forms of school organization require all teachers to adopt whole-school responsibilities as part of the collective staff team (House of Commons, 1986; Alexander *et al.*, 1992, **Reading, 8.1**) and it is thus entirely appropriate to reflect on the overall context. National Curriculum requirements for continuity and progression also call for whole-school co-operation and the continuing pace of change and pressure for development means that all schools need to maximize the use of their innovative and adaptive resources. In this context, then, reflective teachers have both a right and a direct responsibility to consider the school context in which they work and should not avoid it. Nevertheless, for a classroom teacher or a student teacher to investigate and reflect on a whole-school basis could cause difficulties, and we would advise that the practical activities which are suggested in this chapter might be discussed with the headteacher and appropriate colleagues prior to embarking upon them. Ultimately, there can be no side-stepping of the issues. However, the initial approach should be open-minded, seeking to understand perspectives and the constraints which may have influenced the development of existing policies and practices. Such understanding should provide a sound foundation for acting strategically and with positive value-commitments to contribute to future developments.

We begin this chapter by focusing on the new structures of autonomy and accountability in which primary schools are placed, and on the role of professionalism.

1 SCHOOLS AND LOCAL ACCOUNTABILITY

Before the legislation of the late 1980s, educational administration was based on a so-called 'partnership model' in which government, local education authorities and schools worked together, at different levels of organization, to provide community education. As we saw in Chapter 2, this model was challenged in the 1980s and 1990s for being dominated by professionals and for failing to produce sufficiently high standards of education. An alternative conception of schools responding directly to their client consumers was suggested and it is this 'market model' which has begun to dominate. The market model is based on the belief that, if schools are made autonomous and exposed to market forces, then competition between schools will produce steadily increasing standards of education (Chubb and Moe, 1990; Conservative Party, 1992; DFE, 1992).

To make schools more autonomous the influence of local education authorities has been dramatically decreased and schools have been required to embark on Local Management of Schools (LMS), in which the school governors have responsibility for the entire budget, staffing and curricular provision of their schools. Some 2 per cent of English primary schools have also 'opted out' of LEA systems altogether, to become 'grant maintained schools (GMS)' and they now receive annual funding direct from a government funding agency. LMS has given governors and headteachers considerable scope for imaginative decision-making and most headteachers value this and have been able to use it to enhance educational provision. However, many headteachers are also severely pressurized by the enormous number and complexity of administrative, financial and managerial tasks which are associated with LMS. This can compromise their vital role as educational leaders, but does it make it possible for headteachers to be more responsive to pupil needs (see Practical Activity 14.1)?

Practical activity 14.1

Aim: To investigate the perception of a primary school headteacher regarding LMS.

Method: Work with a headteacher to produce a list of 'good points' and a list of 'bad points' regarding LMS.

Follow-up: What do you think will be the long-term costs and benefits of LMS?

Legislation of the late 1980s and early 1990s and the associated 'Parents' Charter' of 1991 gave parents significant rights. These include the rights:

- to have access to standard information about aggregated results of school performance (including the standardized tests)
- to select the school which their children attend (subject to certain limits)
- to receive written reports on the performance of their children
- to receive an annual report from the school governors

Such rights provide parents with certain kinds of information and with clear opportunities to exercise choice. The law positions parents as consumers of education and, in so doing, defines parents, for the present, as the group to which teachers and schools should primarily be held to account.

Of course, not all parents see themselves simply as consumers of education and recent research (Hughes *et al.*, 1994, **Reading, 14.6**) has shown that most parents value the happiness and security provided for their child and the community links of primary schools at least as much as academic achievements. Many parents wish to be 'partners' in the education of their child, an argument on which the Labour Party has placed some emphasis (Labour Party, 1995; see Practical Activity 14.2).

Practical activity 14.2

Aim: To investigate the preferences of parents regarding primary schools.

Method: Ask some parents, perhaps 20 individuals, to answer the question: 'What did you consider in choosing a primary school for your child?' Write down their replies, separating different points in your notes.

To analyse this material, cut up your notes to separate each individual point. Then sort the points out into groups. Search for patterns to find the parents' priorities, reservations and concerns.

Follow-up: To what extent did the parents see themselves as educational consumers or as partners? What did they expect or hope for from the school for their child? What views did they have on teacher professionalism and on the accountability of schools? What are the most constructive implications of your enquiry?

Of course, a considerable part of schools' accountability to parents and the community is exercised through governing bodies. In a maintained primary school of between 100 and 299 pupils this would be made up of three parents, three local authority representatives, four co-opted representatives, one teacher and the head-teacher if he or she chose to be a member. Such governing bodies are now legally responsible for many aspects of their schools, including the budget, buildings, staffing and curriculum. This is a challenging role for non-educationalists and leaves an important role for professionals in offering support (Beckett *et al.*, 1991; see Practical Activity 14.3).

Perhaps the most significant part of governors' responsibility under LMS is control of the school budget. Figure 14.1 sets out the budget of an actual medium-sized, six-teacher, primary school in the 1995/6 financial year (see also Practical Activity 14.4). There are three salient points to make:

1. Most of the income (75 per cent) comes in relation to the 145 pupils on roll. This is an average of £1,166 per pupil, though the actual amount per pupil is age weighted – an 'age-weighted pupil unit' (AWPU).

2. Most of the expenditure (80 per cent, if we include the contingency allowed for salary increases) goes to pay for salaries and other staffing costs.

3. After taking out various costs related to the buildings and grounds, there is only £13,000 (6 per cent) left for direct educational expenditure on the 145 children and six staff for the year (£1.72 per week per pupil).

Following extensive research on how governing bodies work, Deem *et al.*, (1995, **Reading, 14.7**) ask whether school governors should be seen as 'empowered citizens' or as 'state volunteers'. Their concern is that, despite the apparently wide-ranging responsiblities of governors, the actual scope for decision-making is severely constrained. National requirements pervade many areas of a school's provision and resource constraints often restrict opportunities for innovation. Thus governors come to act more as passive agents, enacting and seeming to legitimate the requirements of central government, rather than being active, empowered, local decision-makers for their schools.

It is legitimate to expect professionals to be accountable. However, it is necessary to create educationally constructive structures and processes through which

Practical activity 14.3

Aim: To consider the role of a governing body.

Method: Ask if you can study minutes of the governing body meetings of a primary school. Note and classify the range of issues covered – staffing, curriculum, finance, etc. To what extent would you regard the issues covered as 'professional' matters and to what extent were the decisions taken enhanced by the deliberations of the governing body?

Follow-up: Attend a governing body meeting as an observer.
   Did it provide a constructive forum for school management and professional accountability?

INCOME

Age-weighted pupil units	169,100	
School size allowance	28,400	
Special needs allowance	13,500	
Floor area allowance	15,100	
Total income		**226,100**

EXPENDITURE
Staffing expenditure

Permanent teachers	–141,000	
Supply teachers	–4,000	
Teacher assistants	–6,000	
School meal supervisors	–4,600	
Caretaker	–3,200	
School secretary	–11,000	
Staff development	–4,000	
Total staffing		–173,800

Buildings expenditure

Building repair and maintenance	–6,000	
Vandalism repair	–2,000	
Grounds maintenance	–3,500	
Electricity	–4,500	
Gas	–4,500	
Water rates	–300	
Sewerage	–500	
Cleaning	–8,000	
Refuse collection	–500	
Total buildings		–29,800

Direct educational expenditure

Educational equipment	–5,000	
Books	–4,000	
Materials	–4,000	
Total direct educational		–13,000

Miscellaneous expenditure

Governor's clerk	–300	
Postage	–400	
Telephone	–1,000	
School brochure	–100	
Furniture	–300	
Insurance	–400	
Total miscellaneous		–2,500

Contingencies

Staff settlements	–7,000	
General	0	
Total contingencies		–7,000
Total expenditure		**–226,100**

Figure 14.1 *Projected budget for a medium-sized English primary school, 1995/6 financial year*

> ## Practical activity 14.4
>
> *Aim*: To consider the impact of school budget constraints.
>
> *Method*: Consider the budget in Figure 14.1 with a colleague. If you were part of a school governing body, what implications might it have for your policies on:
>
> - pupil enrolment?
> - staff appointments?
> - staff development?
> - curriculum development?
> - buildings maintenance?
> - publication of assessment results?
> - class size?
> - provision for children with special educational needs?
> - liaison with parents?
> - education equipment and materials (e.g. for art)?
> - car boot sales?
>
> *Follow-up*: Enquire about the budget of a school that you know well. Have budgetary constraints and opportunities affected teaching processes? Has budgetary awareness increased the accountability of the school to parents? Have the roles of central and local governments been considered?

such accountability can be expressed. How the systems of the 1990s will develop in the new millennium remains to be seen.

2 | SCHOOL INSPECTION

A national school inspection system has existed from Victorian times (see **Reading, 7.4**) and there is a long tradition of Her Majesty's Inspectors providing professional advice to government. Until 1993 this was achieved by HMI sampling schools for particular purposes and reviewing developments and quality in the system overall. For more specific information on standards of attainment, evidence had been provided by the 'Assessment of Performance Unit' (APU), which regularly tested a representative sample of pupils at different ages. LEA Advisers provided immediate support and advice to schools.

Provision of more specific information to parents about particular schools was sought and in 1992, the Education (Schools) Act established new procedures for the regular inspection of *all* schools, to be co-ordinated by a new body, the Office for Standards in Education (OFSTED). The numbers of HMI were reduced and large numbers of new inspectors were trained. Teams of inspectors, led by a 'Registered Inspector', were then invited to bid for contracts to inspect particular schools, each of which was to be inspected every four years (see **Reading, 14.8** for a rationale for the new approach).

In the mid-1990s, inspection visits to primary schools of an average size often took one week, with a team of between four and six inspectors. The 1995 OFSTED *Handbook* for Nursery and Primary Schools sets out a structure of the inspection schedule. Thus evidence is collected and a final report is written under the following headings:

Context

> Characteristics of the school

Educational standards achieved by pupils

> Attainment and progress

> Attitudes, behaviour and personal development

> Attendance

Quality of education provided

> Teaching

> The curriculum and assessment

> Pupils' spiritual, moral, social and cultural development

> Support, guidance and pupils' welfare

> Partnership with parents and the community

The management and efficiency of the school

> Leadership and management

> Staffing, accommodation and learning resources

> The efficiency of the school

Curriculum areas and subjects

> For pupils under five

> For English, maths and science (in detail)

> For other subjects (where sufficient evidence exists)

Following an inspection visit, the report is made publicly available and a summary is sent to parents. Governors must consider the report and, within 40 days, must produce an 'action plan' which sets out how it is proposed to remedy any weaknesses which have been identified.

This system has not been a complete success, and it is unlikely that it will continue in its present form once the first cycle of inspections of all schools has been completed. There have been practical problems, simply with recruiting sufficient inspectors, and the cost in 1995 was almost £100m. There have been problems of conception, with some influential commentators suggesting that the system highlights problems but fails to provide support for school improvement (e.g. CERI,

1995, **Reading, 14.9**). There have been problems of stress and diversion, with many teachers suffering anxiety and schools feeling that the inspection process interrupts their long-term development plans (see Practical Activity 14.5). There have been problems of trust and legitimacy, with many professionals feeling that the system has been used to undermine public confidence in schools. For instance, a recent report by a large inspection contractor, CfBT Education Services, states:

> Very many still believe that OFSTED's inspections are punitive Government exercises against the teaching profession, and the reports little more than vehicles for reinforcing Government dogma.

> (Cited in *TES,* 2 Jan. 1996, p. 3)

This feeling has not been helped by the promotion, from both major political parties, of the concept of 'failing schools'. This concept derives from the Education Act 1993 and is developed in Labour's policy statement, *Excellence for Everyone* (1995).

It is likely that a revision of inspection arrangements will reduce the frequency of formal inspection. However, this will be complemented by new requirements for regular school-based self-evaluation and provision for external inspection of schools which appear to be having difficulties. There may be an increased role for LEA advisers and inspectors, working within an LEA development plan.

3   SCHOOL CULTURE

We continue this chapter by discussing the social character of schools. This is an important initial consideration because of the way in which perspectives, behaviour and action in schools are very often influenced by established conventions, expectations and norms. Such norms usually remain tacit (Nias *et al.*, 1989, **Reading, 14.2**) and may easily be taken for granted by people who know a school well. Other people, as relative 'strangers', are likely to be more explicitly aware them.

Practical activity 14.5

Aim: To consider teacher perceptions of inspection.

Method: Talk with a classroom teacher and a head or deputy head about the four 'problems' with inspection which were discussed above:

- practicality
- conception
- stress and diversion
- trust and legitimacy

What concerns do they raise? Also ask them about the positive aspects of inspection, and consider if the benefits outweigh the difficulties.

Follow-up: Study an inspection report of your school, or of another school known to you. Consider what you can learn from in which would help you in improving your practice.

'School ethos' or 'school culture' are well-established notions but they are not always easy to describe. Practical Activity 14.6 suggests one way in which this might be done. The work of Nias and her colleagues on primary school cultures has developed our understanding of this issue (Nias *et al.*, 1989, 1992, **Reading, 14.2**). They see it referring to subjective perceptions, understandings, conventions, habits and routines which are held collectively by school staff. Such a school culture can thus be seen as having been negotiated over time between all those who are, or have been, involved in the school.

On this argument a school is seen as an institution to which new staff bring their perspectives, opinions, skills and enthusiasms. These are used, over time and in interaction with others, to construct understandings about the 'way the school is' (see also **Reading, 14.1**). Obviously the influence of any one individual will depend on their degree of status, power, charisma and authority. Thus, whilst some people will exert considerable influence, perhaps in alliance or association with others, other people, such as students on a school experience programme, may feel and be more marginal. Clearly, a headteacher has a particular degree of power to initiate and influence the development of a school culture. It is hard to underestimate the influence of headteachers in this respect and some research has suggested that management styles have become more 'systems based' as head-

Practical activity 14.6

Aim: To describe a school ethos.

Method: Rate the school on the mapping device below derived from Roger and Richardson, 1985. Ask some colleagues to do the same and discuss the results.

inactive	1 2 3 4 5	busy
happy	1 2 3 4 5	miserable
purposeful	1 2 3 4 5	aimless
relaxed	1 2 3 4 5	tense
enthusiastic	1 2 3 4 5	apathetic
noisy	1 2 3 4 5	quiet
messy	1 2 3 4 5	tidy
chaotic	1 2 3 4 5	organized
welcoming	1 2 3 4 5	formidable
open	1 2 3 4 5	closed
disciplined	1 2 3 4 5	unruly
confident	1 2 3 4 5	insecure

Follow-up: Use of the mapping device and the conversations with colleagues which follow should provide a good idea of the subjective feel of the school ethos. An excellent extension would be to ask children, parents or non-teaching staff to carry out the exercise too. They are likely to have different perspectives. All sorts of issues for school practice and provision might follow if particular patterns emerge from the exercise.

teachers feel more exposed to external market pressures (Menter *et al.*, 1996, **Reading, 14.5**). Practical Activity 14.7 suggests two particular ways of developing an understanding of a headteacher's point of view.

Clearly, it is important to understand the views and actions of headteachers but it is certainly not the case that they are the only influence on a school culture. Many other individuals and groups within a school also have power to influence events and contribute to the formation of expectations. For instance, it is likely that the deputy head, postholders with curricular responsibilities, other teachers, the care-taker and school secretary will all have some influence. Parents and governors are likely to have a more long-term influence on the nature of the school in that they will reflect the priorities and concerns of the community which the school serves. The emergence of understandings about the 'way the school is' should thus be seen as a result of negotiation between a number of different and competing influences and interests. It follows that a school culture may change and develop over time.

The concept of school culture thus leads to an analysis of the micro-politics of schools as a constantly developing and adapting set of negotiated practices and expectations (see Pollard, 1987a, Ball; 1987; Nias *et al.*, 1989). Interestingly, Nias has argued that some primary schools are able to develop a particular 'culture of collaboration' in which there is a very high degree of consensus amongst staff about values, goals and practices. Underpinning this, it is suggested, is a close identification by individual staff with collective beliefs. Thus the 'self' of teachers (see Chapter 4 and **Reading, 4.1**) is reflected in and affirmed through the develop-ment of the school culture (see **Reading, 14.2**).

Such a culture of collaboration could be related to the educational quality of the school, for there is some evidence that teamwork and purposive coherence are effective (MacGilchrist *et al.*, 1995). However, a lot depends on the educational aims and values which are adopted. If these are ill-judged, inappropriate or closed, then a culture of collaboration may reduce to a collective inertia to necessary

Practical activity 14.7

Aim: To understand a headteacher's perspectives and aims for her/his school.

Method: The first method is simply to ask. An interview or series of conversa-tions, perhaps structured around statements of aims which may be contained in a school brochure, will produce a valuable account of the head's perspec-tive and goals. Second, we would suggest that the headteacher's account is triangulated with some data of actual behaviour. An excellent source of data here are assemblies. Assemblies have symbolic and ritual functions as well as being used for practical managerial purposes. Because large numbers of chil-dren are involved, the control and discipline conventions in the school are likely to be evident and the normative structure of the school and expecta-tions of the headteacher are likely to be made explicit.

Follow-up: This exercise will produce a clearer understanding of the way the key leadership figure in the school conceptualizes goals and attempts to enact them. For reflective teachers the application of such understanding derives from the way in which it can inform decisions about future action.

change, rather than providing a means of development. Similarly, a culture of collaboration may turn out to be more apparent than real – a case of 'contrived collegiality' (Hargreaves and Fullan, 1992, **Reading, 14.1**; see Practical Activity 14.8).

Whether or not one believes that a 'collaborative culture' exists in a school, or can be created, there are many good reasons for doing everything one can to understand the roles, work experience and perspectives of other people who work at or are associated with the school. In this we would include school ancillary helpers, dinner supervisors, catering staff, road-crossing patrol helpers, the school secretary, the school cleaners and caretaker. The contributions which they make to school life often go relatively unnoticed and yet they provide essential services without which no school could operate smoothly. People who work in such jobs have particular concerns, interests and feelings about school and their work and these are well worth exploring directly (see Practical Activity 14.9).

Similar activities could profitably be devised by a student teacher to explore the concerns of the governors and of parents. One simple suggestion here, once data has been collected (as suggested in Practical Activity 14.10), is to focus on the

Practical activity 14.8

Aim: To describe and analyse a school culture.

Method: This is a long-term activity which draws on ethnographic methods. It will take several weeks to do. We suggest that all possible opportunities are taken to listen, observe and understand the perspectives, assumptions and taken-for-granted understandings of the various people who are involved in the school (see also Practical Activities 12.6 and 12.8). Make notes so that these are not forgotten. Review these notes and look for patterns in the understandings. Consider if the patterns relate to particular groups of people and use this awareness to orientate your future observations. Make comparisons between the views of different people and/or groups. This should help to refine your understanding. Try to produce a summary analysis. You might distinguish:

1. The main individuals and/or groups and their perspectives.

2. The shared understandings which exist about policy and practice in the school.

3. The degree of agreement with these understandings which exists from individual to individual or group to group.

Follow-up: Through this activity you should produce a clearer understanding of the school culture, of the groups in the school and of the degree of agreement between them. Such understanding is a very useful starting-point for taking a new initiative which is strategically well judged or simply for 'fitting in' to a school.

Practical activity 14.9

Aim: To identify the main concerns, interests and feelings of various non-teaching staff regarding school.

Method: We suggest that time is spent with non-teaching staff. In conversation, some issues could be explored such as the nature of their job, the aspects of the job which they like best, the main problems which are encountered and the constraints within which they work, such as time, resources, pay and conditions.

Follow-up: For a reflective teacher who wishes to contribute to and to develop the strength of the whole-school team, establishing such links and an appreciation of other's concerns is important. In its simplest terms it helps to understand why getting 'chairs up' at the end of each day may be important, why it may be helpful to get the children 'out' for dinner on time and many other small but significant points.

opinions of the various people as they affect the teaching role.

It is possible to distinguish between 'pressures' to do certain things and 'constraints' not to do certain things. For instance, the staff-room culture of a school provides a very significant example of this. If a teacher or student teacher is accepted into a staff group then a considerable source of support and advice is provided. However, there may also be pressure to conform in such things as dress, speech, opinion and practice. Constraints may take the form of a withdrawal of support and a questioning of membership if conformity is not observed. Sometimes, a collaborative culture can become oppressive and can even stifle innovation rather than underpin constructive teamwork. In such circumstances a reflective teacher is likely to want to work towards change.

Practical activity 14.10

Aim: To monitor the support, pressure and constraint which results from relationships with other staff.

Method: One appropriate way to collect data on this is through a private diary over a period of time. Clearly the issue should provide a focus when making entries. After a period, reflection on the diary and memories of various incidents should make it possible to review the support, pressures and constraints which are perceived.

Follow-up: Bearing in mind one's aims and value position, it may or may not be a good thing to be drawn into an existing staff culture. Carrying out this exercise may make one more conscious of staff relationships and may provide a basis for actively contributing to future understandings, developments and innovation.

4 | CURRICULUM, POLICIES AND PRACTICE

A range of whole-school issues is raised here, for a reflective teacher is likely to be concerned both with the overt, officially stated National Curriculum, as implemented in the school and also with curricular practices which, whilst they may remain tacit and hidden in normal teaching and learning processes, still influence the curriculum as experienced by children. In addition, a reflective teacher will be concerned with the processes by which policy and practice is evaluated and reviewed.

This suggests a cyclical model for curriculum development (Figure 14.2), similar to the model for reflective teaching which we suggested in Chapter 1. We will simplify it here into three elements and consider each in turn.

4.1 Evaluating the whole-school curriculum

The first stage, that of evaluating the present curriculum, has received considerable attention in the past few years. It is a process of reviewing policies and implementation on a whole-school basis so that priorities for future development can be identified.

The National Curriculum Council in England offered a useful framework for reviewing the primary curriculum (NCC, 1989a, 1990a). They recommend evaluation in the form of a 'Curriculum Audit' involving teachers, governors, parents and pupils. Their check-lists are the basis of Practical Activity 14.11.

Of course, a major curriculum audit is likely to be a challenging process and will need careful and sensitive management. However this process is so important that it justifies careful monitoring so that constructive adjustments can be made (Practical Activity 14.12).

There are some documents which may offer particularly quick insights into the values and philosophy of schools. The most obvious here are policies concerned with special educational needs, relationships with parents and with equal opportunities

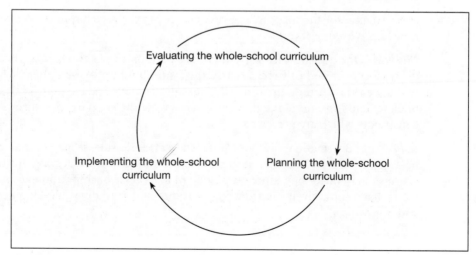

Figure 14.2 *A cyclical model for whole-school curricular development*

Practical activity 14.11

Aim: To explore the issues raised in carrying out a whole-school curriculum audit.

Method: This is a major task and cannot really be undertaken except by the staff team. Nevertheless, a reflective teacher could begin the process, and get a feel for the complexities of the issues which are involved by focusing on one particular subject.

First, consider how the planned curriculum relates to National Curriculum subject and cross-curricular requirements.

Second, consider how the planned curriculum relates to the curriculum as it is experienced by the children.

Follow-up: Such a preliminary review is likely to provide insights into the complexity of whole-school curriculum planning and could lead towards a general evaluation from which priorities can be identified.

Practical activity 14.12

Aim: To describe and review the process for the whole-school evaluation of curriculum and practice in a school.

Method: In order to describe evaluation processes it is possible to study available documents, attend meetings and talk to the people who are, or have been, involved.

To form judgements about such processes a set of clear criteria is required. One might include criteria such as:

- Producing clear curriculum and policy guidelines.
- Introducing socially and educationally worthwhile developments.
- Acting as a means of individual staff development.
- Bringing important issues into open discussion.
- Producing greater cohesion and a clearer sense of purpose among the staff.

Follow-up: This activity will facilitate judgements of the quality of school evaluation processes and may suggest areas in which they might be developed further.

(particularly regarding sexism and racism). Studying guidelines and policy documents which might relate to such issues is an excellent way of understanding the overt plans and intentions which have been officially endorsed by the staff of a school (see Practical Activity 14.13).

The second stage of the curriculum development cycle (Figure 14.2) concerns planning.

Practical activity 14.13

Aim: To study school documentation relating to policy on some important, indicative issues.

Method: There are various possible sources of documentation which may be available. For instance:

- school brochures
- internal curriculum and policy statements
- records of staff and governors meetings

The issues on which one might seek information might include:

- special educational needs
- relationships with parents
- equal opportunities

Follow-up: Study of such documents provides immediate insights into the degree of awareness and quality of thinking as well as the substantive nature of the planning of curriculum and practice in a school. It thus indicates starting-points for further enquiries, for discussions with staff who have particular responsibilities and for policy and curriculum development.

4.2 Planning the whole-school curriculum

Schools now produce annual School Development Plans and these have been seen as enabling schools to become 'empowered' (Hargreaves and Hopkins, 1991, **Reading, 14.3**). These are the prime means by which staff and governors can exercise coherent and forward-looking control over curriculum and school development. In most schools, development plans include consideration of:

1. Aims and philosophy.

2. The present situation.
    - catchment and enrolment
    - organization
    - staffing
    - curriculum provision
    - resources
    - achievements

3. Assessed needs for future development.
    - organizational development
    - staff development
    - curriculum development
    - resource development

4. Plans of how the assessed needs are to be met.

The last point is a significant one, for it brings the planning process up against practicalities – for instance of budgets. School budgeting should be 'curriculum-led' rather than be driven by financial considerations but this is not always possible. Nevertheless, in the words of HMI (1992) development planning provides 'a more rational and coherent framework in which to identify priorities, plan for change and allocate resources. In the best practice, development plans paid attention to teaching and learning, specified manageable time scales, and outlined arrangements for monitoring and evaluation' (HM Senior Chief Inspector of Schools, 1992, p. 20; see also Practical Activity 14.14).

4.3 Implementing the whole-school curriculum

Part of the value both of guidelines and policy documents is that they are recognized as being statements of goals and as specifications of plans for development (Skelton *et al.*, 1991). Nevertheless one would expect some variation when focusing on what actually happens. Indeed, whatever the effort and commitment, in schools, as in many other walks of life, there is often a gap between rhetoric and reality, between intention and implementation. Anning (1983) suggested that new headteachers attempting curriculum innovation face a course rather like that of the Grand National. The first jump, the improvement of the environment, and the second, that of producing new curriculum guidelines, are accomplished smoothly. Becher's Brook looms when it is realized that actual practice in the classrooms may not be changing as fast and cannot be influenced by aesthetics and policy documents alone. This is a problem which faces everyone – for it is never easy to bring practice into line with ideals, let alone in the difficult circumstances which schools have faced in recent years. Indeed, many head-teachers have found that the apparent ordered rationality of school development planning is disrupted by the turbulence of external events (Wallace, 1994, **Reading, 14.4**), so that it becomes something of a diversion from managing the 'real world'.

In an insightful research study, MacGilchrist and her colleagues (1995) identified four types of school development plan: the 'rhetorical plan', the 'singular plan' (produced by the headteacher alone), the 'co-operative plan' (with partial involvement of teaching staff) and the 'corporate plan'. The latter was 'characterised by a united effort to improve ... and a focus on teaching and learning' (p. 195). Clearly, implementing a school development plan is far from easy, and is intimately connected with the school culture (see section 3).

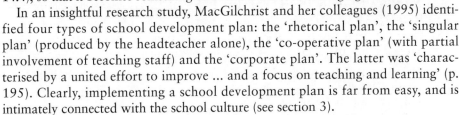

Practical activity 14.14

Aim: To consider a School Development Plan.

Method: Ask a headteacher if you may study the School Development Plan for his or her school. Consider it in the light of HMI observations quoted above. If possible, discuss with the headteacher the circumstances of the plan's production and the reasons for the priorities given.

Follow-up: Talk with other staff in the school and consider how they are able to identify purposefully with the plan.

Such practical difficulties have to be faced with openness if adjustments and further developments are to be soundly based. A reflective teacher will thus want to follow up official statements by enquiring into what actually happens in teaching and learning processes – an enquiry which may identify both expected and unintended outcomes and both overt and hidden aspects of the curriculum which is experienced by the children (Practical activity 14.15).

Practical activity 14.15

Aim: To study the implementation of an area of the observed curriculum or an issue of policy across the school.

Method: The basic strategy here is to select one curriculum area or a relatively discrete issue to focus on and then to observe and document it through each class and in other school contexts. One relatively easy example would be to focus on the application of a handwriting policy. To study the application of an anti-racist or anti-sexist policy would obviously be much more difficult. The co-operation of teachers would be very important for the successful completion of this activity.

Follow-up: This activity will give an indication of the degree of continuity and coherence which exists in the application of the school policy which is studied. It will thus provide a basis for follow-up action and further review.

5 | STRATEGIES FOR WHOLE-SCHOOL DEVELOPMENT

The notion of reflective teaching implies a willingness to adapt and a commitment to contribute towards social and educational developments. The basic stages advocated in this book begin with identifying, understanding and describing actual practice. We then suggest judging the worth of that practice against specific criteria deriving from carefully identified educational aims and value-commitments. This should provide a basis for taking decisions about how best to improve practice where changes are called for.

This is a good deal more difficult to do in a school as a whole than it is in the context of our own classrooms and yet it is clearly the long-term responsibility of reflective teachers, with an awareness of issues beyond their classroom, to contribute towards whole-school developments. In this section we therefore discuss strategies and procedures by which such contributions might be made.

There are two main ways in which this issue can be approached. One officially recommended approach (Hargreaves and Hopkins, 1991, **Reading, 14.3**; Skelton *et al.*, 1991) builds on school development planning processes to create logical procedures for identifying problems collectively as a staff team and for producing ways of resolving them. However, as we have seen, research is accumulating to show that such neat procedures do not describe what tends actually to happen (e.g. Hargreaves, 1992, **Reading, 14.1**; Wallace, 1994, **Reading, 14.4**; MacGilchrist *et al.*, 1995). Indeed, a less prominent and perhaps more sceptical approach, considers ways of acting if such wholehearted collaboration is only partially forthcoming. We would suggest that both approaches may be necessary.

There are several reasons for suggesting consideration of the best forms of strategic action should systematic review procedures falter. The first lies in the nature of evaluation itself. As Adelman and Alexander (1982) argue in their book on the 'self-evaluating institution', all evaluations or school reviews are 'political'. As they put it:

> an evaluation involves acts of valuing, of making judgements of worth or effectiveness, and this presupposes the existence of other... values and judgements. If some judgements prevail over others... [they] ... will have consequences for the distribution of resources and the status of individuals and groups. An evaluation ... offers a critique of and a potential threat to [established] processes and interests and to the balance of institutional power. (p. 146)

Change, review or evaluation is thus political both substantively, in that particular values and judgements are given priority, and interpersonally, in that personal interests are likely to be affected.

As we have seen, a school culture represents normative conventions which are a negotiated product of the existing balance of power and influence in a school. It is exactly these conventions, policies and practices which are, implicitly, likely to come under review in school evaluation and development processes. If such issues are clearly recognized then it is easier to understand the responses of an individual teacher who is involved in processes of change. Doyle and Pounder (1976) identified three typical responses.

1. The 'rational adapter' who, by recognizing problems or issues and enacting logical procedures to tackle them, accepts innovation and helps to bring it about.

2. The 'pragmatic sceptic' who assesses the consequences of change in a calculative way by considering the gains and losses from change in time, energy and personal development before deciding how to act.

3. The 'Stone-Age obstructionist' who, by rejecting the value-position and judgements upon which a need for change is based and by refusing to become fully involved, attempts to retain the *status quo*.

Clearly these are caricatures which simplify the complexity of people's motivations and involvements but they do begin to describe the essence of three basic sorts of compliance (Etzioni, 1966).

Moral: in which commitment is based on intrinsic acceptance of purposes and value concerns.

Calculative: in which compliance is based on extrinsic judgements of personal interests.

Alienative: in which compliance is reluctant and is based on a powerlessness to resist.

The existence of such different types of perspectives and commitment clearly has serious implications for those who may wish to bring about changes in schools.

Having focused on the importance of the political and interpersonal context within a school we now turn to consider a procedure for whole-school evaluation. We start from the point of a reflective teacher having identified an issue or problem, perhaps from a National Curriculum requirement, which is judged to require attention by the whole school. The following five stages might then be considered:

1. Focusing colleagues' attention on the issue and achieving agreement regarding its importance and the necessity of change.

2. Analysing the issue in detail.

3. Analysing factors constraining change and factors which will facilitate change.

4. Considering ideas for innovation and deciding collectively on a coherent programme of actions to introduce change.

5. Monitoring the change process – being prepared to amend plans and even to redefine the problem.

For each of these stages we could suggest some practical activities which might be engaged in as a staff group. However, it is the first stage which is likely to be most difficult and yet is also most important because it involves establishing the platform and rationale for change from which all else follows.

The key strategy which we would suggest here is that of liaising with and sounding out other colleagues, including senior management. This raises the issues and also invites people to involve themselves. Clearly, alliances will be relatively easy to form with those who share similar value-positions but it remains important to establish links with those who may have a more pragmatic, calculative view of suggested changes.

Alliances, however, can be formed with people both inside the school and with those beyond it. In this respect it is vital to remember that schools are open systems and are influenced from outside. For instance, within a school the position of the headteacher is likely to be crucial and, as we suggested above, any reflective teacher in a relatively junior position is likely to want to enlist his or her support when suggesting any innovation. In this respect, it is fortunate that, since headteachers occupy a difficult position and must act at the interface of internal and external pressures, they are likely to be exceptionally aware of events and concerns outside their school. Fullan and Hargreaves' book, *What's Worth Fighting for in Your School?* (1992), has made an important contribution here (see also Fullan 1982, **Reading, 14.10**).

It is thus open to a reflective teacher, however junior in status, to make positive suggestions to a headteacher regarding innovations which would enable the school to contribute more fully to developments in the community and society generally. They could then, together, seek the views of external groups who may be involved. The issues of parental involvement in reading and of school policies on multiracial education provide examples where external participation of this sort has helped to bring about internal developments in many schools. Of course, alliances are possible with a whole range of other external groups, such as industrialists, unionists, advisers, academics, other teachers, community groups, politicians, governors, etc. A reflective teacher or a headteacher acting strategically may consciously aim to affect the range of immediate influences on the school and thus set up conditions for new developments.

When it comes to action within a school there are four basic strategic possibilities for a reflective teacher to consider:

- *Radical innovation.* A strategy which is probably only possible with the strong support of those in very senior positions and is arguably only sensible with a solid measure of agreement among staff as a whole.

- *Reform.* A gradualist strategy with the support of senior staff which, by phasing changes slowly, reduces the immediate threat to vested interests. The overall purposes of innovations can be subject to dilution in the process.

- *Subversion.* A strategy where support from senior staff is lacking and in which individuals or groups in alliance seek to bring about change covertly by undermining the *status quo*.

- *Challenge.* An overt strategy in which individuals or groups in alliance confront the *status quo* directly.

Consideration of the use of these strategies obviously requires careful thought, in particular by placing the importance of the issue under review in the context of other social and educational issues and by considering long-term as well as short-term consequences. It is also almost inevitable that one will have to take some hard, personal decisions about one's loyalties and responsibilities. After all, there is no reason why the views and interests of staff colleagues, headteacher, children, parents, etc., should overlap and choices thus often become necessary. Having considered such issues it is the responsibility of a reflective teacher, we would argue, to decide on a position and to act (Practical Activity 14.16).

Practical activity 14.16

Aim: Given a concern, to review strategies for action.

Method: The most profitable ways forward here are likely to come from discussions with sympathetic colleagues and other allies. It will be necessary to consider the people involved and features of the school culture, of policies and of practice, in relation to desired developments. Some may be constraining, others facilitating. There may even be contradictions which might provide initial ways forward.

Follow-up: Having reviewed such factors a judgement about the best strategies to adopt should be easier to make. One has to consider not only which strategy might be most effective but also what side-effects each might have.

CONCLUSION

In this chapter, we have looked at the local accountability context to which schools are subject, school inspection systems, school culture, processes of curriculum review and school development, and at the part which reflective teachers might play. Having argued that reflective teachers should be active in whole-school development we conclude with an important qualification. This is to point out that insensitive action or innovation can be counter-productive. It is relatively easy to force change in one area only to find that so much goodwill has been lost that other areas have been adversely affected. School life is complex and if one can negotiate with colleagues to develop shared perspectives on issues and collective strategies for action then many problems may be avoided.

Notes for further reading

The outstanding introduction to the importance of school contexts for the quality of educational provision is:

Fullan, M. (1982)
The New Meaning of Educational Change,
London: Cassell.   📖 Reading, 14.10

Constructive collections of articles on school-based management and professional development are:

Biott, C. and Nias, J. (1992)
Working and Learning Together for Change,
Buckingham: Open University Press.

Chapman, J. (ed.) (1990)
School-based Decision Making and Management,
London: Falmer.

Southworth, G. (1987)
Readings in Primary School Management,
London: Falmer.

Day, C., Whitaker, P. and Johnston, D. (1990)
Managing Primary Schools in the 1990s,
London: Paul Chapman.

Local Management of Schools (LMS) has brought particular challenges, including a need for close working with governors. On this see:

Cave, E. and Wilkinson, C. (1990)
Local Management of Schools: Some Practical Issues,
London: Routledge.

Nightingale, D. (1990)
Local Management of Schools at Work in the Primary School,
London: Falmer.

Beckett, C., Bell, L. and Rhodes, C. (1991)
Working with Governors in Schools: Developing a Professional Partnership,
Buckingham: Open University Press.

Deem, R., Brehony, K. and Heath, S. (1995)
Active Citizenship and the Governing of Schools,
Buckingham: Open University Press.

📖 Reading, 14.7

Regarding relationships with parents in the 1990s, see:

Hughes, M. Wikeley, F. and Nash, T. (1994)
Parents and Their Children's Schools,
Oxford: Blackwell.

📖 Reading, 14.6

Vincent, C. (1996)
Parents and Teachers: Power and Participation,
London: Falmer Press.

On developments in the provision of inspection and advice, see:

Ouston, J., Earley, P. and Fidler, B. (1996)
OFSTED Inspections: The Early Experience,
London: David Fulton.

Centre for Educational Research and Innovation (1995)
Schools Under Scrutiny,
Paris: OECD.

📖 Reading, 14.9

There has been considerable emphasis on making schools function more like businesses. In one manifestation, the ideas of 'total quality management' are being applied. For instance, see:

West-Burnham, J. (1992)
Managing Quality in Schools,
London: Longman.

Murgatroyd, S. and Morgan, C. (1992)
Total Quality Management and the School,
Buckingham: Open University Press.

Warnings of the dangers of such developments are provided by:

Bottery, M. (1992)
The Ethics of Educational Management,
London: Cassell.

Menter, I., Muschamp, Y., Nicholls, P., Ozga, J. and Pollard, A. (1996)
Work and Identity in the Primary School: A Post-Fordist Analysis,
Buckingham: Open University Press.

📖 Reading, 14.5

On the challenges which headteachers have faced, see:

Grace, G. (1995)
School Leadership: Beyond Education Management,
London: Falmer Press.

For good reviews of research on the influential concept of school climate see:

Anderson, C. S. (1982)
The search for school climate: a review of the research,
Review of Educational Research, 52, 368–420.

Strivens, J. (1985) School climate: a review of a problematic concept. In D. Reynolds
Studying School Effectiveness,
London: Falmer.

For interpretive approaches using the concepts of school culture:

Hargreaves, A. (1992) Cultures of teaching. In A. Hargreaves, and M. G. Fullan, (eds)
Understanding Teacher Development,
London: Cassell.   📖 **Reading, 14.1**

Nias, J., Southworth, G. and Yeomans, R. (1989)
Staff Relationships in the Primary School:
A Study of Organisational Cultures,
London: Cassell.   📖 see **Reading, 14.2**

Pollard, A. (1987a) Primary school-teachers and their colleagues. In S. Delamont, (ed.)
The Primary School Teacher,
London: Falmer.

For the influential micro-political perspective on school organizations see:

Ball, S. (1987)
Micropolitics of the School: Towards a Theory of School Organisation,
London: Routledge.

On establishing new relationships in a primary school, see:

Mills, J. and Mills, R. (1995)
Primary School People: Getting to Know Your Colleagues,
London: Routledge.

Constructive books on the topic of school-based planning and development are indicated below:

MacGilchrist, B., Mortimore, P., Savage, J. and Beresford, C. (1995)
Planning Matters: The Impact of Development Planning in Primary Schools,
London: Paul Chapman.

Hargreaves, D. H. and Hopkins, D. (1991)
The Empowered School: The Management and
Practice of Development Planning,
London: Cassell.   📖 **Reading, 14.3**

Skelton, M., Playfoot, D. and Reeves, G. (1991)
Development Planning for Schools,
London: Routledge

Nias, J., Southworth, G. and Campbell, P. (1992)
Whole-School Curriculum Development in the Primary School,
London: Falmer.   📖 see **Reading, 14.2**

For an indication of some of the many difficulties in managing schools in recent years, see:

Wallace, M. (1991)
Coping with multiple innovations in schools,
School Organisation, 11(2), 187–209.   📖 **Reading, 14.4**

One of the best recent accounts of development in education has been provided by Ruddock, who sees change 'not as a technical problem, but as a cultural problem'. The reference below is followed by a suggestion of an excellent example of the importance of this point.

Ruddock, J. (1991)
Innovation and Change,
Buckingham: Open University Press.

Keel, P. (1987)
An outline of multicultural educational development in an area of North-east England.
In T. S. Chivers, (ed.)
Race and Culture in England,
Windsor: NFER-Nelson.

For an engaging example of how a reflective teacher can influence her workplace, see:

Dadds, M. (1995)
Passionate Enquiry and School Development: A Story about Teacher Action Research,
London: Falmer Press.

An important publication from the National Commission on Education sets out how schools in disadvantaged areas can maintain effectiveness.

National Commission on Education (1995)
Success Against the Odds,
London: Routledge.

For a international perspectives on school change, effectiveness and quality see:

Husen, T., Tuijnman, A. and Halls, W. D. (eds) (1992)
Schooling in Modern European Society,
Oxford: Pergamon.

Bolam, R. (1982)
Strategies for School Improvement,
Paris: OECD.

The latter report identified the major issues involved in the development of 'problem-solving schools' and has provided the basis for co-operative international research efforts. On the outcomes, see:

Hopkins, D. (1987)
Improving the Quality of Schooling: Lessons from the OECD International School Improvement Project,
London: Falmer.

Finally, a principled polemic on how teachers and headteachers should pull together is:

Fullan, M. and Hargreaves, A. (1992)
What's Worth Fighting for in Your School? Working Together for School Improvement,
Buckingham: Open University Press.

CHAPTER 15

Reflective teaching and society

INTRODUCTION

In many parts of this book we have considered the internal workings of schools and classrooms with relatively few references to the social, economic, cultural and political contexts within which they are located. While this may be necessary for a book of this sort, is not sufficient for a reflective teacher who is, hopefully, aware of the ways in which educational processes are influenced by, and contribute to, wider social forces, processes and relationships (Archer 1979, **Reading, 15.1**). In Chapter 2 we introduced the idea of social development being based on a dialectical process, as individuals respond to and act within the situations in which they find themselves. Actions in the present are thus influenced by the past, but they also contribute to new social arrangements for the future. All teachers, as individuals, are members of society and we hope that reflective teachers will be particularly capable of acting in society to initiate and foster morally and ethically sound developments.

There are three sections in this chapter. The first discusses the relationship between education and society and reviews the theoretical framework which was first introduced in Chapter 2. The second considers the classroom responsibilities of a socially aware and reflective teacher and discusses the formation of classroom policies. The final section focuses on the actions which a reflective teacher could take as a citizen in trying to influence democratic processes of decision-making by local, regional and national governments.

1 EDUCATION AND SOCIETY

Two major questions have to be faced with regard to the relationship between education and society. The first is, 'What should an education system be designed to do?' The second is, 'What can actually be achieved through education?' We will address these in turn and draw out the implications for reflective teachers.

Education has very often been seen as a means of influencing the development of societies, and we will identify three central areas of purpose. These are:

- wealth creation through preparation for economic production
- cultural production and reproduction
- developing social justice and individual rights

Wealth creation. One educational priority is certainly likely to be wealth creation. For instance, in the latter part of the Industrial Revolution in Great Britain, an important part of the argument for the establishment of an elementary school system was that it should provide a workforce which was more skilled and thus more economically productive. The idea became the linchpin of 'human capital' theory in the 1960s (Schultz, 1961), and many new nations, influenced by analyses such as Rostow's *The Stages of Economic Growth* (1962), put scarce resources into their education systems. The economics of education is still a flourishing area of policy and research (Aldcroft, 1992). In Britain, the links between education and economic productivity are constantly being drawn by the government, with particular attention to the standard of basic skills achieved in schools and to the proportion of young people acquiring advanced knowledge and skills in higher education. See **Reading, 15.2** for a liberal manifestation of this concern from the National Commission on Education (1993). There are parallel developments in the USA, Europe, Australasia and elsewhere.

Cultural reproduction. Alternatively, there are those who would highlight the 'function' of education in the production and reproduction of a national culture. Again there were elements of the nineteenth-century British experience which illustrate this. For instance, the arguments and influence of Arnold (1986) helped to define the traditional classical curriculum which remains influential today. Indeed, the necessity for pupils to study Shakespeare and key episodes in English history was insisted upon in the construction of the National Curriculum. Even so, some remain concerned about the erosion of national identity in modern society (see Tate, 1995, **Reading, 15.3**).

A particularly clear example of cultural production is that of the USA in the twentieth century where the education system was required to 'assimilate' and 'integrate' successive groups of new immigrants into an 'American culture'. The education system was seen as a vital part of the 'melting-pot'. Of course, a highly questionable assumption here was that there was a single American culture, but the notion of the existence of a set of 'central values' was important in this formative period of the development of the USA. There are thus costs in the use of education to develop or assert a national culture, and these costs are usually borne by minority or less powerful groups. The historical case of the education provided in the colonies of the British Empire provides a particularly graphic example of this last point (Mangan, 1993).

However, use of an education system for the production of a sense of shared national identity is common in many parts of the world, particularly where independent or democratic states have been established relatively recently. Of course, other forms of political structure can also be supported by education. Thus, at the turn of the century, we have many emergent forms of regional identity within the nations which make up the European Union. Education plays a part in producing and reproducing culture at each of these levels. For example, the people of Wales preserve an important part of their culture through the teaching of Welsh in their schools, but, at the same time, their education system inducts Welsh children into the culture of the United Kingdom and Europe. Another educational priority can thus be an integrative one, relating to the production or reproduction of 'culture' within political structures.

Social justice. Contributing to social justice is a third central purpose which is often identified for education systems. This concern was very much at the forefront of thinking in the production of the 1944 Education Act in the UK and also in the subsequent introduction of comprehensive schools. It has been an important element of policy in the USA and features prominently in the educational goals which are set by many countries in Europe and across the world (for a European exam- ple, see the 1985 Memorandum of the Council of Europe, **Reading, 15.4**). One critical point to make is that 'equality of opportunity' and the meritocratic ideal, which often lie behind policies on this issue, are concepts which are vulnerable to rhetoric. They can be used in ways which ignore the structural inequalities of wealth, status and power which exist. If such issues are glossed, then the promotion of social justice through education policy is very unlikely to be successful. For example, politicians have made much of the rhetoric of 'parental choice' in establishing market competition between schools, but see Dale's analysis (1996, **Reading, 15.5**) of the ways in which this creates inequality.

The concern for social justice through education can partly be seen as a desire to ensure that there is an acceptable and legitimated system for allocating jobs in democratic societies and for facilitating social mobility. However, there are more individualized and fundamental concerns which are perhaps more relevant to reflective teaching. A very clear exposition of such issues is contained in the United Nations Universal Declaration of Human Rights made in 1948. Article 1 of the Declaration states that:

> All human beings are born free and equal in dignity and rights. They are endowed with reason and conscience.

These rights are to be enjoyed, according to Article 2:

> Without distinction of any kind, such as race, colour, sex, language, religion, political or other opinion, national or social origin, property, birth or other status.

There then follow many articles dealing with rights and fundamental freedoms of movement, thought, religion, assembly, political participation, work, leisure and an adequate standard of living. Article 26 deals with education and asserts that:

> Education shall be directed to the full development of the human personality and the strengthening of respect for human rights and fundamental freedoms. It shall promote understanding, tolerance and friendship among all nations, racial and religious groups.

Education was expected to have a crucial role in the dissemination of the UN Declaration across the world, for it was to be 'displayed, read and expanded principally in schools and other educational institutions' in all member states. Needless to say, the achievement of social justice and individual rights for all citizens remains a noble and appropriate goal, but one which will probably always be with us, for it is optimistic to think that educational provision alone can overcome structural inequalities in society. Indeed the necessity of adopting a United Nations Convention on the Rights of the Child in 1989 underlines that fact.

Education policies and systems can thus be designed to emphasize economic production, cultural production or reproduction, social justice or individual rights. Whilst such goals are not necessarily conflicting, various tensions and dilemmas are often posed. One obvious issue concerns the rights of minority groups to maintain an independent culture and sense of identity within a majority culture. Another is the dilemma between the demands of individual development and those of economic production. We have raised these issues in Chapter 4 and argued that a reflective teacher should make informed and responsible judgements about them. The ways in which action might follow will be discussed further below.

We now move on to the second question: 'What can actually be achieved through education?'

There has been a long running debate on this topic. Some people, such as Coleman *et al.,* (1966), Jencks *et al.,* (1972), and Bowles and Gintis (1976, **Reading, 13.1**), have argued that education can make little difference to social development. Although coming to the issue from different theoretical perspectives, they argue that educational processes reflect and reproduce major features of existing society, particularly with regard to distinctions related to social class. The suggestion is that relationships of power, wealth, status and ideology are such that education should be seen as a part of the dominant social system, rather than as an autonomous force within it.

Others, such as Berger and Luckman (1967), may be seen as taking a more idealistic theoretical position. They argue that, since our sense of reality is 'socially constructed' by people as they interact together, there is, therefore, scope for individuals to make an independent impact on the course of future social development. Thus there is potential for education to influence change. What we have here are the competing positions of those who believe in social determinism ranged against those who believe in individual voluntarism. As we have already seen, education is very often expected to bring about social and economic developments and it is an area which tends to attract idealists. However, we also have to recognize that the major structural features of societies are extremely resistant to change. What is needed is a theoretical position which recognizes the importance of action and of constraint. Such a position would accept that education has a degree of relative autonomy and would thus legitimate action by individuals to contribute to future social development.

Such a theoretical framework is provided by what we call the dialectic of the individual and society (see Chapter 2 and, in particular, **Readings, 2.1** and **2.2**). As Berlak and Berlak (1981, **Reading, 1.3**) put it:

> Conscious creative activity is limited by prevailing social arrangements, but human actions and institutional forms are not mere reflections of them. (p. 121)

The clear implication is that people can make their own impact and history but must do so in whatever circumstances they find themselves. If this theoretical framework is adopted, social developments can be seen as the product of processes of struggle and contest between different individuals and groups in society

(**Readings, 15.1** and **15.7**). Such processes are ones in which education must, inevitably, play a part.

Our answer to the question of what education can actually achieve must thus be based on a guarded and realistic optimism. The dialectical model of the influence of individuals and social structures recognizes constraints but asserts that action remains possible. This places a considerable responsibility on a reflective teacher.

2 | CLASSROOM TEACHING AND SOCIETY

One implication of the adoption of a dialectical model of the relationship between individuals and society is that it highlights the possible consequences, for the 'macro' world of society, of actions, experiences and processes which take place in the 'micro' world of the classroom. In Chapter 1, we raised this issue with the assertion that 'reflective teaching implies an active concern with aims and consequences as well as with technical efficiency' and we must pick up the themes again here. One of the most important issues concerns the influence of a reflective teacher's own value-commitments.

In Chapter 1, we argued that reflective teachers should accept democratically determined decisions but should act both as responsible professionals and as autonomous citizens to contribute to such decision-making processes. We also suggested that attitudes of 'open-mindedness' and 'responsibility' are essential attributes. Open-mindedness involves a willingness to consider evidence and argument from whatever source it comes. It is thus the antithesis of closure and of habituated or ideological thinking. There are parallels here with the guidelines issued by the UK Politics Association regarding teaching politics in school (Jones, 1986). Jones suggests that the objective should be to achieve a 'comprehensive awareness' and an 'overall understanding of political processes and issues'. On the basis of such awareness, children should be encouraged to form their own views and participate in the democratic process. An open-minded tolerance to the exposition of a variety of views and opinions is obviously an initial necessity here and we would say the same for reflective teaching.

However, the Politics Association also asserts the importance of a teachers' social responsibility with its guideline that 'the teacher cannot be neutral towards those values which underpin liberal democracy'. But what are such values? Clear guidance on this has been provided by the Council of Europe (1985, **Reading, 15.4**). In a recommendation to all member states of the European Union, the Council of Ministers reaffirmed the understandings embodied in the United Nations' Universal Declaration of Human Rights and the European Convention on Human Rights. The Council suggested that study in schools should 'lead to an understanding of, and sympathy for, the concepts of justice, equality, freedom, peace, dignity, rights and democracy' (Council of Europe, 1985, Appendix). These are seen as being fundamental to democratic societies and all schools, including those for young children, are encouraged to introduce them to their pupils and to develop their understanding. Hugh Starkey (1987) claims that the United Nations' Declaration is accepted as a world-wide moral standard and that fundamental freedoms are what make effective political democracies possible.

This brings us directly back to the issues of individual dignity, equality and freedom. It again raises issues such as sexism, racism and other forms of discrimination on the basis of social class, age, disability or sexual orientation and it focuses attention once more on the quality of relationships and the use of power in classrooms. These are issues upon which, we would argue, children have rights about which socially responsible teachers should not compromise. We take this to constitute a 'bottom line', a value-commitment to the fundamental rights of citizens in a democratic society and a necessary underpinning for professionality.

Such a value-commitment by reflective teachers might be manifested in two ways. First, classroom processes might be monitored with such specific issues in mind; indeed we have made various suggestions of this sort with regard to race, disability and gender. The second way of manifesting this value-commitment follows logically from such monitoring. It is to develop classroom social policies for the long term, so that actions which are taken in the immediacy of classroom decision-making support concerns with individual dignity, equality and freedom rather than undercut them. As we have suggested in Chapter 10, classroom social policies may be seen as attempts to anticipate, plan and prestructure activities and procedures so that teacher actions reflect a consistent and socially responsible value-position.

We will illustrate these steps through the suggestion of practical activities. We begin with Practical Activity 15.1, designed to monitor the care of a child with a special educational need.

Having monitored an existing situation it is then necessary to take action and to establish policy. The establishment of classroom policy is by no means easy. It requires a sound analysis of the issues both in terms of the specific situation and

> ## Practical activity 15.1
>
> *Aim:* To monitor the experience of a child with a physical disability in the classroom.
>
> *Method:* We would suggest a form of focused child study here. Data collection methods might include observation and field notes, collecting examples of work, sociometry and discussions with the child. A colleague might also observe and provide comments on teacher–child interaction.
>
> *Follow-up:* The criteria for analysis might ultimately be in terms of maximizing the child's dignity, equality and freedom but more specific questions which could be used to interrogate the data might be:
>
> 1. to what extent is the child able to participate in class activities?
>
> 2. to what extent is tolerance and understanding of the child's disability shown by other children?
>
> 3. what is the quality of the relationship between the teacher and the child?

in the light of alternative approaches, experiences and research findings from elsewhere. Above all it requires knowledge of oneself and personal commitment to implementation. In our view, it is very hard to develop such understanding without the insights of others and opportunities to discuss the issues with colleagues and 'critical friends'. The establishment of a classroom policy might then take the form as suggested in Practical Activity 15.2. Again we use the example of provision for children with special educational needs.

Activities such as these should help in the development of socially aware teaching and can be applied to issues such as race, social class, beliefs, moral values and gender. Classroom practice can never, following a dialectical model, fail to have some influence on the development of society at large – in particular through the ways in which it influences the identity, values and life-chances of individuals. The development of classroom social policies thus enables the reflective teacher to take conscious control and to contribute productively to micro–macro linkages and to the future of both individual biographies and social history.

3   REFLECTIVE TEACHING AND THE DEMOCRATIC PROCESS

In Chapter 1 we suggested that, in addition to professional responsibilities to implement democratically determined decisions, teachers as citizens also have responsibilities to act to influence the nature of such decisions. Teachers have rights and it is perfectly reasonable that they should be active in contributing to the formation of public policy. This role, as White (1978) suggested, is close to that of the activist and the methods to be utilized are those which have been well developed in recent years by a variety of pressure groups (Practical Activity 15.3). However, teachers' work has become increasingly controlled in recent years (Ball 1994, **Reading, 15.6**), so the challenge of such activities must be faced.

Practical activity 15.2

Aim: To develop a classroom policy to maximize the participation of children with special educational needs.

Method: We would suggest the following stages:

1. Read some of the literature about provision for children with special educational needs in classrooms (e.g. Ashdown, *et al.*, 1991; Jones and Charlton, 1992).

2. Discuss with colleagues how they make provision. Gather examples of practice elsewhere.

3. Consider your present provision. Are the physical resources, the learning activities and the quality of interactions in the classroom such that all children can participate, feel valued and maintain their dignity?

4. Discuss these issues with colleagues. Brainstorm on ways of providing support for children with particular needs. Sort out the ideas which seem to be both productive and practical.

5. Draw out the implications for practice so that explicit policy decisions for one's actions are identified.

Follow-up: Attempt to develop classroom action which is guided by policy. Monitor your degree of success.

Practical activity 15.3

Aim: To investigate processes of political activity and decision-making with regard to an educational issue.

Method: A necessary basic strategy here is to focus on one issue and to trace the debates in the media and elsewhere. This is best done with colleagues so that the work-load is shared. The issue could be local or national.

Newspapers provide useful sources of easily retrievable information. Some, such as *The Times*, publish an index and this is particularly helpful.

Having gathered a variety of statements about the issue in question, an attempt should be made to classify them so that the competing positions are identified. From this point, it may be possible to gather policy statements directly from the participants, by letter, discussion, interview or library search.

Finally, the decision point can be studied. Were the public arguments influential? What interests seem to have prevailed when decisions were taken?

Follow-up: Having studied an example of political influence on decision-making, it is worth taking stock of what has been learned. Did you feel that the debate reflected appropriate educational concerns? Could educationalists have made more constructive contributions?

There are six basic elements of successful pressure group activity:

1. Identifying decision-makers
2. Preparing the case
3. Forming alliances
4. Managing the media
5. Lobbying decision-makers
6. Following up

Such techniques have been evident in UK debates about the curriculum in primary schools where lobbying of Members of Parliament has taken place. For instance, members of the National Association for Primary Education were encouraged to write to MPs and the views of the association were made clear to education ministers and to the House of Commons Select Committee on Primary Education. The techniques have also been deployed on more general educational issues such as cutbacks in educational expenditure, the growth of the private sector, the abolition of corporal punishment in schools and the introduction of formal assessment for young children. Some national educational pressure groups are now well established. These include CASE (the Campaign for the Advancement of State Education), NCNE (the National Campaign for Nursery Education), NAPE (the National Association for Primary Education) and NAME (the National Anti-racist Movement in Education). Professional associations such the NUT, NAS/UWT, AMMA and PAT are also active, though the most influential in recent years have been the headteacher associations NAHT and SHA.

At the more local level, pressure group activity and lobbying by individuals of councillors and education officials also takes place regularly. As two specific examples we can cite a 1992 campaign by parents of a school in Avon to oppose a proposal that their school should 'opt out' of the local education authority and the very successful lobbying of Oxfordshire County Council by parents and the community around Barton First School, Oxford, which had been threatened with closure.

In the Avon case statistical information and educational arguments showing the benefits provided by the local education authority were assembled with the help of union officials, colleagues and academics. The support of parents was enlisted and the campaign was publicized. Key political figures representing each of the major political parties were identified on the County Council and were lobbied and invited to a seminar to discuss the issues. Continued lobbying led to a reappraisal of school policies and a new ordering of priorities for expenditure by the Council.

At Barton First School on the outskirts of Oxford, the proposal to close the school met with the united opposition of the community. Parents, local councillors, clergymen and other community leaders developed a strong and determined campaign. This included letter writing, petitioning, lobbying education officials and councillors, providing publicity material for the press and demonstrating outside the Council Chamber. The school remained open.

Pressure group activity and collective action by individuals can thus both bring about new policy priorities and lead to a reappraisal of existing policies. This is an essential feature of democratic decision-making and we would suggest that reflective teachers have both the right and responsibility to contribute to such processes.

Given that this is a book which is primarily designed to support student teachers during periods of school-based work, activities to influence wider policies may seem inappropriate. They are included here because such activity is a logical consequence of taking reflective teaching seriously and because some preparation for such activity is perfectly possible before taking up a full-time teaching post. One of the most important aspects of this is to demystify the democratic process itself and various suggestions on this can be made with regard to the six elements of pressure group activity which have been identified. These might be followed up by small groups of students or teachers, perhaps by taking an educational issue as a case-study, or indeed by facing a real current issue.

Demystifying the democratic process

There is a tendency to regard decision-making as something which is done by 'them' – an ill-defined, distant and amorphous body. In fact, decisions in democracies are taken by people who are elected representatives and the connection between the ordinary citizen and decision-makers can be much more close, direct and specific. Some possible ways forward here are:

- Visit a relevant meeting of your local or regional council or the House of Commons. Council committee meetings are normally open to the public and attendance at an education committee meeting is likely to be very interesting to reflective teachers.
- Visit a local elected representative, MP, councillor or a candidate. Alternatively set up a meeting which they can attend. Discuss their views on educational issues and get them to explain the constraints and pressures within which they serve.
- Attend a meeting of the governing body of your school. Note who the governors are and their powers over the affairs of the school. Consider the potential for partnership between teachers and governors.

Identifying decision-makers

Lists of MPs and councillors are normally available in local libraries and from council offices. It is then necessary to identify those who have a particular interest in education and those who have a particular degree of influence over decisions. A list of members of the education committee on a council or of members of the House of Commons with an interest in education will be helpful. The names of school governors will be available in your school.

It is also often appropriate to identify the leaders of political groups and those who speak on education issues. In addition, the chair of the finance committee on a local council or Treasury ministers in the House of Commons are likely to be worth identifying – depending, of course, on the issue under consideration.

A further group to identify are the education officers and civil servants who advise decision-makers and implement many decisions. Chief education officers, for instance, can be extremely influential.

Preparing the case

It is essential to prepare a case well. This requires at least three things:

1. Appropriate factual information about the issue.
2. Good educational arguments in support of whatever is being advocated.
3. Some understanding and responses to the interests and concerns of those whom it is hoped to influence.

Statistical information can be gathered from various sources at a local or national level. For instance, in England the Statistics Branch of the Department for Education publishes a *Statistical Bulletin* every month and other important statistics on more general issues are available from *Social Trends* and *Regional Trends*, both of which are annual government publications from the Central Statistical Office and should be available in good libraries. Similar statistics are available from the Scottish Office, Welsh Office and Northern Ireland Office.

Other sorts of information can be collected through discussion with those people who may be involved locally with the issue under consideration. Sources within your school should be one starting-point. Newspapers also offer a regular source of reports and comment on educational developments and can be monitored for relevant material. Bearing in mind the nature of some journalism, it is worth checking stories if possible.

For good educational arguments, one might want to consult the literature and certainly would wish to discuss the issues under consideration with colleagues. Regarding the interests of those whom one wishes to influence, a good place to start is with any published policy statements or manifestos. This could be followed up by discussion and by making judgements regarding the pressures and constraints which they face.

Forming alliances

Representative democracy is designed as a system which links decision-making with the views of a majority. It follows that the most successful type of campaigning is likely to be one which is broadly based – one which is produced by an alliance of interested parties bringing concerted pressure to bear on policy-makers.

Reflective teachers may thus wish to act with others if and when they wish to influence public policy. Obvious places to look for allies are:

- Other colleagues, perhaps through professional association, trade union links or a General Teaching Council if one exists. The fragmentation of the profession into different unions has been a considerable source of weakness on some issues in the past.
- Parents. The importance of parental support cannot be underestimated. It can help to establish the legitimacy of educational arguments and is a source of much energy and commitment to educational quality.
- Other workers in the public services.
- Existing national pressure groups such as those listed earlier in this section.
- Local community and interest groups who may be directly or indirectly affected by the issues under consideration.

Managing the media

Possibilities here include:

- Carrying out a review of the types of media which might be interested in educational issues – press, radio, television, etc.
- Holding discussions with people who have had experience of managing publicity to learn from them.
- Carrying out an analysis of the types of stories or news that each media outlet is likely to be interested in and, crucially, of the ways in which they are likely to handle educational issues.

- Considering the timing constraints which appropriate media outlets face.
- Holding discussions with selected journalists to get firsthand knowledge of their concerns.
- Preparing some press releases and considering suitable images for photographic or filming purposes.
- Identifying and supporting a spokesperson for press follow-up.

Lobbying decision-makers

There are any number of possibilities here such as:

- Discrete lobbying through discussion
- Letter writing by individuals
- Letter writing campaigns
- Delegations to put arguments
- Petitions
- Leafleting meetings
- Demonstrating with supporters
- Attending council or House of Commons debates to observe

One important strategy is to try to ensure, for as long as possible, that any policy changes can be introduced by politicians with dignity. Not many politicians enjoy being forced to change course, but most are open to persuasion if they have not previously taken up a hard, public position.

Following up

There is no mystery here. If agreement for changes in policy or practice is reached, it is simply necessary to check that the agreement is enacted (see Practical Activity 15.4.)

Practical activity 15.4

Aim: To reflect on some of the difficult realities of attempting to influence political decisions.

Method: Consider the account below, of events leading up to a ballot of parents on whether a primary school should 'opt out' of LEA control and become a grant-maintained school.

THE SCHOOL THAT DIDN'T 'OPT OUT'
By Jenny Wills, a parent

A couple of parents at my son's primary school (who just happened to be governors) started up a petition in order to apply for the school to obtain grant-maintained status. The first instance I became aware of the situation was when a note came home from school asking parents to check if their names were on the school's parents' register in order to be eligible to vote, and that voting would take place in three weeks' time. I found this an alarmingly short time in which to make an informed decision when, at this stage, I was completely 'in the dark' with regard to the implications and potential consequences of such an act.

I first spoke to the head who thought that opting out would release him from the control of the LEA with which he felt deep dissatisfaction. Other teachers were less inclined to comment as they felt they might be implicated at a later stage. Leaflets arrived home from school printed by the DES informing us of the 'advantages' of opting out. Parents received *one* sheet direct from the school on the 'disadvantages' printed by LSI (Local Schools Information). On the following Saturday morning the LEA-appointed governors arranged to have more comprehensive leaflets from LSI to be delivered through parents' doors.

A parents' meeting was arranged at which the governors and a selection of speakers were present including the assistant director of education, representatives from LSI and the government plus the head of a nearby secondary school that had opted out. The meeting turned into a fiasco as there were teachers in the audience who had resigned from the nearby secondary school as a result of it becoming grant-maintained and they were shouting disapproval at what their ex-head had to say, and quite a row developed between the governors about the way in which the leaflets had been distributed.

After this noisy and non-constructive meeting I wrote to the chairman of the governors asking for another parents' meeting – without the presence of uninvolved parties – and for the voting day to be moved to a later date. A lot of other parents must have had the same idea as the requests were granted.

The second meeting was a much more orderly and constructive affair involving just parents, governors and the head. Parents were told that the governors wishing to opt out were doing so in order to acquire money to carry out building and repair works and to appoint a crossing patrol person. The head also wanted to erect a new classroom to take in more reception children.

The ballot closed on 6 December 1991; 303 parents voted out of a possible 432. Fifty seven voted yes and 246 voted no.

Six months later the school has a new lollipop man, all the required repairs have been carried out and building work has been started.

- What were the main issues involved here?
- Can you identify the main interest and pressure groups?
- Could the necessary decision-making process have been handled to produce less anguish?
- What might the role of a reflective teacher have been in a situation of this sort?

Follow-up: Such events go on all the time and deciding on the most appropriate course of action is usually difficult. However, being clear about one's own values helps enormously (see Practical Activity 4.3). What actions are you prepared to take to support your values?

CONCLUSION

Education is inevitably concerned not just with 'what is' but also with what 'ought to be' (Kogan, 1978). I hope that this book will help teachers and student teachers to develop not only the necessary skills of teaching but also the awareness and commitment which will ensure the positive nature of their contribution to the education service in the future.

Notes for further reading

Many of the books suggested as further reading for Chapters 1 and 2 will also be relevant here. Two of those books which are particularly challenging are:

Apple, M. (1982)
Education and Power,
London: Routledge & Kegan Paul.

Stenhouse, L. (1982)
Authority, Education and Emancipation,
London: Heinemann.

One more general way of following up many of these issues, particularly to gather information, would be through the use of textbooks in the sociology of education. For two of the most recent see:

Burgess, R. G. (1986)
Sociology, Education and Schools,
London: Batsford.

Reid, I. (1986)
The Sociology of School and Education,
London: Fontana.

For an important analysis of the impact of market competition between schools, see:

Dale, R. (1996)
Mechanisms of Differentiation between schools: the four 'Ms'. Mimeo,
Auckland: University of Auckland.   📖 **Reading, 15.5**

For optimistic assessments of the contribution to education which sociologists might make in collaboration with teachers see:

Woods, P. and Pollard, A. (eds) (1988)
Sociology and Teaching: A New Challenge for the Sociology of Education,
London: Croom Helm.

Human rights is an extremely important topic. The most important documents to consider are:

The Universal Declaration of Human Rights,
New York: United Nations.

This Declaration was initially agreed in 1948 and is available through United Nations Associations.

The European Convention on Human Rights,
Strasbourg: Council of Europe.

This Convention represents a collective guarantee of a number of the principles contained in the Universal Declaration. It came into force in 1953 and all of the 21 member states of the Council of Europe have ratified it. It is backed by the European Court of Human Rights. Copies of the Convention and further information are available from: Directorate of Human Rights, Council of Europe, F-67006 Strasbourg, France.

The United Nations Convention on the Rights of the Child is another important international statement. For an excellent account of both it and its implications for the UK, see:

Newell, P. (1991)
The UN Convention and Children's Rights in the UK,
London: National Children's Bureau.

For specific guidance and ideas on classroom practice see also:

Council of Europe (1985)
Teaching and Learning about Human Rights in Schools, Recommendation No. R (85)7 of the Committee of Ministers to Member States.
Strasbourg: Council of Europe.   Reading, 15.4

Steiner, M. (1994) *Learning from Experience: World Studies in the Primary Curriculum,* Stoke: Trentham Books.

Lyseight-Jones, P. (1985)
Human Rights Education in Primary Schools,
Report of Council of Europe Teacher's Seminar No. 28, Donaueschingen,
Strasbourg: Council of Europe.

Starkey, H. (1987)
Practical Activities for Teaching and Learning about Human Rights in Schools,
Strasbourg: Council of Europe.

There is also a considerable literature which is more specifically about children's rights. For an important handbook, see:

Franklin, B. and Hammarberg, T. (1995)
The Handbook of Children's Rights: Comparative Legislation and Practice,
London: Routledge.

For consideration of some of the issues to do with political balance which may be raised, see:

Jones, B. (1986)
Politics and the pupil,
Times Educational Supplement, 30 May 1986.

Wellington, J. J. (ed.) (1986)
Controversial Issues in the Curriculum,
Oxford: Blackwell.

Action by reflective teachers within the democratic process calls for some knowledge of political structures and processes. For excellent introductions, see:

Coxall, B. and Robins, L. (1991)
Contemporary British Politics,
London: Macmillan.

Kingdom, J. (1991)
Government and Politics in Britain,
Oxford: Polity Press.

Byrne, T. (1992)
Local Government in Britain,
London: Penguin.

For analyses of recent conditions among local authority policy-makers, advisers and school governors respectively, see:

Hewton, E. (1986)
Education in Recession: Crisis in County Hall and Classroom,
London: Allen and Unwin.

Heller, H. and Edwards, P. (1992)
Policy and Power in Education: The Rise and Fall of the LEA,
London: Routledge.

Ranson, S. (1992)
The Role of Local Government in Education,
London: Longman.

Winkley, D. (1985)
Diplomats and Detectives: LEA Advisers at Work,
London: Robert Royce.

Kogan, M., Johnson, D., Packwood, T. and Whitaker, T. (1984)
School Governing Bodies,
London: Heinemann.

Beckett, C., Bell, L. and Rhodes, C. (1991)
Working with Governors in Schools: Developing a Professional Partnership,
Buckingham: Open University Press.

An element of struggle between central government and the teaching profession has been clear in the last decade. On this see:

Ball, S. J. (1994)
Education Reform: A Central and Post-Structural Approach,
Buckingham: Open University Press.   ◻ **Reading, 15.6**

Pollard, A., Broadfoot, P., Croll, P., Osborn, M. and Abbott, D. (1994)
Changing English Primary Schools?
London: Cassell.

BIBLIOGRAPHY

Abbott, D. and Croll, P. (1991) 'Whole school change'. Paper presented to the annual conference of the American Educational Research Association, Chicago, April.

ACAS (1986) *Report of the Appraisal/Training Working Group*. London: ACAS.

Acker, S. (ed.) (1989) *Teachers, Gender and Careers*. London: Falmer.

Adam Smith Institute (1984) *Omega Report – Education Policy*. London: Adam Smith Institute.

Adelman, C. (ed.) (1981) *Uttering, Muttering: Collecting, Using and Reporting Talk for Social and Educational Research*. London: Grant McIntyre.

Adelman, C. and Alexander, R. J. (1982) *The Self-Evaluating Institution*. London: Methuen.

Adelman, C. and Walker, R. J. (1975) *A Guide to Classroom Observation*. London: Methuen.

Adler, A. (1927) *The Practice and Theory of Individual Psychology*. New York: Harcourt.

Ainscow, M. (1991) *Effective Schools for All*. London: David Fulton.

Ainscow, M. and Tweddle, D. (1984) *Early Learning Skills Analysis*. London: David Fulton.

Aldcroft, D. H. (1992) *Education, Training and Economic Performance. 1984 – 1990* Manchester: Manchester University Press.

Alexander, R. J. (1984) *Primary Teaching*. London: Holt, Rinehart & Winston.

Alexander, R. J. (1992) *Policy and Practice in Primary Education*. London: Routledge.

Alexander, R. J., Rose, J. and Woodhead, C. (1992) *Curriculum Organisation and Classroom Practice in Primary Schools: A Discussion Paper*. London: Department of Education and Science.

Alexander, R. J., Wilcocks, J. and Kinder, K. M. (1989) *Changing Primary Practice*. London: Falmer.

Alexander R. J., Wilcocks, J., Kinder, K and Nelson, N. (1995) *Versions of Primary Education*. London: Routledge.

Alladina, S. and Edwards, V. (eds) (1991) *Multilingualism in the British Isles*. 2 vols. London: Longman.

Allen, I. *et al.,*(1975) *Working an Integrated Day*. London: Ward Lock.

Altbach, P. G. and Kelly, G. P. (eds) (1986) *New Approaches to Comparative Education*. Chicago: University of Chicago.

Althusser, L. (1971) Ideology and the ideological state apparatuses. In B. R. Cosin (ed.) *Education, Structure and Society*. Harmondsworth: Penguin.

Altrichter, H., Posch, P. and Somekh, B. (1993) *Teachers Investigate Their Work: An Introduction to the Methods of Action Research*. London: Routledge.

Anderson, A. J. B. (1989) *A First Course in Statistics*. London: Routledge.

Anderson, C. S. (1982) The search for school climate: a review of the research, *Review of Educational Research*. 52, 368–420.

Anning, A. (1983) The three year itch, *Times Educational Supplement*. 24 June 1983.

Anning, A. (1991) *The First Years at School: Education 4 to 8*. Milton Keynes: Open University Press.

Anning, A. (ed.) (1995) *A National Curriculum for the Early Years*. Buckingham: Open University Press.

Anthony, W. (1979) Progressive learning theories: the evidence. In G. Bernbaum (ed.) *Schooling in Decline*, London: Macmillan.

Apple, M. (1982) *Education and Power*. London: Routledge & Kegan Paul.

Apple, M. (1986) *Teachers and Texts*. London: Routledge.

Apple, M. W. (1993) *Official Knowledge: Democratic Education in a Conservative Age*. London: Routledge.

Apple, M. W. and Christian-Smith, L. K. (1991) *The Politics of the Textbook*. London: Routledge.

Archer, M. (1979) *The Social Origins of Educational Systems*. London: Sage Publications.

Armstrong, M. (1981) *Closely Observed Children: The Diary of a Primary Classroom*. London: Writers and Readers.

Armstrong, M. (1989) Another way of looking, *Forum*. 33, (1), 181–8.

Arnold, M. (1986) *Selected Works*. Oxford: Oxford University Press.

Arnold, R. (ed.) (1991) *Topic Planning and the National Curriculum*. London: Longman.

Arnot, M. and Barton, L. (1992) *Voicing Concerns: Sociological Perspectives on Contemporary Education Reforms*. Wallingford: Triangle.

Ashdown, R., Carpenter, B. and Bovair, K. (1991) *The Curriculum Challenge: Access to the National Curriculum for Pupils with Learning Difficulties*. London: Falmer.

Athey, C. (1990) *Extending Thought in Young Children: A Parent–Teacher Partnership*. London: Paul Chapman.

Audit Commission (1990) *Rationalising Primary School Provision*. London: HMSO.

Audit Commission (1991) *Management Within Primary Schools*. London: HMSO.

Avann, P. (ed.) (1985) *Teaching Information Skills in the Primary School*. London: Edward Arnold

Avon County Council (1990) *Developing Economic and Industrial Understanding in Primary Schools*. Bristol: Avon CC.

Avon County Council (1992) *Guidance for Curriculum Planning*. Bristol: Avon CC.

Baddeley, G. *et al.*, (1991) *Teaching, Talking and Learning in Key Stage Two*. York: National Curriculum Council.

Ball, S. J. (1981a) Initial encounters in the classroom and the process of establishment. In P. F. Woods (ed.) *Pupil Strategies*. London: Croom Helm.

Ball, S. J. (1981b) *Beechside Comprehensive*. Cambridge: Cambridge University Press.

Ball, S. J. (1987) *Micropolitics of the School: Towards a Theory of School Organisation*. London: Routledge.

Ball, S. J. (1990) *Politics and Policy Making in Education: Explorations in Policy*. London: Routledge.

Ball, S. J. (1994) *Education Reform: A Critical and Post-Structural Approach*. Buckingham: Open University Press.

Ball, S. J. and Goodson, I. F. (1985) *Teachers' Lives and Careers*. London: Falmer.

Bantock, G. H. (1980) *Dilemmas of the Curriculum*. Oxford: Martin & Robertson.

Barber, M. (1991) *Education and the Teacher Unions*, London: Cassell.

Barker, R. G. (1978) *Habitats, Environments and Human Behaviour*. San Francisco: Jossey-Bass.

Barker Lunn, J. C. (1970) *Streaming in the Primary School*. Slough: NFER.

Barnes, D. (1975) *From Communication to Curriculum*. London: Penguin Books.

Barnes, D., Britton, J. and Rosen, H. (1969) *Language, the Learner and the School*. Harmonsworth: Penguin.

Barr, M., D'Arcy, P. and Healy, M. K. (eds) (1982) *What's Going On? Language/Learning Episodes in British and American Classrooms, Grades 4–13*. Montclair, NJ: Boynton/Cook.

Barrett, E., Barton, L., Furlong, J., Galvin, C., Miles, S. and Whitty, G. (1992) *Initial Teacher Education in England and Wales: A Topography*. Mimeo, London: University of London: Institute of Education.

Barrett, G. (ed.) (1989) *Dissaffection from School: The Early Years*. London: Falmer.

Barrow, R. (1984) *Giving Teaching Back to Teachers*. Brighton: Wheatsheaf.

Barrow, R. and Woods, R. (1988) *An Introduction to Philosophy of Education*. London: Routledge.

Barton, L. and Lawn, M. (1980/81) Back inside the whale: a curriculum case study, *Interchange*. **11** (4).

Barton, L., Barrett, E., Whitty, G., Miles, S. and Furlong, J. (1994) Teacher education and teacher professionalism in England: some emerging issues, *British Journal of Sociology of Education*. **15**, 4. 529–44.

Bassey, M. (1978) *Practical Classroom Organization*. London: Ward Lock Educational.

Bassey, M. (1990) Creating education through research, *Research Intelligence*. Autumn. 40– 4.

Bauman, Z. (1990) *Thinking Sociologically*. Oxford: Blackwell.

Bazalgette, C. (1988) They changed the picture in the middle of the fight ... New kinds of literacy. In M. Meek and C. Mills (eds) *Language and Literacy in the Primary School*. London: Falmer Press.

Beckett, C., Bell, L. and Rhodes, C. (1991) *Working with Governors in Schools: Developing a Professional Partnership*. Buckingham: Open University Press.

Bell, A. and Sigsworth, A. (1987) *The Small Rural Primary School: A Matter of Quality*. London: Falmer.

Bellotti, E. (1975) *Little Girls*. London: Readers and Writers.

Bennett, K. and Kastor, T. (1988) *Analysing Children's Language*. Oxford: Blackwell.

Bennett, N. (1976) *Teaching Styles and Pupil Progress*. London: Open Books.

Bennett, N. (1979) Recent research on teaching: a dream, a belief and a model. In S. N. Bennett and D. McNamara (eds) *Focus on Teaching*. London: Longman.

Bennett, N. (1992) Unpublished contribution to the British Education Research Association's Primary Education Policy Task Group.

Bennett, N. (1994) *Class Size in Primary Schools: Perceptions of Headteachers, Chairs of Governors, Teachers and Parents*. NASUWT Birmingham.

Bennett, N. and Carré, C. (eds) (1993) *Learning To Teach*. London: Routledge.

Bennett, N. and Dunne, E (1992) *Managing Classroom Groups*. Hemel Hempstead: Simon & Schuster.

Bennett, N., Desforges, C., Cockburn, A. and Wilkinson, B. (1984) *The Quality of Pupil Learning Experiences*. London: Lawrence Erlbaum Associates.

Bennett, N. and Kell, J. (1989) *A Good Start? Four Year Olds in Infant Schools*. Oxford: Blackwell.

Bennett, N., Wragg, E. C., Carré, C. G. and Carter, D. S. G. (1992) A longitudinal study of primary teachers' perceived competence in, and concerns about, National Curriculum implementation, *Research Papers in Education*, 7 (1), 53–78.

Berger, P. L. (1963) *Invitation to Sociology: A Humanistic Perspective*. New York: Doubleday.

Berger, P. L. and Luckman, T. (1967) *The Social Construction of Reality*. London: Allen Lane.

Berlak, H. and Berlak, A. (1981) *Dilemmas of Schooling*. London: Methuen.

Bernstein, B. (1971) On the classification and framing of educational knowledge. In M. F. D. Young (ed.) *Knowledge and Control: New Directions for the Sociology of Education*. London: Collier-Macmillan.

Biott, C. (1990) *Semi-detached Teachers: Building Support and Advisory Relationships in Classrooms*. London: Falmer.

Biott, C. and Easen, P. (1994) *Collaborative Learning in Staffrooms and Classrooms*. London: David Fulton.

Biott, C. and Nias, J. (1992) *Working and Learning Together for Change*. Buckingham: Open University Press.

Biott, C., Easen, P. and Atkins, M. (1992) School development planning, participation and staff membership. Paper presented to the annual conference of the British Educational Research Association, Stirling.

Black, P. (1994) Performance, assessment and accountability: the experience in England and Wales, *Educational Evaluation and Policy Analysis*, **16** (2), 200–1.

Blatchford, P. (1989) *Playtime in the Primary School: Problems and Improvements*. London: Routledge.

Blatchford, P. (1992) Children's attitudes to work at 11 years, *Educational Studies*, **18** (1), 107–8.

Blenkin, G. M. and Kelly, A. V. (1981) *The Primary Curriculum*. London: Harper & Row.

Blenkin, G. M. and Kelly, A. V. (eds) (1992) *Assessment in Early Childhood Education*. London: Paul Chapman.

Blishen, E. (1969) *The School That I'd Like*. Harmondsworth: Penguin.

Blyth, W. A. L. (1965) *English Primary Education*. Vol. II: Background. London: Routledge.

Blyth, W. A. L. (1975) *Place, Time and Society*, 8–11. London: Collins.

Blyth, W.A.L. (1984) *Development, Experience and Curriculum in Primary Education*. London: Croom Helm.

Board of Education (1931) *Report of the Consultative Committee on the Primary School*. (The Hadow Report), London: HMSO.

Bolam, R. (1982) *Strategies for School Improvement*. Paris: OECD.

Bollington, R., Hopkins, D. and West, M. (1990) *An Introduction to Teacher Appraisal*. London: Cassell.

Bolster, A. (1983) Towards a more effective model of research on teaching, *Harvard Educational Review*, **53** (3), 294–308.

Bonnett, M. (1993) *Thinking and Understanding in the Primary School Curriculum*. London: Cassell.

Booth, M., Furlong, J. and Wilkin, M. (1990) *Partnership in Initial Teacher Training*. London: Cassell.

Borg, W. R. (1981) *Applying Educational Research: A Practical Guide for Teachers*. New York: Longman.

Bossert, S. T. (1979) *Tasks and Social Relationships in Classrooms*. Cambridge: Cambridge University Press.

Bottery, M. (1990) *The Morality of the School*. London: Cassell.

Bottery, M. (1992) *The Ethics of Educational Management*. London: Cassell.

Bourdieu, P. and Passeron, J. C. (1977) *Reproduction in Education, Society and Culture*. London: Sage.

Bourne, J. (1989) *Moving into the Mainstream, LEA Provision for Bilingual Pupils*. London: Routledge.

Bowe, R. and Ball, S., with Gold. A. (1992) *Reforming Education and Changing Schools*. London: Routledge.

Bowles, S. and Gintis, H. (1976) *Schooling in Capitalist America*. London: Routledge & Kegan Paul.

Boyson, R. (1975) Maps, chaps and your hundred best books, *Times Education Supplement*. 17 October 1975.

Breakwell, G. M. (1986) *Coping with Threatened Identities*. London: Methuen.

Brierley, J. (1992) *Growth in Children*. London: Cassell.

Broadfoot, P. (ed.) (1984) *Selection, Certification and Control: Social Issues in Educational Assessment*. London: Falmer.

Broadfoot, P. (ed.) (1986) *Profiles and Records of Achievement*. London: Cassell.

Broadfoot, P. (1996) Do we really need to write it all down? Managing the challenge of National Assessment at Key Stage 1 and Key Stage 2. In P. Croll (ed.) *Teachers, Pupils and Primary Schooling: Continuity and Change*. London: Cassell.

Broadfoot, P., Abbott, D., Croll, P., Osborn, M., Pollard, A. and Towler, L. (1991) Implementing national assessment: issues for primary teachers, *Cambridge Journal of Education*, **21** (2), 153–68.

Broadfoot, P., Gilly, M., Osborn, M., and Paillet, A. (1993) *Perceptions of Teaching: Primary School Teachers in England and France*. London: Cassell.

Broadfoot, P., James, M., McMeeking, S., Nuttall, D. and Stierer, B. (1988) *Records of Achievement*. Report of the National Evaluation of Pilot Schemes, London: HMSO.

Bronfenbrenner, U. (1979) *The Ecology of Human Development; Experiments in Nature and Design*. Cambridge, MA: Harvard University Press.

Brophy, J. E. and Good, T. L. (1974) *Teacher–Student Relationships*. New York: Cassell.

Brown, G. (1978) *Lecturing and Explaining*. London: Methuen.

Brown, G. and Wragg, T. (1993) *Questioning*. London: Routledge.

Brown, M. (1989) Graded assessment and learning hierarchies: an alternative view, *British Educational Research Journal*, **15** (2), 121–8.

Brown, M. E. and Precious, G. N. (1968) *The Integrated Day in the Primary School*. London: Ward Lock Educational.

Brown, S. and McIntyre, D. (1992) *Making Sense of Teaching*. Buckingham: Open University Press.

Browne, N. and France, P. (1986) *Untying the Apron Strings*. Buckingham: Open University Press.

Bruner, J. S. (1966) *Towards a Theory of Instruction*. Cambridge, MA: Harvard University Press.

Bruner, J. S. (1986) *Actual Minds, Possible Worlds*. Cambridge, MA: Harvard University Press.

Bruner, J. S. (1990) *Acts of Meaning*. Cambridge, MA: Harvard University Press.

Bruner, J. S. and Haste, H. (1987) *Making Sense: The Child's Construction of the World*. London: Methuen.

Bruner, J. S., Goodnow, J. and Austin, G. A. (1956) *A Study of Thinking, Studies in Cognitive Thought*. New York: Wiley.

Burgess, H., Southworth, G. and Webb, R. (1994) Whole school planning in the primary school. In A. Pollard (ed.) *Look Before You Leap? Research Evidence for the Curriculum at Key Stage Two*. London: Tufnell Press.

Burgess, R. G. (ed.) (1982) *Field Research: A Sourcebook and Field Manual*. London: Allen & Unwin.

Burgess, R. G. (1984) *In the Field: An Introduction to Field Research*. London: Allen & Unwin.

Burgess, R. G. (1986) *Sociology, Education and Schools*. London: Batsford.

Burns, R. B. (1982) *Self-Concept Development and Education*. London: Routledge & Kegan Paul.

Byrne, T. (1992) *Local Government in Britain*. London: Penguin.

Calderhead, J. (1984) *Teachers' Decision Making*. London: Cassell.

Calderhead, J. (1987) *Exploring Teachers' Thinking*. London: Cassell.

Calderhead, J. (1988) *Teachers' Professional Learning*. London: Falmer.

Calderhead, J. (1994) Can the complexities of teaching be accounted for in terms of competences? Contrasting views of professional practice from research and policy. Mimeo produced for an ESRC symposium on teacher competence.

Callaghan, J. (1976) Towards a national debate, *Education*, **148**, (17).

Calvert, B. (1975) *The Role of the Pupil*. London: Routledge & Kegan Paul.

Campbell, J. (1985) *Developing the Primary School Curriculum*. London: Holt, Rinehart & Winston.

Campbell, J. (ed) (1988a) *The Routledge Compendium of Primary Education*. London: Routledge.

Campbell, J. (1988b) *Cashmore School*. Block ED352, Milton Keynes: Open University.

Campbell, J. (1993) A dream at conception: a nightmare at delivery. In J. Campbell (ed.) *Breadth and Balance in the Primary Curriculum*. London: Falmer.

Campbell, J. and Neill, S. R. St J. (1992) *Teacher Time and Curriculum Manageability at Key Stage 1*. London: AMMA.

Campbell, R. J. and Neill, S. R. St J. (1994) *Primary Teachers at Work*. London: Routledge.

Cane, B. and Schroeder, C. (1970) *The Teacher and Research*. Slough: NFER.

Capra, F. (1982) Buddist physics. In S. Kumar (ed.) *The Schumacher Lectures*, London: Abacus.

Carnoy, M. and Levin, H. M. (1985) *Schooling and Work in the Democratic State*. Stanford, CA: Stanford University Press.

Carr, W. and Kemmis, S. (1986) *Becoming Critical: Education, Knowledge and Action Research*. London: Falmer Press.

Carrington, B. and Short, G. (1989) *Race and the Primary School: Theory into Practice*. Windsor: NFER-Nelson.

Carter, R. (ed.) (1990) *Knowledge about Language and the National Curriculum*. London: Hodder and Stoughton.

Cattell, R. B. and Kline, P (1977) *The Scientific Analysis of Personality and Motivation*. London: Academic Press.

Cave, E. and Wilkinson, C. (1990) *Local Management of Schools: Some Practical Issues*. London: Routledge.

Central Advisory Council for Education (CACE)(England) (1967) *Children and their Primary Schools*. London: HMSO.

Central Statistical Office (1995) *Population Trends 80*. London: HMSO.

Centre for Educational Research and Innovation (1995) *Schools Under Scrutiny*. Paris: OCED.

Chapman, J. (ed.) (1990) *School-based Decision Making and Management*. London: Falmer.

Child, D. (1986) *Psychology and the Teacher*. London: Cassell.

Chubb, T. E. and Moe, T. M. (1990) *Politics, Markets and America's Schools*. Washington DC: Brookings.

Clandinin, D. J. (1986) *Classroom Practice: Teacher Images In Action*. London: Falmer.

Clarkson, M. (1988) *Emerging Issues in Primary Education*. London: Falmer.

Clarricoates, K. (1978) Dinosaurs in the classroom – a re-examination of some aspects of the 'hidden' curriculum in primary schools, *Women's Studies International Quarterly*, 1 353–64.

Clarricoates, K. (1981) The experience of patriarchal schooling, *Interchange*, 12 (2–3), 185–205.

Clarricoates, K. (1987) Child culture at school: a clash between gendered worlds? In A. Pollard (ed.) *Children and Their Primary Schools*. London: Falmer.

Claxton, G. (1989) *Being a Teacher: A Positive Approach to Change and Stress*. Milton Keynes: Open University Press.

Cleave, S. and Brown, S. (1992) *Early to School: Four Year Olds in Infant Classes*. London: Routledge.

Clegg, D. and Billington, S. (1994) *The Effective Primary Classroom: Management and Organisation of Teaching and Learning*. London: David Fulton.

Clift, P., Weiner, G. and Wilson, E. (1981) *Record Keeping in the Primary School*. London: Macmillan.

Cockburn, A. (1996) *Teaching Under Pressure: Looking at Primary Teachers' Stress*. London: Falmer Press.

Cohen, D. and MacKeith, S. (1991) *The Development of Imagination: The Private Worlds of Childhood*. London: Routledge.

Cohen, L. (1976) *Educational Research in Classrooms and Schools: A Manual of Materials and Methods*. London: Harper & Row.

Cohen, L. and Holliday, M. (1979) *Statistics for Education*. London: Harper & Row.

Cohen, L. and Manion, L. (1994) *Research Methods in Education* (4th edn). London: Croom Helm.

Cohen, L., Thomas, J. and Manion, L. (1982) *Educational Research and Development in Britain, 1970–1980*. Slough: NFER.

Cohen, S. (1972) *Folk Devils and Moral Panics*. Oxford: Martin Robinson.

Cole, M. and Walker, S. (eds) (1989) *Teaching and Stress*. Milton Keynes: Open University Press.

Coleman, J. S., Coser, L. A. and Powell, W. W. (1966) *Equality of Educational Opportunity*. Washington DC: US Government Printing Office.

Collett, P. (ed.) (1977) *Social Rules and Social Behaviour*. Oxford: Blackwell.

Collins, R. (1977) Some comparative principles of educational stratification, *Harvard Educational Review*, 47 (1), 1–27.

Combs, P. H. (1985) *The World Crisis in Education: The View from the Eighties*. Oxford: Oxford University Press.

Commission for Racial Equality (1987) *Learning in Terror: A Survey of Racial Harassment in Schools*. London: CRE.

Committee of Enquiry on Discipline in Schools (1989) *Discipline in Schools: Report of the Committee of Enquiry chaired by Lord Elton*. London: HMSO.

Connell, R. W. (1985) *Teachers' Work*. London: Allen & Unwin.

Connell, R. W., Ashden, D. J., Kessler, S. and Dowsett, G. W. (1982) *Making the Difference: Schools, Families and Social Divisions*. Sidney: Allen & Unwin.

Conner, C. (1990) *Assessment and Testing in the Primary School*. London: Falmer.

Conservative Party (1992) *Manifesto for the General Election*. London: Conservative Party.

Consultative Committee on Primary Education (1931) *Report of the Consultative Committee on Primary Education*. (Hadow Report). London: HMSO.

Cooper, P. and McIntyre, D. (1996) *Effective Teaching and Learning: Teachers' and Students' Perspectives*. Buckingham: Open University Press.

Coopers & Lybrand Deloitte (1991) *Costs of the National Curriculum in Primary Schools*. London: National Union of Teachers.

Corbett, H. D. and Wilson, B. L. (1991) Unintended and unwelcome: the local impact of state testing. In G. W. Niblett, and W. T. A. Fink(eds) *Testing, Reform and Rebellion*. New York: Ablex Publishing Corporation.

Cortazzi, M. (1990) *Primary Teaching How It Is: A Narrative Account*. London: David Fulton.

Council for National Academic Awards, Committee for Teacher Education (1991) *Competency-based Approaches to Teacher Education: Viewpoints and Issues*. London: CNAA.

Council of Europe (1985) *Teaching and Learning about Human Rights in Schools*. Recommendation No. R (85)7 of the Committee of Ministers to Member States. Strasbourg: Council of Europe.

Cox, C. B. and Dyson, A. E. (eds) (1969) *Fight for Education: A Black Paper*. London: Critical Quarterly Society.

Cox, C. B. and Marks, J. (eds) (1982) *The Right to Learn*. London: Centre for Policy Studies.

Coxall, B. and Robins, L. (1991) *Contemporary British Politics*. London: Macmillan.

Craft, A. (ed.) (1996) *Primary Education: Assessing and Planning Learning*. London: Routledge.

Cranfield, J. and Wells, H. (1976) *100 Ways to Enhance Self-Concept in the Classroom*. Englewood Cliffs, NJ: Prentice-Hall.

Croll, P. (1986) *Systematic Classroom Observation*. London: Falmer.

Croll, P, (1990) Norm and criterion referenced assessment. *Redland Papers*, 1, Summer, 8–11.

Croll, P. (ed.) (1996) *Teachers, Pupils and Primary Schooling: Continuity and Change*. London: Cassell.

Croll, P. and Moses, D. (1985) *One in Five: The Assessment and Incidence of Special Educational Needs*. London: Routledge & Kegan Paul.

Cullingford, C. (ed.) (1985) *Parents, Teachers and Schools*. London: Robert Royce.

Cullingford, C. (1990) *The Nature of Learning*. London: Cassell.

Cunningham, P. (1988) *Curriculum Change in the Primary School Since 1945: Dissemination of the Progressive Ideal*. London: Falmer.

Curriculum Council for Wales (CCW) (1991) *The Whole Curriculum in Wales*. Cardiff: CCW.

Curriculum Council for Wales (1993) *Records of Achievement in Primary Schools*. Cardiff, CCW.

Dadds, M. (1995) *Passionate Enquiry and School Development: A Story about Teacher Action Research*. London: Falmer Press.

Dale, R. (1977) Implications of the rediscovery of the hidden curriculum. In D. Gleedson (ed.) *Identity and Structure*. Driffield: Nafferton.

Dale, R. (1989) *The State and Education Policy*. Milton Keynes: Open University Press.

Dale, R. (1996), Mechanisms of differentiation between schools: the four 'Ms'. Mimeo. Auckland: University of Auckland.

Davey, A. (1983) *Learning to be Prejudiced*. London: Edward Arnold.

David, T. (1990) *Under Five – Under Educated*. Buckingham: Open University Press.

Davies, B. (1982) *Life in the Classroom and Playground*. London: Routledge & Kegan Paul.

Davies, B. (1993) *Shards of Glass: Children Reading and Writing Beyond Gendered Identities*. Sydney: Allen and Unwin.

Day, C., Johnston, D. and Whitaker, P. (1985) *Managing Primary Schools*. London: Harper & Row.

Day, C., Whitaker, P. and Johnston, D. (1990) *Managing Primary Schools in the 1990s*. London: Paul Chapman.

Dean, J. (1973) *Display*. London: Evans.

Dean, J. (1991) *Organizing Learning in the Primary School Classroom*. London: Routledge.

Dearden, R. F. (1968) *The Philosophy of the Primary Education*. London: Routledge & Kegan Paul.

Dearing, R. (1993) *The National Curriculum and its Assessment: A Final Report*. London: School Curriculum and Assessment Authority.

De Bono, E. (1972) *Children Solve Problems*. London: Penguin.

Deem, R. (1994) School governing bodies: public concerns and private interests. In D. Scott (ed.) *Accountability and Control in Educational Settings*. London: Cassell.

Deem, R., Brehony, K. and Heath, S. (1995) *Active Citizenship and the Governing of Schools*. Buckingham: Open University Press.

Delamont, S. (1980) *Sex Roles and the School*. London: Routledge.

Delamont, S. (ed.) (1987) *The Primary School Teacher*. London: Falmer.

Delamont, S. (1990) *Interaction in the Classroom*. London: Routledge.

De Lyon, H. and Migniuolo, F. (1989) *Women Teachers: Issues and Experiences*. Milton Keynes: Open University Press.

Department for Education (1992) *Choice and Diversity: A New Framework for Schools*. London: DFE.

Department for Education (1993a) *Criteria for Initial Teacher Training* (Primary Phase), DFE Circular 14/93. London: DFE.

Department for Education (1993b) *Reporting on Pupils' Achievements to Parents*. Circular 16/93. London: DES.

Department for Education (1994) *The Code of Practice on the Identification and Assessment of Special Educational Needs*. London: DFE.

Department for Education (1995) *Value Added in Education: A Briefing Paper*. London: DFE.

Department for Education and Employment (1995) *Desirable Outcomes*. London: DFEE.

Department for Education and Employment (1996) *Results of the 1995 National Curriculum Assessments of 11 Year Olds in England*. London: DFEE.

Department for Education/Welsh Office (1992) *Initial Teacher Training (Secondary Phase)*. DFE Circular 9/92, WO Circular 35/92, London: DFE.

Department of Education and Science (1975) *A Language for Life*. (The Bullock Report). London: HMSO.

Department of Education and Science (1978a) *Primary Education In England: A Survey by HMI*. London: HMSO.

Department of Education and Science (1978b) *Special Educational Needs* (The Warnock Report). London: HMSO.

Department of Education and Science (1980) *A View of the Curriculum*. London: HMSO.

Department of Education and Science (1981a) *The School Curriculum*. London: HMSO.

Department of Education and Science (1981b) *West Indian Children in Our Schools* (The Rampton Report). London: HMSO

Department of Education and Science (1984) *Records of Achievement: A Statement of Policy*. London: DES.

Department of Education and Science (1985a) *The Curriculum from 5 to 16*. HMI, Curriculum Matters Series. London: HMSO.

Department of Education and Science (1985b) *Better Schools: A Summary*. London: HMSO.

Department of Education and Science (1985c) *The Curriculum 5–16*. Curriculum Matters 2, HMI Series. London: HMSO.

Department of Education and Science (1985d) *Education For All*. Report of the Committee of Enquiry into the Education of Children from Ethnic Minority Groups (The Swann Report). London: HMSO.

Department of Education and Science (1987) *The National Curriculum 5–16: A Discussion Document*. London: DES.

Department of Education and Science (1989a) *National Curriculum: From Policy to Practice*. London: DES.

Department of Education and Science (1989b) *Discipline in Schools*. Report of the Committee of Enquiry chaired by Lord Elton. London: HMSO.

Department of Education and Science (1990–1) *Language in the National Curriculum (LINC): Materials for Professional Development*. London: HMSO.

Department of Education and Science (1990a) *Starting with Quality: Report of the Committee of Enquiry into the Quality of Educational Provision for Under Fives* (The Rumbold Report). London: HMSO.

Department of Education and Science (1990b) *Records of Achievement*. Circular 8/90, London: DES.

Department of Education and Science (1992a) *The Parent's Charter*. London: DES.

Department of Education and Science (1992b) *Reporting Pupils' Achievements to Parents*. Circular 5/92, London: DES.

Department of Education and Science (1992c) *Choice and Diversity: A New Framework for Schools*. London: HMSO.

Department of Health (DHSS) (1989) *On the State of the Public Health 1988*. London: HMSO.

Desforges, C. (1989) *Testing and Assessment*. London: Cassell

Desforges, C. (1992) The application of subject knowledge in the primary school. Mimeo. School of Education, University of Exeter.

Dewey, J. (1916) *Democracy and Education*. New York: Free Press

Dewey, J. (1933) *How We Think: A Restatement of the Relation of Reflective Thinking to the Educative Process*. Chicago: Henry Regnery.

Dickson, W. P. (ed.) (1981) *Children's Oral Communication Skills*. New York: Academic Press.

Dillon, J. (1983) Problem solving and findings, *Journal of Creative Behaviour*, **16** (2), 97–111.

Dixon, B. (1977) *Catching Them Young: Sex, Race and Class in Children's Fiction*. London: Pluto Press.

Docking, J.M. (1980) *Control and Discipline in Schools*. London: Harper & Row.

Docking, J. (ed.) (1990a) *Education and Alienation in the Junior School*. London: Falmer.

Docking, J. (1990b) *Managing Behaviour in the Primary School*. London: David Fulton.

Donaldson, M. (1978) *Children's Minds*. Glasgow: Collins/Fontana.

Dowling, M. (1992) *Education 3–5*. London: Paul Chapman.

Doyle, W. (1977) Learning the classroom environment: an ecological analysis, *Journal of Teacher Education*, **XXVIII** (6), 51–4.

Doyle, W. and Pounder, C. A. (1976) The practicality ethic in teacher decision-making, *Interchange*, **8**.

Dreeben, R. (1968) *On What is Learned in School*. Reading, MA: Addison-Wesley.

Dreyfus, S. E. (1981) *Four Models v. Human Situational Understanding*. US Air Force, Office of Scientific Research.

Drummond, M. J. (1993) *Assessing Children's Learning*. London: David Fulton.

Dunham, J. (1992) *Stress in Teaching*. London: Routledge.

Dunn, J. (1988) *The Beginnings of Social Understanding*. Oxford: Blackwell.

Dunne, E. and Bennett, N. (1990) *Talking and Learning in Groups*. London: Routledge.

Dweck, C. S., (1986) Motivational processes affecting learning, *American Psychologist*, October, 1040–6.

Dweck, C. and Bempechat, J. (1983) Children's theories of intelligence: consequences for learning. In S.G. Paris, G.M. Olson and H.W. Stevenson (eds) *Learning and Motivation in the Classroom*. Hillsdale, NJ: Lawrence Erlbaum Associates.

Easen, P. (1985) *Making School-Centred INSET Work*. London: Croom Helm.

EATE (1991) *Student Primary Teachers: Their Economic and Industrial Background, Understanding and Attitudes*. EATE Dissemination Study No 2. Bath: EATE, University of Bath.

Ede, J. and Wilkinson, J. (1980) *Talking, Listening and Learning*. London: Longman.

Educational Resources Information Center (ERIC). United States Department of Education.

Edwards, A. D. and Westgate, D. P. G. (1987) *Investigating Classroom Talk*. London: Falmer.

Edwards, D. and Mercer, N. (1987) *Common Knowledge: The Development of Understanding in Classrooms*. London: Methuen.

Edwards, V. (1983) *Language in the Multicultural Classroom*. London: Batsford.

Edwards, V. and Redfern, A. (1988) *Parental Participation in Primary Education*. London: Routledge.

Egan, K. (1979) *Educational Development*. Oxford: Oxford University Press.

Egan, K. (1991a) *Romantic Understanding*. London: Routledge.

Egan, K. (1991b) *Primary Understanding*. London: Routledge.

Egan, M. and Bunting, B. (1991) The effects of coaching on 11+ scores, *British Journal of Eductional Psychology*, **61** (1), 85–91.

Eisner, E. W. (1979) *The Educational Imagination*. New York: Macmillan.

Eisner, E. W. (1985) *The Art of Educational Evaluation*. London: Falmer.

Eisner, E. W. and Vallance, E. (eds) (1974) *Competing Conceptions of the Curriculum*. Berkeley CA: McCutchan.

Eke, R. and Croll, P. (1992) Television formats and children's classifications of their viewing, *Journal of Educational Television*, **18** (1–2), 97–105.

Elbaz, F.(1983) *Teacher Thinking: A Study of Practical Knowledge*. London: Croom Helm.

Elliot, J., Menter, I., Mortimore, T., Newman, E., Pollard, A., Triggs, P., White, E. and Woodruffe, B. (1991) *Equal Opportunities*. Bristol: University of the West of England.

Elliott, J. (1991a) A model of professionalism and its implications for teacher education, *British Educational Research Journal*, **17** (4), 309–18.

Elliott, J. (1991b) *Action Research for Education Change*. Buckingham: Open University Press.

Elliott, J. and Adelman, C. (1973) Reflecting where the action is; the design of the Ford Teaching Project, *Education for Teaching*, **9** (2), 8–20.

Elliott, M. (ed.) (1992) *Bullying: A Practical Guide to Coping for Schools*. London: Longman.

Ely, M. (1990) *Doing Qualitative Research: Circles within Circles*. London: Falmer.

Entwistle, N. (1981) *Styles of Learning and Teaching*. London: Wiley.

Entwistle, N. (ed.) (1985) *New Directions in Educational Psychology: Learning and Teaching*. London: Falmer.

Entwistle, N. (1987) *Understanding Classroom Learning*. London: Hodder and Stoughton.

Epstein, D. (1993) *Changing Classroom Cultures: Anti-Racism, Politics and Schools*. Stoke-on-Trent: Trentham Books.

Ernest, P. (1991a) *The Philosophy of Mathematics Education*. London: Falmer.

Ernest, P. (1991b) Does the National Curriculum in mathematics need revising?, British Educational Research Association, *Research Intelligence*, Autumn, 49–50.

Etzioni, A. (1966) *A Comparative Analysis of Complex Organisations*. New York: Free Press of Glencoe.

European Convention on Human Rights, Strasbourg: Council of Europe.

Evans, J., Lunt, I. and Wedell, K. (1992) *Special Needs and the 1988 Act*. London: Cassell.

Evans, K. M. (1962) *Sociometry and Education*. London: Routledge & Kegan Paul.

Evans, T. (1988) *A Gender Agenda: A Sociological Study of Teachers, Parents and Pupils in their Primary Schools*. Sydney: Allen and Unwin.

Evetts, J. (1990) *Women in Primary Teaching: Career, Contexts and Strategy*. London: Routledge.

Eysenck, H. J. and Cookson, D. (1969) Personality in primary school children, I: Ability and achievement, *British Journal of Educational Psychology*, **39**, 109–22.

Farmer, A., Cowin, M., Freeman, L., James, M., Drent, A. and Arthur, R. (1991) *Positive School Discipline: A Practical Guide to Developing Policy*. London: Longman.

Farnham-Diggory, S. (1990) *Schooling*. Cambridge, MA: Harvard University Press.

Feuerstein, R. (1979) *The Dynamic Assessment of Retarded Performance*. Baltimore, MD: University Park Press.

Filer, A. (1993) Contexts of assessment in a primary classroom, *British Educational Research Journal*, **19** (1), 95–108.

Finch, J. (1986) *Research and Policy*. London: Falmer Press.

Fine, G. A. and Sandstrom, K. L. (1988) *Knowing Children: Participant Observations with Minors*. New York: Sage.

Fink, A. and Kosecoff, J. (1986) *How to Conduct Surveys: A Step by Step Guide*. London: Sage.

Fisher, R. (1990) *Teaching Children to Think*. Oxford: Blackwell.

Fisher, S. and Hicks, D. (1985) *World Studies 8–13: A Teacher's Handbook*. Edinburgh: Oliver and Boyd.

Flanders, N. (1970) *Analysing Teaching Behavior*. Reading, MA: Addison-Wesley.

Flavell, J. H. (1970) Developmental studies of mediated memory. In H. W Reese and L. P. Lipsett (eds) *Advances in Child Development and Behavior*. New York: Academic Press.

Fontana, D. (1986) *Classroom Control: Understanding and Guiding Classroom Behaviour*. London: Routledge.

Fontana, D. (1988) *Psychology for Teachers*. London: Macmillan.

Foucault, M. (1977) *Discipline and Punish*. London: Peregrine Books.

Franklin, B. (ed.) (1986) *The Rights of Children*. Oxford: Blackwell.

Franklin, B and Hammarberg, T (1995) *The Handbook of Children's Rights: Comparative Legislation and Practice*. London: Routledge.

Fraser, B. J. (1986) *Classroom Environment*. London: Croom Helm.

Fraser, B. J. and Fisher, D. L. (1984) *Assessment of Classroom Psychosocial Environment: Workshop Manual*. Bentley: Western Australia Institute of Technology.

Fraser, B. J. and Walberg, H. J. (eds) (1991) *Educational Environments: Evaluation, Antecedents and Consequences*. Oxford: Pergamon Press.

Freeman, J. (1991) *Gifted Children Growing Up*. London: Cassell.

Freeman, P. L. (1986) Don't talk to me about lexical meta-analysis of criterion-referenced clustering and lap-dissolve spatial transformations: a consideration of the role of practising teachers in educational research, *British Education Research Journal*, **12** (2), 197–206.

Fullan, M. (1982) *The New Meaning of Educational Change*. London: Cassell.

Fullan, M. and Hargreaves, A. (1992) *What's Worth Fighting for in Your School? Working Together for School Improvement*. Buckingham: Open University Press.

Furlong, J. and Maynard, T. (1995) *Mentoring Student Teachers: The Growth of Professional Knowledge*. London: Routledge.

Gagné, R. M. (1965) *The Conditions of Learning*. New York: Holt, Rinehart & Winston.

Galton, M. (1989) *Teaching in the Primary School*. London: David Fulton.

Galton, M. and Blyth, A. (1989) *Handbook of Primary Education in Europe*. London: David Fulton.

Galton, M. and Williamson, J. (1992) *Groupwork in the Primary Classroom*. London: Routledge.

Galton, M., Simon, B. and Croll, P. (1980) *Inside the Primary Classroom*. London: Routledge & Kegan Paul.

Gamble, A. (1986) The political economy of freedom. In R. Levitas (ed.) *The Ideology of the New Right*. Oxford: Polity Press.

Gardner, H. (1985) *Frames of Mind: The Theory of Multiple Intelligences*. London: Paladin Books.

Garvey, C. (1990) *Play*. Cambridge, MA: Harvard University Press.

Giddens, A. (1989) *Sociology*. Oxford: Polity Press.

Giddens, A. (1991) *Modernity and Self-Identity*. Cambridge: Polity Press.

Giles, R.H. (1977) *The West Indian Experience in British Schools*. London: Heinemann.

Ginsberg, H. and Opper, S. (1969) *Piaget's Theory of Intellectual Development*. New York: Prentice Hall.

Gipps, C. (1990) *Assessment: A Teachers' Guide to the Issues*. London: Hodder and Stoughton.

Gipps, C. and Murphy, P. (1994) *A Fair Test? Assessment, Achievement and Equity*. Buckingham: Open University Press.

Gipps, C., Brown, M., McCallum, B. and McAlister, S. (1995) *Intuition or Evidence?* Buckingham: Open University Press.

Gipps, C., McCallum, B., McAllister, S. and Brown, M. (1991) National assessment at seven: some emerging themes. In C. Gipps (ed.) *Developing Assessment for the National Curriculum*. Bedford Way Series. London: Kogan Page.

Gipps, C., Steadman, S. Blackstone, T. and Stierer, B. (1983) *Testing Children: Standardised Testing in LEAs and Schools*. London: Heinemann.

Glaser, B and Strauss, A. (1967) *The Discovery of Grounded Theory*. Chicago: Aldine.

Glass, G. V. (1982) *School Class Size: Research and Policy*. Beverly Hills, CA: Sage.

Glass, G. V., Cahan, L. S., Smith, M. and Filby, N. (1979) *School Class Size, Research and Policy*. Beverly Hills: Sage.

Goffman, E. (1959) *The Presentation of Self in Everyday Life*. Garden City: Doubleday.

Goldthorpe, J.H. (1987) *Social Mobility and Class Structure in Modern Britain*. Oxford: Oxford University Press.

Golombok, S. and Fivush, R. (1994) *Gender development*. Cambridge: Cambridge University Press.

Good, T. and Brophy, J. (1978) *Looking in Classrooms*. New York: Harper & Row.

Goodman, E. (1952) *Race Awareness in Young Children*. New York: Collier

Goodnow, J. and Burns, A. (1985) *Home and School: A Child's Eye View*. Sydney: Allen & Unwin.

Government Statistical Service (1991) *Social Trends*. London: HMSO.

Grace, G. (1978) *Teachers, Ideology and Control*. London: Routledge & Kegan Paul.

Grace, G. (1985) Judging teachers; the social and political contexts of teacher evaluation, *British Journal of Sociology of Education*, 6 (1), 3–16.

Grace, G. (1995) *School Leadership: Beyond Education Management*. London: Falmer Press.

Graddul, D., Cheshire, J. and Swann, J. (1987) *Describing Language*. Milton Keynes: Open University Press.

Graham, D. (1992) *A Lesson for Us All: The Making of the National Curriculum*. London: Routledge.

Gramsci, A. (1978) *Selections from Political Writings*. Vols 1 and 2, London: Lawrence and Wishart.

Grant, D. (1989) *Learning Relations*. London: Routledge.

Grant, G. A. (ed.) (1984) *Preparing for Reflective Thinking*. Boston: Allyn & Bacon.

Gray, J. and Sime, N. (1989) Findings from the national survey of teachers in England and Wales. In DES/WO *Discipline in Schools*. Report of the Committee of Enquiry chaired by Lord Elton. London: DES.

Green, A. (1990) *Education and State Formation*. London: Macmillan.

Grieve, R. and Hughes, M. (1990) *Understanding Children*. Oxford: Blackwell.

Griffiths, M. and Davies, C. (1995) *In Fairness to Children*. London: David Fulton.

Gross, M. (1992) *Exceptionally Gifted Children*. London: Routledge.

Grugeon, E. and Woods, P. (1990) *Educating All: Multicultural Perspectives in the Primary School*. London: Routledge.

Gunning, D., Gunning, S., and Wilson, J. (1981) *Topic Teaching in the Primary School*. London: Croom Helm.

Gunter, B. and McAleer, J. L. (1990) *Children and Television: The One Eyed Monster?* London: Routledge.

Haigh, G. (1990) *Classroom Problems in the Primary School*. London: Paul Chapman.

Hall, G. (ed.) (1992) *Themes and Dimensions of the National Curriculum: Implications for Policy and Practice*. London: Kogan Page.

Halsey, A. H. (1986) *Change in British Society*. Oxford: Oxford University Press.

Halsey, A. H., Heath, A. F. and Ridge, J. M. (1980) *Origins and Destinations*. Oxford: Oxford University Press.

Hamilton, D. (1977) *In Search of Structure*. Edinburgh: Scottish Council for Research in Education.

Hammersley, M. (1986) *Controversies in Classroom Research*. Milton Keynes: Open University Press.

Hammersley, M. and Atkinson, P. (1983) *Ethnography: Principles in Practice*. London: Tavistock.

Hampson, S. E. (1988) *The Construction of Personality: An Introduction*. London: Routledge.

Harding, L. and Beech, J. (1991) *Educational Assessment of the Primary School Child*. London: Routledge.

Hargreaves, A. (1978) The significance of classroom coping strategies. In L. Barton and R. Meighan (eds) *Sociological Interpretations of Schooling and Classrooms*. Driffield: Nafferton.

Hargreaves, A. (1989) *Curriculum and Assessment Reform*. Milton Keynes: Open University Press.

Hargreaves, A. (1992) Cultures of teaching. In A. Hargreaves and M. G. Fullan (eds) *Understanding Teacher Development*. London: Cassell.

Hargreaves, A. and Fullan, M. G. (eds) (1992) *Understanding Teacher Development*. London: Cassell.

Hargreaves, D. H. (1967) *Social Relations in a Secondary School*. London: Routledge & Kegan Paul.

Hargreaves, D. H. (1972) *Interpersonal Relationships and Education*. London: Routledge & Kegan Paul.

Hargreaves, D. H. and Hopkins, D. (1991) *The Empowered School: The Management and Practice of Development Planning*. London: Cassell.

Hargreaves, D. H. *et al.*, (1989) *Planning for School Development*. London: DES.

Hargreaves, D. H., Hestor, S. K. and Mellor, F. J. (1975) *Deviance in Classrooms*. London: Routledge & Kegan Paul.

Harlen, W. (1985) *Primary Science: Taking the Plunge*. London: Heinemann.

Harlen, W., Gipps, C., Broadfoot, P. and Nuttall, D. (1992) Assessment and the improvement of education, *Curriculum Journal*, 3 (3), 217–25.

Harnett, A., Carr, W. and Naish, M. (1992) *Understanding the National Curriculum*. London: Cassell.

Harré, R. (1974) Rule as a scientific concept. In T. Mischel (ed.) *Understanding Other Persons*. Oxford: Blackwell.

Hartley, D. (1985) *Understanding the Primary School*. London: Croom Helm.

Hartley, D. (1992) *Understanding the Nursery School*. London: Cassell.

Hartnett. A (ed.)(1982) *The Social Sciences in Educational Studies: A Selective Guide to the Literature*. London: Heinemann.

Haviland, J. (1988) *Take Care, Mr Baker!* London: Fourth Estate.

Heads Legal Guide. London: Croner Publications.

Heller, H. and Edwards, P. (1992) *Policy and Power in Education: The Rise and Fall of the LEA*. London: Routledge.

Henry, M., Taylor, S., Knight, J. and Lingard, R. (1990) *Understanding Schooling*. London: Routledge.

Her Majesty's Inspectors (1978) *Primary Education in England*. London: HMSO.

Her Majesty's Chief Inspector of Schools (1995) *Standards and Quality in Education 1993/94*. London: HMSO.

Her Majesty's Senior Chief Inspector of Schools (1991) *Standards in Education. 1989–90: Annual Report*. London: HMI/DES.

Her Majesty's Senior Chief Inspector of Schools (1992) *Education in England. 1990–91: Annual Report*. London: HMI/DES.

Hewton. E. (1986) *Education in Recession: Crisis in County Hall and Classroom*. London: Allen and Unwin.

Hextall, I., Lawn, M., Menter, I., Sidgwick, S. and Walker, S. (1991) Imaginative projects: arguments for a new teacher education, *Evaluation and Research in Education*, 5 (1) and (2) 79–95.

Hillgate Group (1986) *Whose Schools? A Radical Manifesto*. London: Hillgate Group.

Hillgate Group (1987) *The Reform of British Education*. London: Hillgate Group.

Hilsum, S. and Cane, B. S (1970) *The Teacher's Day*. Slough: NFER.

Hirst, P. H. (1965) Liberal education and the nature of knowledge. In R. Archambault (ed.) *Philosophical Analysis and Education*. London: Routledge & Kegan Paul.

Hirst, P. H. and Peters, R. S. (1970) *The Logic of Education*. London: Routledge & Kegan Paul.

Hitchcock, G. (1986) *Profiles and Profiling*. London: Longman.

Hitchcock, G. and Hughes, D. (1995) *Research and the Teacher: A Qualitative Introduction to School-Based Research* (2nd edn). London: Routledge.

Hodgson, N. (1988) *Classroom Display*. Diss: Tarquin Publications.

Hohmann, M., Banet, B. and Weikart, D. (1979) *Young Children in Action*. Ypsilanti, MI: High Scope Educational Research Foundation.

Holden, C. and Smith, L. (1992) Economic and industrial understanding in primary education: problems and possibilities, *Education and Training*, 34 (3), 11–14.

Holt, J. (1967) *How Children Learn*. London: Penguin.

Holt, J. (1982) *How Children Fail*. London: Penguin.

Hook, C. (1981) *Studying Classrooms*. Victoria: Deakin University Press.

Hopkins, D. (1986) *A Teacher's Guide to Classroom Research*. Milton Keynes: Open University Press.

Hopkins, D. (1987) *Improving the Quality of Schooling: Lessons from the OECD International School Improvement Project*. London: Falmer.

Hopkins, D. and Bollington, R. (1989) Teacher appraisal for professional development: a review of research, *Cambridge Journal of Education*, **19** (2), 163–82.

House of Commons, Select Committee on Education, Science and the Arts (1986) *Achievement in Primary Schools*. London: HMSO.

Howe, M. J. A. (1990) *The Origins of Exceptional Abilities*. Oxford: Blackwell.

Howe, M. J. A. (1991) Review of Richardson, K. 1991, 'Understanding Intelligence', *British Journal of Educational Psychology*, **61** (3), 382–3.

Hughes, M, Wikeley, F. and Nash, T. (1990) Parents and the National Curriculum: An Interim Report. Mimeo. University of Exeter.

Hughes, M., Wikeley, F. and Nash, T. (1991) Parents and SATs: A Second Interim Report: Mimeo. University of Exeter.

Hughes, M., Wikeley, F. and Nash, T. (1994) *Parents and Their Children's Schools*. Oxford: Blackwell.

Humphreys, T. (1995) *A Different Kind of Teacher*. London: Cassell

Humphries, S. (1982) *Hooligans or Rebels?* Oxford: Blackwell.

Hunter, R. and Scheirer, E. A. (1988) *The Organic Curriculum: Organizing for Learning 7–12*. London: Falmer Press.

Hurst, V. (1992) *Planning for Early Learning: The First Five Years*. London: Paul Chapman.

Husen, T., Tuijnman, A. and Halls, W. D. (eds) (1992) *Schooling in Modern European Society*. London: Pergamon.

Hustler, D., Cassidy, T. and Cuff, T. (eds) (1986) *Action Research in Schools and Classrooms*. London: Allen & Unwin.

Hustler, D. and McIntyre, D (1996) *Developing Competent Teachers: Approaches to Professional Competence in Teacher Education*. London: David Fulton

Hutton, W. (1995) *The State We're In*. London: Jonathan Cape.

Ingram, J. and Worrall, N. (1993) *Teacher–Child Partnership: The Negotiating Classroom*. London: David Fulton

Inman, S. and Buck, M. (1995) *Adding Value: Schools' Responsibility for Pupils' Personal Development*. Stoke: Trentham Books

Inner London Education Authority (1987) *Language Courses*. London: ILEA Research and Statistics.

Institute for Fiscal Studies (1995) *Low Income Statistics: Low Income Families 1989–92*. London: HMSO.

Jackson, B. (1964) *Streaming: An Education System in Miniature*. London: Routledge & Kegan Paul.

Jackson, M. (1993) *Literacy*. London: David Fulton.

Jackson, P. W. (1968) *Life in Classrooms*. New York: Holt, Rinehart & Winston.

James, A. and Prout, A. (eds) (1990) *Constructing and Reconstructing Childhood: Contemporary Issues in the Sociological Study of Childhood*. London: Falmer.

Jencks, C. *et al.,* (1972) *Inequality: A Reassessment of the Effect of Family and Schooling in America*. New York: Basic Books.

Johnson, D. (1990) *Parental Choice in Education*. London: Routledge.

Johnson, G., Hill, B. and Tunstall, P. (1992) *Primary Records of Achievement*. London: Hodder and Stoughton.

Johnson, P. (1992) Assessing the links, *Junior Education*. October.

Jones, B. (1986) Politics and the pupil, *Times Educational Supplement*, 30 May.

Jones, K. and Charlton, T. (1992) *Learning Difficulties in the Primary Classroom*. London: Routledge.

Joseph Rowntree Foundation (1995) *Inquiry into Income and Wealth*. York: JRF.

Jowett, S. and Baginsky, M. (1991) *Building Bridges: Parental Involvement in Schools*. London: Routledge.

Kagan, J. and Kogan, N. (1970) Individual variation in cognitive processes. In P. Mussel (ed.) *Carmichael's Manual of Child Psychology* (3rd edn). New York: Wiley.

Kagan, J. *et al.*, (1964) Information processing in the child: significance and reflective attitudes, *Psychological Monographs*, 78.

Kay-Shuttleworth, J. (1868) *Memorandum on Popular Education* (1969 edn). London: Woburn Books.

Keel, P. (1987) An outline of multicultural educational development in an area of North-east England. In T. S Chivers (ed.) *Race and Culture in England*. Windsor: NFER-Nelson.

Kegan, R. (1982) *The Evolving Self: Problem and Process in Human Development*. London: Harvard University Press.

Kellmer-Pringle, M, (1974) *The Needs of Children*. London: Hutchinson.

Kelly, A.V. (1986) *Knowledge and the Curriculum*. London: Harper & Row.

Kelly-Byrne, D. (1989) *A Child's Play Life: An Ethnographic Study*. New York: Teachers' College Press.

Kemmis, S. and McTaggert, R. (1981) *The Action Research Planner*. Victoria: Deakin University.

Kerry, T. (1982) *Effective Questioning*. London: Macmillan.

Kerry, T. and Eggleston, J. (1988) *Topic Work in the Primary School*. London: Routledge.

Kerry, T. and Sands, M. K. (1982) *Handling Classroom Groups*. London: Macmillan.

King, R. (1978) *All Things Bright and Beautiful*. Chichester: Wiley.

King, R. (1989) *The Best of Primary Education? A Sociological Study of Junior Middle Schools*. London: Falmer.

Kingdom, J. (1991) *Government and Politics in Britain*. Cambridge: Polity Press.

Klemp, G. O. (1977) *Three Factors of Success in the World of Work*. Boston: McBer & Co.

Kline, P. (1991) *Intelligence: The Psychometric View*. London: Routledge.

Kogan, M. (1978) *The Politics of Educational Change*. London: Fontana.

Kogan, M., Johnson, D., Packwood, T. and Whitaker, T. (1984) *School Governing Bodies*. London: Heinemann.

Kohl, H. (1986) *On Becoming a Teacher*. London: Methuen.

Kounin, J. S. (1970) *Discipline and Group Management in Classrooms*. New York: Holt, Rhinehart & Winston.

Labour Party (1994) *Opening Doors to a Learning Society*. London: Labour Party

Labour Party (1995) *Excellence for Everyone: Labour's Crusade to Raise Standards*. London: Labour Party.

Labov, W. (1973) The logic of non-standard English. In N. Keddie (ed.) *Tinker. Tailor .... the Myth of Cultural Deprivation*. Harmondsworth: Penguin.

Lacey. C. (1970) *Hightown Grammar*. Manchester: Manchester University Press.

Lang. P. (ed.) (1988) *Thinking About Personal and Social Education in the Primary School*. Oxford: Blackwell.

Lang, R. (1986) *Developing Parental Involvement in Primary Schools*. London: Macmillan.

Lareau, A. (1989) *Home Advantage: Social Class and Parental Intervention in Elementary Education*. London: Falmer.

Laslett, R. and Smith, C. (1992) *Effective Classroom Management: A Teacher's Guide*. London: Routledge.

Lawlor, S. (1988) *Correct Core: Simple Curricula for English, Maths and Science*. Policy Study No. 93, London: Centre for Policy Studies.

Lawn, M. and Grace, G. (eds) (1987) *Teachers: The Culture and Politics of Work*. London: Falmer.

Lawn, M. and Ozga, J. (1981) The educational worker: a reassessment of teachers. In J. Ozga (ed.) *Schoolwork: Approaches to the Labour Process of Teaching*. Milton Keynes: Open University Press.

Lawrence, D. (1987) *Enhancing Self-Esteem in the Classroom*. London: Paul Chapman.

Lawson, H. (1992) *Practical Record Keeping for Special Schools*. London: David Fulton.

Lawton, D. (1975) *Class, Culture and the Curriculum*. London: Routledge & Kegan Paul.

Lawton, D. (1977) *Education and Social Justice*. Beverly Hills: Sage.

Lawton, D. (1980) *The Politics of the School Curriculum*. London: Routledge & Kegan Paul.

Lee, V. (ed.) (1990) *Children's Learning in School: Behaviourism, Piaget and Vygotsky*. London: Hodder and Stoughton.

Levine, J. (ed.) (1990) *Bilingual Learners and the Mainstream Curriculum*. London: Falmer.

Lewin, K. (1946) Action research and minority problems, *Journal of Social Issues*, **2**, 34–6.

Lewis, A. (1991) *Primary Special Needs and the National Curriculum*. London: Routledge.

Light, P. and Butterworth, G. (eds) (1992) *Context and Cognition: Ways of Learning and Knowing*. Hemel Hempstead: Harvester Wheatsheaf.

Light, P., Sheldon, S. and Woodhead, M. (1991) *Learning to Think*. London: Routledge.

Lindsay, G. (1991) The assessment of cognitive abilities. In L. Harding and J. R. Beech (eds) *Educational Assessment of the Primary School Child*. Windsor: NFER-Nelson.

Linguistic Minorities Project (1985) *The Other Languages of England*. London: Routledge & Kegan Paul.

Lloyd, B. and Duveen, G. (1992) *Gender Identities and Education: The Impact of Starting School*. London: Harvester Wheatsheaf.

Lobban,G. (1975) Sex roles in reading schemes, *Forum*, **16** (2), 57–60.

Lubeck, S. (1985) *Sandbox Society*. London: Falmer Press.

Lyseight-Jones, P. (1985) *Human Rights Education in Primary Schools*. Report of Council of Europe Teachers' Seminar No. 28, Donaueschingen, Strasbourg: Council of Europe.

McCallum, B., McAlister, S., Brown, M. and Gipps, C. (1992) Teacher assessment at Key Stage One, *Research Papers in Education*, 8 (3), 308–18.

McClelland (1963) The achievement motive in economic growth. In B. F. Hoselitz and W. E. Moore (eds) *Industrialisation and Society*. The Hague: UNESCO.

MacGilchrist, B., Mortimore, P., Savage, J. and Beresford, C. (1995) *Planning Matters: The Impact of Development Planning in Primary Schools*. London: Paul Chapman.

McIntyre, D. and Hagger, H. (1996) *Mentors in Schools: Developing the Profession of Teaching*. London: David Fulton

MacLure, M. and Elliott, J. (1993) Packaging the primary curriculum: textbooks and the English national curriculum, *The Curriculum Journal*, 4 (1), 91–115.

MacLure, M., Phillips, T. and Wilkinson, A. (1988) *Oracy Matters: The Development of Talking and Listening in Education*. Milton Keynes: Open University Press.

McManus, M. (1989) *Troublesome Behaviour in the Classroom: A Teacher's Survival Guide*. London: Routledge.

McMullen, H. (1992) *Assessment in the Primary School*. London: Cassell.

McNamara, D. (1994) *Classroom Pedagogy and Primary Practice*. London: Routledge.

McNamara, D. and Desforges, C. (1978) The social sciences, teacher education and the objectification of craft knowledge, *British Journal of Teacher Education*, 4 (1), 17–36.

McNamara, S. and Moreton, G. (1995) *Changing Behaviour: Teaching Children with Emotional and Behavioural Difficulties in Primary and Secondary Classrooms*. London: David Fulton.

McNay, I. and Ozga, J. (1985) *Policy Making in Education*. Oxford: Pergamon.

McNiff, J. (1988) *Action Research: Principles and Practice*. London: Routledge.

McNiff, J. (1992) *Teachers as Learners*. London: Routledge.

McPherson, A and Raab, C. D (1988) *Governing Education: A Sociology of Policy since 1945*. Edinburgh: Edinburgh University Press.

Maines, B. (1991) *Challenging Behaviour in the Primary School: A School Development Programme*. Bristol: Redland Centre for Professional Development, University of the West of England.

Major, J. (1991) Education – all our futures. Speech to the Centre for Policy Studies, Café Royal, London, 3 July.

Makins, V. (1969) Child's eye view of teachers, *Times Educational Supplement*, 19 and 26 September.

Mangan, J. A (ed.) (1993) *The Imperial Curriculum: Racial Images and Education in the British Colonial Experience*. London: Routledge.

Marks, J. (1992) *Value for Money in Education*. York: Campaign for Real Education.

Marks, J. and Pomian-Srzednicki, M. (1985) *Standards in English Schools: Second Report*. London: National Council for Educational Standards.

Marriott, S. (1985) *Primary Education and Society*. London: Falmer.

Marsh, L. (1970) *Alongside the Child*. London: Black.

Maslow, A. H. (1954) *Motivation and Personality*. New York: Harper & Row.

Massey, I. (1991) *More Than Skin Deep: Developing Multicultural Education in Schools*. London: Hodder and Stoughton.

Mayall, B. (1994) *Negotiating Health: Children at Home and Primary School*. London: Cassell.

Maylor, U. (1995) Identity, migration and education. In M. Blair and J. Holland (eds) *Identity and Diversity*. Clevedon: Multilingual Matters.

Mead, G. H. (1934) *Mind, Self and Society*. Chicago: University of Chicago.

Meadows, S. (1992) *Children's Cognitive Development: The Development and Acquisition of Cognition in Childhood*. London: Routledge.

Meighan, R. (1978) *A Sociology of Education*. London: Holt, Rinehart & Winston.

Meighan, R. (1981) *The Sociology of Educating*. London: Holt, Rinehart & Winston.

Menter, I. (1989) Teaching practice stasis: racism, sexism and school experience in initial teacher education, *British Journal of Sociology of Education*, 10 (4), 459–73.

Menter, I., Muschamp, Y. and Pollard, A., with Nicholls, P. and Ozga, J. (1995) The primary market place: a study of small service providers in an English city. Mimeo, presented to the American Educational Research Association, San Francisco.

Menter, I. Muschamp, Y., Nicholls, P. and Ozga, J. with Pollard, A. (1996) *Work and Identity in the Primary School: A Post-Fordist Analysis*. Buckingham: Open University Press.

Mercer, N. (1992) Culture, context and the appropriation of knowledge. In P. Light and G. Butterworth (eds) *Context and Cognition: Ways of Learning and Knowing*. Hemel Hempstead: Harvester Wheatsheaf.

Merrett, F. (1993) *Encouragement Works Best: Positive Approaches to Classroom Management*. London: David Fulton.

Merrett, F. and Wheldall, K. (1990) *Identifying Troublesome Classroom Behaviour*. London: Paul Chapman.

Merttens, R. and Vass, J. (1990) *How to Plan and Assess the National Curriculum in the Primary Classroom*. London: Heinemann.

Messenger Davies, M. (1989) *Television is Good for your Kids*. London: Hilary Shipman.

Meyer, J. W. and Kamens, D. H. (1992) Conclusion: accounting for a world curriculum. In J. W. Meyer, D. H. Kamens and A. Benavot with Y. K. Cha and S. Y. Wong (eds) *School Knowledge for the Masses: World Models and National Primary Curricular Categories in the Twentieth Century*. London: Falmer.

Meyer, J. W., Kamens, D. H. and Benavot, A. (1992) *School Knowledge for the Masses: World Models of National Primary Curricular Categories in the Twentieth Century*. London: Falmer.

Miles, T. and Miles, E. (1990) *Dyslexia: A Hundred Years On*. Buckingham: Open University Press.

Miliband, R. (1991) *Divided Societies*. Oxford: Oxford University Press.

Miller, J. (1983) *Many Voices: Bilingualism, Culture and Education*. London: Routledge.

Mills, C. W. (1959) *The Sociological Imagination*. New York: Oxford University Press.

Mills, J. and Mills, R. (1995) *Primary School People: Getting to Know Your Colleagues*. London: Routledge.

Moos, R. H. (1979) *Evaluating Educational Environments: Procedures, Measures, Findings and Policy Implications*. San Francisco: Jossey-Bass.

Mortimore, P. and Mortimore, J. (1992) *The Primary Head: Roles, Responsibilities and Reflections*. London: Paul Chapman.

Mortimore, P., Sammons, P., Stoll, L., Lewis, D. and Ecob, R. (1986) *Report of The Junior School Project*. London: Inner London Education Authority.

Mortimore, P., Sammons, P., Stoll, L., Lewis, D. and Ecob, R. (1988) *School Matters: The Junior Years*. Wells: Open Books.

Moyles, J. R. (1989) *The Role and Status of Play in Early Childhood*. Buckingham: Open University Press.

Moyles, J. R. (1992) *Organising for Learning in the Primary Classroom: A Balanced Approach to Classroom Organisation*. Buckingham: Open University Press.

Moyles, J. R. (ed) (1994) *The Excellence of Play*. Buckingham, Open University Press.

Munn, P., Johnstone, M. and Chalmers, V. (1992) *Effective Discipline in Primary Schools and Classrooms*. London: Paul Chapman.

Murgatroyd, S. and Morgan, C. (1992) *Total Quality Management and the School*. Buckingham: Open University Press.

Murphy, P., and Moon, B. (eds) (1989) *Developments in Learning and Assessment*. London: Hodder and Stoughton.

Murphy, P., Selijnger, M., Bourne, J. and Briggs, M. (eds) (1995) *Subject Learning in the Primary Curriculum*. London: Routledge.

Muschamp, Y. (1991) Pupil Self Assessment. *Practical Issues in Primary Education*, No 9. Bristol: National Primary Centre (South West).

Muschamp, Y., Pollard, A. and Sharpe, R. (1992) Curriculum management in primary schools, *The Curriculum Journal*, 3 (1), 21–39.

Myers, K. (1992) *Genderwatch*. Cambridge: Cambridge University Press.

Nash, R. (1976) *Teacher Expectations and Pupil Learning*. London: Routledge & Kegan Paul.

National Children's Homes (1991) *Poverty and Nutrition Survey*. London: National Children's Homes.

National Commission on Education/Paul Hamlyn Foundation (1993) *Learning to Succeed: A Radical Look at Education Today and A Strategy for the Future*. London: Reed Consumer Books.

National Commission on Education (1995) *Success Against the Odds*. London: Routledge.

National Curriculum Council (1989a) *A Framework for the Primary Curriculum*. Curriculum Guidance 1. York: National Curriculum Council.

National Curriculum Council (1989b) *A Curriculum for All*. Curriculum Guidance 2. York: NCC.

National Curriculum Council (1990a) *The Whole Curriculum*. Curriculum Guidance 3. York: NCC.

National Curriculum Council (1990b) *Education for Economic and Industrial Understanding*. Curriculum Guidance 4. York: NCC.

National Curriculum Council (1991) *Managing Economic and Industrial Understanding in Schools*. York: NCC.

National Curriculum Council (1992) *Starting Out with the National Curriculum*. York: NCC.

National Curriculum Council (1993a) *School Teacher Appraisal: A National Framework*. London: HMSO.

National Curriculum Council (1993b) *The National Curriculum at Key Stages 1 and 2*. Advice to the Secretary of State for Education, January.

National Curriculum Council and National Oracy Project (1991) *Assessing Talk in Key Stages One and Two*. Occasional Papers in Oracy, No 5. York: NCC/National Oracy Project.

National Primary Centre (South West) (1991a) *Constructive Teacher Assessment: Progression in Children's Understanding*. PIPE No 6. Bristol: NPC (SW).

National Primary Centre (South West) (1991b) *Strategies for Classroom Assessment*. INSET Pack. Bristol: National Primary Centre (SW).

National Primary Centre (South West) (1991c) Pupil Self Assessment. *Practical Issues in Primary Education*, No 9. Bristol: NPC (SW).

National Steering Group (1989) *School Teacher Appraisal: A National Framework*. London: HMSO.

National Writing Project (1989a) *A Question of Writing*. Walton-on-Thames: Nelson.

National Writing Project (1989b) *Becoming a Writer*. Walton-on-Thames: Nelson.

National Writing Project (1989c) *Writing and Learning*. Walton-on-Thames: Nelson.

Neave, G. (1992) *The Teaching Nation: Prospects for Teachers in the European Community*. Oxford: Pergamon.

Newell, P. (1991) *The UN Convention and Children's Rights in the UK*. London: National Children's Bureau.

Newman, J. W. (1990) *America's Teachers*. New York: Longman.

Nias, J. (1989a) *Primary Teachers Talking: A Study of Teaching as Work*. London: Routledge.

Nias, J. (1989b) Refining the cultural perspective, *Cambridge Journal of Education*, **19** (2) 143–6.

Nias, J., Southworth, G. and Campbell, P. (1992) *Whole-School Curriculum Development in the Primary School*. London: Falmer.

Nias, J., Southworth, G. and Yeomans, R. (1989) *Staff Relationships in the Primary School: A Study of Organisational Cultures*. London: Cassell.

Nicholls, J. G. (1983) Conceptions of ability and achievement motivation: a theory and its implications for education. In S. G. Paris, G. M. Olson and H. W. Stevenson *Learning and Motivation in the Classroom*. Hillsdale, NJ: Lawrence Erlbaum Associates.

Nightingale, D. (1990) *Local Management of Schools at Work in the Primary School*. London: Falmer.

Nisbet, J. and Shucksmith, J. (1986) *Learning Strategies*. London: Routledge.

Nixon, J. (ed.) (1981) *A Teachers' Guide to Action Research*. London: Grant McIntyre.

Norman, K. (1990) *Teaching, Talking and Learning in Key Stage One*. York: NCC.

Noss, R., Goldstein, H. and Hoyles, C. (1989) Graded assessment learning hierachies in mathematics, *British Educational Research Journal*, **15**, 109–20.

No Turning Back Group of MPs (1986) *Save Our Schools*. London: Conservative Party Centre.

Office for Standards in Education (1993) *Curriculum Organisation and Classroom Practice in Primary Schools: A Follow-up Report*. London: OFSTED.

Office for Standards in Education (1995) *Guidance on the Inspection of Nursery and Primary Schools: The OFSTED Handbook*. London: OFSTED.

O'Hear, A. (1981) *An Introduction to the Philosophy of Education*. London: Routledge.

O'Hear, A. (1991) *Education and Democracy: Against the Educational Establishment*. London: Claridge.

O'Keeffe, D. (1988) A critical look at the National Curriculum and testing: a libertarian view. Paper presented to the American Educational Research Association, New Orleans, April.

Olson, J. (1991) *Understanding Teaching: Beyond Expertise*. Buckingham: Open University Press.

Olweus, D. (1989) *Aggression in the Schools*. New York: Wiley.

Open University (1979) *Research Methods in Education and the Social Sciences*. Course DE304. Buckingham: Open University Press.

Open University (1980) *Curriculum in Action: Practical Classroom Evaluation*. Milton Keynes: Open University Press.

Open University (1992) *Principles of Social and Educational Research*. Course DEH313. Buckingham: Open University Press.

Opie, I. and Opie, P. (1959) *Children's Games in Street and Playground*. Oxford: Oxford University Press.

Orlick, T. (1979) *Cooperative Sports and Games Book: Challenge without Competition*. London: Readers and Writers.

Osborn, A. H., Butler, N. R. and Morris, A. C. (1984) *The Social Life of Britain's Five-Year-Olds*. London: Routledge & Kegan Paul.

Ouston, J., Earley, P. and Fidler, B. (1996) *OFSTED Inspections: The Early Experience*. London: David Fulton.

Paley, V. G. (1981) *Wally's Stories*. Cambridge, MA: Harvard University Press.

Paley, V. G. (1990) *The Boy Who Would Be a Helicopter*. Cambridge, MA: Harvard University Press.

Parsons, T. (1951) *The Social System*. London: Routledge & Kegan Paul.

Parsons, T. (1959) The school class as a social system, *Harvard Educational Review*, **29**, 297–318.

Pask, G. (1976) Styles and strategies of learning, *British Journal of Educational Psychology*, **46**, 128–48.

Pate-Bain, H., Achilles, C., Boyd-Zaharias, J. and McKenna, B. (1992) Class size does make a difference, *Phi Delta Kappan*, November, 253–5.

Pattanayak, D. P. (1991) Forward. In S. Alladina and V. Edwards (eds) *Multilingualism in the British Isles*. Vol. 1. London: Longman.

Perera, K. (1987) *Understanding Language*. London: National Association of Advisers in English.

Perrot, E. (1982) *Effective Teaching: A Teaching Guide to Improving Your Teaching*. London: Longman.

Peters, R. S. (1966) *Ethics and Education*. London: Allen & Unwin.

Phelps, R. (1969) *Display in the Classroom*. Oxford: Blackwell.

Phillips, T. (1985) Beyond lip service: discourse development after the age of nine. In G. Wells and J. Nicholls, (eds) *Language and Learning: An Interactional Perspective*. London: Falmer.

Piaget, J. (1926) *The Language and Thought of the Child*. New York: Basic Books.

Piaget, J. (1950) *The Psychology of Intelligence*. London: Routledge & Kegan Paul.

Piaget, J. (1951) *Play, Dreams and Imitation*. New York: Norton.

Piaget, J. (1961) A genetic approach to the psychology of thought, *Journal of Educational Psychology*, **52**. 151–61.

Pinsent, P. (1992) *Language. Culture and Young Children*. London: David Fulton.

Pollard, A. (1980) Teacher interests and changing situations of survival threat in primary school classrooms. In P. Woods (ed.) *Teacher Strategies*. London: Croom Helm.

Pollard, A. (1982) A model of coping strategies, *British Journal of Sociology of Education*, **3** (1), 19–37.

Pollard, A. (1985) *The Social World of the Primary School*. London: Cassell.

Pollard, A. (1987a) Primary school-teachers and their colleagues. In S. Delamont (ed.) *The Primary School Teacher*. London: Falmer.

Pollard, A. (ed.) (1987b) *Children and their Primary Schools: A New Perspective*. London: Falmer.

Pollard, A (1987c) Studying children's perspectives: a collaborative approach. In G. Walford, *Doing Sociology of Education*. London: Falmer.

Pollard, A. (1987d) Social differentiation in primary schools, *Cambridge Journal of Education*, **17** (3), 158–61.

Pollard, A. (1992) Teachers' responses to the reshaping of primary education. In M. Arnot and L. Barton (eds) *Voicing Concerns: Sociological Perspective on Contemporary Education Reforms*. Wallingford: Triangle.

Pollard, A. (1993) Balancing priorities: children and the curriculum in the nineties. In J. Campbell (ed.) *Breadth and Balance in the Primary Curriculum*. London: Falmer.

Pollard, A. (1996) *An Introduction to Primary Education*. London: Cassell.

Pollard, A. with Filer, A. (1996) *The Social World of Children's Learning*. London: Cassell.

Pollard, A. and Filer, A (forthcoming) *The Social World of Pupil Careers*. London: Cassell.

Pollard, A., Thiessen, D. and Filer, A. (eds) (forthcoming) *Children and the Curriculm: The Perspectives of Primary and Elementary School Pupils*. London: Falmer.

Pollard, A., Broadfoot P., Croll P., Osborn, M. and Abbott, D (1994) *Changing English Primary Schools? The Impact of the Education Reform Act at Key Stage One*. London: Cassell.

Popkewitz, T. (ed.) (1993) *Changing Patterns of Power: Social Regulation and Teacher Education Reform in Eight Countries*. New York: State University of New York Press.

Popper, K. R. (1968) *The Logic of Scientific Discovery*. London: Hutchinson.

Pring, R. (1976) Curriculum integration. In R. Hooper (ed.) *The Curriculum; Context, Design and Development*. London: Oliver & Boyd.

Pring, R. (1984) *Personal and Social Education in the Curriculum*. London: Hodder and Stoughton.

Pring, R. (1995) *The New Curriculum* (2nd. edn). London: Cassell.

Prisk, T (1987) Letting them get on with it: a study of unsupervised group talk in an infant school. In A. Pollard (ed.) *Children and their Primary Schools*. London: Falmer.

Proctor, N. (ed.) (1990) *The Aims of Primary Education and the National Curriculum*. London: Falmer.

Prutzman, P., Burger, M. L., Bodenhamer, G. and Stern, L. (1978) *The Friendly Classroom for a Small Planet*. New Jersey: Avery Publishing.

Putnam, J. and Burke, J. B. (1992) *Organising and Managing Classroom Learning Communities*. New York: McGraw Hill.

Quicke, J. (1988) The 'New Right' and education, *British Journal of Educational Studies*, **36** (1), 5–20.

Radical Statistics Education Group (1982) *Reading Between the Numbers: A Critical Guide to Educational Research*. London: BSSRS publications.

Ranson, S. (1992) *The Role of Local Government in Education*. London: Longman.

Reason, R. (1993) Primary special needs and National Curriculum assessment. In S. Wolfendale (ed.) *Assessing Special Educational Needs*. London: Cassell.

Reid, I. (1986) *The Sociology of School and Education*. London: Fontana.

Reid, I. (1989) *Social Class Differences in Britain: Life Chances and Life-Styles*. London: Fontana.

Resnick, L. and Resnick, D. (1991) Assessing the thinking curriculum: new tools for educational reform. In B. Gifford and M. O'Connor (eds) *Future Assessments: Changing Views of Aptitude, Achievement and Instruction*. New York: Kluwer Academic Publishers.

Richards, C. (1991) Children and subjects: a national perspective. Papers of the third annual conference of the Association for the Study of Primary Education, ASPE.

Richards, J. (1979) *Classroom Language: What Sort?* London: George Allen and Unwin.

Richards, M. and Light, P. (1986) *Children of Social Worlds*. Cambridge: Polity Press.

Richardson, K. (1991) *Understanding Intelligence*. Buckingham: Open University Press.

Rieser, R. and Mason, M. (1990) *Disability, Equality in the Classroom: A Human Rights Issue*. London: ILEA.

Rist, R. (1970) Student social class and teacher expectations, *Harvard Education Review*, 40, 411–51.

Ritchie, R. (ed.) (1991) *Profiling in Primary Schools*. London: Cassell.

Roaf, C. and Bines, H. (1989) Needs, rights and opportunities in special education. In C. Roaf and H. Bines (eds) *Needs, Rights and Opportunities*. London: Falmer Press.

Roberts, T. (1983) *Child Management in the Primary School*. London: Allen & Unwin.

Robinson, E. (1983) Meta-cognitive development. In S. Meadows (ed.) *Developing Thinking*. London: Methuen.

Roger, I. A. and Richardson, J. A. S. (1985) *Self-Evaluation for Primary Schools*. London: Hodder and Stoughton.

Rogers, C. (1961) *On Becoming a Person*. London: Constable.

Rogers, C. (1969) *Freedom to Learn*. New York: Merrill.

Rogers, C. (1980) *A Way of Being*. Boston: Houghton Mifflin.

Rogers, C. and Kutnick, P. (1990) *The Social Psychology of the Primary School*. London: Routledge.

Rogoff, B. and Lave, J. (ed.) (1984) *Everyday Cognition: Its Development in Social Context*. London: Harvard University Press.

Romberg, T. A. and Zavinnia, E. A. (1989) *The Influence of Mandated Testing on Mathematical Instruction*. Madison, WI: National Centre for Mathematical Science Foundation, University of Wisconsin.

Rosenberg, M. (1989) *Society and the Adolescent Self-Image*. Connecticut: Wesleyan University Press.

Rosenthal, R. and Jacobsen, L. (1968) *Pygmalion in the Classroom*. New York: Holt, Rinehart & Winston.

Rostow, W. W. (1962) *The Stages of Economic Growth*. Cambridge: Cambridge University Press.

Rottenberg, C. and Smith, M. L. (1990) Unintended effects of external testing in elementary schools. Paper presented to the annual conference of the American Educational Research Association, Boston, April.

Rowland, S. (1984) *The Enquiring Classroom*. London: Falmer.

Rowland, S. (1987) An interpretive model of teaching and learning. In A. Pollard (ed.) *Children and their Primary Schools*. London: Falmer.

Rubin, Z. (1980) *Children's Friendships*. London: Fontana.

Ruddock, J. (1991) *Innovation and Change*. Buckingham: Open University Press.

Runnymede Trust (1993) *Equality Assurance in Schools*. Stoke-on-Trent: Trentham Books.

Rutter, M. and Madge, N. (1976) *Cycles of Disadvantage*. London: Heinemann.

Salmon, P. and Claire, H. (1984) *Classroom Collaboration*. London: Routledge & Kegan Paul.

Sammons, P. and Nuttall, D. (1992) Differential school effectiveness: results from a reanalysis of the ILEA's Junior School Project data. Paper presented at the annual conference of the British Educational Research Association, Stirling, August.

Sammons, P., Lewis, A., MacLure, M., Riley, J., Bennett, N. and Pollard, A. (1994) Teaching and learning processes. In A. Pollard (ed) *Look Before You Leap? Research Evidence for the Curriculum at Key Stage Two*. London: Tufnell Press.

Sayer, J. (1992) *The Future Governance of Education*. London: Cassell.

Schmuck, R. A. (1985) Groupwork. In E. R. Slavin (ed.) *Learning to Cooperate, Cooperating to Learn*. New York: Plenum.

Schön, D. A. (1983) *The Reflective Practitioner: How Professionals Think in Action*. London: Maurice Temple Smith.

School Curriculum and Assessment Authority (1995a) *Annual Report April 1994 – March 1995*. London: SCAA.

School Curriculum and Assessment Authority (1995b) *Planning the Curriculum at Key Stages 1 and 2*. London: SCAA.

School Curriculum and Assessment Authority (1996) *A Guide to the National Curriculum*. London: SCAA.

Schools Council (1983) *Primary Practice, Working Paper 75*. London: Methuen Educational.

Schultz, T. (1961) Investment in human capital, *American Economic Review*, **51**, 1–17.

Scottish Office Education Department (SOED) (1989) *Curriculum and Assessment in Scotland: A Policy for the 90's*. Working Paper 1. Edinburgh: Scottish Office.

Scottish Office Education Department (1992) *Revised Guidelines for Teacher Training Courses*. Scottish Office Education Department: Edinburgh.

Scruton, R. (1986) The myth of cultural relativism. In F. Palmer. *Anti-racism: An Assault on Education and Value*. London: Sherwood.

Secord, P. F. and Backman, C. W. (1964) *Social Psychology*. New York: McGraw Hill.

Sedgwick, F. (1988) *Here Comes the Assembly Man*. London: Falmer.

Serbin, L.A., Powlishta K. K. and Gulko, J. (1993) *The Development of Sex Typing in Middle Childhood*. Monogragh of the Society for Research in Child Development, Serial No. 232, 58 (2).

Sexton, S. (1987) *Our Schools: A Radical Policy*. Warlington: Institute of Economic Affairs.

Sexton, S. (1988) No nationalised curriculum, *The Times*, 9 May.

Sharp, R. and Green, A. (1975) *Education and Social Control*, London: Routledge & Kegan Paul.

Sharpe, K. (1992) Educational homogeneity in French primary education: a double case study, *British Journal of Sociology of Education*, **13** (3), 329–48.

Shepard, L. A. (1987) The harm of measurement driven instruction. Paper presented to the annual conference of the American Educational Research Association, Boston, April.

Shephard, G. (1994) Speech to the Annual Conference of the National Union of Teachers, Easter.

Shipman, M. (1981) *The Limitations of Social Research*. London: Longman.

Shipman, M. (ed.) (1985) *Educational Research: Principles, Policies and Practice*. London: Falmer Press.

Shorrocks, D. *et al.*, (1991) *The Evaluation of National Curriculum Assessment at Key Stage One*. Final Report. Leeds: University of Leeds.

Shulman, L. S. (1986) Those who understand: knowledge and growth in teaching, *Educational Researcher*, **15**, 4–14.

Siegel, H. (1990) *Educating Reason: Rationality, Critical Thinking and Education*. London: Routledge.

Sikes, P. J., Measor, L. and Woods, P. (1985) *Teachers' Careers*. London: Falmer.

Silver, H. (1980) *Education and the Social Condition*. London: Methuen.

Simon, B. (1953) *Intelligence Testing and the Comprehensive School*. London: Lawrence and Wishart.

Simon, B. (1985) *Does Education Matter?* London: Lawrence and Wishart.

Simon, B. (1992) *What Future for Education?* London: Lawrence and Wishart.

Simpson, E. (1988) *Review of Curriculum-Led Staffing*. Windsor: NFER.

Simpson, M. (1989) *A Study of Differentiation and Learning in Primary Schools*. Aberdeen: Northern College of Education.

Siraj-Blatchford, J. and Siraj-Blatchford, I. (1995) *Educating the Whole Child: Cross-Curricular Skills, Themes and Dimensions*. Buckingham: Open University Press.

Skelton, M., Playfoot, D. and Reeves, G. (1991) *Development Planning for Schools*. London: Routledge.

Skinner, B. F. (1953) *Science and Human Behavior*. New York: Macmillan.

Skinner, B. F. (1954) The science of learning and the art of teaching, *Harvard Educational Review*, **24**, 86–97.

Skinner, B. F. (1968) *The Technology of Teaching*. New York: Appleton.

Slavin, R. E. (1987) Ability grouping and student achievement in elementary schools: a best-evidence synthesis, *Review of Educational Research*, **57** (3), 293–336.

Slukin, A. (1981) *Growing Up in the Playground*. London: Routledge & Kegan Paul.

Smith, F. (1990) *To Think*. New York: Teachers' College Press.

Smyth, J. (1991) *Teachers as Collaborative Learners*. Buckingham: Open University Press.

Southworth, G. (1987) *Readings in Primary School Management*. London: Falmer.

Southworth, G., Nias, J. and Campbell, P. (1992) Rethinking collegiality: teachers' views. Mimeo presented to the American Educational Research Association, New Orleans.

Spaulding, C. L. (1992) *Motivation in the Classroom*. New York: McGraw Hill.

Spender, D. (1980) *Man Made Language*. London: Routledge & Kegan Paul.

Spender, D. and Sarah, E. (eds) (1980) *Learning to Lose: Sexism and Education*. London: Women's Press.

Spring, J. (1991) *American Education: An Introduction to Social and Political Aspects*. New York: Longman.

Squibb, P. (1973) The concept of intelligence: a sociological perspective, *Sociological Review*, **21** (1), 147–66.

Stacey, M. (1991) *Parents and Teachers Together: Partnership in Primary and Nursery Education*. Buckingham: Open University Press.

Stainthorp, R. (1989) *Practical Psychology for Primary Teachers*. London: Falmer.

Starkey, H. (1987) *Practical Activities for Teaching and Learning about Human Rights in Schools*. Strasbourg: Council of Europe.

Steedman, J. and MacKinnon, D. (1991) *The Education Factfile*. London: Hodder and Stoughton.

Steiner, M. (1994) *Learning from Experience: World Studies in the Primary Curriculum*. Stoke: Trentham Books.

Stenhouse, L. (1975) *An Introduction to Curriculum Research and Development*. London: Heinemann.

Stenhouse, L. (1982) *Authority, Education and Emancipation*. London: Heinemann.

Stewart, J. (1986) *The Making of the Primary School*. Milton Keynes: Open University Press.

Stierer, B. M. (1985) School reading volunteers; results of a postal survey of primary school heads, *Journal of Research in Reading*, **8** (1), 21–31.

Stinton, J. (1979) *Racism and Sexism in Children's Books*. London: Writers and Readers.

Stott, D. H. (1976) *Bristol Social Adjustment Guides Manual*. London: Hodder and Stoughton.

Straughan, R. (1988) *Can We Teach Children to be Good? Basic Issues in Moral, Personal and Social Education*. Milton Keynes: Open University Press.

Strauss, A. and Corbin, J. (1990) *Basics of Qualitative Research*. New York: Sage.

Strivens, J. (1985) School climate: a review of a problematic concept. In D. Reynolds *Studying School Effectiveness*. London: Falmer.

Stubbs, M. (1983) *Language, Schools and Classrooms*. London: Routledge.

Stubbs, M. and Hillier, H. (eds) (1983) *Readings on Language and Classrooms*, London: Methuen.

Styan, D. *et al.* (1990) *Developing School Management: The Way Forward*. Report by the School Management Task Force. London: HMSO.

Sutton, R. (1991) *Assessment: A Framework for Teachers*. London: Routledge.

Tabachnik, R. and Zeichner, K. (eds) (1991) *Issues and Practices in Inquiry-Oriented Teacher Education*. London: Falmer.

Tann, S. (1981) Grouping and group-work. In B. Simon, and J. Willcocks (eds) *Research and Practice in the Primary School*. London: Routledge & Kegan Paul.

Tann, S. (ed.) (1988) *Developing Topic Work in the Primary School*. London: Falmer.

Tann, S. (1991) *Developing Language in the Primary Classroom*. London: Cassell.

Tann, S. and Armitage, M. (1986) Time for talk, *Reading*, **20** (3), 184–9.

Tanner, J. M. (1978) *Education and Physical Growth*. London: University of London Press.

Task Group on Assessment and Testing (1987) *National Curriculum, Report*. London: DES.

Task Group on Assessment and Testing (1988) *Three Supplementary Reports*. London: DES.

Tate, N. (1995) National cultures. Mimeo, speech to the annual conference of Shropshire secondary headteachers annual conference, July.

Tattum, D. P. (ed.) (1986) *The Management of Disruptive Pupil Behaviour in Schools*. Chichester: Wiley.

Tattum, D. P. and Lane, D. A. (1989) *Bullying in Schools*. Stoke-on-Trent: Trentham Books.

Taylor, P. (1986) *Expertise and the Primary School Teacher*. Windsor: NFER-Nelson.

Taylor, P. (1990) The aims of primary education in world perspective. In N. Proctor (ed.) *The Aims of Primary Education and the National Curriculum*. London: Falmer.

Teacher Training Agency (1995) *Corporate Plan*. London: TTA.

Tharp, R. and Gallimore, R. (1988) *Rousing Minds to Life: Teaching. Learning and Schooling in Social Context*. New York: Cambridge University Press.

Thomas, G. (1989) The teacher and others in the classroom. In C. Cullingford (ed.) *The Primary Teacher: The Role of the Educator and the Purpose of Primary Education*. London: Cassell.

Thomas, G. (1992) *Effective Classroom Teamwork: Support or Intrusion?* London: Routledge.

Thomas, N. (1989) The aims of primary education in member states of the Council of Europe. In M. Galton and A. Blyth (eds) *Handbook of Primary Education in Europe*. London: David Fulton.

Thomas, N. (1990) *Primary Education from Plowden to the 1990s*. London: Falmer.

Thorndike, E. L. (1911) *Human Learning*. New York: Prentice Hall.

Thorne, B. (1993) *Gender Play: Girls and Boys in School*. Buckingham, Open University Press.

Tizard, B. and Hughes, M. (1984) *Young Children Learning*. London: Fontana.

Tizard, B., Blatchford, P., Burke, J., Farquhar, C. and Plewis, I. (1988) *Young Children at School in the Inner City*. Hove: Lawrence Erlbaum Associates.

Tomlinson, P. (1995) *Understanding Mentoring*. Buckingham: Open University Press.

Topping, K. and Wolfendale S. (1985) *Parental Involvement in Children's Reading*. London: Croom Helm.

Torrance, E. P. (1962) *Guiding Creative Talent*. Englewood Cliffs, NJ: Prentice Hall.

Torrance, H. (1991) Evaluating SATs: the 1991 pilot, *Cambridge Journal of Education*, **21** (2), 129–40.

Triggs, P. and Newman, E., with Prestidge, J. (1993) Closing the distance, *Managing Schools Today*, **2** (5), 42–4.

Troyna, B. and Carrington, B. (1988) *Children and Controversial Issues: Strategies for the Early and Middle Years of Schooling*. London: Falmer.

Troyna, B. and Hatcher, R. (1992) *Racism in Children's Lives: A Study of Mainly White Primary Schools*. London: Routledge.

Tutchell, E. (ed.) (1990) *Dolls and Dungarees: Gender Issues in the Primary School Curriculum*. Buckingham: Open University Press.

United Nations 48: European Convention on Human Rights (UN Convention on Children's Rights). C14.

Van Manen, M. (1990) *The Tact of Teaching: The Meaning of Pedagogical Thoughtfulness*. London, Ontairio: Althouse Press.

Verma, M. K., Corrigan K. P. and Firth, S. (1995) *Working with Bilingual Pupils*. Clevedon: Multilingual Matters

Vincent, C. (1996) *Parents and Teachers: Power and Participation*. London: Falmer Press.

Vulliamy, G. and Webb. R. (1992) *Teacher Research and Special Educational Needs*. London: David Fulton.

Vygotsky, L. S. (1962) *Thought and Language*. Cambridge, MA: Massachusetts Institute of Technology.

Vygotsky, L. S. (1978) *Mind in Society: The Development of Higher Psychological Processes*. Cambridge, MA: Harvard University Press.

Waksler, F. C. (ed.) (1991) *Studying the Social Worlds of Children: Sociological Readings*. London: Falmer.

Walberg, H. J. (ed.) (1979) *Educational Environments and Effects: Evaluation, Policy and Productivity*. Berkeley, CA: McCutchan.

Walford, G. (1991) *Doing Educational Research*. London: Routledge.

Walker, R. (1986) *Doing Research: A Handbook for Teachers*. London: Routledge.

Walkerdine, V. (1981) Sex power and pedagogy, *Screen Education*, **38**, 14–23.

Walkerdine, V. (1983) It's only natural: rethinking child-centred pedagogy. In A. M. Wolpe and J. Donald (eds) *Is There Anyone There from Education?* London: Pluto Press.

Walkerdine, V. (1988) *The Mastery of Reason: Cognitive Development and the Production of Rationality*. London: Routledge.

Wallace, M. (1991) Coping with multiple innovations in schools, *School Organisation*, **11** (2), 187–209.

Wallace, M. (1994) Towards a contingency approach to development planning in schools. In D. H. Hargreaves and D. Hopkins (eds) *Development Planning for School Improvement*. London: Cassell.

Walton, J. (ed.) (1971) *The Integrated Day: Theory and Practice*. London: Ward Lock.

Waterhouse, P. (1983) *Managing the Learning Process*. London: McGraw-Hill.

Waterhouse, S. (1991) *First Episodes: Pupil Careers in the Early Years of School*. London: Falmer.

Webb, R. (1990) The processes and purposes of practitioner research. In R. Webb (ed.) *Practitioner Research in the Primary School*. London: Falmer Press.

Webb, R. (ed.) (1991) *Practitioner Research in the Primary School*. London: Falmer.

Webb. R. (ed.) (1996) *Cross-curricular Primary Practice: Taking a Leadership Role*. London: Falmer Press.

Webb, R. and Vulliamy, G. (1996) *Roles and Responsibilities in the Primary School: Changing Demands, Changing Practices*. Buckingham: Open University Press.

Weiner, G. (1990) Developing educational policy on gender in the primary school. In G. Weiner (ed.) *The Primary School and Equal Opportunities: International Perspectives on Gender Issues*. London: Cassell.

Wellington, J. J. (ed.) (1986) *Controversial Issues in the Curriculum*. Oxford: Blackwell.

Wells, G. (1986) *The Meaning Makers: Children Learning Language and Using Language to Learn*. London: Hodder and Stoughton.

Wertsch, J. V. (1985) *Vygotsky and the Social Formation of Mind*. Cambridge, MA: Harvard University Press.

West-Burnham, J. (1992) *Managing Quality in Schools*. London: Longman.

Wheldall, K. (1991) *Discipline in Schools: Psychological Perspectives on the Elton Report*. London: Routledge.

Whetton, C. *et al.* (1991) *National Curriculum Assessment at Key Stage One: 1991 Evaluation.* Report 4. Slough: NFER.

White, D. and Woollett, A. (1991) *Families: A Context for Development.* London: Falmer.

White, J. (1978) The primary teacher as servant of the state, *Education, 3–13,* 7 (2), 18–23.

White, R. T. and Gunstone, R. F. (1992) *Probing Understanding.* London: Falmer.

Whitty, G. (1985) *Sociology and School Knowledge.* London: Methuen.

Whitty, G. (1989) The New Right and the National Curriculum: state control or market forces? *Journal of Education Policy,* **4,** (4), 329–42.

Whitty, G (1992) Education, economy and national culture. In R. Bocock and K. Thompson (eds) *Social and Cultural Forms of Modernity.* Oxford: Polity.

Whitty, G. and Willmott, E. (1991) Competence-based teacher education: approaches and issues, *Cambridge Journal of Education,* 21 (3), 309–18.

Willes, M. (1983) *Children into Pupils.* London: Routledge & Kegan Paul.

Winkley, D. (1985) *Diplomats and Detectives: LEA Advisers at Work.* London: Robert Royce.

Winter, R. (1989) *Learning From Experience: Principles and Practice in Action-Research.* London: Falmer.

Withall, J. and Lewis, W. (1963) Social/emotional climate in the classroom. In N. L. Gage (ed.) *Handbook of Research on Teaching.* American Educational Research Association.

Withall, J. (1949) The development of a technique for the measurement of social-emotional climate in classrooms, *Journal of Experimental Education,* **17,** 347–61.

Witkin, H. A., Moore, C. A., Goodenough, D. R. and Cos, P. W. (1977) Field-dependent cognitive styles and their educational implications, *Review of Educational Research,* 1–64.

Wolfendale, S. (1989) *Parental Involvement.* London: Cassell.

Wolfendale, S. (1992a) *Involving Parents in Schools.* London: Cassell.

Wolfendale, S. (1992b) *Primary Schools and Special Needs.* London: Cassell.

Wolff, S. (1989) *Childhood and Human Nature: The Development of Personality.* London: Routledge.

Wood, D. (1988) *How Children Think and Learn.* Oxford: Blackwell.

Woods, P. (1977) Teaching for survival. In P. Woods and M. Hammersley, (eds) *School Experience.* London: Croom Helm.

Woods, P. (1983) *Sociology and the School: An Interactionist Viewpoint.* London: Routledge & Kegan Paul.

Woods, P. (1986) *Inside Schools.* London: Routledge & Kegan Paul.

Woods, P. (1987) Managing the primary school teacher's role. In S. Delamont (ed.) *The Primary School Teacher.* London: Falmer.

Woods, P. (1990) *The Happiest Days? How Pupils Cope with School.* London: Falmer.

Woods, P. (1995) *Creative Teachers in Primary Schools.* Buckingham, Open University Press.

Woods, P. and Jeffrey, B. (1996) *Teachable Moments: The Art of Teaching in Primary Schools.* Buckingham, Open University Press.

Woods, P. and Pollard, A. (eds) (1988) *Sociology and Teaching: A New Challenge for the Sociology of Education.* London: Croom Helm.

Wragg, E. C. (1993a) *Primary Teaching Skills*. London: Routledge.

Wragg, E. C. (1993b) *Class Management*. London: Routledge.

Wragg, E. C. (1993c) *An Introduction to Classroom Observation*. London: Routledge.

Wragg, T. and Brown, G. (1993) *Explaining*. London: Routledge.

Wray, D. and Medwell, J. (1991) *Literacy and Language in the Primary Years*. London: Routledge.

Wright, C. (1992) *Race Relations in the Primary School*. London: David Fulton.

Yeo, E. (1992) *The Rise and Fall of Primary Education*. York: Campaign for Real Education.

Yeomans, R. and Sampson, J. (eds) (1994) *Mentorship in the Primary School*. London: Falmer Press.

Young, M. D. (ed.) (1971) *Knowledge and Control*. London: Collier-Macmillan.

Yussen, S. R. (ed.) (1985) *The Growth of Reflection in Children*. New York: Academic Press.

Zeichner, K. (1981–2) Reflective teaching and field-based experience in pre-service teacher education, *Interchange*, **12**, 1–22.

Zeichner, K. (1986) Content and contexts: neglected elements in studies of student teaching as an occasion for learning to teach, *Journal of Education for Teaching*, **12** (1), 5–24.

Zimmet, S. G. and Hoffman, M. (1980) *Print and Prejudice*. London: Hodder and Stoughton.

PRACTICAL ACTIVITIES INDEX

NAME INDEX

Name index

SUBJECT INDEX